SHAPED BY THE WEST

VOLUME 2

A History of North America since 1850

William Deverell and Anne Hyde

UNIVERSITY OF CALIFORNIA PRESS

D1533797

University of California Press, one of the most distinguished
university presses in the United States, enriches lives around
the world by advancing scholarship in the humanities, social
sciences, and natural sciences. Its activities are supported by the
UC Press Foundation and by philanthropic contributions from
individuals and institutions. For more information, visit
www.ucpress.edu.

University of California Press
Oakland, California

Library of Congress Cataloging-in-Publication Data

Names: Deverell, William F., 1962- author. | Hyde, Anne Farrar,
    1960- author.
Title: Shaped by the West / William F. Deverell and Anne F. Hyde.
Description: Oakland, California : University of California Press,
    [2018] | Includes bibliographical references and index. |
Identifiers: LCCN 2017060975 (print) | LCCN 2018002204 (ebook) |
    ISBN 9780520964372 (ebook) | ISBN 9780520290044 (v. 1 ; pbk. :
    alk. paper) | ISBN 9780520964372 (v. 1 ; ebook) |
    ISBN 9780520291416 (v. 2 ; pbk. : alk. paper) |
    ISBN 9780520965201 (v. 2 ; ebook)
Subjects: LCSH: West (U.S.)—History. | Frontier and pioneer life—
    West (U.S.) | United States—History. | Indians of North
    America—Great Plains—History.
Classification: LCC F591 (ebook) | LCC F591 .D395 2018 (print) |
    DDC 978—dc23
LC record available at https://lccn.loc.gov/2017060975

Manufactured in the United States of America

27 26 25 24 23 22 21 20 19 18
10 9 8 7 6 5 4 3 2 1

Contents

Preface

These two volumes on the history of the American West first came about because of a really good idea that did not work. Twenty years ago, the two of us agreed to sign up for an innovative project aimed at tying regional history to the broadest sweeps of US history. The elegant intention for a two-volume annotated reader on the West was that it would supplement American history survey courses taught at colleges and universities *in* the West.

Broad-brush national issues—war, slavery, conquest, labor, gender and the family, cities, etc.—would be elaborated upon by documents and images drawn from, and interpreted within, western settings. Students learning about Prohibition, for example, would address that topic and its long history by reading temperance and Prohibition sources alongside stories from western places: Colorado, California, Wyoming, Oregon, and others. Specific settings would shed light on the overriding topic, and students in the West would get to know their region's history better and more broadly.

Good idea, right? It was. And the first edition of these two volumes offered the two of us, friends and colleagues now for half our lives, a great opportunity to work on something together.

So what happened? The easy answer is that, for whatever reason or reasons, the survey courses on campus in the US West did not much bend to the regional illumination our books offered. Maybe the survey-course instructors did not want to alter the way they taught their courses. Maybe a textbook-driven syllabus could not easily accommodate two additional volumes of readings and exercises. Maybe the innovative idea required a bit more public relations energy than a busy publisher could be expected to provide.

But the books did not fail. They just hit a different target than the one we first imagined. Not long after they were published in 2000, we began to hear from our western history colleagues all over the country, who told us that our two volumes were a hit in their courses. Not their US survey courses but their western, or various versions of regional, history courses. The documents and images brought the West's complex, chaotic history to life and to the ground. Voices of real people could be heard in the primary source records we had mined for the books. And our brief annotations and introductions helped our colleagues by adding context and scholarly perspective to history's themes, moments, and episodes.

The "hook" was unintended, but no less gratifying because of it. The books got out there, they got taught, and our colleagues told us that they liked using them.

So here we are, two decades later, launching them again. We're different, our students are different, the concerns of historians who focus on the West have changed, so these books are different. With a new publisher, everything had to be rethought, reorganized, and revised in light of how much the field of western history has changed in this century.

It still makes sense to pull the long history of the West apart, to make this a two-volume reader. There is an early West and a later West, though the dividing line is a slippery concept. We opted, once again, for a division deep into the American period, roughly at the Civil War moment. We expect that the books will be taught apart and together. One aspect of western history that has invigorated the field in recent times has been the brilliant scholarship illuminating the indigenous histories of the West, before and after Spanish contact, before and after American conquest. We have been careful to bring much of that work to bear in our documents, short essays, and bibliographies, which close each chapter in both volumes.

The West has grown since we wrote the first edition of these books. Western historians who were once pretty content with the continental and national outlines of the American West must now, thanks again to bold, new scholarship, look beyond conventional boundaries of the West as a trans-Mississippi or trans-Rockies terrestrial place. Our West, and our students' West, is capacious and boundary-breaking, because the human beings who lived there and the ideas they carried with them crossed borders. We incorporate a West that is not defined by terra firma but is instead oceanic. The rise of transnational and Pacific histories within the western historical canons of scholarship have added much to our field. Now we ask how the West looked, and how people lived their lives, in and around "the great Ocean" that borders the western edges of a West we ought no longer delimit at high tide.

There are other ways in which the West has grown richer as a field of historical inquiry. Our field's embrace of environmental history, long strong, has only gotten more ambitious and interesting, and those prisms of analysis and those stories are reflected in these pages. Western history has long been a field in which breakthrough scholars have helped us better understand such concepts as gender and masculinity. Researchers whose work addresses sexuality have added magnificently to those foundations, and we are indebted to them here, just as we are to historians and others who address LGBTQ histories in the archives and narratives of western America. They bring us a stunningly human West, where people learned new things about themselves, did awful things to each other, and sometimes took great care. Throughout this project, our aim has been to make these books speak to a new western audience, using up-to-date scholarship, and simultaneously to relay to students just how exciting it is to be working in western history at this moment in American historical writing. Our archives grow, the people in them change, and our access to that knowledge gets easier every day. The stories and puzzles they yield have never been more compelling.

We also find obligation in opportunity. We have tried to bring contemporary concerns and problems into sharper view by way of context and history. The West is a troubled place in early twenty-first-century America. It is a place where many of the nation's uncertainties and tensions seem to get wrestled with first out in the open, in ways both inspiring and repulsive. Our West, and the West of the students who will read these volumes, has—as it always has—problems atop possibilities, troubles atop triumphs. But the stakes seem, to us, higher now. What the West will do or not do, what the West will collectively say to the nation and to the world, matters greatly. Think of challenging issues in contemporary America: immigration, the environment, the carceral state, native sovereignty, global change, race and racism, gender and power. These are not just western issues—of course not. But they have western valences, they have western contexts, and that particular history ought to help us all to better understand them.

So in a way we have come full circle. We're still friends, we still disagree about aspects of the West and its history, but we care about it deeply. This little two-volume project about the history of the region reflects our passion and experience. We still believe, as we did twenty years ago, that the West provides a sharply focused lens to view national and international issues. And it remains a distinctive region because of its physical setting and particular histories. We hope that in learning about that region and its wild history you will be shaped by the West. We hope you take that knowledge far beyond your classrooms.

ACKNOWLEDGMENTS

Because western history and the West have not grown simpler over the years, it took us a while to reimagine these volumes and to wrestle them into useful shape and size. We are very grateful to Niels Hooper at the University of California Press for thinking these volumes were a good idea and for not saying too much when they took longer than we ever thought they would. Bradley Depew, Niels's able assistant, has shaped these volumes and corralled the authors.

Copyeditors Ann Donahue and Lindsey Westbrook did wonderful work in correcting errors, finding inconsistencies, and making the volumes look terrific.

We owe a lot to reviewers, who looked at initial proposals and then first and second drafts of both volumes. As experienced teachers and western scholars, they gave us excellent and detailed advice that pushed us to reconfigure these volumes. Susan L. Johnson, from the University of Wisconsin; Adam Arenson of Manhattan College; Greg Hise from the University of Nevada, Las Vegas; and Shana Bernstein of Northwestern University all read carefully and convinced us to make significant changes. We can't thank them enough, and we hope these volumes begin to represent their efforts. In Southern California, Bill would like to thank Taryn Haydostian, Elizabeth Logan, Brian Moeller, Erin Chase, and Aaron Hodges for their efforts in tracking down images, rekeying documents, and getting permissions. In Oklahoma, Anne would like to thank the staff at the Western History Collection, Laurie Scrivener, Curtis Foxley, and History 1493, for test driving documents and ideas.

William Deverell, University
of Southern California
Anne Hyde, University of Oklahoma

Introduction

This document collection is many years, we might say hundreds of years, in the making. It is the product of centuries of historical change and upheaval, triumph and tragedy, in the region we now call the American West. It offers hundreds of voices from the past to represent a range of human beings that enable you to see both glimmers of yourself in the past and worlds and ideas that are breathtakingly different.

As we think about how these will be used in classrooms, by you and your classmates, we are confident in two major ideas. The first is that you, your classmates, and your instructors will shape these volumes by your collective ideas, wrapped around history and region. We know also that reading and thinking about the history of the West is best done if you can sit with the words and images of the people who are no longer around. Some of these are written documents that have been translated many times, but some are objects, photographs, maps, or buildings. We have an obligation as historians to guide you in that work, almost to sit alongside you as you read.

The West we take you through is far more than what eventually becomes the US West. Those borders and that idea of a region didn't always exist. Some of your experiences will tilt earlier, to a West not yet conquered by Anglo-America, to a West of overlapping claims, global ambitions, and Native systems of governance, both roving and rooted in western places and spaces. Other classes, other students of the West, will find more to grapple with in a "later West," when conquest morphed into the colonialism of taking gold, oil, coal, or water on unprecedented scales, when cities arose to marshal commodities, people, and capital. And some of you will focus more attention on the West of the most recent vintage, the West of your own lifetimes, a West of roiling demographic and political change (not so new, actually), a West at the center of some of the most vexing and divisive issues in contemporary American life.

So we take you to places where different ideas about how people should live and who should control resources bump up against each other. Sometimes that makes a border, sometimes a frontier, sometimes a war zone, or sometimes a place of peaceful diplomacy. In moving through these zones of contention or collaboration, the people actually there do the speaking. Our job is to ask you to think about this or think about that as you read. We frame the documents and pictures within the context of their making, and we introduce you to the circumstances that led to that letter or that law or that photograph.

The real meaning of all this is in the exchanges you have with the western past. If we know what we are talking about, our annotations, captions, and miniessays will help you as you move through western time and space. But it is your give and take with the actual sources of history that we hope this book inspires. The past is both like and utterly unlike the present we inhabit. Listen to the voices of the West. See how language is the same, yet different. Understand the circumstances people, groups, and nations found themselves in, how they made decisions, what those decisions ultimately meant. Ask questions of these sources—why did this happen? What might have happened differently? How can two people see the same moment so divergently? What were the best ideas of the past? What were the worst? How does the past, and all those decisions made by people who came before us, still influence the present and the future?

Where does the past stop, and where does the present begin? And what is our present other than the future's past?

History offers fascinating terrain to exercise your ideas and come up with new ones. It is hard work, the answers are never easy to come by, and history has neither a neat beginning nor a neat end. The West, only one of an infinite number of ways in which to carve up the past, is a place that has fascinated us for the entirety of our careers. We hope that this same excitement, along with ideas we haven't even thought of, accompanies you as you think your way through these volumes.

Alfred A. Hart, Chinese Camp, Central Pacific Railroad, ca. 1869. Railroad building and photographic technology rose together in the second half of the nineteenth century. After the Civil War, the nation watched the progress of the expanding railway web with great fascination and wonder, and photographers, working on their own or for the railroads as freelance artists, produced thousands of images. They captured not only the ties and tracks, but the spaces and landscapes of the American West. Sometimes, as in this image by Alfred A. Hart, they captured glimpses of the workers who put the western railroads together. Were it not for imported Chinese workers like those whose tents we see here, the western portion of the transcontinental railroad would not have been built.

These side-by-side photographs are not exactly the same—they differ in that the photographer moved the camera just a few degrees. Mounted on cardboard and inserted into a viewing device called a stereoscope or stereopticon, they gave the impression of three-dimensional depth. How might Hart have captioned this photograph differently? Can you imagine him framing it differently? If yes, how?

Railroads West

Beginning in the first third of the nineteenth century, Americans began to wonder if the new technology of fixed-track railroading (what they at first, appropriately, called the "Rail Road") might reach across vast reaches of the continent. While those who called for such expansion were initially ridiculed—even called insane—the idea took hold quickly. Railroads expanded in the West, and the technology of tracks and trains improved, especially in New England. In short order, Americans entered into what more than one observer at the time called the Railroad Age, and that epoch proved exciting, disruptive, chaotic, violent, and remarkable all at once.

Railroads, even those that traveled only a few hundred yards or maybe a mile or two, overwhelmed their surroundings. What could at first have been powered by a horse, a mule, a man, or even simple gravity rapidly took shape by the 1840s into steam-powered locomotion that traveled at great and, for those who experienced it at the time, often terrifying velocity. Railroads were loud, smoky, and sometimes dangerous intrusions into previously quieter, safer landscapes. At eighteen miles an hour, their early top speed, trains could induce what people in the middle of the century often described as the sensation of flying, *really* flying.

Americans linked railroads to the exuberance of the early republic. Railroads rose with the nation. They underlined American faith in progress linked to technology, and they seemed to be a particularly useful tool by which to conquer nature, alter perceptions of time and space (because they moved across space more quickly than anything people had yet experienced), and imagine the young country stretching beyond earlier borders of the imagination or the nation itself. As railroads expanded, so too did Americans expand their vision of the size and purpose of the young nation.

And so what had once been brushed off as crazy talk became, certainly by the 1850s, the stuff of serious interest: Could railroads traverse the nation, the entire nation, from East to West? Could the railroad be the most powerful manifestation and mechanism of Manifest Destiny?

The answer was yes. But the reality and the history of it all would prove to be very complicated. As the North and the South pulled increasingly apart, as sectional tensions over the expansion of slavery into the new territories gained by way of warfare and violence escalated, railroads became more and more entwined with that larger story. Westward-moving railroads hastened the incorporation of parts of the then West (now the Midwest) into the nation, which in turn exacerbated the antagonisms between South and North about the future of the nation, its land, its people, and its labor systems. By the 1850s, as the building of a transcontinental railroad network from the Atlantic to the Pacific actually began to look possible, if not probable, disagreements arose that hastened the coming of the Civil War. Where would such a transcontinental railroad be built? Should it be placed on a latitude more northerly across the continent? More southerly? More in the middle? Should there be more than one cross-country rail route? How would even just one of these railroads be paid for? Could the environmental, labor, and technological obstacles of such a gargantuan effort be surmounted?

Southerners who thought about the West and the railroad invariably wished that any transcontinental project go west from the South. In that way, Southern ambitions to control western trade could be enhanced. What's more, Southern beliefs about the necessity to expand slavery into western territories could be kept alive, as some thought that slaves could be transported west to new landscapes given over to unfree labor *and* that the products of that labor could be then shipped east to the South or be launched across the ocean from trade networks established on the Pacific at the railroad terminus.

The North was not about to let the railroad fall to an increasingly hostile South to run, build, or influence. Once the Confederacy was formed, and secession under way, President Abraham Lincoln launched the building of the transcontinental railroad by way of vast incentives in land and money to the two corporations willing to make a go of it. Within seven years of the passage of the Pacific Railroad Acts in 1862, and after the Civil War had ended, the merger of the westward-building Union Pacific Railroad and the eastward-building Central Pacific Railroad occurred in a lonely expanse of treeless hill country just north of the Great Salt Lake.

AS YOU READ: Think about the ways in which the South may have pinned slavery hopes to the railroad, how the North eventually blocked these (mostly by way of the Civil War itself), and about the ironies of using what we might call "barely free" Chinese laborers to build so much of the western end of the giant rail project. Think, too, of how fast change came to the first half of nineteenth-century America by way of experiences in the West. If Lewis and Clark went west in the first decade of that century in search of the fabled Northwest Passage, did railroad workers end up building an iron version of it only a few generations later? Was that a move to modernity, leaving behind an Enlightenment dream of a waterway west, in favor of an industrial marvel that spanned the continent ocean to ocean?

1. INDUSTRIALIZING THE WESTERN LANDSCAPE *(SEE P. 4)*

This remarkable photograph was taken by the same photographer who captured the Chinese camp shown at the start of this chapter (from the same railroad project). It gives us some idea of the hive of activity that surrounded railroad construction in the West immediately after the Civil War. Remember that each mile of track laid meant that much more money, land, and loans going to one railroad corporation over another. Construction was a race, with all the attendant incentives to build cheaply and dangerously. How might you caption this image differently? What can you make out in the picture, and how would you crop it to highlight particular aspects? What would a contemporary photograph taken from the same spot reveal today?

2. RATIONALIZING WESTERN SPACE *(SEE P. 5)*

This map was created the very same year (1869) that the transcontinental railroad project linked up in northern Utah. Look here at the reach and claims and ambition of the young nation, not yet one hundred years old, as it incorporates, surveys, plants, and sells land in the far West. Literally on top of that expanding empire, won by way of near wholesale destruction of Native peoples, the nation and its corporate railroad partners inscribed, in the handwriting of industrial technology, the straight lines of property, jurisdictional boundaries, and railroad tracks. How many years separated this image, and all that it represents,

Alfred A. Hart, *"End of the Track. Near Humboldt River Canyon, Nevada." Campsite and Train of the Central Pacific Railroad at Foot of Mountains*, 1868

National Archives and Records Administration, 165-XS-28.

from the overland expeditions of Lewis and Clark? How wishful of western conquest do you find a map such as this, or does it depict the aftermath of conquest already accomplished? How would you find out?

3. CONQUERING NATURE BY VIOLENCE *(SEE P. 6)*

Nineteenth-century Americans often referred to the railroad as a tool by which the centuries-old struggle to subdue nature in North America could be furthered and even accomplished. The kind of activity pictured here makes those assumptions look all too real. Not only were the large animals of the Plains and far West increasingly set upon by hunters tasked with feeding railroad gang workers from the 1860s onward, but others got quickly into the act. Tourists and travelers of all kinds saw in their railroad journeys westward a chance to get in on the excitement, hence images like this. While we can assume that the locomotive is idling

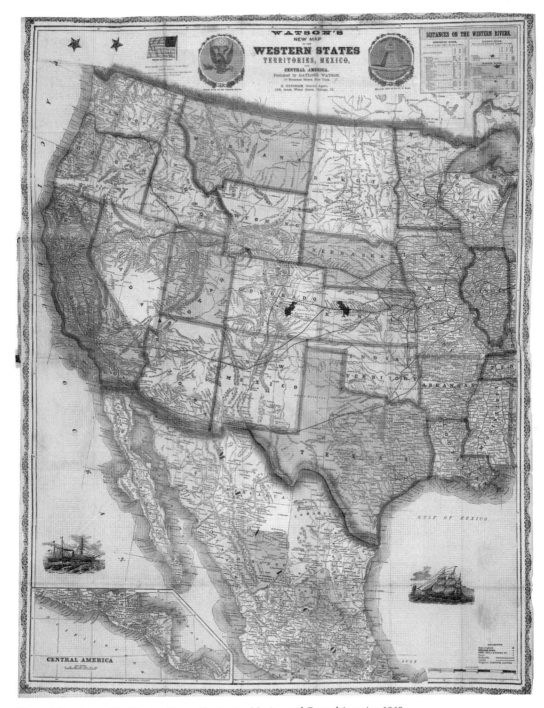

Watson's New Map of the Western States, Territories, Mexico, and Central America, 1869

Courtesy the Huntington Library, San Marino, California.

SHALL THE BUFFALO GO ?—SLAUGHTERED FOR A PASTIME.

"Shall the Buffalo Go?—Slaughtered for a Pastime," 1883
Frank Leslie's Popular Monthly 15 (May 1883): 557.

here, or perhaps moving at a very slow pace, we can also assume that it didn't linger so that the bison victims of this "hunt" would be harvested as meat. On the contrary, it's likely that this show of force and weaponry and wanton destruction was all about the excitement of simply killing buffalo and letting the dead and wounded animals lie where they had fallen, as the train continued down the line. Do you think nineteenth-century Americans would have found reasons to object to the actions that images such as these present? Why or why not?

4. RAILROAD WORK AND THE INDISPENSABILITY OF CHINESE LABOR *(SEE P. 7)*

With so many Chinese (certainly ten thousand and maybe closer to twenty thousand) at work on the western half of the transcontinental railroad project and its smaller tributaries, we might expect to have more photographic evidence of their labor and their lives, as hinted at in the image that opens this chapter. But the Chinese were not often captured in pictures as they worked on, or lived near, the growing transit of the transcontinental railroad. This picture—and if you look closely, you will see it has a lot of people in it (including children)—shows a

Alfred A. Hart, *End of Track, on Humboldt Plains*, ca. 1865–69
Courtesy the Library of Congress Prints and Photographs Division.

Chinese labor team out in the desolate wide open of Nevada, probably in the late 1860s. The photographer stood on something to make this image, perhaps a locomotive engine. Look at the perpendicular lines made by the relation of the ties and track to the telegraph poles alongside. Some of the people depicted here are ghost images: they did not hold still long enough for Hart's camera to capture them with clarity. What do you think the life stories were of those you see in this picture? Who are the children?

5. RAILROAD GRAFT AND INFLUENCE *(SEE P. 8)*

As the brains behind the Central and Southern Pacific railroad empire stretching out across the American West and south into Mexico in the last third of the nineteenth century, tycoon Collis P. Huntington wielded tremendous political and financial clout. He was rarely shy about using it, or threatening to use it, in advancing the conjoined interests of his future, his fortune, and his railroad network. At times he could do much with the simple gift of railroad passes, doled out to this or that politician or newspaperman so that those Huntington wanted in his debt could ride the rails hither and yon for free. At other times, the price exacted for favors could loom higher, as Huntington hints at in this 1876 letter to subservient business partner David Colton. Graft, influence peddling, and combinations of political and financial ruthlessness all fell together in the world of "big railroading" in the American West. The railroads may have indeed democratized transit across the nation, but it would be too narrow a view of history to see them only in that light.

Collis Potter Huntington and David Doulty Colton
From *The Colton Letters*
1876[1]

New York
January 17, 1876

Friend Colton;

I have received several letters and telegrams from Washington to-day, all calling me there, as Scott will certainly pass his Texas Pacific bill *if I do not come over*, and I shall go over to-night, but I think he should not pass his bill if I should help him; but of course I cannot know this for certain, and just what effort to make against him is what troubles me. *It costs money to fix things so that I would know his bill would not pass. I believe with $200,000 I can pass our bill, but I take it that it is not worth that much to us.*

---

1. Collis Potter Huntington and David Doulty Colton, *The Colton Letters: Declaration of Huntington That Congressmen are for Sale*, n.p., n.d. [1894], 7, italics in original.

6. PICTURING THE WEST AND THE RAILS *(SEE PP. 10–11)*

Alongside the coincident timing of photographic technology's development and railroad expansion westward, innovations in printing—color and mass production most prominent among them—created great opportunities for railroad promotion. These maps and flyers are examples of that promotionalism: for tourists, settlers, businesspeople, and more. Documents such as these were easy to produce, easy to ship, and very effective at sparking the imaginations of people who might previously never even have thought of the West, much less of going there.

7. HARDLY ROMANTIC: A FAMED TRAVEL WRITER GOES WEST IN THE 1870S

Among the most famous writers of his era, and surely the best known travel writer, Robert Louis Stevenson was already well known in the late 1870s when he took a train to California. His fame would grow in later years following the publication of such books as Strange Case of Dr. Jekyll and Mr. Hyde *(1886);* Treasure Island *(1882); and* Kidnapped *(1886). Stevenson took the new railroad from New York all the way west. Even in this early era of the transcontinental railroad, it was possible to ride in at least some luxury afforded by money or status. Stevenson chose otherwise, by necessity and adventurousness. His stories from the rough settings of railroad steerage made for spellbinding reading, but at a real cost. The journey broke his already fragile health. The full account of his trip was not published until after Stevenson's 1894 death, and his descriptions of the rough conditions (and rough people) he encountered shocked his family and friends. As you read this, imagine the sights, sounds, and smells of the journey. Other than the most general sense of travel by rail, does Stevenson's trip seem anything at all like train trips you have taken? What is the same, and what has changed?*

Robert Louis Stevenson
From *The Amateur Emigrant*
1895[1]

It was about two in the afternoon of Friday that I found myself in front of the Emigrant House, with more than a hundred others, to be sorted and boxed for the journey. A white-haired official, with a stick under one arm, and a list in the other hand, stood apart in front of us, and called name after name in the tone of a command. At each name you would see a family gather up its brats and bundles and run for the hindmost of the three cars that stood awaiting us, and I soon concluded that this was to be set apart for the women and children. The second or central car, it turned out, was devoted to men travelling alone, and the third to the Chinese.

I suppose the reader has some notion of an American railroad-car, that long, narrow wooden box, like a flat-roofed Noah's ark, with a stove and a convenience, one at either end, a passage down the middle, and transverse benches upon either hand.

Those destined for emigrants on the Union Pacific are only remarkable for their extreme plainness, nothing but wood entering in any part into their constitution, and for the usual inefficacy of the lamps, which often went out and shed but a dying glimmer even while they burned. The benches are too short for anything but a young child. Where there is scarce elbow-room for two to sit, there will not be space enough for one to lie. Hence the company, or rather, as it appears from certain bills about the Transfer Station, the company's servants, have conceived a plan for the better accommodation of travellers. They prevail on every two to chum together. To each of the chums they sell a board and three square cushions stuffed with straw, and covered with thin cotton.

The benches can be made to face each other in pairs, for the backs are reversible. On the approach of night the boards are laid from bench to bench, making a couch wide enough for two, and long enough for a man of the middle height;

---

1. Robert Louis Stevenson, *The Amateur Emigrant: From the Clyde to Sandy Hook* (Chicago: Stone and Kimball, 1895), 115–20.

Map of the Central Pacific Railroad and Its Connections, ca. 1870

Courtesy the Huntington Library, San Marino, California.

and the chums lie down side by side upon the cushions with the head to the conductor's van and the feet to the engine. When the train is full, of course this plan is impossible, for there must not be more than one to every bench, neither can it be carried out unless the chums agree.

A great personage on an American train is the newsboy. He sells books (such books!), papers, fruit, lollipops, and cigars; and on emigrant journeys, soap, towels, tin washing-dishes, tin coffee pitchers, coffee, tea, sugar, and tinned eatables, mostly hash or beans and bacon.

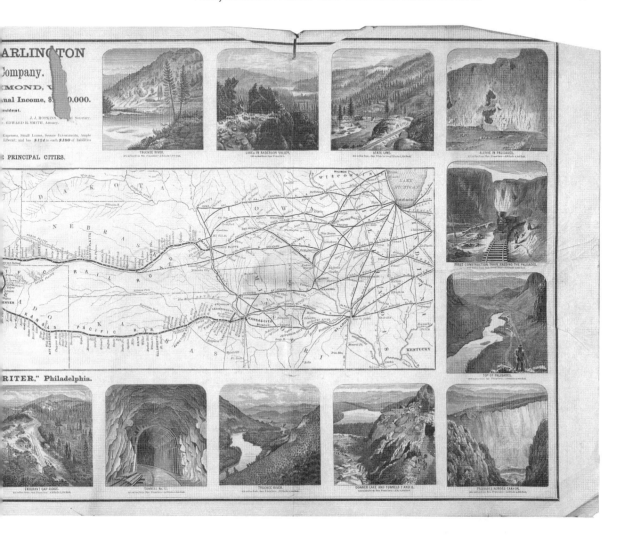

Early next morning the newsboy went around the cars, and chumming on a more extended principle became the order of the hour. It requires but a co-partnery of two to manage beds; but washing and eating can be carried on most economically by a syndicate of three. I myself entered a little after sunrise into articles of agreement, and became one of the firm of Pennsylvania, Shakespeare, and Dubuque.

Shakespeare was my own nickname on the cars; Pennsylvania that of my bedfellow; and Dubuque, the name of a place in the State of Iowa, that of an

"Up in the Mountains of Colorado, Down on the Atlantic Coast, and Out on the Pacific Slope We Hear the People All Talking about the New Line Just Opened Up Composed of the Grand 'Burlington Route' C.B. & Q.R.R.," ca. 1883

Courtesy the Huntington Library, San Marino, California.

"Frisco Line, St. Louis and San Francisco Ry," ca. 1890

Courtesy the Huntington Library, San Marino, California.

amiable young fellow going west to cure an asthma, and retarding his recovery by incessantly chewing or smoking, and sometimes chewing and smoking together. I have never seen tobacco so sillily abused.

Shakespeare bought a tin washing-dish, Dubuque a towel, and Pennsylvania a brick of soap. The partners used these instruments, one after another, according to the order of their first awaking; and when the firm had finished there was no want of borrowers. Each filled the tin dish at the water filter opposite the stove, and retired with the whole stock in trade to the platform of the car. There he knelt down, supporting himself by a shoulder against the woodwork, or one elbow crooked about the railing, and made a shift to wash his face and neck and hands—a cold, an insufficient, and, if the train is moving rapidly, a somewhat dangerous toilet.

FURTHER READING

Aldrich, Mark. *Death Rode the Rails: American Railroad Accidents and Safety, 1828–1965*. Baltimore: Johns Hopkins University Press, 2006.

Dearinger, Ryan. *The Filth of Progress: Immigrants, Americans, and the Building of Canals and Railroads in the West*. Berkeley: University of California Press, 2015.

Deverell, William. *Railroad Crossing: Californians and the Railroad, 1850–1910*. Berkeley: University of California Press, 1994.

Fogel, Robert. *Railroads and American Economic Growth*. Baltimore: Johns Hopkins University Press, 1964.

Friedricks, William. *Henry E. Huntington and the Creation of Southern California*. Columbus: Ohio State University Press, 1992.

Hyde, Anne F. *An American Vision: Far Western Landscape and National Culture, 1820–1920*. New York: New York University Press, 1990.

Isenberg, Andrew C. *The Destruction of the Bison: An Environmental History, 1750–1920*. New York: Cambridge University Press, 2000.

Lewis, Daniel. *Iron Horse Imperialism: The Southern Pacific of Mexico, 1880–1951*. Tucson: University of Arizona Press, 2007.

Licht, Walter. *Working for the Railroad: The Organization of Work in the Nineteenth Century*. Princeton, NJ: Princeton University Press, 1983.

Orsi, Richard J. *Sunset Limited: The Southern Pacific Railroad and the Development of the American West, 1850–1930*. Berkeley: University of California Press, 2005.

Schivelbusch, Wolfgang. *The Railway Journey: The Industrialization of Time and Space in the Nineteenth Century*. Berkeley: University of California Press, 2014.

Stevenson, Robert Louis. *The Amateur Emigrant: From the Clyde to Sandy Hook*. Chicago: Stone and Kimball, 1895.

Strom, Claire. *Profiting from the Plains: The Great Northern Railway and Corporate Development of the American West*. Seattle: University of Washington Press, 2003.

White, Richard. *Railroaded: The Transcontinentals and the Making of Modern America*. New York: W. W. Norton, 2011.

Wohaw, *Self-Portrait,* 1878. This drawing was made by the Kiowa warrior Wohaw ("Spotted Cow") while he was a prisoner at Fort Marion in St. Augustine, Florida. Captured along with other Kiowa, Cheyenne, and Comanche Indians following the 1874 Red River War in the Texas Panhandle, Wohaw produced many drawings during his imprisonment, some depicting the life he once knew on the southern Plains, some showing his new life of confinement. Here, Wohaw, who has written his name above the self-portrait, pictures himself caught between two worlds and offering a peace pipe to each. Such was the fate of thousands of Native Americans in the years following the Civil War, as the relentless invasion of their former lands continued. What are some of the symbols of Wohaw's dilemma of identity? Who is his intended audience?

Missouri Historical Society, St. Louis.

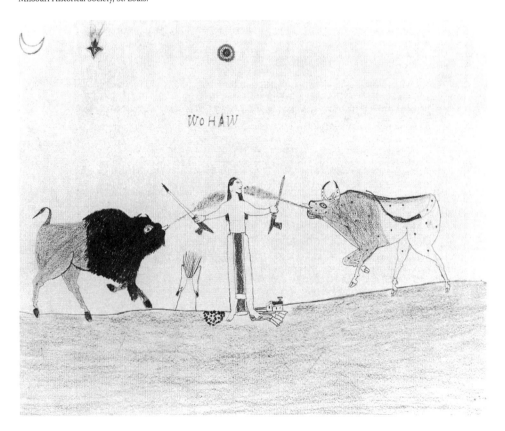

Western Conquest

2

The War against Native America

Although American migration to and across the Rocky Mountains and into what we now know as the American West had begun well before the Civil War, the end of that conflict accelerated the process. Traveling on ever-widening transportation networks provided by railroads, better roads, even western steamships on rivers big enough to accommodate them, and lured by hopes for a better life (or at least an adventurous journey), tens of thousands of native-born Americans and foreign-born immigrants sought new opportunities across western cities, towns, and landscapes.

But whose West was it? The federal government both claimed and coveted the vast West, and through legislative tools like the Homestead Act of 1862 actively encouraged settlement and growth. Settlers responded. All across the West, from the Canadian border down through the Plains on one side of the Rockies and the Great Basin on the other, from the Pacific Northwest to the American Southwest and to the very shores of the Pacific, homesteaders took up federal land, and the obligations that they "improve" it, in one land rush after another. Some land rushes featured thousands of settlers clamoring for their public land stake, and others happened more gradually: settlers here and there, families moving, communities coalescing over time. Miners chased mineral dreams from mountain to mountain, river to river, claim to claim. Politicians and newspaper editors, writers and boosters, trumpeted the West and its seductive democratic or rejuvenating promises. Others saw in the West a way and a place for the country, so damaged by the Civil War, to heal. It was in the West that broken bodies and a broken nation might find new life after the horrors of the war, after all the blood, the sickness, the sadness, the death. It was in the West, such thinking went, that the wide-open spaces and vast beautiful vistas could be harnessed to put America and Americans back together.

But there was at least one very big challenge to this kind of thinking: the West was anything but empty. It was not uninhabited, it was not unclaimed. Beauty and vistas it had in great supply, but it also already had people all over it, people whom the vast majority of Americans, along with their government, saw as simply in the way. Native Americans, possessing hundreds of different cultures, histories, and tribal groups, lived everywhere in the West. Some had stayed close to where ancient migratory patterns stretching back thousands of years (if not more) had put them; some answered the dictates of their own migrations or hunting and gathering imperatives; others occupied places new to their cultures, having been pushed there by warfare with other indigenous peoples or with the United States. There was a time, before the Civil War, when the US government and the US military figured that the trans-Mississippi West could become the vessel in which troublesome Indians could be put. That "solution" was hardly a solution at all; beyond its cultural cruelty and attendant violence, the coercive movement of indigenous peoples westward meant only that the Indian "in-the-way-ness" would simply be put off for a generation or less, sure to come back with the passage of time and increased growth of the post–Civil War West by way of American settlement, railroads, urbanization, and industrial expansion.

The history of the Indian wars of the American West has been distorted in film, print, and popular culture. Cowboys and Indians did not clash in great numbers or innumerable contests, nor did Indians massacre untold numbers of westering settlers cowering behind their Conestoga wagons as they plodded across the prairies and plains. In reality, Indian-settler conflict was both more mundane and more complicated. Cattle, for instance, played an important role in the decline of Native American cohesion and survival in the post–Civil War. The relentless beef markets that demanded ever more range and range cattle helped to drive the American bison, the critical nutrient resource for Plains Indians, to the edge of extinction. This process, exacerbated by the bison demands of westering railroad companies that had to feed big work crews, helped in turn to weaken and drive Native peoples from such places as Kansas, Wyoming, and Nebraska as once-vast buffalo herds thinned from uncountable to not many.

Assaults on Native America came from all sides. US military leaders, civilian politicians, and various religious and humanitarian groups often differed over what to do about the so-called Indian Problem. On the ground, settlers, railroad workers and officials, prospectors and mining companies, farmers, ranchers, and others only added to the chaos and the ultimate tragedy of it all. Reformers and missionaries saw in Native America opportunities and obligations to push Christianization and Americanization goals. Miners and farmers and railroad barons wanted the land or what lay beneath it, and they often attached western water to the list of resources they wished to possess and exploit. Tourists wanted Indians to play roles that made them exotic, though not dangerous, western attractions. As culturally and geopolitically complicated as it was, the Indian Problem could also be understood in simple, tragic terms. Indians were Indians, and that was a problem. And Indians were in the way, and that also was a problem. The solutions were as obvious as they were cruel: remove the Indian, remove his or her Indian-ness, or both.

Native peoples responded to these crises, as they always had, in different ways. Some tribes adopted, or tried to adopt, "white" ways, attempting with greater and lesser success to assimilate or at least integrate with the surrounding farms, villages, or towns. How well this worked usually had more to do with the reaction of local whites than it did with any particular efforts on the part of the Indians. Others retreated to the isolation of the reservations, adopting some aspects of the dominant culture, resisting others, or creating hybrid practices and folkways. Reservations, which would come to dominate federal Indian policy, were, in the words of historian Richard White, "paradoxical places where Indians were to be temporarily segregated in order to prepare them for ultimate integration into the larger society." Such was the theory, but what constituted "temporary" was uncertain and, in the end, undecided.

Other tribes, particularly those on the Plains and in the Southwest, fought back. Often they had little or no choice. In 1865, one general in the US Army ordered his Montana Territory command to accept "no overtures of peace or submission from Indians" but to "attack and kill every male Indian over twelve years of age." Several treaties signed in 1865, which deeded huge chunks of Montana's Powder River country to Indians, fell apart as gold miners refused to honor the boundaries and rules. Sioux bands, in league with Cheyenne and Arapahoe allies, lashed back at whites. One infamous event was the Fetterman Massacre, in which Captain William J. Fetterman and eighty men under his command rode out from Fort Phil Kearny in the Dakota Territory on a winter's day in 1866, and not a single one came back. This humiliating defeat—rendered ironic by Fetterman's alleged earlier boast that, with eighty men, he could ride through the entire Sioux nation—foreshadowed the even more stunning destruction of General George Armstrong Custer and his command at Little Bighorn a decade later. Both defeats gave politicians and the military the leverage to adopt even harsher measures against Indian enemies as the century waned.

Brutal and spasmodic warfare erupted elsewhere as well. Cheyenne and Arapahoe warriors attacked white settlements in Kansas. Apaches on the relatively new border with Mexico carried on a running battle with US and Mexican troops until they were finally subdued in the late 1880s and sent to military prisons in Florida. In Colorado, Arapahoe and Ute Indians fought against farmers, other settlers, and miners. In the Black Hills of Dakota Territory, gold miners trampled on another treaty that had presumably set aside land sacred to the Lakota Sioux. The federal government's inability and unwillingness to enforce the treaty or to hold back the miners set off renewed warfare that led to the annihilation of Custer and his men in the summer of 1876. Custer died a martyr, if a blundering and arrogant one, and public opinion demanded vengeance. Within a year, those Indians who had fought at Little Bighorn were captured or killed, along with so many others who had resisted reservation exile.

By the last decade of the nineteenth century, significant Native American opposition to western territorial and demographic expansion had all but ended. The vast majority of the indigenous people of the West had either been killed, run off to reservations, or shunted into boarding schools run by Christian missionaries. The Dawes Act of 1887, a hybrid of humanitarian reform and coercion, tried to make farmers (and hence "good Americans") of reservation Indians. The act was audacious in its simplistic solution to enduringly complex problems: it would chop up reservations into individual parcels of farmland, where Indians would farm their own land, grow food, earn money, and, in the process, learn what were considered the appropriate traits of full citizenship. In turn, Indians were to give up tribal lives and tribal ways, and renounce claims on ancestral lands. Clumsy and wrongheaded, if at times graced by good intentions, the Dawes Act was but the latest of any number of approaches to the Indian Problem, and it did not work well.

Sporadic conflict continued to break out, even into the early twentieth century. The most notorious and brutal event occurred at Wounded Knee Reservation in South Dakota, where, in the frigid winter of 1890, US troops massacred nearly 150 Sioux men, women, and children who had gathered in the hopeful expectation of the coming of a new world. All they got for their dreams was death.

AS YOU READ: The documents reproduced here illustrate at least some of the complexities of the post–Civil War "Indian Problem" in the American West. Consider how and in what ways the various statements contradict one another. Such contradictions are further proof of the crosscutting and, in the end, hopeless confusion marking US Indian policy. How do the words of John Chivington, for example, mesh with those of Henry Carrington? How might a figure such as Wooden Leg respond to these men? Or Chief Joseph?

8. A MILITARY OFFICER JUSTIFIES THE SAND CREEK MASSACRE

During the Civil War, Governor John Evans of Colorado Territory embarked on his own war against the Cheyenne Indians in order to gain political prestige. The governor's ally in this war was Colonel John Milton Chivington, a former Methodist minister seeking fame as an Indian fighter and the head of the Colorado militia. The Cheyenne Chief Black Kettle, however, desired peace. He did not get it. In the winter of 1864, while camped peacefully alongside Sand Creek in the flatlands of eastern Colorado—beneath an American flag—Black Kettle's band of more than one hundred Cheyenne women and children (most of the men were absent) were massacred by Chivington and the Colorado militia. The Sand Creek Massacre shocked even those accustomed to the horrors of warfare between Native Americans and American settlers and soldiers. "It is difficult to believe," a government investigative panel later stated, "that beings in the form of men could commit or countenance the commission of such acts of cruelty and barbarity." Chivington was subsequently removed from his command. In this statement, designed to justify his actions, Chivington addresses the events that led up to the massacre and proclaims that, under the circumstances, his attack was appropriate and legitimate. What is Chivington's attitude toward the Cheyennes, and what claims does he make about his innocence? Are the claims credible? What other sources would you wish to examine before you made up your mind?

John Milton Chivington
"To the People of Colorado"
1865[1]

When I arrived at Fort Lyon on an expedition against the Indians in November, 1864, I was informed that the Indians on Sand Creek were hostile. Major Anthony, commanding the post, whom I thought was better acquainted than any one else with the relations that existed between the Government and the Indians as regarded peace or war, informed me, on different occasions, that the Indians were hostile, that he had repeatedly fired upon them; that the Indians had sent him word that if he wanted a fight to come out to Sand Creek and they would give him as big a fight as he wanted; that every man of his command would go gladly, and urged an immediate departure. Anthony after the battle of Sand Creek, exulted over the fight, and thought it was the biggest thing on record, and witnesses say they never heard him speak of it except exultingly.

---

1. John Milton Chivington, "To the People of Colorado," synopsis of the Sand Creek investigation, Denver, June 1865, 5–8.

Have I not shown all these facts by witnesses under oath, and can the people of Colorado, or the world, say, that though I had been governed by the most rigid rules of civilized warfare, that with such statements from the commanding officer of a fort made to me, that my conduct could be adjudged anything but honorable. I am but human, and the same means of knowledge by which the public have been informed of the "Chivington massacre," I was informed of the hostility of the Indians on Sand Creek. If Major Anthony, in representing the relations that existed between the troops and the Indians, wilfully lied, then Major Anthony is the responsible party, and the world cannot consistently punish me for the crimes of others, for certainly, from all accounts, I will have enough to answer for without them.

The morning of the 29th day of November 1864 finds us before the village of the Indian foe. The first shot is fired by them. The first man who falls is white. No white flag is raised. None of the Indians show signs of peace, but flying to rifle pits already prepared, they fight with a desperation unequalled, showing their perfect understanding of the relations that existed as regards peace or war, as forty-nine killed and wounded soldiers too plainly testified. Our command consisted of nearly six hundred men. The fight continued till nearly three o'clock in the afternoon. Stephen Decatur swears that being detailed as clerk, in company with Lieut. Col. Bowen, he rode over the field where the fight had occurred and counted four hundred and fifty dead warriors, and that no more women and children were killed than would have been killed in a white village under like circumstances; that the women and children that were killed could not have been saved if the troops had tried; that they were in the rifle pits with the warriors; that there were very few women and children killed; that after he returned to the village he saw things that made him desire to kill more Indians; that he saw great numbers of white scalps, daguerreotypes, part of a ladies toilet, and children's wearing apparel. Would not such sights make any person feel as Stephen Decatur did? Stephen Decatur is a husband and a father, and how many harrowing thoughts of murder and suffering would a spectacle like this call up, and how many endearing reminiscences would be swept into the gulf of horror on an occasion like this. Stephen Decatur has spent seven years among the Indians and is acquainted with them. He had been a soldier before, and speaks of this fight as being the hardest he ever saw, on both sides. He had seen the Lipan or Camanche Indians scalp their own dead. Husbands and fathers, under similar circumstances what would you have done? *Coaxed* the chiefs to have taken their warriors away, or like white men and true soldiers accepted their wager of battle and whipped them if you could. Yet this is all that was done at Sand Creek. Though hundreds of Colorado soldiers are to-day branded as murderers, and that in many instances by men without knowing or caring whether the charge be false or true. It is sufficient if he be a soldier, in the eyes of these malignant cowards. He must as a natural consequence be a murderer, while others wearing the uniform of officers, without the courage to perform a brave deed themselves, are the loudest to condemn the conduct of a brother soldier who wins a single laurel that they cannot steal. Such men are more to be feared than the crawling viper. Perjury, larceny or robbery are no obstacles in their road to vengeance, venomous as reptiles and cowardly as curs. But what is the cause of all this trouble—whence the source of this cry of holy horror that has been rung with such startling effect upon the minds of the unsophisticated people of New England, the people generally of the States, and especially the billious old maids in the United States Senate and the House of Representatives? Why it originates in the fertile minds of two Government employees conspiring together to swindle the Government, as one of them states, out of $25,000. Through the influence of friends he has in Washington, and by whom he expects to get his claims allowed, probably some high official who is desirous of making an honest dollar by advocating the cause of the honest old men of the wilderness, the veracious John Smith, Indian interpreter and that reliable, respectable old gentleman, Major Colley, Indian Agent.[2] But under the solemn and binding obligations of an oath, what does Major Talbott say? Simply that Major Colley and John Smith stated to him that they would do anything to ruin Col. Chivington; that they were even equally interested in their trade with the Indians—one an Indian Agent, the other Indian Interpreter; that they had lost one hundred and five buffalo robes and two white ponies by Col. Chivington's attack on the Indian village at Sand Creek; that they would collect $25,000 for it of the Government, and eventually damn Col. Chivington; that John Smith boastingly stated that the eastern papers would be filled with accounts of Sand Creek, as a massacre; that they would go to Washington and represent to the committee on the Conduct of the War that Sand Creek was a massacre. What did they mean when they said they would do *anything* to ruin Col. Chivington? The word has a broad signification, and did they not include *perjury*? It appears to us without any stretch of the imagination, they did take the expression "we will go to Washington and represent Sand Greek as a massacre; the eastern papers will be filled with accounts of Sand Creek as a massacre, by letters from Fort Lyon, and we will do *anything* to ruin Col. Chivington," and draw your own conclusions. If it appears to you as it does to me, perjury would be no obstacle to these worthies in their road to vengeance. If they would deliberately conspire to rob the Government out of $25,000 through the influence of their friends would they not also be guilty of *perjury*, to ruin their enemies? Then what conclusions are we compelled to arrive at? That perjury has been perpetrated by these worthies, abetted by their friends and the honorable gentlemen who compose the Committee on the Conduct of the War,—they whose piercing criticism has been a terror to evil doers in the States,—they who, from their high order of intelligence have been supposed to be able to draw aside the

---

2. **Indian Agent:** an official representative of the US government.

thick curtain that concealed the dark deeds of the adepts in crime and allow the sunlight of truth and justice to shine in upon it, are made the *innocent tools* of two ignorant old Indian trappers and traders, to wreak disgrace and ruin upon Col. Chivington and Colorado soldiers generally. Truly these two old gentlemen, Colley and Smith, must have read the Scriptures, for they appear to have been, in Washington, "as innocent as lambs and as wary as foxes."[3]

Now, fellow citizens, what do you think of the Chivington massacre, whose horrors have filled so many columns of the papers in the States and called down upon Colorado so many disgraceful epithets, while at the same time our enterprising freighters, emigrants and settlers, with their wives and children, have been murdered, scalped and their bodies horribly mutilated by these much abused sons of the plains. . . .

Lo, the poor Indian, in thy untutored greatness, you have proved yourself, with the assistance of high officials, your friends, a good diplomat. You have long been a bone of contention and many a villainous swindle has been perpetrated upon the Government in thy name and humanity, which would put to blush the unparalelled commander of the sons of sin, His Satanic Majesty, the Devil.

J. M. Chivington,
Late Col. 1st Cavalry of Colorado,
Com'd'g Dist. of Colorado

---

3. **"innocent as lambs and as wary as foxes":** a biblical reference, perhaps to Matthew 10:16.

9. INSTRUCTIONS TO WHITES IN INDIAN COUNTRY

Emigrant wagon trains and miners fanned out across the wide spaces of the American West once the Civil War had ended. Army commanders at various frontier forts and outposts issued orders to wagon masters and leaders of other settler and miner parties not to interfere with the local Native American populations in hopes that contact between groups might remain peaceful. In this selection, Colonel Henry B. Carrington, who had charge of a vast chunk of the northern Great Plains, tries to get settlers, miners, and other emigrant parties to behave peaceably when they cut through Indian country. Yet, although the document stated that peace could be maintained, it was a hopeless cause. Settlers, miners, and adventurers commonly disregarded such orders, and their stubborn insistence on going where they should not go and doing what they should not do only exacerbated tensions between Indians and whites. Within months of issuing these orders, Colonel Carrington would have to explain how the Fetterman Massacre could have taken place on his watch. According to Carrington, what are the important reasons why trouble breaks out between Indians and whites? How do you think he planned to enforce these rules? Do you think any other methods of addressing the "Indian Problem" would have worked in the second half of the nineteenth century?

Henry B. Carrington

"Orders to Civilian Wagon Trains in Montana"
1866[1]

1. All trains, whether large or small, must stop at Reno Station, formerly Fort Reno,[2] on Powder River, and report to the post commander.

2. Thirty armed men constitute a party which, upon selection of its commander or conductor, will be allowed to proceed. The reduction of this number will depend upon the general conduct of trains and the conditions and safety of the route, of which due notice will be given.

3. When a train shall have organized, the conductor will present to the post commander a list of the men accompanying the said train, upon which list, if satisfactory, he will endorse, "Permission given to pass to Fort Reno." Upon arrival of a train at Fort Reno, the conductor will report with his list, indorsed[3] as above mentioned, to the post commander to receive the same indorsed approval as in the first instance to pass to the next post. This examination and approval must be had at each post, so that the last post commander on the Upper Yellowstone will have the evidence that the train has passed all posts.

4. The constant separation and scattering of trains pretending to act in concert must be stopped; and for the information of emigrants and well-disposed citizens the following reasons are given: viz:

> First, nearly all danger from Indians lies in the recklessness of travelers. A small party when separated, either sell whisky to or fire upon scattering Indians, or get in dispute with them, and somebody is hurt. An insult to an Indian is resented by the Indians against the first white men they meet, and innocent travelers suffer.
>
> Again, the new route is short and will be made perfectly secure. The cooperation of citizens is therefore essential for their own personal comfort as well as for the interests of the public at large; and if citizens ask, as they will of course rightly expect, the protection and aid from Government troops, they must themselves be equally diligent in avoiding difficulties with Indians, or among themselves, and the consideration paid to any complaint will be measured by the apparent good faith with which citizens regard the regulations for the management of the route.

5. When trains scatter and upon reporting at any post there shall be found a substantial variation from the list furnished, all of the remaining teams will be stopped until the residue of the train arrives, or is accounted for; and until this is done they will not be permitted to unite with other trains to complete numbers, which their insubordination or haste has lost or scattered.

---

1. Dee Brown, *The Fetterman Massacre: An American Saga* (London: Barrie and Jenkins, 1972), 60–61.
2. **Fort Reno:** older name for Fort Phil Kearny.
3. **indorsed:** endorsed.

6. The main object being perfect security to travel, all citizens are cautioned against any unnecessary dealings with Indians, against giving or selling ardent spirits, against personal quarrels with them, or any acts having a tendency to irritate them, or develop hostile acts or plans. A faithful and wise regard for these instructions will, with the aid of the Government troops, insure peace, which is all important and can be made certain.

7. A copy of these instructions will be properly and publicly posted at the office of each post or station commandant, and all conductors of trains will have their attention called thereto, with instructions to notify all who travel in their charge.

10. A MILITARY OFFICER'S VIEW OF THE BLACK HILLS

Lieutenant Colonel Richard Dodge's book The Black Hills: A Minute Description of the Routes, Scenery, Soil, Climate, Timber, Gold, Geology, Zoology, Etc., *published in 1876, was a virtual tourists' and miners' guide to a region supposedly off-limits, in perpetuity, to non-Indians. Dodge's claims—that Indians had not established permanent settlement rights in the region and that the "Indian Problem" had not been dealt with effectively by the United States government— were commonly held assumptions. On the heels of publications such as these and the Black Hills gold rush of 1874, more and more adventurous, greedy, and often foolhardy (not to say murderous) miners penetrated the Black Hills, crossing treaty lines in the process. Sentiments from supposed authorities like Colonel Dodge, whose perspective on the territory ("a true oasis," he called it) is reproduced here, did little to lessen tensions or the likelihood of violence. In what ways does Dodge hint at his own solution to the "Indian Problem"? What reasons does Dodge offer for why the Black Hills ought to be thrown open to settlement, mining, and growth? What counterarguments could have been made by Native Americans or their white allies?*

Richard I. Dodge
"Indians and the Indian Question"
1876[1]

It is believed by some persons that the Crow Indians, the former owners, actually occupied and lived in the Black Hills before being driven out by the Sioux. I do not think so, for two reasons; First, If this country had been used as a residence, even thirty years ago, some marks of its occupation would still be visible.

---

1. Richard Irving Dodge, *The Black Hills:* A *Minute Description of the Routes, Scenery, Soil, Climate, Timber, Gold, Geology, Zoology, Etc.* (New York: James Miller, Publisher, 1876), 136–41, 149–51.

Second, The mountain Crows are known to be determined fighters, in their own fastnesses.[2] Had even a small band occupied and defended the Hills, they could have held it until now against the whole Sioux nation, who, though excellent horseback fighters, are worth nothing on foot; and though most dangerous, aggressive enemies on the plains, are timid as hares in woods and mountains.

My opinion is, that the Black Hills have never been a permanent home for any Indians. Even now small parties go a little way into the Hills to cut spruce lodge-poles, but all the signs indicate that these are mere sojourns of the most temporary character.

The "teepe," or lodge, may be regarded as the Indian's house, the wickyup[3] as his tent. One is his permanent residence, the other the make-shift shelter for a night. Except in one single spot, near the head of Castle Creek, I saw nowhere any evidence whatever of a lodge having been set up, while old wickyups were not unfrequent in the edge of the Hills. There is not one single teepe or lodge-pole trail, from side to side of the Hills, in any direction, and these poles, when dragged in the usual way by ponies, soon make a trail as difficult to obliterate as a wagon road, visible for many years, even though not used.

Several small parties of Indians, overcome by curiosity, and reassured by the presence of the "soldiers,"[4] came into the Hills this summer. The most intelligent of these, an Indian named Robe Raiser, was quite communicative, and informed the interpreter that, though fifty years old, and though he had been around the Hills almost every year of his life, he had never before ventured inside; that when passing north or south in the fall, the squaws come in sometimes to cut lodge-poles, the bucks venturing to hunt a little, but that these stops are very short. His reasons for the Indians not coming in were: First, That the Hills are "bad medicine," and the abode of spirits. Second, That there is nothing to come for except lodge-poles, the game being scarce and more difficult to kill than that on the plains. Third, That the thickets are so dense that their ponies are soon lost if turned loose, and the flies are so bad that they are tormented and worried out, if kept tied up. Fourth, That it rains very frequently, and that the Indian does not like rain. Fifth, That it thunders and lightens with terrible force, tearing trees to pieces and setting fire to the woods. He said, moreover, that the Indians had never lived here, and did not and would not live here now; that they did not want the country, and would have sold or given it away long ago to the whites, but for the "squaw men" about the reservations, who urged them to make a "big fuss" and they would be sure to get a "big price" for the country.

These statements are borne out by those of every Indian communicated with, and by the observation of every man of our party. The Indians do not live

---

2. **fastnesses:** secure places or fortifications.
3. **wickyup:** a framed structure, often very mobile, with a covering of bark or brush.
4. **"soldiers":** It is unclear what Dodge means by the quotation marks. He may be referring to Indian warriors accompanying other Indians into the Black Hills.

in, occupy, or use the country in any way (except for lodge-poles, as stated); they do not want it; the large majority would willingly give it to the whites, but for the exertions and influence of as rascally a set of white men as curse the earth. It appears probable that there will be a war on this question. Some homes will be ruined, some good men and valuable citizens will be murdered, some women ravished, some babies brained against burning door-posts, and all because a few miscreants want to make money.

The Black Hills are closed to settlers by virtue of a treaty with the Indians, which treaty, the settlers claim, has been violated by the Indians time and again. By it the Indians agreed to abstain from robbery and murder of the whites. Within a very short time after it was made, the very Indians making it murdered an officer of the army, and though (I am told) the individual Indians who committed the crime are well known, though the jewelry and other articles of the murdered man are worn openly by the murderers, not only is nothing said about it, but the murderers and their families are "good Indians," living at the reservation and drawing their rations with excellent regularity. . . .

It may appear very singular to most persons that a question so easy of solution as this Indian problem should have been allowed to disturb and agitate the country for so many years.

It must appear strange, the facts being known to almost every intelligent person of the land, that agents of the Government have been permitted to starve and swindle the Indian year after year with impunity.

The murder of a family by white ruffians, with the accompaniment of rape and arson, would send a thrill of horror through every breast. No stone would be left unturned to capture the villains and bring them to the gallows. Yet every year murders, arsons, rapes are permitted to the Indian as pastimes, the murderers, though known, not only remaining unmolested, but being fed and petted by the agents of a Government which owes protection to all its citizens.

The impunity which surrounds all these abuses is, however, easily accounted for, when we reflect on the enormous power of money, and the desperate passion with which some men pursue gain.

There is more money in this Indian question than in any other which agitates the country, and where money is, there power is also.

Some of the greatest fortunes of this country have been founded on Indian contracts, Indian agencies, Indian trade.

Some of our wealthiest and most powerful citizens are, at this moment, pecuniarily interested in having this matter remain just as it is, and the Indian Ring[5] is the wealthiest and most powerful in the land. . . .

---

5. **Indian Ring:** Dodge is charging that a syndicate of US officials, Indian agents, and commercial vendors have gotten wealthy through illegal or questionable activity in filling the contracts that supply food and other goods to Indians on reservations.

Conclusion

The "Black Hills" country is a true oasis in a wide and dreary desert. The approaches from every direction are through long stretches of inhospitable plains, treeless and broken, in which the supply of water is so saturated with bitter and nauseous alkalies as to be unfit for the continuous use of the white man. . . .

I but express my fair and candid opinion when I pronounce the Black Hills, in many respects, the finest country I have ever seen.

The beauty and variety of the scenery, the excellence of the soil, the magnificence of the climate, the abundance of timber and building-stone, make it a most desirable residence for men who want good homes.

As a grazing country it cannot be surpassed; and small stock-farms of fine cattle and sheep cannot, I think, fail of success.

In a few years, when this wilderness shall have been made to "blossom as the rose," with cozy farms and comfortable residences, when rocky crags shall have been crowned with palatial hotels, the tourist will find an ample reward in climbing the rugged heights, or exploring the dark defiles of this wonderful land.

Gold there is, everywhere in the granitic areas; gold enough to make many fortunes, and tempt to the loss of many more. The very uncertainty has a fascination for many men. It is a grand lottery! Only a few draw prizes, but each may be the favorite of the "fickle goddess."

This hope, this barest chance, will draw thousands of men from comfortable homes and sorrowing friends.

In a few weeks or months the eager thirst for "pot-holes"[6] will have deserted the better class, and they will settle down into valuable citizens of a country destined in a few years to be an important and wealthy portion of the great American Republic.

---

6. **"pot-holes"**: mining strikes.

11. A CHEYENNE VIEW OF BATTLE

In 1874, troops under the command of George Armstrong Custer found gold in the Black Hills. Miners soon began to stream into the area, in stark violation of the Laramie Treaty of 1868. Sioux Indians and their allies retaliated, and Custer and other military officers and units were sent out to push the Indians onto reservations. But things did not work out as the US Army planned. On June 25, 1876, Custer, along with several hundred of his men, died in a brief but fierce battle near the banks of the Little Big Horn River in Montana. The humiliating defeat galvanized the army, which quickly conquered the Native Americans of the northern Plains. Nearly sixty years after the battle, the Cheyenne warrior Wooden Leg recalled the event and his role in it. In this excerpt from the transcription of his reminiscences, the aged Cheyenne remembers the tumult and excitement of that fateful day when Custer and his few hundred men blundered into a gathering of four thousand Indians, the largest congregation of Native American warriors ever assembled in North America. As you read Wooden Leg's account, think of the sights and sounds of the battle he is describing. How would his viewpoint influence the portrayal of this battle in a film? Do Wooden Leg's memories of the battle and the behavior of the Indians fit what Chivington believed about Native Americans? What does this reminiscence reveal about codes of conduct among Indian warriors?

Wooden Leg

Account of the Battle of Little Bighorn
1931[1]

In my sleep I dreamed that a great crowd of people were making lots of noise. Something in the noise startled me. I found myself wide awake, sitting up and listening. My brother too awakened, and we both jumped to our feet. A great commotion was going on among the camps. We heard shooting. We hurried out from the trees so we might see as well as hear. The shooting was somewhere at the upper part of the camp circles. It looked as if all of the Indians there were running away toward the hills to the westward or down toward our end of the village. Women were screaming and men were letting out war cries. Through it all we could hear old men calling:

"Soldiers are here! Young men, go out and fight them."

We ran to our camp and to our home lodge. Everybody there was excited. Women were hurriedly making up little packs for flight. Some were going off northward or across the river without any packs. Children were hunting for their mothers. Mothers were anxiously trying to find their children. I got my lariat and my six shooter. I hastened on down toward where had been our horse herd. . . .

My father had caught my favorite horse from the herd brought in by the boys and Bald Eagle. I quickly emptied out my war bag and set myself at getting ready to go into battle. I jerked off my ordinary clothing. I jerked on a pair of new breeches that had been given to me by an Uncpapa Sioux. I had a good cloth shirt, and I put it on. My old moccasins were kicked off and a pair of beaded moccasins substituted for them. My father strapped a blanket upon my horse and arranged the rawhide lariat into a bridle. He stood holding my mount.

"Hurry," he urged me. . . .

---

1. Thomas Marquis, ed., *Wooden Leg: A Warrior Who Fought Custer* (Lincoln: University of Nebraska Press, 1962), 217–28, 231, 236–37, 240, 247–48, 256.

The air was so full of dust I could not see where to go. But it was not needful that I see that far. I kept my horse headed in the direction of movement by the crowd of Indians on horseback. I was led out around and far beyond the Uncpapa camp circle. Many hundreds of Indians on horseback were dashing to and fro in front of a body of soldiers. The soldiers were on the level valley ground and were shooting with rifles. Not many bullets were being sent back at them, but thousands of arrows were falling among them. I went on with a throng of Sioux until we got beyond and behind the white men. By this time, though, they had mounted their horses and were hiding themselves in the timber. A band of Indians were with the soldiers. It appeared they were Crows or Shoshones. Most of these Indians had fled back up the valley. Some were across east of the river and were riding away over the hills beyond.

Our Indians crowded down toward the timber where were the soldiers. More and more of our people kept coming. Almost all of them were Sioux. There were only a few Cheyennes. Arrows were showered into the timber. Bullets whistled out toward the Sioux and Cheyennes. But we stayed far back while we extended our curved line farther and farther around the big grove of trees. Some dead soldiers had been left among the grass and sagebrush where first they had fought us. It seemed to me the remainder of them would not live many hours longer. Sioux were creeping forward to set fire to the timber.

Suddenly the hidden soldiers came tearing out on horseback, from the woods. I was around on that side where they came out. I whirled my horse and lashed it into a dash to escape from them. All others of my companions did the same. But soon we discovered they were not following us. They were running away from us. They were going as fast their tired horses could carry them across an open valley space and toward the river. We stopped, looked a moment, and then we whipped our ponies into swift pursuit. A great throng of Sioux also were coming after them. My distant position put me among the leaders in the chase. The soldier horses moved slowly, as if they were very tired. Ours were lively. We gained rapidly on them.

I fired four shots with my six shooter. I do not know whether or not any of my bullets did harm. I saw a Sioux put an arrow into the back of a soldier's head. Another arrow went into his shoulder. He tumbled from his horse to the ground. Others fell dead either from arrows or from stabbings or jabbings or from blows by the stone war clubs of the Sioux. Horses limped or staggered or sprawled out dead or dying. Our war cries and war songs were mingled with many jeering calls, such as:

"You are only boys. You ought not to be fighting. We whipped you on the Rosebud. You should have brought more Crows or Shoshones with you to do your fighting."

Little Bird and I were after one certain soldier. Little Bird was wearing a trailing warbonnet. He was at the right and I was at the left of the fleeing man. We were lashing him and his horse with our pony whips. It seemed not brave to shoot him. Besides, I did not want to waste my bullets. He pointed back his revolver, though, and sent a bullet into Little Bird's thigh. Immediately I whacked the white man fighter on his head with the heavy elk-horn handle of my pony whip. The blow dazed him. I seized the rifle strapped on his back. I wrenched it and dragged the looping strap over his head. As I was getting possession of this weapon he fell to the ground. I did not harm him further. I do not know what became of him. . . .

Indians mobbed the soldiers floundering afoot and on horseback in crossing the river. I do not know how many of our enemies might have been killed there. With my captured rifle as a club I knocked two of them from their horses into the flood waters. Most of the pursuing warriors stopped at the river, but many kept on after the men with the blue clothing. I remained in the pursuit and crossed the river. . . .

Another enemy Indian was behind a little sagebrush knoll and shooting at us. His shots were returned. I and some others went around and got behind him. We dismounted and crept toward him. As we came close up to him he fell. A bullet had hit him. He raised himself up, though, and swung his rifle around toward us. We rushed upon him. I crashed a blow of my rifle barrel upon his head. Others beat and stabbed him to death. I got also his gun. . . .

I returned to the west side of the river. Lots of Indians were hunting around there for dead soldiers or for wounded ones to kill. I joined in this search. I got some tobacco from the pockets of one dead man. I got also a belt having in it a few cartridges. All of the weapons and clothing and all other possessions were being taken from the bodies. The warriors were doing this. No old people nor women were there. They all had run away to the hill benches to the westward. I went to a dead horse, to see what might be found there. Leather bags were on them, behind the saddles. I rummaged into one of these bags. I found there two pasteboard boxes. I broke open one of them.

"Oh, cartridges!" . . .

Now I need not be so careful in expending ammunition. Now I felt very brave. I jumped upon my horse and went again to fight whatever soldiers I might find on the east side of the river. . . .

From our hilltop position I fired a few shots from my newly obtained rifle. I aimed not at any particular ones, but only in the direction of all of them. I think I was too far away to do much harm to them. I had been there only a short time when somebody said to me:

"Look! Yonder are other soldiers!"

I saw them on distant hills down the river and on our same side of it. The news of them spread quickly among us. Indians began to ride in that direction. . . .

Not many people were in the lodges of our camp. . . .

More and more Indians were flocking from the camps to that direction. Some were yet coming along the hills from where the first soldiers had stopped.

The soldiers now in view were spreading themselves into lines along a ridge. The Indians were on lower ridges in front of them, between them and the river, and were moving on around up a long coulee to get behind the white men. . . .

The slow long-distance fighting was kept up for about an hour and a half, I believe. The Indians all the time could see where were the soldiers. . . .

After the long time of the slow fighting, about forty of the soldiers came galloping from the east part of the ridge down toward the river, toward where most of the Cheyennes and many Ogallalas were hidden. The Indians ran back to a deep gulch. The soldiers stopped and got off their horses when they arrived at a low ridge where the Indians had been. Lame White Man, the Southern Cheyenne chief, came on his horse and called us to come back and fight. In a few minutes the warriors were all around these soldiers. Then Lame White Man called out:

"Come. We can kill all of them." . . .

A Sioux wearing a warbonnet was lying down behind a clump of sagebrush on the hillside only a short distance north of where now is the big stone having the iron fence around it. He was about half the length of my lariat rope up ahead of me. Many other Indians were near him. Some boys were mingled among them, to get in quickly for making coup blows[2] on any dead soldiers they might find. A Cheyenne boy was lying down right behind the warbonnet Sioux. The Sioux was peeping up and firing a rifle from time to time. At one of these times a soldier bullet hit him exactly in the middle of the forehead. His arms and legs jumped in spasms for a few moments, then he died. The boy quickly slid back down into a gully, jumped to his feet and ran away. . . .

The shots quit coming from the soldiers. Warriors who had crept close to them began to call out that all of the white men were dead. All of the Indians then jumped up and rushed forward. All of the boys and old men on their horses came tearing into the crowd. The air was full of dust and smoke. Everybody was greatly excited. It looked like thousands of dogs might look if all of them were mixed together in a fight. . . .

Seven of these last soldiers broke away and went running down the coulee sloping toward the river from the west end of the ridge. I was on the side opposite from them, and there was much smoke and dust, and many Indians were in front of me, so I did not see these men running, but I learned of them from the talk afterward. They did not get far, because many Indians were all around them. . . .

I took one scalp. As I went walking and leading my horse among the dead I observed one face that interested me. The dead man had a long beard growing from both sides of his face and extending several inches below the chin. He had also a full mustache. All of the beard hair was of a light yellow color, as I now

---

2. **making coup blows:** delivering final blows to the dead or wounded enemy.

recall it. Most of the soldiers had beard growing, in different lengths, but this was the longest one I saw among them. I think the dead man may have been thirty or more years old. "Here is a new kind of scalp," I said to a companion. I skinned one side of the face and half of the chin, so as to keep the long beard yet on the part removed. . . .

I rode away from the battle hill in the middle of the afternoon. Many warriors had gone back across the hills to the southward, there to fight again the first soldiers. But I went to the camps across on the west side of the river. I had on a soldier coat and breeches I had taken. I took with me the two metal bottles of whisky. At the end of the arrow shaft I carried the beard scalp.

I waved my scalp as I rode among our people. The first person I met who took special interest in me was my mother's mother. She was living in a little willow dome lodge of her own. "What is that?" she asked me when I flourished the scalp stick toward her. I told her. "I give it to you," I said, and I held it out to her. She screamed and shrank away. "Take it," I urged. "It will be good medicine for you." Then I went on to tell her about my having killed the Crow or Shoshone at the first fight up the river, about my getting the two guns, about my knocking in the head two soldiers in the river, about what I had done in the next fight on the hill where all of the soldiers had been killed. We talked about my soldier clothing. She said I looked good dressed that way. I had thought so too, but neither the coat nor the breeches fit me well. The arms and legs were too short for me. . . .

There was no dancing nor celebrating of any kind in any of the camps that night. Too many people were in mourning, among all of the Sioux as well as among the Cheyennes. Too many Cheyenne and Sioux women had gashed their arms and legs, in token of their grief. The people generally were praying, not cheering. . . .

12. A NEZ PERCÉ'S CALL FOR PEACE

A year after Custer's humiliating defeat, the army went after a band of the Nez Percé Indians of eastern Oregon. Led by Hin-mah-too-yah-lat-kekt (Thunder Traveling over the Mountains), or "Young Joseph" (as whites called him to distinguish him from his father), the Wallowa Valley band of the Nez Percés wanted nothing to do with reservation life. Following a series of clashes with white settlers, Joseph's band began a remarkable sprint eastward, first toward the countryside surrounding Yellowstone (which had been made the nation's first national park in 1872) and then north to Canada. Just forty miles short of the border, the majority of the band, exhausted, cold, and hungry, surrendered to General Nelson Miles. From there, the Nez Percés were shuttled off to imprisonment in interior camps, forts, and reservations in the West. Only in 1885 were they allowed to move to the Nez Percé reservation in Idaho. In this document, published in the pages of a leading magazine not long after his capture, Young Joseph discusses his views of Indian affairs, especially as they relate to the dramatic story of the Nez Percés. "An Indian's View of Indian Affairs" was originally delivered as a speech in Washington, DC. Though Chief Joseph's remarks called for an ambitious rethinking of the government's Indian policies, the speech, in the end, accomplished little other than to make him a well-known, well-respected tribal leader. In this excerpt he relates how his band of Wallowa Nez Percés felt forced into flight. Given his remarks in this speech, what decisions do you think Chief Joseph would have made if he were able to influence US Indian policy? How would Lieutenant Colonel Richard Dodge have responded to this speech? What would Colonel Chivington propose? How does religion influence Joseph's perspective?

Chief Joseph

"An Indian's View of Indian Affairs"
1879[1]

My friends, I have been asked to show you my heart. I am glad to have a chance to do so. I want the white people to understand my people. Some of you think an Indian is like a wild animal. This is a great mistake. I will tell you all about our people, and then you can judge whether an Indian is a man or not. I believe much trouble and blood would be saved if we opened our hearts more. I will tell you in my way how the Indian sees things. The white man has more words to tell you how they look to him, but it does not require many words to speak the truth. What I have to say will come from my heart, and I will speak with a straight tongue. . . .

We did not know there were other people besides the Indian until about one hundred winters ago, when some men with white faces came to our country. They brought many things with them to trade for furs and skins. They brought tobacco, which was new to us. They brought guns with flint stones on them, which frightened our women and children. Our people could not talk with these white-faced men, but they used signs which all people understand. These men were Frenchmen, and they called our people "Nez Percés," because they wore rings in their noses for ornaments. Although very few of our people wear them now, we are still called by the same name. These French trappers said a great many things to our fathers which have been planted in our hearts. Some were good for us, but some were bad. Our people were divided in opinion about these men. Some thought they taught more bad than good. An Indian respects a brave man, but he despises a coward. He loves a straight tongue, but he hates a forked tongue. . . .

---

1. Young Joseph, "An Indian's View of Indian Affairs," *North American Review* 269 (April 1879): 415–16, 419–25, 432–33.

For a short time we lived quietly. But this could not last. White men had found gold in the mountains around the land of winding water. They stole a great many horses from us, and we could not get them back because we were Indians. The white men told lies for each other. They drove off a great many of our cattle. Some white men branded our young cattle so they could claim them. We had no friend who would plead our cause before the law councils. It seemed to me that some of the white men in Wallowa were doing these things on purpose to get up a war. They knew that we were not strong enough to fight them. I labored hard to avoid trouble and bloodshed. We gave up some of our country to the white men, thinking that then we could have peace. We were mistaken. The white man would not let us alone. We could have avenged our wrongs many times, but we did not. Whenever the Government has asked us to help them against other Indians, we have never refused. When the white men were few and we were strong we could have killed them all off, but the Nez Percés wished to live at peace. . . .

On account of the treaty made by the other bands of the Nez Percés, the white men claimed my lands. We were troubled greatly by white men crowding over the line. Some of these were good men, and we lived on peaceful terms with them, but they were not all good.

Nearly every year the agent came over from Lapwai[2] and ordered us onto the reservation. We always replied that we were satisfied to live in Wallowa. We were careful to refuse the presents or annuities which he offered.

Through all the years since the white men came to Wallowa we have been threatened and taunted by them and the treaty Nez Percés. They have given us no rest. We have had a few good friends among white men, and they have always advised my people to bear these taunts without fighting. Our young men were quick-tempered, and I have had great trouble in keeping them from doing rash things. I have carried a heavy load on my back ever since I was a boy. I learned then that we were but few, while the white men were many, and that we could not hold our own with them. We were like deer. They were like grizzly bears. We had a small country. Their country was large. We were contented to let things remain as the Great Spirit Chief made them. They were not; and would change the rivers and mountains if they did not suit them.

Year after year we have been threatened, but no war was made upon my people until General Howard[3] came to our country two years ago and told us that he was the white war-chief of all that country. He said: "I have a great many soldiers at my back. I am going to bring them up here, and then I will talk to you

---

2. **Lapwai:** the Lapwai Reservation in Idaho where the Nez Percés had been ordered to move. Some Nez Percé bands had signed an earlier treaty agreeing to go to the reservation; Joseph's Wallowa Valley Nez Percés had not signed the treaty.
3. **General Howard:** O. O. Howard, an army officer and one-armed Civil War veteran who had earlier headed up the Freedman's Bureau in the South.

again. I will not let white men laugh at me the next time I come. The country belongs to the Government, and I intend to make you go upon the reservation."

I remonstrated with him against bringing more soldiers to the Nez Percés country. He had one house full of troops all the time at Fort Lapwai.

The next spring the agent at Umatilla agency sent an Indian runner to tell me to meet General Howard at Walla Walla. I could not go myself, but I sent my brother and five other head men to meet him, and they had a long talk.

General Howard said: "You have talked straight, and it is all right. You can stay in Wallowa." He insisted that my brother and his company should go with him to Fort Lapwai. When the party arrived there General Howard sent out runners and called all the Indians in to a grand council. I was in that council. I said to General Howard, "We are ready to listen." He answered that he would not talk then, but would hold a council next day, when he would talk plainly. I said to General Howard: "I am ready to talk to-day. I have been in a great many councils, but I am no wiser. We are all sprung from a woman, although we are unlike in many things. We can not be made over again. You are as you were made, and as you were made you can remain. We are just as we were made by the Great Spirit, and you can not change us; then why should children of one mother and one father quarrel—why should one try to cheat the other? I do not believe that the Great Spirit Chief gave one kind of men the right to tell another kind of men what they must do."

General Howard replied: "You deny my authority, do you? You want to dictate to me, do you?"

Then one of my chiefs—Too-hool-hool-suit—rose in the council and said to General Howard: "The Great Spirit Chief made the world as it is, and as he wanted it, and he made a part of it for us to live upon. I do not see where you get authority to say that we shall not live where he placed us."

General Howard lost his temper and said: "Shut up! I don't want to hear any more of such talk. The law says you shall go upon the reservation to live, and I want you to do so, but you persist in disobeying the law" (meaning the treaty). "If you do not move, I will take the matter into my own hand, and make you suffer for your disobedience."

Too-hool-hool-suit answered: "Who are you, that you ask us to talk, and then tell me I sha'n't talk? Are you the Great Spirit? Did you make the world? Did you make the sun? Did you make the rivers to run for us to drink? Did you make the grass to grow? Did you make all these things, that you talk to us as though we were boys? If you did, then you have the right to talk as you do."

I said: "War can be avoided, and it ought to be avoided. I want no war. My people have always been the friends of the white man. Why are you in such a hurry? I can not get ready to move in thirty days. Our stock is scattered, and Snake River is very high. Let us wait until fall, then the river will be low. We want time to hunt up our stock and gather supplies for winter."

General Howard replied, "If you let the time run over one day, the soldiers will be there to drive you on to the reservation, and all your cattle and horses outside of the reservation at that time will fall into the hands of the white men."

I knew I had never sold my country, and that I had no land in Lapwai; but I did not want bloodshed. I did not want my people killed. I did not want anybody killed. Some of my people had been murdered by white men, and the white murderers were never punished for it. I told General Howard about this, and again said I wanted no war. I wanted the people who lived upon the lands I was to occupy at Lapwai to have time to gather their harvest.

I said in my heart that, rather than have war, I would give up my country. I would give up my father's grave. I would give up everything rather than have the blood of white men upon the hands of my people.

General Howard refused to allow me more than thirty days to move my people and their stock. I am sure that he began to prepare for war at once. . . .

There were bad men among my people who had quarreled with white men, and they talked of their wrongs until they roused all the bad hearts in the council. Still I could not believe that they would begin the war. I know that my young men did a great wrong, but I ask, Who was first to blame? They had been insulted a thousand times; their fathers and brothers had been killed; their mothers and wives had been disgraced; they had been driven to madness by whisky sold to them by white men; they had been told by General Howard that all their horses and cattle which they had been unable to drive out of Wallowa were to fall into the hands of white men; and, added to all this, they were homeless and desperate.

I would have given my own life if I could have undone the killing of white men by my people. I blame my young men and I blame the white men. I blame General Howard for not giving my people time to get their stock away from Wallowa. I do not acknowledge that he had the right to order me to leave Wallowa at any time. I deny that either my father or myself ever sold that land. It is still our land. It may never again be our home, but my father sleeps there, and I love it as I love my mother. I left there, hoping to avoid bloodshed. . . .

My friends among white men have blamed me for the war. I am not to blame. When my young men began the killing, my heart was hurt. Although I did not justify them, I remembered all the insults I had endured, and my blood was on fire. Still I would have taken my people to the buffalo country without fighting if possible. . . .

When I think of our condition my heart is heavy. I see men of my race treated as outlaws and driven from country to country, or shot down like animals.

I know that my race must change. We can not hold our own with the white men as we are. We only ask an even chance to live as other men live. We ask to be recognized as men. We ask that the same law shall work alike on all men. If the Indian breaks the law, punish him by the law. If the white man breaks the law, punish him also.

Let me be a free man—free to travel, free to stop, free to work, free to trade where I choose, free to choose my own teachers, free to follow the religion of my fathers, free to think and talk and act for myself—and I will obey every law, or submit to the penalty.

Whenever the white man treats the Indian as they treat each other, then we will have no more wars. . . .

For this time the Indian race are waiting and praying. I hope that no more groans of wounded men and women will ever go to the ear of the Great Spirit Chief above, and that all people may be one people.

[Hin-mah-too-yah-lat-kekt] has spoken for his people.

[Young Joseph]
Washington City, DC

FURTHER READING

Blackhawk, Ned. *Violence Over the Land: Indians and Empires in the Early American West*. Cambridge, MA: Harvard University Press, 2008.

Brown, Dee. *The Fetterman Massacre: An American Saga*. London: Barrie and Jenkins, 1972.

Calloway, Colin G., ed. *Our Hearts Fell to the Ground: Plains Indian Views of How the West Was Lost*. Boston: Bedford Books, 1996.

Delay, Brian. *War of a Thousand Deserts*. New Haven, CT: Yale University Press, 2009.

Hämäläinen, Pekka. *The Comanche Empire*. New Haven, CT: Yale University Press, 2009.

Hutton, Paul. *Phil Sheridan and His Army*. Lincoln: University of Nebraska Press, 1985.

Jacobs, Margaret D. *Engendered Encounters: Feminism and Pueblo Cultures, 1879–1934*. Lincoln: University of Nebraska Press, 1999.

Josephy, Alvin. *The Nez Percé and the Opening of the Northwest*. New Haven, CT: Yale University Press, 1965.

Madley, Benjamin. *An American Genocide: The United States and the California Indian Catastrophe, 1846–1873*. New Haven, CT: Yale University Press, 2016.

Paul, Rodman. *The Far West and the Great Plains in Transition, 1850–1900*. New York: Harper and Row, 1988.

Reeve, Paul. *Making Space on the Western Frontier: Mormons, Miners, and Southern Paiutes*. Urbana: University of Illinois Press, 2006.

Reséndez, Andrés. *The Other Slavery: The Uncovered Story of Indian Enslavement in America*. Boston: Houghton Mifflin Harcourt, 2016.

Richardson, Heather Cox. *West from Appomattox: The Reconstruction of America after the Civil War*. New Haven, CT: Yale University Press, 2008.

Schultz, Duane P. *Month of the Freezing Moon: The Sand Creek Massacre*. New York: St. Martin's, 1991.

Utley, Robert. *The Indian Frontier of the American West, 1846–1890*. Albuquerque: University of New Mexico Press, 1984.

West, Elliott. *The Contested Plains: Indians, Goldseekers, and the Rush to Colorado*. Lawrence: University Press of Kansas, 1998.

———. *The Last Indian War: The Nez Perce Story*. New York: Oxford University Press, 2009.

Wickett, Murray R. *Contested Territory: Whites, Native Americans, and African Americans in Oklahoma, 1865–1907*. Baton Rouge: Louisiana State University Press, 2000.

Wooster, Robert. *The Military and United States Indian Policy, 1865–1903*. New Haven, CT: Yale University Press, 1988.

Victims of the Chinese massacre, Los Angeles, 1871. In October 1871, a mob of white and Latino men in the plaza district of Los Angeles perpetrated a horrific massacre. The tragedy began when rival Chinese factions engaged in gunfire over what was said to be the fate of a Chinese woman who had been kidnapped. A local saloon owner entered the fray, only to be shot dead. Following that, a mob of as many as five hundred men, along with some women and children, set upon the Chinese, hanging and shooting them. When it was over, as many as twenty-two Chinese lay dead, many of them further mutilated after death. The "Chinese massacre" remains one of the largest mass lynchings in American history; certainly it is the most horrific spasm of murder aimed at this ethnic group in the history of the nation. This photograph of dead men and boys only begins to describe the horror.

Courtesy Los Angeles Public Library

The Unwelcome

When the gold rush brought the world's attention to California in the late 1840s and 1850s, the world responded by joining in the frenzied search for gold in the state's mountains, streams, and rivers. Among those who came were Chinese, who, having heard the same tales about unfathomable mineral wealth in the Sierra Nevada mountains, took to calling California by a Chinese phrase that translates as "gold mountain."

The Chinese journey to California and across the American West is fraught with tragedy and violence. But there is heroism and courage in the story, tales of striving and success, and narratives of pride and accomplishment. Above all, the story of the Chinese in the far West from the 1850s onward is characterized by constant struggle. The struggle of being a young man thousands of miles away from home, seeking gold in a foreign place. The struggle of Chinese miners forced off mineral claims by discriminatory laws, local regulations, or tax practices. The stinging struggle of racial violence aimed at those miners who might have done too well in the eyes of nearby non-Chinese miners. The struggle of those Chinese who chose to push back or used the wrong words at the wrong moment and offended those who were quick to resort to violence in the face of challenge or perceived insult. The endemic, unending struggle to eke out a living in an economy in which Chinese work was quickly categorized around household or feminized labor—cooking, housekeeping, and laundry chief among them. Or the struggle of a very different kind of labor: dangerous, sometimes absurdly dangerous, railroad work in an era when mountains had to be conquered by a combination of crude explosives and brutalizing human labor. Pyramids of the far West, in a way, the railroads of the second half of the nineteenth century were put together, and brought under, over, and around the great mountains, by a sea of Chinese workers: largely anonymous, underpaid, little regarded, and, at the same time, indispensable.

Once the West had been conquered—once the railroads had been built, the cities established, the indigenous people vanquished (more or less)—the Chinese themselves proved, in the eyes of the dominant society, simply in the way, unassimilable, foreign, just plain too different for the dominant society to bear. With most of the great railroad building done by the late 1870s, the Chinese migrated to the only place they could migrate to: the western cities. China-towns small and large grew up around them and, despite seeking infusions of exoticism by way of food, culture, prostitutes, and narcotics as they would, whites grew increasingly intolerant as more and more Chinese appeared in the urban population centers of California, Colorado, Washington, Oregon, and Wyoming.

Get rid of them, people insisted. Politicians sensed a groundswell, religious leaders grabbed hold of the non-Christian cudgel made from Chinese religions, and by the early 1880s, the American West—the supposedly "freer" American West, the land of rejuvenation and new beginnings—had set loose a juggernaut of political, social, and legal discrimination that did what the people shouting the loudest said to do: kick them out.

13. THE CHINESE QUESTION IN A CALIFORNIA CITY

Willard Glazier, a writer and military officer who claimed to have lived in more than one hundred cities in the United States, wrote Peculiarities of American Cities *in the early 1880s, when agitation over "the Chinese question" had reached a fever pitch in the West. The Pacific coast was a hotbed of anti-Chinese feeling, and San Francisco the capital of racial intolerance. Although it was home to as much as a third of California's Chinese population, the city relegated the Chinese to poorly paid work in laundries and factories. Yet many white workers still feared Chinese competition and charged the Chinese with driving down the cost of labor. Anti-Chinese sentiments prompted the formation of political parties whose platform and slogan was "The Chinese Must Go!" Other western cities displayed attitudes that were little better and sometimes much worse. Both Rock Springs, Wyoming, and Los Angeles witnessed race riots in which mobs invaded local Chinatowns and killed dozens of people. In large measure in response to such vehemence, Congress passed the Chinese Exclusion Act in 1882, which barred further Chinese immigration to the United States. In this selection, Glazier describes his impressions of San Francisco and the city's Chinese population. Although he falls into conventional racial stereotypes, he also recognizes the ironies in the anti-Chinese movement. How would you characterize Glazier's view of the Chinese? How does he connect the "Chinese question" to the growth of San Francisco?*

Willard Glazier

"San Francisco"
1883[1]

. . . The Chinese problem is one which is agitating the country and giving a coloring to its politics. The Pacific States seem, by a large majority of their population, to regard the presence of the Mongolian among them as an unmitigated evil, to be no longer tolerated. Eastern capitalists have hailed their coming as inaugurating the era of cheap labor and increased fortunes for themselves. Hence the discussion and the disturbances. A lady who had made her home in San Francisco for several years past, says, in a letter to the writer of this article, "A person not living in California can form no conception of the curse which the Chinese are to this section of the world."

Yet without them some of the great enterprises of the Pacific coast, notably the Central Pacific Railroad, would have remained long unfinished; and they came also to furnish manual labor at a time when it was scarce and difficult to obtain at any price. The Chinaman is a strange compound of virtue and vice, cleanliness and filth, frugality and recklessness, simplicity and cunning. He is scrupulously clean as to his person, indulging in frequent baths; yet he will live contentedly with the most wretched surroundings, and inhale an air vitiated by an aggregation of breaths and stenches of all kinds. He is a faithful worker and a wonderful imitator. He cannot do the full work of a white man, but he labors steadily and unceasingly. He takes no time for drunken sprees, but he is an inveterate opium smoker, and sometimes deliberately sacrifices his life in the enjoyment of the drug. He is frugal to the last degree, but will waste his daily earnings in the gambling hell and policy shop.[2] Scrupulously honest, he is yet the victim of the vilest vices which are engrafting themselves upon our western coast. Living upon one-third of what will keep a white man, and working for one-half the wages the latter demands, he is destroying the labor market of that quarter of our country, reducing its working classes to his own level, in

---

1. Captain Willard Glazier, *Peculiarities of American Cities* (Philadelphia: Hubbard Brothers, 1886), 469–71.
2. **gambling hell and policy shop:** references to gambling practices and customs, usually involving numbers running and illicit lotteries.

which in the future the latter, too, will be forced to be contented on a diet of "rice and rats," and to forgo all educational advantages for their children, becoming, like the Chinese themselves, mere working machines; or else enter into a conflict of labor against labor, race against race.

The latter alternative seems inevitable, and it has already begun. China, with her crowded population, could easily spare a hundred million people and be the better for it. Those one hundred million Chinamen, if welcomed to our shores, would speedily swamp our Western civilization. They might not become the controlling power—the Anglo-Saxon is always sure to remain that—but as hewers of wood and drawers of water, as builders of our railroads, hands upon our farms, workers in our factories, and cooks and chambermaids in our houses, a like number of American men and women would be displaced, and wages quickly reduced to an Asiatic level; and such a time of distress as this country never saw would dawn upon us.

There seems to be no assimilation between the Caucasian and the Mongolian on the Pacific slope. In the East an Irish girl recently married a Chinaman; but in San Francisco, though every other race under the sun has united in marriage, the Chinaman is avoided as a pariah. White and yellow races may meet and fraternize in business, in pleasure, and even in crime; but in marriage never. Chinamen rank among the most respected merchants of San Francisco, and these receive exceptional respect as individuals; but between the two races as races a great gulf is fixed. The Chinese immigrant takes no interest in American affairs. His world is on the other side of the Pacific. And the American people return the compliment by taking no interest in him. It is undeniable that, by a certain class of San Francisco citizens, popularly known as Hoodlums, the treatment of the Chinese population has been shameful in the extreme. A Chinaman has no rights which a white man is bound to respect. Insult, contumely,[3] abuse, cruelty, and injustice he has been forced to bear at the hands of the rougher classes, without hope of redress. He has been kicked, and cheated, and plundered, and not a voice has been raised on his behalf; but if he has been guilty of the slightest peccadillo, how quickly has he been made to feel the heavy hand of justice!

It seems a pity that before the cry was raised with such overwhelming force, "The Chinese must go!"[4] some little effort had not been made to adapt them to Western civilization. They are quick to take ideas concerning their labor; why not in other things? We have received and adopted the ignorant, vicious hordes from foreign lands to the east of us, and are fast metamorphosing them into intelligent, useful citizens. We are even trying our hand upon the negro, as a

---

3. **contumely:** insolent or insulting language, treatment, or behavior.
4. **"The Chinese must go!":** a racial and political rallying cry of the 1870s, used most effectively by white working-class politicians and activists in San Francisco worried about competition from Chinese labor. Sentiments such as these led to the 1882 Chinese Exclusion Act.

late atonement for all the wrong we have done him. But the Indian and the Chinaman seem to be without the pale of our mercy and our Christianity. It might not have been possible, but still the experiment was worth the trying, of attempting to lift them up industrially, educationally and morally, to a level with our own better classes, instead of permitting them to drag us down. Returning to their own country, and carrying back with them our Western civilization, as a little leaven, they might have leavened the whole lump. It is too late for that now, and the mandate has gone forth: "The Chinese must go!" Considering all things as they are, rather than as they might have been, it is undoubtedly better so, and the only salvation of our Pacific States. . . .

14. THE CHINESE QUESTION IN CARTOON

The controversy over the presence of the Chinese in the cities and towns of the West played out in innumerable newspaper columns, editorials, pamphlets, and posters during the 1870s and early 1880s. The question also prompted cartoonists to weigh in on one side or the other. Most often, the Chinese found themselves viciously lampooned in racist cartoons that derided everything about them: their physical appearance, their social practices, their living conditions, even their eating habits. This cartoon is an exception to the general trend of racial antagonism, in that it emphasizes an economic basis for the West's virulent anti-Chinese feeling. In view of Willard Glazier's comments and this cartoon, how do you think economic incentives influenced the anti-Chinese movement in the West? What other period sources might tell you more about the situation? How does the tone of the cartoon's caption compare with the way the cartoonist has depicted the Chinese immigrant?

15. SEALING THE BORDERS

Think of what the West meant as a place in the era following the Civil War. On the one hand, with new rail connections and burgeoning cities, with its mines and farms and ranches, the West looked to many to be synonymous with opportunity, renewal, maybe even redemption. But the West could mean the opposite of those things; the prosperity of the few was built upon the lives and backs of the many. Native American resistance to western conquest underwent perhaps its most tragic chapters in the later years of the nineteenth century. And what of the Chinese? Those thousands of laborers who searched first for gold in the 1850s, then blasted mountains out of the way to lay railroad track in the 1860s, found themselves more detested and mistrusted than ever in the 1870s (see again the image that opens this chapter) and the 1880s. The West led an ignominious

UNCLE SAM'S HOSPITALITY.

Keep off! You are so industrious and economical that our boys
can't compete with you.

George Augustus Sala, *America Revisited: From the Bay of New York to the Gulf of Mexico* (London: Vizetelly, 1882), 237.

national charge: the Chinese must go. And go they did: by acts such as the one printed here, which was formally renewed again and again for decades, the United States, guided by western racism and votes, entered into a dark place of racial and national exclusion. Land of opportunity? For whom, and when?

From the Chinese Exclusion Act
"An Act to Execute Certain Treaty Stipulations Relating to Chinese"
1882[1]

Whereas, in the opinion of the Government of the United States the coming of Chinese laborers to this country endangers the good order of certain localities within the territory thereof:

Therefore,

Be it enacted by the Senate and House of Representatives of the United States of America in Congress assembled, That from and after the expiration of ninety days next after the passage of this act, and until the expiration of ten years next after the passage of this act, the coming of Chinese laborers to the United States be, and the same is hereby, suspended; and during such suspension it shall not be lawful for any Chinese laborer to come, or having so come after the expiration of said ninety days, to remain within the United States.

SEC. 2. That the master of any vessel who shall knowingly bring within the United States on such vessel, and land or permit to be landed, any Chinese laborer, from any foreign port or place, shall be deemed guilty of a misdemeanor, and on conviction thereof shall be punished by a fine of not more than $500 for each and every such Chinese laborer so brought, and may be also imprisoned for a term not exceeding one year.

SEC. 3. That the two foregoing sections shall not apply to Chinese laborers who were in the United States on the 17th day of November, 1880, or who shall have come into the same before the expiration of ninety days next after the passage of this act. . . .

SEC. 6. That in order to the faithful execution of articles one and two of the treaty in this act before mentioned, every Chinese person other than a laborer who may be entitled by said treaty and this act to come within the United States, and who shall be about to come to the United States, shall be identified as so entitled by the Chinese Government in each case, such identity to be evidenced by a certificate issued under the authority of said government, which certificate shall be in the English language or (if not in the English language) accompanied by a translation into English, stating such right to come, and which certificate shall state the name, title, or official rank, if any, the age, height, and all physical peculiarities, former and present occupation or

1. https://www.ourdocuments.gov/doc.php?flash=false&doc=47.

profession, and place of residence in China of the person to whom the certificate is issued and that such person is entitled conformably to the treaty in this act mentioned to come within the United States. . . .

SEC. 8. That the master of any vessel arriving in the United States from any foreign port or place shall, at the same time he delivers a manifest of the cargo, and if there be no cargo, then at the time of making a report, of the entry of the vessel pursuant to law, in addition to the other matter required to be reported, and before landing, or permitting to land, any Chinese passengers, deliver and report to the collector of customs of the district in which such vessels shall have arrived a separate list of all Chinese passengers taken on board his vessel at any foreign port or place, and all such passengers on board the vessel at that time. . . .

SEC. 9. That before any Chinese passengers are landed from any such vessel, the collector, or his deputy, shall proceed to examine such passengers, comparing the certificates with the list and with the passengers; and no passenger shall be allowed to land in the United States from such vessel in violation of law. . . .

SEC. 11. That any person who shall knowingly bring into or cause to be brought into the United States by land, or who shall knowingly aid or abet the same, or aid or abet the landing in the United States from any vessel of any Chinese person not lawfully entitled to enter the United states, shall be deemed guilty of a misdemeanor, and shall, on conviction thereof, be fined in a sum not exceeding $1,000, and imprisoned for a term not exceeding one year.

SEC. 12. That no Chinese person shall be permitted to enter the United States by land without producing to the proper officer of customs the certificate in this act required of Chinese persons seeking to land from a vessel. . . .

SEC. 14. That hereafter no State court or court of the United States shall admit Chinese to citizenship; and all laws in conflict with this act are hereby repealed.

SEC. 15. That the words "Chinese laborers," wherever used in this act, shall be construed to mean both skilled and unskilled laborers and Chinese employed in mining.

Approved, May 6, 1882

FURTHER READING

Faragher, John Mack. *Eternity Street: Violence and Justice in Frontier Los Angeles.* New York: W. W. Norton, 2016.

Jew, Victor. "The Anti-Chinese Massacre of 1871 and Its Strange Career." In *A Companion to Los Angeles*, edited by William Deverell and Greg Hise, 110–28. London: Wiley-Blackwell, 2010.

Johnson, Susan Lee. *Roaring Camp: The Social World of the California Gold Rush.* New York: W. W. Norton, 2000.

Ngai, Mae. *Impossible Subjects: Illegal Aliens and the Making of Modern America.* Princeton, NJ: Princeton University Press, 2004.

———. *The Lucky Ones: One Family and the Extraordinary Invention of Chinese America.* Boston: Houghton Mifflin Harcourt, 2010.

Paddison, Joshua. *American Heathens: Religion, Race, and Reconstruction in California.* Berkeley: University of California Press, 2012.

Saxton, Alexander. *The Indispensable Enemy: Labor and the Anti-Chinese Movement in California*. Berkeley: University of California Press, 1995.

See, Lisa. *On Gold Mountain: The One-Hundred-Year Odyssey of My Chinese-American Family*. New York: Vintage, 1996.

Sinn, Elizabeth. "Pacific Ocean: Highway to Gold Mountain, 1850–1900." *Pacific Historical Review* 83, no. 2 (May 2014): 220–37.

Zesch, Scott. *The Chinatown War: Chinese Los Angeles and the Massacre of 1871*. New York: Oxford University Press, 2012.

San Francisco, ca. 1890. At the time of this photograph, San Francisco was home to nearly three hundred thousand people, making it the eighth largest city in America. Like its urban counterparts in the East, San Francisco owed its growth to immigration and industrial expansion. In 1890, with more than a third of its population born outside the United States, the city was one of the most ethnically diverse places in the country, if not the world. These identical side-by-side images are mounted on a card meant to be viewed through a device called a stereopticon, which produced a three-dimensional effect. Stereographic photography, all the rage in the latter part of the nineteenth century, offered people the illusion of visiting new places. This street scene would convey to viewers in other parts of the country a vivid sense of bustling prosperity. No longer a rough-and-ready gold rush town, San Francisco boasted tall buildings, paved sidewalks, and fashionably dressed people. Miners' dungarees, the uniform of the forty-niners, are conspicuously absent. Why do you think a photograph like this might be interesting to someone in the East or South? Does this look like a city in the West? Why or why not?

The Rise of the Western Metropolis

4

In the generation after the Civil War, America reinvented itself as an urban nation. Always tied to commerce and trade, cities became centers of rampant industrial expansion. Fueled by technological breakthroughs and innovations—railroads, more efficient factory machinery, trolley systems, and an increased use of electricity for light and power, for instance—late nineteenth-century American cities mushroomed. Already huge by 1870, New York had grown fivefold by 1910. Chicago made that look small: the brash young city of the Midwest grew ten times during that same period. Farther to the west, cities such as Denver, Seattle, and Los Angeles also witnessed rapid growth.

Many factors combined to propel urbanization forward, but none were as important as the twin engines of immigration and industrialization. American cities were people magnets in the late nineteenth and early twentieth centuries, drawing immigrants from every corner of the globe—Russians, Germans, Poles, Irish, Italians, Slavs, Brits, and countless others—longing to start new, better lives in the United States. Factory jobs beckoned, but it would be a stretch to say that things were easy. On the contrary, the arrivals had to contend with crowded living conditions, dangerous jobs, urban pollution on unprecedented scales, and the none-too-subtle racial and ethnic antagonism of those who would have preferred that they not come in the first place.

Still they came. Their labor met the needs of cities bent on matching population growth with industrial output. Chicago grew fast and it grew big, in large measure because its industries found ways to align all that human labor with productive work. Chicago took in the natural resource bounty of millions of acres surrounding it in every direction, and the newly arrived immigrants processed all those trees into lumber, all those cattle into beef, all that grain into bread and beer. Once transformed into commodities, all that stuff then went out from Chicago by way of a sophisticated rail network that connected the city to markets hither and yon. Dangerous, often grim and brutal, the system nonetheless hummed, and the modern city grew from it.

This pattern repeated across the nation and into the far West. Industry needed workers; immigrants answered the call; urbanization followed. Native-born Americans came too, leaving their family farms and the countryside in record numbers in the post–Civil War era, chased off the land by falling farm prices, depleted soils, and the sheer allure of life in the big city. By the end of the nineteenth century, the American West, and especially its cities, had been utterly transformed. The process—people gathering first in hamlets, which often grew into villages, then into towns and cities—had been ongoing for a long time, in the West as elsewhere. But the velocity of urbanization in the post–Civil War West made things look markedly different there. By the 1870s a web of iron railroad tracks had formed interlocking connections across the region, and the arrival of the rails could make a town bloom quickly into a city—or wither if they went someplace else.

Aiding the growth of western cities, or at least adding their words and their voices to the din, were the innumerable "boosters" who championed the finer points of this or that place. Boosters papered the nation with maps, photographs, advertisements, flyers, and posters extolling the delights of Denver, the charms of Seattle, the promise of Boise, and every would-be city in between. Every western city, or wannabe city, had its booster corps. Here the water was sweeter, there the sunshine more brilliant. At this place, the air could do wonders for the health. At that place, industrial jobs were plentiful. Boosters usually had skin in the game: they were real estate speculators, perhaps, or had a hand in this or that business, or they aimed at turning their booster skills to politics. No single person boosted with anything like the power and pull of the railroads, which had entire departments devoted to singing—loudly—the praises of exactly those cities that they served in trade and tourism.

People answered the call. They listened, they read, they saw, and they came. Denver, already a good-size American city with more than thirty thousand residents in 1880, more than tripled in size in ten years. San Francisco was already the nation's tenth largest city in 1870, thanks to the gold rush twenty years earlier, and it kept growing in population and power. To the south, Los Angeles proved an urban marvel. A few thousand people made up tiny Los Angeles in 1850, when California became a state. A generation later, Los Angeles had railroad connections to the outside world, and the region had grown to include some thirty thousand people. Boosters boosted, and a diversified economy added allure. One hundred thousand people were in the Los Angeles basin by 1890, and by 1920, one million.

Growth came with what we now think of as typical urban concerns: the spread of disease and challenges to public health, ever-present fire dangers, overcrowding, sewage and water supply and delivery problems, labor disputes, crime. Racial intolerance and violence also plagued western cities. African American emigrants to the West, trying to escape the ever-present dangers of the post–Civil War South, often encountered the West as anything but egalitarian. Many a western African American found him- or herself attracted instead to all-black western urban experiments nestled far from the discriminatory hurts and dangers posed by white neighbors in western cities. Anti-immigrant activities in thought, word, and deed sprouted from ugly seeds sown in western cities. As they finished their labors on the transcontinental and other railroad projects, as we have seen, Chinese laborers fell into western cities and western Chinatowns, but they could not escape the condemnation and vicious attacks of those who did not want them there and did all they could to get them out.

AS YOU READ: The passages that follow examine aspects of post–Civil War western city building. Listen as travelers describe the look and feel of two very different, though perhaps similarly ambitious, western cities: Denver and Salt Lake. Think what life was like in an all-black place like Boley, a place of refuge perhaps every bit as much as of opportunity. Consider how urbanization changed the horizons of people's lives, their hopes, dreams, and experiences. Where America had once been so defined by the vantages and views of farms and countryside, that had changed by the end of the nineteenth century. The West, with its brash, young, and nearly instant cities, played a key role in that transition.

16. A TOURIST'S VIEW OF THE UTAH TERRITORY

An eastern writer who was extremely fond of the West, Samuel Bowles wrote numerous books and articles extolling the virtues of the region. In this document, Bowles writes of time he spent in Salt Lake City, the capital of the Utah Territory. Founded in the late 1840s by Mormons fleeing persecution in other parts of the nation, Salt Lake City grew with the faith of those who settled it. Like many travelers before and after him, Bowles was fascinated by the Mormon capital, finding it at once exotic and mundane. He was bemused by Mormon practices and the city's mixture of civil and religious government, but also clearly appreciative of its neatness and tidy urban plan. In what ways does Bowles compare Salt Lake City to other American cities of the period? How does he describe the city's diversity of population and opinion?

Samuel Bowles

"A Week in Salt Lake"
1869[1]

The city has, indeed, a most charming location, and is happily laid out and improved. Coming out of the mountains on the east and north, we enter upon a high plateau or "bench" of land, commanding the valley for forty or fifty miles to the south, and west to Salt Lake and the mountains that seem to rise from out of the water, and, stretching southward, guard the valley in that direction. The city lies directly below, . . . under the highest mountains, on what seems almost a level plain, but holding a grade that keeps the irrigating streams in quick motion, and promotes dryness and health,—with wide sweep of fertile valley before it, Salt Lake shimmering with the sunlight in the far distance, and the delaying Jordan ribboning the gardens of grain and grass below,—with mountains behind white-capped in snow even under the summer's sun, and hills in front that often rival them in height and garniture,—Salt Lake City spreads itself with luxuriance of space, and with luxuriance of garden and orchard growth, that almost hides its buildings.

The streets are broad and regular,—one hundred feet from curb to curb,—dividing the town into squares of just ten acres, and these again are divided into eighths, which leaves an acre and a quarter for each home. Only in the business streets and in the lower and poorer quarters are these home lots sub-divided. The houses were originally altogether of adobe, or mud bricks dried in the sun; now, stone and red brick are introduced for the larger buildings and stores, and lumber varies with the earlier material in dwellings and second-rate business establishments. The houses are mostly small, and a story or a story and a half in height; they often suggest the peculiar institution of the country by a long frontage with numerous distinct entrances. The number of wives a man has is frequently indicated by the number of front doors to his house.

A full square of ten acres in the center of the city is devoted to the central church edifices. Here is the old Tabernacle, a large, low, barn-like structure, holding several thousand people; also the new Tabernacle, which will contain from ten to fifteen thousand, is two hundred and fifty feet long, one hundred and fifty feet wide, and ninety high, built of stone, covered by a grand arched

---

1. Samuel Bowles, *Our New West: Records of Travel between the Mississippi River and the Pacific Ocean* (Hartford, CT: Hartford, 1869), 219–25.

dome, and looks in the distance like a huge deep platter turned bottom up. In the most conspicuous location of the same square lie the foundations of the Grand Temple, begun many years ago, and to be finished when the church has leisure and money enough. The plan proposes a structure that rivals the cathedrals of Europe, and is grander than any church edifice in America. This square is surrounded by a strong, high wall of adobe brick and plaster.

Similarly guarded from cunning eyes or profane entrance by a high, strong wall, is Brigham Young's[2] entire square, opposite. Within this are the "tithing-house," where are gathered in the tenth part of every man's yearly productions or profits, the other offices and store-houses of the church, two large houses for Young and his extensive family and his private offices, a school-house with cupola for his children, immense barns and sheds for his animals, and far in the rear his grand model flouring-mill. Fine gardens and orchards fill up the vacant places. Here is the central life and authority of the State. The telegraph of the church, extending all over the Territory, centers here, and here is the office of the special church newspaper organ.

The principal business street is long and well built. There are a few stores of the very first character, both in size, amount and variety of goods, and extent of business done. There are several firms, some Mormon, others not, that do a business of a million and over each every year. The great Mormon establishments often connect manufacturing of some kind with their business, and frequently have branch stores all over the territory; but they are all in the hands of close allies, relatives, or subservient instruments of Brigham Young, and are under his sharp surveillance. The hotels, two of which are large and well managed, are all kept by Mormons; and so far as possible, all the avenues to money-making, all the instrumentalities of life in the city, are in the hands of creatures of the head of this Church and State organization. If a Mormon is suspected of unsoundness, or is getting too rich and powerful, he is persecuted out of the way, or "called of God" to go as missionary somewhere, and leave his business in somebody else's hands, or the "tithings" are applied so sharply as to keep his fortune within reasonable bounds. Many cases are given in illustration of these and other ways of enriching the church and preventing the growth of individual power.

Within the last few months, a new plan has been devised for extending and compacting the business affiliations of the church. It is that of putting all extensive trade and manufacturing operations into coöperative associations, and inviting all the Mormon population to take shares in them. The great Mormon stores in Salt Lake City have been thus converted, and the principle is rapidly extending to all business enterprises in every part of the Territory. It

---

2. **Brigham Young's:** Brigham Young succeeded Joseph Smith as the spiritual and political leader of the Mormon Church and led the Mormons to Salt Lake City in the 1840s.

has two advantages,—that of extending the common interests of the grand organization, and ensuring the enforcement of the rule that Mormons shall buy only of Mormons, and that of distributing the losses of any revulsions in business, or any break-down of the Mormon rule, growing out of the revolutionary influences of the Railroad. It strengthens the power of the leaders, and it enables them to change their investments, or, as they say in Wall Street, to "unload."

The long dry summers of all our New West render irrigation a necessity to all diversified culture of the soil. . . . The streams that come out from the mountains are diverted and divided through the streets of the town, and among the farms of the valley above the River Jordan. Thus lively brooks course down the gutters of the streets, keeping the shade trees alive and growing, supplying drink for animals and water for household purposes, and delightfully cooling the summer air; besides being drawn off in right proportion for the use of each garden. . . . Under this regular stimulus, with a strong soil, made up of the wash of the mountains, the finest of crops are obtained; the vegetable bottom lands of the New England rivers or of the interior prairies cannot vie with the products of the best gardens and farms of these western valleys and plains under this system of irrigation. There needs to be enough rain in the spring or winter moisture remaining to start the seeds, and there generally is; after that, the regular supply of water keeps the plants in a steady and rapid growth. . . .

The soil of this and the smaller neighboring valleys is especially favorable to the small grains. Fifty and sixty bushels is a very common crop of wheat, oats and barley; and over ninety have been raised. President Young once raised ninety-three and a half bushels of wheat on a single acre. I should say the same soil located in the East, and taking its chances without irrigation, would not produce half what it does here with irrigation. Laborious and expensive as the process must be, the large crops and high prices obtained for them have made it a very profitable recourse.

But a singular change seems to be creeping over all our Western regions under settlement, in this matter of climate and of rain. Summer rains are palpably on the increase, and the necessity of irrigation is lessening, especially for the grains and slow-growing vegetables. When the Mormons first came here, there was no rain from April to November; but now summer showers are of frequent occurrence. . . . Connected with this change, it is observed here that Salt Lake is growing in size and freshness, and the Jordan increasing in width and sluggishness of movement. In broader phrase, the whole basin, once evidently filled with water, is slowly returning to its old condition. The Lake is rising at the rate of a foot a year. General Connor's little steamboat, that has been carrying ties for the Railroad across the Lake during the last year, certainly rode for a mile over what was good grazing-ground five years before. Does Providence propose to drown the Mormons out, and with water solve the problem that is puzzling our moral philosophers and statesmen? . . .

17. A DAY IN DENVER

*The British lawyer W. R. Russell traveled throughout the United States and parts
of Canada in 1881 and 1882 as a member of a small company of wealthy tourists.
Like thousands of others who could afford to do so, Russell and his companions
toured the country by train. Such tourist excursions became extremely popular
once the transcontinental railroad was completed, and an entire tourist economy
developed around them: travel agencies made bookings and other arrangements
for the entire trip, luxury hotels sprang up in formerly out-of-the-way places, and
the railroad companies published guidebooks and brochures describing various
journeys and sights. Tourists expected to see the West's natural grandeur, but
they were also surprised by the size and appearance of its cities. In this selection,
Russell describes a day he spent in the capital of Colorado. What surprises him
about Denver? What comparisons does he make between Denver and cities elsewhere in the world? Are these comparisons meaningful or simply descriptive
flourishes? What do you think Russell expected the city to look like?*

W. R. Russell
"Denver City"
1882[1]

... The evidences of a bustling city were not wanting in the approaches to the
capital of Colorado. There were tall chimneys vomiting out smoke in the distance, and near at hand trains of wagons were toiling over the dusty plain—still
5000 feet above the sea-level—fast trotters and people on horseback, beergar-
dens, factories of all kinds, brick-kilns, and then a fringe of log houses and
wooden shanties, before the train stopped at the imposing and substantial depot.

It was a quarter-past eight, nearly dark, when we reached Denver, and glad
were we to get into the hall of the Windsor Hotel, which was crowded with a
mixed multitude—miners, and speculators, and traders, and some travellers
like ourselves—a very busy scene indeed. In the hotel were all human comforts
nearly; hot and cold baths, and good rooms, and more appliances of civilised
existence, for those who could pay for them, than could be found in many hos-
telries of approved reputation in venerable towns at home. . . . As we peered out
of our windows over the roofs of the wide-spread houses of the town, we could
see the snow on the lofty ranges of hills, watered by the South Platte River and
Cherry Creek, which surround the cup in which Denver has been built in obedience to the impulses of the increasing population, which now numbers,
I believe, 38,000 souls. There was a bright glare from the gas-lighted streets,

1. W. R. Russell, *Hesperothen; Notes from the West: A Record of a Ramble in the United States and
Canada in the Spring and Summer of 1881*, vol. 2 (London: Sampson Low, Marston, Searle and
Rivington, 1882), 91–97.

sounds of music, and a tumult of life in the town which would have been cred-
itable to an ancient metropolis. In the morning from the hotel windows
appeared a beautiful and wide-spread panorama of the hills we had seen the
evening before, peak above peak, . . . all capped with snow, now bathed in a
flood of fervent sunshine, the snow lighted up by the peculiar crimson tints
common in Alpine regions. . . . There were, perhaps, at that moment some hundreds, if not thousands, out of the population of 37,000 or 38,000 of the city,
who belonged to the adventurous classes—sporting-men, betting-men, ring-
men, bar-keepers, hell-proprietors,[2] and their satellites, and the scum of the
saloons attracted from the great cities of the States for hundreds of miles, by
the prey which miners with belts full of gold, half mad with drink, and always
fond of excitement, frequently are; and if to these be added the dissolute loafers
and broken-down mining speculators, the strength of the army arrayed against
the law may be estimated; and the wonder is that among a population armed to
the teeth there are not more cases of such violent deeds as we were reading of at
breakfast. To the stranger there was no evidence of the existence of these disturbing elements, unless the bearded and booted men with speculation in their
eyes, in the hotel passages and halls, belonged to the dangerous, as they certainly did to the mining, classes. As to the resources of the city, . . . [there] is
everything that any one can want to be had for money in the place, and much
more than most people need. Paris fashions and millinery are in vogue. There
are fine shops, handsome churches, a theatre, breweries, factories, banks,
insurance offices.

The principal street exhibits pretty young people, who would have no occasion to fear comparison with the *beau monde* in Eastern or European capitals.
The thoroughfares are crowded with vehicles, and spruce carriages and well
turned-out horses may be seen in the favourite drive, that has been made over
an indifferent road to the base of the Rocky Mountains, which appear to be
close at hand, though they are thirteen miles away. But here and there in the
well-dressed crowd may be seen a Bohemian *pur sang*,[3] or a miner in his every
day clothes, bent on a rig out and a good time of it. The streets, unpaved, dusty,
and rugged, are very wide, and bordered with trees, and the houses generally
are built of good red brick instead of wood; and there are runnels of water like
those one sees in Pretoria and other Dutch towns in South Africa. . . .

There are many ready-made clothing establishments in the main streets, and
there is a heavy trade in tinned provisions. Through the Western States, as in
South Africa, the débris of provision-tins constitutes a certain and considerable
addition to the objects to be seen in the vicinity of every house, and to the
mounds of rubbish in the street of every village. How indeed could the firstcom-
ers in such regions keep body and soul together without the supplies in such a

---

2. **hell-proprietors:** gambling-house owners.
3. *pur sang:* pure blood.

portable form of the first necessaries of life? Having once run up a town in these remote wastes, the inhabitants are still compelled to make a liberal use of the same sort of food, and mines of tinned iron gradually accumulate around them.

Our first excursion was to the Argo Works. . . . The works are at some distance outside the town, but the lofty chimneys vomit out quite sufficient vaporous fumes and smoke to blight the vegetation and to give the people near at hand a taste of their quality. . . . The Argo Works simply assay and reduce ores on commission, but the business is on a very large scale. Immense piles, in fact small mountains, of brown, cinnamon and earth coloured dust and rock were heaped up in the sheds, to be brought to the furnaces and turned, when divested of the lead, iron, copper, and gold, out in ingots of silver. . . .

The business of assaying here must be profitable, and if the reputation of any firm be once established there is a secure fortune for its members. The miners flock to them, and they can dictate terms. . . . As a specimen of what Messrs. Bush and Tabor of our hotel give their guests for dinner, let me offer you this *menu* of the 5.30 ordinary to-day (June 16). Soup, beef à l'Anglaise; fish, boiled trout, anchovy sauce; corned beef, leg of mutton, sirloin beef, chickens with giblet sauce, fricassee à la Toulouse, veal, kidneys sautés aux croûtons, rice, croquettes, baked pork and beans, saddle of antelope, currant jelly, lamb, tongue, chicken salad, spiced salmon; innumerable "relishes" and vegetables, baked rice pudding, strawberry pie, apricot pie, jelly, blancmange, vanilla ice cream, macaroons, pound cake, fruit, Swiss cheese, nuts, coffee, &c. The wines were not cheap. . . . Orders for "drinks" at the bar after dinner were much more general[4] than orders for wine at dinner.

Denver, in spite of its mineral wealth, is very poor, however, in that of which the want would make life, even in America, intolerable. The supply of drinking-water is scanty and bad, and last year there was nearly a water famine. The *cartes* in the hotel announced "Water used in this room is boiled and filtered." But great efforts have been made to furnish the inhabitants with a store, constant and adequate, of the precious fluid, and we saw very considerable works, the property of an Irish gentleman, erected before the town attained its present dimensions, which were to be supplemented by a new enterprise respecting which we heard much. Perhaps no town of equal size in an equal length of time has ever had so much money and money's worth flowing in and through it as Denver since the Colorado mines were worked. It is asserted that the trade of the town for 1881 will exceed 8,000,000*l*. Colorado in 1879 yielded ores to the value of more than 3,750,000*l*. The output in the present year will exceed that of 1880. In that year $35,417,517 worth of gold and $20,183,889 of silver (more than 11,000,000*l*.) was deposited in the United States Mint and Assay Office. There is, besides, vast wealth in flocks and herds, and Denver is the place where

---

4. **general:** common.

the people resort from Colorado for purposes of trade and pleasure; altogether an astounding place, with a future quite dazzling to think of. . . .

18. AN AFRICAN AMERICAN COMMUNITY IN THE WEST

Booker T. Washington, then head of the African American Tuskegee Institute in Alabama, visited Oklahoma shortly before it became a state in 1907. There he saw firsthand the racial and ethnic diversity of the former Indian Territory. In this essay he describes his impressions of Oklahoma, its inhabitants, and the all-black colony of Boley. He briefly discusses the history of African American migration to the West and writes of the ways in which the young state's Indian, African American, and white populations treat one another. Boley, a growing colony of several thousand people, was of particular interest to the famed educator. Though Washington refers to the colony as a town, the US Census Bureau, with an urbanization scale of 2,500 people, would have considered Boley a city. What ingredients of western city building does Boley have? What is Washington's impression of the levels of western racial tolerance? In his eyes, what makes Boley "western"?

Booker T. Washington
"Boley, a Negro Town in the West"
1908[1]

Boley, Indian Territory, is the youngest, the most enterprising, and in many ways the most interesting of the negro towns in the United States. A rude, bustling, Western town, it is a characteristic product of the negro immigration from the South and Middle West into the new lands of what is now the State of Oklahoma.

The large proportions of the northward and westward movement of the negro population recall the Kansas Exodus of thirty years ago, when within a few months more than forty thousand helpless and destitute negroes from the country districts of Arkansas and Mississippi poured into eastern Kansas in search of "better homes, larger opportunities, and kindlier treatment."

It is a striking evidence of the progress made in thirty years that the present northward and westward movement of the negro people has brought into these new lands, not a helpless and ignorant horde of black people, but land-seekers and home-builders, men who have come prepared to build up the country. In the thirty years since the Kansas Exodus the Southern negroes have learned to build schools, to establish banks and conduct newspapers. They have recovered

---

1. *Outlook*, January 4, 1908, 28–31.

something of the knack for trade that their foreparents in Africa were famous for. They have learned through their churches and their secret orders the art of corporate and united action. This experience has enabled them to set up and maintain in a raw Western community numbering 2,500, an orderly and self-respecting government.

In the fall of 1905 I spent a week in the Territories of Oklahoma and Indian Territory.[2] During the course of my visit I had an opportunity for the first time to see the three races—the Negro, the Indian, and the white man—living side by side, each in sufficient numbers to make their influence felt in the communities of which they were a part, and in the Territory as a whole. It was not my first acquaintance with the Indian. During the last years of my stay at Hampton Institute I had charge of the Indian students there, and had come to have a high respect both for their character and intelligence, so that I was particularly interested to see them in their own country, where they still preserve to some extent their native institutions. I was all the more impressed, on that account, with the fact that in the cities that I visited I rarely caught sight of a genuine native Indian. When I inquired, as I frequently did, for the "natives," it almost invariably happened that I was introduced, not to an Indian, but to a Negro. During my visit to the city of Muskogee I stopped at the home of one of the prominent "natives" of the Creek Nation, the Hon. C. W. Sango, Superintendent of the Tullahasse Mission. But he is a negro. The negroes who are known in that locality as "natives" are the descendants of slaves that the Indians brought with them from Alabama and Mississippi, when they migrated to this Territory, about the middle of the last century. I was introduced later to one or two other "natives" who were not negroes, but neither were they, as far as my observation went, Indians. They were, on the contrary, white men. "But where," I asked at length, "are the Indians?"

"Oh! the Indians," was the reply, "they have gone," with a wave of the hand in the direction of the horizon, "they have gone back!"

I repeated this question in a number of different places, and invariably received the same reply, "Oh, they have gone back!" I remembered the expression because it seemed to me that it condensed into a phrase a great deal of local history.

One cannot escape the impression, in traveling through Indian Territory, that the Indians, who own practically all the lands, and until recently had the local government largely in their own hands, are to a very large extent regarded by the white settlers, who are rapidly filling up the country, as almost a negligible quantity. To such an extent is this true that the Constitution of Oklahoma, as I understand it, takes no account of the Indians in drawing its distinctions

---

2. **Territories of Oklahoma and Indian Territory:** Oklahoma Territory had been carved out of the western part of Indian Territory in 1890. The two merged to become the state of Oklahoma in 1907.

among the races. For the Constitution there exist only the negro and the white man. The reason seems to be that the Indians have either receded—"gone back," as the saying in that region is—on the advance of the white race, or they have intermarried with and become absorbed with it. Indeed, so rapidly has this intermarriage of the two races gone on, and so great has been the demand for Indian wives, that in some of the Nations, I was informed, the price of marriage licenses has gone as high as $1,000.

The negroes, immigrants to Indian Territory, have not, however, "gone back." One sees them everywhere, working side by side with white men. They have their banks, business enterprises, schools, and churches. There are still, I am told, among the "natives" some negroes who cannot speak the English language, and who have been so thoroughly bred in the customs of the Indians that they have remained among the hills with the tribes by whom they were adopted. But, as a rule, the negro natives do not shun the white man and his civilization, but, on the contrary, rather seek it, and enter, with the negro immigrants, into competition with the white man for its benefits.

This fact was illustrated by another familiar local expression. In reply to my inquiries in regard to the little towns through which we passed, I often had occasion to notice the expression, "Yes, so and so? Well, that is a 'white town.'" Or, again, "So and so, that's colored."

I learned upon inquiry that there were a considerable number of communities throughout the Territory where an effort had been made to exclude negro settlers. To this the negroes had replied by starting other communities in which no white man was allowed to live. For instance, the thriving little city of Wilitka, I was informed, was a white man's town until it got the oil mills. Then they needed laborers, and brought in the negroes. There are a number of other little communities—Clairview, Wildcat, Grayson, and Taft—which were sometimes referred to as "colored towns," but I learned that in their cases the expression meant merely that these towns had started as negro communities or that there were large numbers of negroes there, and that negro immigrants were wanted. But among these various communities there was one of which I heard more than the others. This was the town of Boley, where, it is said, no white man has ever let the sun go down upon him.

In 1905, when I visited Indian Territory, Boley was little more than a name. It was started in 1903. At the present time it is a thriving town of two thousand five hundred inhabitants, with two banks, two cotton gins, a newspaper, a hotel, and a "college," the Creek-Seminole College and Agricultural Institute.

There is a story told in regard to the way in which the town of Boley was started, which, even if it is not wholly true as to the details, is at least characteristic, and illustrates the temper of the people in that region.

One spring day, four years ago, a number of gentlemen were discussing, at Wilitka, the race question. The point at issue was the capability of the negro for self-government. One of the gentlemen, who happened to be connected with the Fort Smith Railway, maintained that if the negroes were given a fair chance they would prove themselves as capable of self-government as any other people of the same degree of culture and education. He asserted that they had never had a fair chance. The other gentlemen naturally asserted the contrary. The result of the argument was Boley. Just at that time a number of other town sites were being laid out along the railway which connects Guthrie, Oklahoma, with Fort Smith, Arkansas. It was, it is said, to put the capability of the negro for self-government to the test that in August, 1903, seventy-two miles east of Guthrie, the site of the new negro town was established. It was called Boley, after the man who built that section of the railway. A negro town-site agent, T. M. Haynes, who is at present connected with the Farmers' and Merchants' Bank, was made Town-site Agent, and the purpose to establish a town which should be exclusively controlled by negroes was widely advertised all over the Southwest.

Boley, although built on the railway, is still on the edge of civilization. You can still hear on summer nights, I am told, the wild notes of the Indian drums and the shrill cries of the Indian dancers among the hills beyond the settlement. The outlaws that formerly infested the country have not wholly disappeared. Dick Shafer, the first Town Marshal of Boley, was killed in a duel with a horse thief, whom he in turn shot and killed, after falling, mortally wounded, from his horse. The horse thief was a white man.

There is no liquor sold in Boley, or any part of the Territory, but the "natives" go down to Prague, across the Oklahoma border, ten miles away, and then come back and occasionally "shoot up" the town. That was a favorite pastime, a few years ago, among the "natives" around Boley. The first case that came up before the Mayor for trial was that of a young "native" charged with "shooting up" a meeting in a church. But, on the whole, order in the community has been maintained. It is said that during the past two years not a single arrest has been made among the citizens. The reason is that the majority of these negro settlers have come here with the definite intention of getting a home and building up a community where they can, as they say, be "free." What this expression means is pretty well shown by the case of C. W. Perry, who came from Marshall, Texas. Perry had learned the trade of a machinist and had worked in the railway machine shops until the white machinists struck and made it so uncomfortable that the negro machinists went out. Then he went on the railway as brakeman, where he worked for fifteen years. He owned his own home and was well respected, so much so that when it became known that he intended to leave, several of the County Commissioners called on him. "Why are you going away?" they asked; "you have your home here among us. We know you and you know us. We are behind you and will protect you."

"Well," he replied, "I have always had an ambition to do something for myself. I don't want always to be led. I want to do a little leading." . . .

A large proportion of the settlers of Boley are farmers from Texas, Arkansas, and Mississippi. But the desire for Western lands has drawn into the community not only farmers, but doctors, lawyers, and craftsmen of all kinds. The fame of the town has also brought, no doubt, a certain proportion of the drifting population. But behind all other attractions of the new colony is the belief that here negroes would find greater opportunities and more freedom of action than they have been able to find in the older communities North or South.

Boley, like the other negro towns that have sprung up in other parts of the country, represents a dawning race consciousness, a wholesome desire to do something to make the race respected; something which shall demonstrate the right of the negro, not merely as an individual, but as a race, to have a worthy and permanent place in the civilization that the American people are creating. . . .

19 AND 20. DEMOGRAPHY IN THE WEST

The following two documents, one a brief excerpt from the 1890 census and the other an excerpt of a table from the 1900 census, reflect both the growth and the diversity of the West at the close of the nineteenth century. According to the 1890 census, an unbroken line of frontier no longer existed in the nation. Although census officials could once define a border in the American West between settlement and wilderness, now it was no longer locatable. The concept was itself muddled, for with it came all kinds of preconceived notions about what constituted settlement, civilization, wilderness, and progress. It also assumed that American history was a one-way movement from the East to the West in which "civilization" pushed aside what the nineteenth century called "savagery." This description of a frontierless America prompted the historian Frederick Jackson Turner to ponder the origins of American democratic institutions and the role the West had played in their development. The 1900 census document, a table of demography statistics from the West, shows population growth and diversity. It is important to note this diversity; European and other immigrants arrived in the cities of the East but many headed West either immediately or within a short time. There, they most often ended up in the expanding cities. How would you describe the tone of the 1890 assessment of the nation's progress? What does it imply about western urban growth? What can you determine from the 1900 population figures?

US Census Bureau
Statistics Measuring Progress and Birthrates
1890 and 1900

1890

This census completes the history of a century; a century of progress and achievement unequaled in the world's history. A hundred years ago there were groups of feeble settlements sparsely covering an area of 239,935 square miles, and numbering less than 4,000,000. The century has witnessed our development into a great and powerful nation; it has witnessed the spread of settlement across the continent until not less than 1,947,290 square miles have been redeemed from the wilderness and brought into the service of man, while the population has increased and multiplied by its own increase and by additions from abroad until it numbers 62,622,250.

During the decade just past a trifling change has been made in the boundary between Nebraska and Dakota by which the area of Nebraska has been slightly increased. Dakota territory has been cut in two and the states of North Dakota and South Dakota admitted. Montana, Wyoming, Idaho, and Washington have also been added to the sisterhood of states. The territory of Oklahoma has been created out of the western half of the Indian territory, and to it has been added the strip of public land lying north of the panhandle of Texas.

The most striking fact connected with the extension of settlement during the past decade is the numerous additions which have been made to the settled area within the Cordilleran region. Settlements have spread westward up the slope of the plains until they have joined the bodies formerly isolated in Colorado, forming a continuous body of settlement from the east to the Rocky mountains. Practically the whole of Kansas has become a settled region, and the unsettled area of Nebraska has been reduced in dimensions to a third of what it was ten years ago. What was a sparsely settled region in Texas in 1880 is now the most populous part of the state, while settlements have spread westward to the escarpment of the Staked Plains. The unsettled regions of North Dakota and South Dakota have been reduced to half their former dimensions. Settlements in Montana have spread until they now occupy one-third of the state. In New Mexico, Idaho, and Wyoming considerable extensions of area are to be noted. In Colorado, in spite of the decline of the mining industry and the depopulation of its mining regions, settlement has spread, and two-thirds of the state are now under the dominion of man. Oregon and Washington show equally rapid progress, and California, although its mining regions have suffered, has made great inroads upon its unsettled regions, especially in the south. Of all the western states and territories Nevada alone is at a standstill in this respect, its settled area remaining practically the same as in 1880. When it is remembered that the state has lost one-third of its population during the past ten years, the fact that it has held its own in settled area is surprising until it is understood that the state has undergone a material change in occupations during the decade, and that the inhabitants, instead of being closely grouped and engaged in mining pursuits, have become scattered along its streams and have engaged in agriculture. . . .

20. Native and Foreign Born Population, by States and Territories Arranged Geographically, in 1880, 1890, and 1900, with Increase since 1890

| STATES AND TERRITORIES | NATIVE BORN | | | FOREIGN BORN | | | INCREASE FROM 1890 TO 1900 | | | |
| | | | | | | | Native born | | Foreign born | |
	1900	1890	1880	1900	1890	1880	Number	Percent	Number	Percent
Western division	3,245,028	2,331,359	1,267,635	846,321	770,910	500,062	913,669	39.2	75,411	9.8
Montana	176,262	99,828	27,638	67,067	43,096	11,521	76,434	76.6	23,971	55.6
Wyoming	75,116	47,642	14,939	17,415	14,913	5,850	27,474	57.7	2,502	16.8
Colorado	448,545	329,259	154,537	91,155	83,990	39,790	119,286	36.2	7,165	8.5
New Mexico	181,685	149,023	111,514	13,625	11,259	8,051	82,662	21.9	2,366	21.0
Arizona	98,698	69,448	24,391	24,233	18,795	16,049	29,250	42.1	5,488	28.9
Utah	222,972	157,715	99,969	53,777	53,064	43,994	65,257	41.4	713	1.3
Nevada	32,242	32,649	36,613	10,093	14,706	25,653	[2]407	[2]1.2	[2]4,613	[2]31.4
Idaho	137,168	71,092	22,636	24,604	17,456	9,974	66,076	92.9	7,148	40.9
Washington	406,739	267,227	59,313	111,364	90,005	15,803	139,512	52.2	21,359	23.7
Oregon	347,788	260,387	144,265	65,748	57,317	30,503	87,401	33.6	8,431	14.7
California	1,117,813	847,089	571,820	367,240	366,309	292,874	270,724	32.0	931	0.3
Alaska	50,931	15,381	–	12,661	16,671	–	35,550	231.1	[2]4,010	[2]24.1
Hawaii	63,221	48,117	–	90,780	41,873	–	15,104	31.4	48,907	116.8

SOURCE: Twelfth Census of the United States, 1900, Population, Park I, xcix.

[1] Includes persons in the military and naval service of the United States (including civilian employees, etc.) stationed abroad, not credited to any state or territory.

[2] Decrease.

FURTHER READING

Abbott, Carl. *Portland: Planning, Politics, and Growth in a Twentieth-Century City.* Lincoln: University of Nebraska Press, 1983.

Barth, Gunther. *Instant Cities: Urbanization and the Rise of San Francisco and Denver.* New York: Oxford University Press, 1975.

Hernández, Kelly Lytle. "Hobos in Heaven: Race, Incarceration, and the Rise of Los Angeles, 1880–1910." *Pacific Historical Review* 83, no. 3 (August 2014): 410–47.

Klingle, Matthew. *Emerald City: An Environmental History of Seattle.* New Haven, CT: Yale University Press, 2007.

Larson, Lawrence H. *The Urban West at the End of the Frontier.* Lawrence: Regents Press of Kansas, 1978.

MacDonald, Norbert. *Distant Neighbors: A Comparative History of Seattle and Vancouver.* Lincoln: University of Nebraska Press, 1987.

Miller, Zane L., and Patricia M. Melvin. *The Urbanization of Modern America: A Brief History*. 2nd ed. San Diego, CA: Harcourt, Brace, Jovanovich, 1987.

Monkkonen, Eric. *America Becomes Urban: The Development of U.S. Cities and Towns*. Berkeley: University of California Press, 1988.

Nugent, Walter. *Into the West: The Story of Its People*. New York: Knopf, 1990.

Reps, John W. *Cities of the American West: A History of Frontier Urban Planning*. Princeton, NJ: Princeton University Press, 1979.

Sackman, Doug. *Orange Empires: California and the Fruits of Eden*. Berkeley: University of California Press, 2005.

Sloane, David C., ed. *Planning Los Angeles*. Chicago: American Planning Association, 2012.

Solnit, Rebecca. *Infinite City: A San Francisco Atlas*. Berkeley: University of California Press, 2010.

Starr, Kevin. *Americans and the California Dream*. New York: Oxford University Press, 1973.

Taylor, Quintard. *In Search of the Racial Frontier: African Americans in the American West, 1528–1990*. New York: Norton, 1998.

William Jennings Bryan campaign poster, 1900. William Jennings Bryan ran for president for a second time in 1900, four years after losing in the 1896 campaign that saw the Populists and the Democrats unite on a "fusion" ticket. This poster from the 1900 campaign, displaying symbolic references to the railroad "octopus" and the Liberty Bell, among other things, exemplifies the ways in which Bryan tried to appeal to voters across a wide geographical, occupational, and regional perspective. What other symbols can you find, and what do they mean?

Courtesy the Library of Congress Prints and Photographs Division.

Populism | 5

The Politics of Protest

The magnitude and the scale of urban growth in the latter third of the nineteenth century left its mark across the countryside. So, too, did the coming of a deep national depression in 1893. In the spring of that year the stock market collapsed, much as it would later do at the dawn of the Great Depression in 1929. Crop prices fell, and rural Americans found even more reasons to try both their luck and their lives in the cities growing all across the nation.

On the farms and in the tiny towns they left behind (or returned to, if city life did not meet their needs, expectations, or dreams), down times generated growing discontent. Before long, that discontent boiled over into radical dissent and action. As the nineteenth century drew to a close, the American farm belt, especially in the West and the South, became a hotbed of political and cultural protest that, in certain moments and particular places, threatened to overturn the social order.

Rural antagonism aimed at the cities, aimed at the industrialization of America, aimed at the corporations and banks that arose in service to such industrialization, had been growing since the end of the Civil War. Farmers felt themselves losing ground—culturally, politically, and economically—as powerful (and often unseen) social forces worked to remake America. In the 1860s and 1870s, a loose confederation of farmers' clubs, called the Grange, had arisen across the Midwest and West. Grange members were interested in farm economics, in the hopes for cooperative arrangements that could tie them together and build collective clout, and in ways they might push back against the political and economic power coming at them from urban and industrializing America.

The Grange, and its attendant Granger movement, lost ground in the 1880s, in part because of costly and largely failed attempts to manufacture farm equipment for members (and thus bypass the big companies). But in a way, the Grange succeeded even as it failed. Out of its dust came other farmer organizations: better organized, more focused, and driven by increasing anger at the way things were. By the early 1890s, the Alliance movement—a child of the Grange—was busy hustling third-party candidates toward political office in state elections across the nation. That challenge to the conventional two-party allegiance of Republicans or Democrats grew into a national political party, the People's Party, also known as the Populist Party. The leaders of that movement set their sights on nothing less than the White House and the presidency of the United States.

One thing Populists had going for them, which also could work against them, was their sheer diversity of opinion. Populists could be conservative one moment, radical the next. They were open-minded, closed-minded; racially egalitarian, racially exclusive. Just as the Populists did among themselves, historians have disagreed about just what Populism meant, what its political programs signified, and what legacies emerged from its experiments and its dreams. A few things are certain. Like the Grangers before them, Populists were angry, sometimes to the point of violence directed at other people or things, about what they perceived as the declining centrality of rural life in (and to) America, and they banded together to try to do something about it.

So what did they try to do? One of their most ambitious, and in the end largely unsuccessful, efforts was to link city and country in hopes that urban workers might have similar critiques of powerful banks, railroads, and industrial corporations. They were right in thinking that this might be true, and Populists and their urban (and occasional mining) allies tried, across the 1890s, to make common cause in attacks on central banking authorities, on corporate (and especially) railroad hierarchies, and on the political structures and personnel supporting it all. The explicit class-based appeal gave Populism its radical tinge. Populists insisted that workers, farmers, and miners were the true producers of wealth in America, that the nation's political economy should bend in service to them and not to the corporations and banks that hoarded and did not earn that wealth. Band together they did—if briefly—in strikes here and there, in tackling the power of railroads, and in fomenting political antagonism to entrenched industrial or corporate might all over the West.

There is a difference between "brief" and "flash in the pan." Populism was the former, not the latter. James Weaver, the movement's candidate for president in 1892, lost. That was not a surprise. But Weaver polled a million votes, and he won several states outright, all in the West: Colorado, Kansas, Idaho, and Nevada. That was a surprise, and it was meaningful. Some states elected Populist governors, some cities put Populist mayors in office. Such success frightened the leadership of the Democratic and Republican parties, and Populists worked to extend their influence and clout beyond pure politics or electoral results. In California, for example, farmers supported the summer 1894 Pullman Strike of railroad workers. Workers shut down rail traffic in the state, in support of a national call to do so, and they occupied railroad depots up and down the state. In an act of political and economic solidarity, farmers brought them food as the occupation of the depots went on and sided with them in the dispute, seeing both a common railroad enemy and the chance to build that country-city alliance. This kind of solidarity repeated itself in other episodes and events across the West and, had it been sustained, could have fundamentally remade the American political and economic landscape.

Populism pushed the gender envelope, too, in important and lasting ways. The movement offered farming women avenues to political and public action, very far removed from the daily tedium of rural lives and work. In this regard, Populism further distinguished the West as a region of uncommonly egalitarian understandings of women's involvement in public affairs. Beginning in the West, women gained the right to vote well ahead of their eastern or southern counterparts. Idaho, Colorado, Utah, and Wyoming led the way, and it would be decades before the nation caught up. It would take, in fact, another generation for women's suffrage to be recognized as constitutionally protected and authorized. Populism's ahead-of-the-curve progressive response to women as political actors and leaders in their own right, while it can be overemphasized and was not perfect, nonetheless helped pave the way for such advancements in American political and social life writ large.

Populism eventually faded. Weaver was defeated in 1892, and the Populists chose to back a political rocket, Nebraska Democrat William Jennings Bryan, for president in 1896. Bryan ran a strident and oratorically spellbinding campaign that had as its central plank his fervent opposition to the gold standard. This was a monetary approach that tied the US money supply to the gold reserves held by the government. Like Bryan, the Populists, especially those tied to the mining regions of the Rockies, favored "free silver," or the unlimited coinage of silver by the government, which the gold standard would prevent and which would simultaneously send western silver mines into a freefall of lowered prices. The worsening of the 1893 depression raised this issue above all others, at least for the Populists and the Democrats. Populists hoped that federal purchase of silver would sustain their allies at work in western silver mines and would also, by boosting the money supply, drive up farm prices and prop up farmers.

It was a tough sell. Former farm allies felt left out by the platform, which they viewed as too focused on western mines, miners, and monetary policy.

What's more, the alliance with the Democratic Party and its candidate, while rational, meant that Populism lost its third-party punch and panache. Industrial workers in the city could not be convinced that free silver was in their best interests, especially since they viewed an increased money supply as an invitation to inflation. And in the mining towns themselves, miners fell away from the cause when they saw mining bosses and mining corporations begin to back Bryan and his free silver argument. Nothing cut into Populism's working-class legitimacy more than seeing "Bryan for President" banners saluted by mine owners.

A star of the American political landscape already at the young ago of thirty-six, Bryan gave one of the greatest American speeches of all time at the Democratic convention. But even his "Cross of Gold" address was not enough, and Populists could not bring the Democrats enough votes to defeat the Republican William McKinley. An Ohioan tied to conservative interests in the cities of the East (and the last US president to have served in the Civil War), McKinley trounced Bryan on election day. The movement fared similarly.

AS YOU READ: Here we are looking at a number of Populist perspectives and personalities. Think of the regional and other differences in the Populist movement, and think about the national scale of the ambitions that made this into a true movement. Why did Populism take hold in a state like Kansas? What would Populists in Kansas have in common with fellow Populists in California? How would you find out? What legacies do you see from Populism's more egalitarian view of women's roles in public space, public affairs, and politics?

21. WOMEN IN THE POPULIST MOVEMENT

The Alliance movement, which grew out of the Grange, would become the Populist movement with the formation of the People's Party in 1892. The following magazine article, published the same year Populism "went national," describes the role of women in the movement and the ways in which Populism responded to women's political interests. According to Annie Diggs, women were drawn to the Alliance for a number of reasons: political commitment, boredom, loneliness, the desire to associate with other women, and the sheer excitement of the cause. A prominent orator and politician in her own right, Diggs had been active in Kansas temperance and suffrage reform for more than a decade when she wrote this essay. By the mid-1890s, she would become one of the best-known women in the Populist movement and the state librarian of Kansas. What indication, if any, does Diggs give about the possible appeal of Populism among urban or industrial workers, men or women? How does she describe the reaction of opponents to Alliance women?

Annie L. Diggs

"The Women in the Alliance Movement"

1892[1]

The women prominent in the great farmer manifesto[2] of this present time were long preparing for their part; not consciously, not by any manner of means even divining that there would be a part to play. In the many thousands of isolated farm homes the early morning, the noonday, and the evening-time work went on with a dreary monotony which resulted in that startling report of the physicians that American farms were recruiting stations from whence more women went to insane asylums than from any other walk in life.

Farm life for women is a treadmill. The eternal climb must be kept up though the altitude never heightens. For more than a quarter of a century these churning, washing, ironing, baking, darning, sewing, cooking, scrubbing, drudging women, whose toilsome, dreary lives were unrelieved by the slight incident or by-play of town life, felt that their treadmills slipped cogs. Climb as they would, they slipped down two steps while they climbed one. They were not keeping pace with the women of the towns and cities. The industry which once led in the march toward independence and prosperity, was steadily falling behind as to remuneration. Something was wrong.

The Grange came on—a most noble order, of untold service and solace to erstwhile cheerless lives. Pathetic the heart-hunger for the beauty side of life. The Grange blossomed forth in "Floras" and "Pomonas." There was a season of sociability, with much good cookery, enchanting jellies, ethereal angel cakes, and flower-decked tables. There was much burnishing of bright-witted women—not always listeners, often essayists. Sometimes, indeed, leaders of discussion and earnest talk about middlemen, the home market, the railroad problem, and such other matters as would have shed light on the cause of the farmer's declining prosperity had not wary politicians sniffed danger, and, under specious pretence of "keeping out politics lest it kill the Grange," tabooed free speech and thus adroitly injected the fatalest of policies. The Grange is dead. Long live the Grange born again—the Alliance! this time not to be frightened out of politics or choked of utterance; born this time to do far more than talk—to vote.

The Granger sisters through the intervening years, climbing laboriously, patiently, felt their treadmill cogs a slipping three steps down to one step up. Reincarnate in the Alliance the whilom[3] Floras and Pomonas became secretaries and lecturers. The worn and weary treadmillers are anxious, troubled. They have no heart for poetry or play. Life is work unremitting. There is no time for ransacking of heathen mythologies for fashions with which to trig out modern goddesses. Instead of mythologic lore, they read "Seven Financial Conspiracies,"

---

1. *The Arena* 31 (June 1892): 161–63, 165, 179.
2. **manifesto:** a declaration of principles, usually, as in this case, political.
3. **whilom:** formerly, or, in this usage, former.

"Looking Backward," "Progress and Poverty." Alas! of this last word they know much and fear more—fear for their children's future. These once frolicking Floras and playful Pomonas turn with all the fierceness of the primal mother-nature to protect their younglings from devouring, devastating plutocracy.

Politics for the farmer had been recreation, relaxation, or even exhilaration, according to the varying degree of his interest, or of honor flatteringly bestowed by town committeemen upon a "solid yeoman" at caucus or convention. The flush of pride over being selected to make a nominating speech, or the sense of importance consequent upon being placed on a resolution committee to acquiesce in the prepared document conveniently at hand—these high honors lightened much muddy plowing and hot harvest work.

But the farmers' wives participated in no such ecstacies. Hence for them no blinding party ties. And therefore when investigation turned on the light, the women spoke right out in meeting, demanding explanation for the non-appearance of the home market for the farm products, which their good husbands had been prophesying and promising would follow the upbuilding of protected industries. These women in the Alliance, grown apt in keeping close accounts from long economy, cast eyes over the long account of promises of officials managing public business, and said, "Promise and performance do not balance." "Of what value are convention honors, or even elected eloquence in national Capitol, if homelessness must be our children's heritage?"

Carlyle's Menads,[4] hungrier than American women are as yet, penetrated the French Assembly "to the shamefullest interruption of public speaking" with cries of, "Du pain! pas tant de longs discours!" Our Alliance women spake the same in English: "Bread! not so much discoursing!" "Less eloquence and more justice!" . . .

In several states, notably Texas, Georgia, Michigan, California, Colorado, and Nebraska, women have been useful and prominent in the farmer movement, which indeed is now widened and blended with the cause of labor other than that of the farm.

Kansas, however, furnished by far the largest quota of active, aggressive women, inasmuch as Kansas was the theatre where the initial act of the great labor drama was played. . . .

The great political victory of the people of Kansas would not have been won without the help of the women of the Alliance. Women who never dreamed of becoming public speakers, grew eloquent in their zeal and fervor. Farmers' wives and daughters rose earlier and worked later to gain time to cook the picnic dinners, to paint the mottoes on the banners, to practice with the glee clubs, to march in procession. Josh Billings's saying that "wimmin is everywhere" was literally true in that wonderful picnicking, speech-making Alliance summer of 1890.

---

4. **Carlyle's Menads:** a reference to the British historian Thomas Carlyle and his history of the French Revolution.

Kansas politics was no longer a "dirty pool."[5] That marvellous campaign was a great thrilling crusade. It was religious to the core. Instinctively the women knew that the salvation of their homes, and more even, the salvation of the republic, depended upon the outcome of that test struggle. Every word, every thought, every act, was a prayer for victory, and for the triumph of right. Victory was compelled to come.

Narrow ignoramuses long ago stumbled upon the truth, "The home is woman's sphere." Ignoramus said, "Women should cook and gossip, and rock cradles, and darn socks"—merely these and nothing more. Whereas the whole truth is, women should watch and work in all things which shape and mould the home, whether "money," "land," or "transportation." So now Alliance women look at politics and trace the swift relation to the home—their special sphere. They say, "Our homes are threatened by the dirty pool. The pool must go."

Before this question of the salvation of the imperilled homes of the nation, all other questions, whether of "prohibition" or "suffrage," pale into relative inconsequence. For where shall temperance or high thought of franchise be taught the children, by whose breath the world is saved, if sacred hearth fires shall go out? The overtopping, all-embracing moral question of the age is this for which the Alliance came. Upon such great ethical foundation is the labor movement of to-day building itself. How could women do otherwise than be in and of it? . . .

Consider this Kansas record, oh supercilious sneerer at "strong-minded" women. Most of these women have opened their mouths and spake before many people; they have sat in counsel with bodies of men, among whom were their husbands and sons. And oh, Ultima Thule of "unwomanliness," they have voted—actually cast ballot, thereby saying in quietest of human way that virtue shall dethrone vice in municipal government. All these heretical things have they done, and yet are womanliest, gentlest of women, the best of homekeepers, the loyalest of wives, the carefulest of mothers.

What answer to this, oh, most bombastic cavillers—you who would shield woman from the demoralizing ballot? What answer, most ridiculous of theorists, who tremble lest any sort of man-made laws be mightier than nature's laws, who writhe lest statutes should change the loving, loyal mother-nature of woman? Let not such preposterous theorist come into the presence of the six stalwart sons of halofaced Mrs. Davis and suggest that their most revered mother is "unsexed" because of ballot box and politics.

Thus splendidly do the facts about women in politics refute the frivolous theories of timorous or hostile objectors. The women prominent as active, responsible factors in the political arena are those who are characterized by strong common sense, high ideals, and lofty patriotism. . . .

---

5. **"dirty pool"**: a general reference to undemocratic combinations of economic and political power.

22. DEFENDING POPULISM

Daniel Zercher's laundry list of the reasons he supported the Populist Party was part of the 1894 "Manifesto" of the People's Party of Kansas but mixed national issues with local conditions. This is not surprising. Populism, like any even moderately successful national political movement, was elastic enough to incorporate the local with the national, the regional with the federal. Pronouncements like Zercher's, which appeared in a book heralding Populism, were not uncommon to the movement, which depended on the voices of everyday Americans to make the case for its principles. Which reasons seem directed solely at issues in Kansas? in the West? Which seem truly national in scope? How would you compare Populism's regional dimensions to the challenge it posed nationally? Which reasons would William Allen White (see Document 23 on p. 78) find particularly objectionable? What phrases or words are now obscure?

Daniel Zercher
"75 Reasons Why I Am a Populist"
1894[1]

1. Because I am in favor of an increase in the volume of money.
2. Because I am in favor of less taxes.
3. Because I am in favor of the remonetization of silver.
4. Because the Populists in congress vote as a unit on the questions that interest the masses—the gold power being unable to divide them.
5. Because I am in favor of paper, silver and gold comprising the money of this country.
6. Because I am in favor of a graduated income and property tax.
7. Because I am opposed to the issuing of bonds in time of peace for the running expenses of the government or for any other purpose.
8. Because I am opposed to the secretary of the treasury having power to issue bonds, except in times of war.
9. Because I am opposed to the exception clause on the greenback.[2]
10. Because I am in favor of the free coinage of silver.
11. Because I am in favor of the poor man having an equal show with the rich.
12. Because I am opposed to the governmental policy of loaning money to banks at 1 per cent. per annum, and refusing to loan it on farms or other good security at any price.

---

1. Kansas State Central Committee, People's Party of the United States, *Stubborn Facts in a Nutshell: Manifesto by the State Central Committee of the People's Party* (Topeka, KS: Advocate Publishing, 1894), 55–59.
2. **greenback:** paper money. Greenbacks could be used for nearly all transactions, but they were not honored for certain debts of the US government. Supporters of the Greenback movement, or the Greenback Party, many of whom became Populists, wished the government to honor and issue greenbacks more freely and were opposed to the gold standard.

13. Because I am opposed to the granting of subsidies and land grants to railroads or other corporations.
14. Because I am opposed to alien ownership of land in America.
15. Because I am in favor of special privileges to none.
16. Because I am in favor of equal justice to all.
17. Because I am opposed to trusts and combines, the result of the legislation for the past 30 years.
18. Because I am opposed to selling our products in a free-trade market and buying our necessities in a protected market.
19. Because I am opposed to the immigration of pauper labor, without proper restrictions.
20. Because I believe there are several questions which more concern the American people than the tariff.
21. Because I believe that the general government should issue and coin all the money.
22. Because I am opposed to national banks as banks of issue.
23. Because I am in favor of the government establishing postal savings banks in lieu of national banks.
24. Because I am in favor of a service pension to all soldiers or sailors of the union army in addition to a pension for disabilities received.
25. Because I am in favor of our government keeping its credit, honor and promises by paying the soldiers of the union army the $16 per month agreed upon for their services, instead of about $6.84 per month, which the depreciated currency amounted to.
26. Because of Republican extravagance on statehouse contracts.
27. Because I believe in rigid economy in governmental affairs.
28. Because the People's Party of Kansas saved the taxpayers over a million dollars during its administration.
29. Because the People's Party keeps its pledges.
30. Because the Populist board of railroad assessors equalized the assessment of railroad property of the state with other property.
31. Because corporations and the wealthy classes should not be granted favors by courts and relieved in the payment of their taxes when the same are denied to the common people.
32. Because no political party is worthy of support that promises bimetalism[3] in its platform and votes single gold standard in congress.
33. Because I am in favor of government ownership of the means of transportation and communication.
34. Because I am in favor of the municipal ownership of electric street railways, electric-light plants, water works, and other public utilities.

---

3. **bimetalism:** a Populist political plank that urged the government to use both gold and silver as currency; the gold standard would prevent this.

35. Because I believe that, with government ownership of the means of transportation and communication, their employees will receive at least $2.25 per day where they now receive $1.10 per day.

36. Because many Populists in Kansas had courage enough to leave a party that had 82,000 majority for the sake of principle.

37. Because Geo[rge]. L. Douglass, a Republican, battered down the doors of representative hall with a sledge hammer.

38. Because every overt act that caused legislative disturbance and trouble in Kansas was committed by the Republicans.

39. Because the Populist senate and Dunsmore house passed the maximum-freight-rate bill.

40. Because I love the People's Party for the abuse it has received, on the principle that Republicans do not usually "throw clubs into a tree unless there are some good apples growing there."

41. Because a Populist superintendent of insurance is collecting reciprocal taxes due the state from insurance companies to the amount of thousands of dollars.

42. Because the Republican house compelled the payment of a board bill for Republican members and officers of the Douglass house to the amount of $1,460.20.

43. Because the Republican majority of the Supreme Court usurped the constitutional authority of the House of Representatives.

44. Because Populists favor liberal public improvements.

45. Because I am in favor of the government erecting a post-office building in every city of over 5,000 inhabitants in the United States, and increasing the volume of currency sufficient to pay for them, thus giving employment to our starving millions. This would also save rent.

46. Because Populists will enact and enforce good, wholesome laws if given an opportunity.

47. Because under old party rule the prices of silver, wheat and cotton have constantly declined.

48. Because Republicans always lack just a few votes when it comes to enacting legislation in the interest of the common people.

49. Because the Republicans demonetized silver in 1873.

50. Because the Democrats demonetized silver in 1893.

51. Because Republicans had at least 15,000 illegal voters return to Kansas on passes and vote the Republican ticket.

52. Because Republican loan agents refused to renew farm loans for Populists without first extorting from them a pledge to vote the Republican ticket.

53. Because the Republican canvassing boards counted in Republican legislators when Populists were elected.

54. Because I believe that the person receiving the highest number of legal votes cast for him is elected.

55. Because I believe that a citizen of Oklahoma should not sit as a member in a Kansas legislature.

56. Because a Republican county clerk transposed the figures of a Democratic candidate, who was elected, to the Republican candidate.

57. Because I do not think that a certificate of election is sufficient without a majority of legal ballots back of it.

58. Because Republicans printed and sent out, at public expense, documents for campaign purposes in Swede, German, and English.

59. Because the Populist board of railroad commissioners have reduced freight rates on agricultural implements, coal, and other merchandise, to various points.

60. Because Higgins, Humphrey, Hovey & Co., held a secret lottery drawing behind closed doors, contrary to the statute.

61. Because the Populists proposed to arbitrate the points at issue in the legislature of 1893, and proposed as an arbitrating committee nine judges, as follows: five Republicans, two Democrats, and two Populists, which proposition was rejected by the Republicans.

62. Because the Populists afterwards offered to refer their claims to an arbitrating board consisting of two Republican judges and one Populist judge, which was also rejected by the Republicans.

63. Because a third proposition was made by the Populists, proposing Chief Justice Horton (Rep.) and Associate Justice Allen (Pop.), and they two should select a third man, the same to compose an arbitrating committee, whose decision should be final. This was also rejected by the Republicans.

64. Because Sheriff Wilkerson refused to protect state property when called on to do so by Governor Lewelling.

65. Because a Populist law and a Populist state printer have saved the state over $80,000 on state printing in two years.

66. Because a Populist secretary of state has conducted his office without any extra clerk hire and, besides, turned into the state treasury, the first year, $1,894.40.

67. Because a Populist bank commissioner turns into the state treasury more than $1,500 per annum, in fees, more than his Republican predecessor.

68. Because of secret rebates to purchasers and contractors of supplies for our state institutions under Republican rule.

69. Because I am opposed to watered stocks of corporations.

70. Because I am opposed to the waving of the bloody shirt[4] or sectional strife.

---

4. **bloody shirt:** Keeping the sectional crisis alive after the Civil War, especially through the actions of the Democratic Party in the South, was known as "waving the bloody shirt."

71. Because the Populist board of equalization made the lowest state tax levy ever made in Kansas.
72. Because Republican newspapers have injured the credit of Kansas in the East, and driven capital out of the state.
73. Because there are but two great political parties, the People's Party and Wall Street.
74. Because the Republicans and Democrats of New Jersey are driving Western capital out of the state.
75. Because I believe in the principles enunciated in the Omaha platform.

23. A NEWSPAPERMAN OPPOSES POPULISM

Not everyone in the West supported Populism's demands or its description of economic and political distress. One fierce opponent was the young journalist William Allen White of the Kansas newspaper Emporia Gazette. *His editorial "What's the Matter with Kansas?" attacked Populists and their movement as so much bluster, hot air, and wild ideas. White called the Populists "gibbering idiots" who saw conspiracy lurking around every corner, who feared the things they could not understand, and who had no reasonable plan to address the problems they shouted about. White's editorial, which helped make him famous, reveals the class antagonisms that colored much of the opposition to the Populist campaign. What are White's major points? How would one determine whether he was correct in his assumptions about the "who" and "what" of Kansas Populism? How do you think Daniel Zercher would respond to White's criticisms? How would Annie Diggs answer White?*

William Allen White
"What's the Matter with Kansas?"
1896[1]

Today the Kansas Department of Agriculture sent out a statement which indicates that Kansas has gained less than two thousand people in the past year. There are about two hundred and twenty-five thousand families in this state, and there were ten thousand babies born in Kansas, and yet so many people have left the state that the natural increase is cut down to less than two thousand net.

This has been going on for eight years.

If there had been a high brick wall around the state eight years ago, and not a soul had been admitted or permitted to leave, Kansas would be a half million

---

1. Irwin Ungar, ed., *Populism: Nostalgic or Progressive?* (Chicago: Rand McNally, 1964), 50–53.

souls better off than she is today. And yet the nation has increased in population. In five years ten million people have been added to the national population, yet instead of gaining a share of this—say, half a million—Kansas has apparently been a plague spot and, in the very garden of the world, has lost population by ten thousands every year.

Not only has she lost population, but she has lost money. Every moneyed man in the state who could get out without loss has gone. Every month in every community sees someone who has a little money pack up and leave the state. This has been going on for eight years. Money has been drained out all the time. In towns where ten years ago there were three or four or half a dozen money-lending concerns, stimulating industry by furnishing capital, there is now none, or one or two that are looking after the interest and principal already outstanding.

No one brings any money into Kansas any more. What community knows over one or two men who have moved in with more than $5,000 in the past three years? And what community cannot count half a score of men in that time who have left, taking all the money they could scrape together?

Yet the nation has grown rich; other states have increased in population and wealth—other neighboring states. Missouri has gained over two million, while Kansas has been losing half a million. Nebraska has gained in wealth and population while Kansas has gone downhill. Colorado has gained every way, while Kansas has lost every way since 1888.

What's the matter with Kansas?

There is no substantial city in the state. Every big town save one has lost in population. Yet Kansas City, Omaha, Lincoln, St. Louis, Denver, Colorado Springs, Sedalia, the cities of the Dakotas, St. Paul and Minneapolis and Des Moines—all cities and towns in the West—have steadily grown.

Take up the government blue book[2] and you will see that Kansas is virtually off the map. Two or three little scrubby consular places in yellow-fever-stricken communities that do not aggregate ten thousand dollars a year is all the recognition that Kansas has. Nebraska draws about one hundred thousand dollars; little old North Dakota draws about fifty thousand dollars; Oklahoma doubles Kansas; Missouri leaves her a thousand miles behind; Colorado is almost seven times greater than Kansas—the whole west is ahead of Kansas.

Take it by any standard you please, Kansas is not in it.

Go east and you hear them laugh at Kansas; go west and they sneer at her; go south and they "cuss" her; go north and they have forgotten her. Go into any crowd of intelligent people gathered anywhere on the globe, and you will find the Kansas man on the defensive. The newspaper columns and magazines once

---

2. **government blue book:** a listing of those people holding federal office.

devoted to praise of her, to boastful acts and startling figures concerning her resources, are now filled with cartoons, jibes and Pefferian[3] speeches. Kansas just naturally isn't in it. She has traded places with Arkansas and Timbuctoo.

What's the matter with Kansas? We all know; yet here we are at it again. We have an old mossback Jacksonian who snorts and howls because there is a bathtub in the State House; we are running that old jay for Governor. We have another shabby, wild-eyed, rattle-brained fanatic who has said openly in a dozen speeches that "the rights of the user are paramount to the rights of the owner"; we are running him for Chief Justice, so that capital will come tumbling over itself to get into the state. We have raked the old ash heap of failure in the state and found an old human hoop skirt who has failed as a businessman, who has failed as an editor, who has failed as a preacher, and we are going to run him for Congressman-at-Large. He will help the looks of the Kansas delegation at Washington. Then we have discovered a kid without a law practice and have decided to run him for Attorney General. Then, for fear some hint that the state had become respectable might percolate through the civilized portions of the nation, we have decided to send three or four harpies out lecturing, telling the people that Kansas is raising hell and letting the corn go to weed.

Oh, this is a state to be proud of! We are a people who can hold up our heads! What we need is not more money, but less capital, fewer white shirts and brains, fewer men with business judgment, and more of those fellows who boast that they are "just ordinary clodhoppers, but they know more in a minute about finance than John Sherman";[4] we need more men who are "posted," who can bellow about the crime of '73, who hate prosperity, and who think, because a man believes in national honor, he is a tool of Wall Street. We have had a few of them—some hundred fifty thousand—but we need more.

We need several thousand gibbering idiots to scream about the "Great Red Dragon" of Lombard Street.[5] We don't need population, we don't need wealth, we don't need well-dressed men on the streets, we don't need cities on the fertile prairies; you bet we don't! What we are after is the money power. Because we have become poorer and ornerier and meaner than a spavined, distempered mule, we, the people of Kansas, propose to kick; we don't care to build up, we wish to tear down.

"There are two ideas of government," said our noble Bryan at Chicago. "There are those who believe that if you legislate to make the well-to-do pros-

---

3. **Pefferian:** a reference to United States Senator William A. Peffer (1831–1912), a Populist from Kansas.
4. **John Sherman:** US senator from Ohio and author of the Sherman Anti-Trust Act of 1890, which outlawed trusts or associations that restrained trade.
5. **Lombard Street:** a term for London's financial district.

perous, this prosperity will leak through on those below. The Democratic idea has been that if you legislate to make the masses prosperous their prosperity will find its way up and through every class and rest upon them."

That's the stuff! Give the prosperous man the dickens! Legislate the thriftless man into ease, whack the stuffing out of the creditors and tell the debtors who borrowed the money five years ago when money "per capita" was greater than it is now, that the contraction of currency gives him a right to repudiate.

Whoop it up for the ragged trousers; put the lazy, greasy fizzle, who can't pay his debts on the altar, and bow down and worship him. Let the state ideal be high. What we need is not the respect of our fellow men, but the chance to get something for nothing.

Oh, yes, Kansas is a great state. Here are people fleeing from it by the score every day, capital going out of the state by the hundreds of dollars; and every industry but farming paralyzed, and that crippled, because its products have to go across the ocean before they can find a laboring man at work who can afford to buy them. Let's don't stop this year. Let's drive all the decent, self-respecting men out of the state. Let's keep the old clodhoppers who know it all. Let's encourage the man who is "posted." He can talk, and what we need is not mill hands to eat our meat, nor factory hands to eat our wheat, nor cities to oppress the farmer by consuming his butter and eggs and chickens and produce. What Kansas needs is men who can talk, who have large leisure to argue the currency question while their wives wait at home for a nickel's worth of bluing.

What's the matter with Kansas?

Nothing under the shining sun. She is losing her wealth, population and standing. She has got her statesmen, and the money power is afraid of her. Kansas is all right. She has started in to raise hell as Mrs. Lease[6] advised, and she seems to have an over-production. But that doesn't matter. Kansas never did believe in diversified crops. Kansas is all right. There is absolutely nothing wrong with Kansas. "Every prospect pleases and only man is vile."

---

6. **Mrs. Lease:** Mary Elizabeth Lease, Kansas Populist leader and speaker.

24. SILVER POPULISM AND "THE CROSS OF GOLD"

This speech ranks as one of the greatest in American history. William Jennings Bryan, whose youth and vigor captivated the nation, stormed into the national political limelight off the flat farmlands of Nebraska. As the Democratic nominee for president in 1896, Bryan agreed with the Populists only on the silver issue; he championed a plan for the government to go forward with the unlimited production of silver money, which farmers hoped would drive up inflation and raise fallen crop prices. Western mine owners were eager to supply the silver.

This speech, given at the Democratic convention in Chicago, electrified listeners and made it clear that the Democrats and Populists would win or lose the presidency on the silver issue. They lost. William McKinley, the Republican nominee, got the votes where they mattered most—in the East. The East did not care about silver, or Populism, the way the West did. Bryan made a remarkable speech, blasting the moneyed, urban East for ignoring the rural West and South. But the speech succeeded far more as oratory than as policy and, ironically, its sheer success helped sink the Populist cause as Bryan became identified with the silver issue and not broader Populist issues. What makes this such a successful speech? What points does Bryan drive home the hardest? In what ways does he appeal to westerners?

William Jennings Bryan
"The Cross of Gold" Speech to the Democratic National Convention
1896[1]

. . . Never before in the history of this country has there been witnessed such a contest as that through which we have just passed. Never before in the history of American politics has a great issue been fought out as this issue has been, by the voters of a great party. On the fourth of March, 1895, a few Democrats, most of them members of Congress, issued an address to the Democrats of the nation, asserting that the money question was the paramount issue of the hour; declaring that a majority of the Democratic party had the right to control the action of the party on this paramount issue; and concluding with the request that the believers in the free coinage of silver in the Democratic party should organize, take charge of, and control the policy of the Democratic party. Three months later, at Memphis, an organization was perfected, and the silver Democrats went forth openly and courageously proclaiming their belief, and declaring that, if successful, they would crystallize into a platform the declaration which they had made. Then began the conflict. With a zeal approaching the zeal which inspired the crusaders who followed Peter the Hermit,[2] our silver Democrats went forth from victory unto victory until they are now assembled, not to discuss, not to debate, but to enter up the judgment already rendered by the plain people of this country. In this contest brother has been arrayed against brother, father against son. The warmest ties of love, acquaintance and association have been disregarded; old leaders have been cast aside when they have refused to give expression to the sentiments of those whom they would lead, and new leaders have sprung up to give direction to this cause of truth.

---

1. Donald K. Springen, *William Jennings Bryan, Orator of Small-Town America* (New York: Greenwood, 1991), 133–39.
2. **Peter the Hermit:** Christian evangelist of the Crusades.

Thus has the contest been waged, and we have assembled here under as binding and solemn instructions as were ever imposed upon representatives of the people. . . .

We say to you that you have made the definition of a business man too limited in its application. The man who is employed for wages is as much a business man as his employer, the attorney in a country town is as much a business man as the corporation counsel in a great metropolis; the merchant at the cross-roads store is as much a business man as the merchant of New York; the farmer who goes forth in the morning and toils all day—who begins in the spring and toils all summer—and who by the application of brain and muscle to the natural resources of the country creates wealth, is as much a business man as the man who goes upon the board of trade and bets upon the price of grain; the miners who go down a thousand feet into the earth, or climb two thousand feet upon the cliffs, and bring forth from their hiding places the precious metals to be poured into the channels of trade are as much business men as the few financial magnates who, in a back room, corner the money of the world. We come to speak for this broader class of business men.

Ah, my friends, we say not one word against those who live upon the Atlantic coast, but the hardy pioneers who have braved all the dangers of the wilderness, who have made the desert to blossom as the rose—the pioneers away out there [pointing to the West], who rear their children near to Nature's heart, where they can mingle their voices with the voices of the birds—out there where they have erected schoolhouses for the education of their young, churches where they praise their Creator, and cemeteries where rest the ashes of their dead—these people, we say, are as deserving of the consideration of our party as any people in this country. It is for these that we speak. We do not come as aggressors. Our war is not a war of conquest; we are fighting in the defense of our homes, our families, and posterity. We have petitioned, and our petitions have been scorned; we have entreated, and our entreaties have been disregarded; we have begged, and they have mocked when our calamity came. We beg no longer; we entreat no more; we petition no more. We defy them.

The gentleman from Wisconsin has said that he fears a Robespierre.[3] My friends, in this land of the free you need not fear that a tyrant will spring up from among the people. What we need is an Andrew Jackson to stand, as Jackson stood, against the encroachments of organized wealth.

They tell us that this platform was made to catch votes. We reply to them that changing conditions make new issues; that the principles upon which Democracy rests are as everlasting as the hills, but that they must be applied to new conditions as they arise. Conditions have arisen, and we are here to meet

---

3. **Robespierre:** Maximilien Robespierre, a French revolutionary executed in 1794.

these conditions. They tell us that the income tax ought not to be brought in here; that it is a new idea. They criticize us for our criticisms of the Supreme Court of the United States. My friends, we have not criticized; we have simply called attention to what you already know. If you want criticism, read the dissenting opinions of the court. There you will find criticisms. They say that we passed an unconstitutional law; we deny it. The income tax law was not unconstitutional when it was passed; it was not unconstitutional when it went before the Supreme Court for the first time; it did not become unconstitutional until one of the judges changed his mind, and we cannot be expected to know when a judge will change his mind. The income tax is just. It simply intends to put the burdens of government justly upon the backs of the people. I am in favor of an income tax. When I find a man who is not willing to bear his share of the burdens of the government which protects him, I find a man who is unworthy to enjoy the blessings of a government like ours.

They say that we are opposing national bank currency; it is true. If you will read what Thomas Benton said, you will find he said that, in searching history, he could find but one parallel to Andrew Jackson, that was Cicero, who destroyed the conspiracy of Cataline and saved Rome. Benton said that Cicero only did for Rome what Jackson did for us when he destroyed the bank conspiracy and saved America. We say in our platform that we believe that the right to coin and issue money is a function of government. We believe it. We believe that it is a part of sovereignty, and can no more with safety be delegated to private individuals than we could afford to delegate to private individuals the power to make penal statutes or levy taxes. Mr. Jefferson, who was once regarded as good Democratic authority, seems to have differed in opinion from the gentleman who has addressed us on the part of the minority. Those who are opposed to this proposition tell us that the issue of paper money is a function of the bank, and that the Government ought to go out of the banking business. I stand with Jefferson rather than with them, and tell them, as he did, that the issue of money is a function of government, and that the banks ought to go out of the governing business. . . .

And now, my friends, let me come to the paramount issue. If they ask us why it is that we say more on the money question than we say upon the tariff question, I reply that, if protection has slain its thousands, the gold standard has slain its tens of thousands. If they ask us why we do not embody in our platform all the things that we believe in, we reply that when we have restored the money of the constitution all other necessary reforms will be possible; but that until this is done there is no other reform that can be accomplished.

Why is it that within three months such a change has come over the country? Three months ago, when it was confidently asserted that those who believe in the gold standard would frame our platform and nominate our candidates, even the advocates of the gold standard did not think that we could elect a President. And they had good reason for their doubt, because there is scarcely a

State here to-day asking for the gold standard which is not in the absolute control of the Republican party. But note the change. Mr. McKinley was nominated at St. Louis upon a platform which declared for the maintenance of the gold standard until it can be changed into bimetallism by international agreement. Mr. McKinley was the most popular man among the Republicans, and three months ago everybody in the Republican party prophesied his election. How is it to-day? Why, the man who was once pleased to think that he looked like Napoleon—that man shudders to-day when he remembers that he was nominated on the anniversary of the battle of Waterloo. Not only that, but as he listens he can hear with ever-increasing distinctness the sound of the waves as they beat upon the lonely shores of St. Helena.

Why this change? Ah, my friends, is not the reason for the change evident to any one who will look at the matter? No private character, however pure, no personal popularity, however great, can protect from the avenging wrath of an indignant people a man who will declare that he is in favor of fastening the gold standard upon this country, or who is willing to surrender the right of self-government and place the legislative control of our affairs in the hands of foreign potentates and powers.

We go forth confident that we shall win. Why? Because upon the paramount issue of this campaign there is not a spot of ground upon which the enemy will dare to challenge battle. If they tell us that the gold standard is a good thing, we shall point to their platform and tell them that their platform pledges the party to get rid of the gold standard and substitute bimetallism. If the gold standard is a good thing, why try to get rid of it? I call your attention to the fact that some of the very people who are in this convention to-day and who tell us that we ought to declare in favor of international bimetallism—thereby declaring that the gold standard is wrong and that the principle of bimetallism is better—these very people four months ago were open and avowed advocates of the gold standard, and were then telling us that we could not legislate two metals together, even with the aid of all the world. If the gold standard is a good thing, we ought to declare in favor of its retention and not in favor of abandoning it; and if the gold standard is a bad thing why should we wait until other nations are willing to help us to let go? Here is the line of battle, and we care not upon which issue they force the fight; we are prepared to meet them on either issue or on both. If they tell us that the gold standard is the standard of civilization, we reply to them that this, the most enlightened of all the nations of the earth, has never declared for a gold standard and that both the great parties this year are declaring against it. If the gold standard is the standard of civilization, why, my friends, should we not have it? If they come to meet us on that issue we can present the history of our nation. More than that; we can tell them that they will search the pages of history in vain to find a single instance where the common people of any land have ever declared themselves in favor of the gold standard. They can find where the holders of fixed investments have declared for a gold standard, but not where the masses have. . . .

You come to us and tell us that the great cities are in favor of the gold standard; we reply that the great cities rest upon our broad and fertile prairies. Burn down your cities and leave our farms, and your cities will spring up again as if by magic; but destroy our farms and the grass will grow in the streets of every city in the country.

My friends, we declare that this nation is able to legislate for its own people on every question, without waiting for the aid or consent of any other nation on earth; and upon that issue we expect to carry every State in the Union. I shall not slander the inhabitants of the fair State of Massachusetts nor the inhabitants of the State of New York by saying that, when they are confronted with the proposition, they will declare that this nation is notable to attend to its own business. It is the issue of 1776 over again. Our ancestors, when but three millions in number had the courage to declare their political independence of every other nation; shall we, their descendants, when we have grown to seventy millions, declare that we are less independent than our forefathers? No, my friends, that will never be the verdict of our people. Therefore, we care not upon what lines the battle is fought. If they say bimetallism is good, but that we cannot have it until other nations help us, we reply that, instead of having a gold standard because England has, we will restore bimetallism, and then let England have bimetallism because the United States has it. If they dare to come out in the open field and defend the gold standard as a good thing, we will fight them to the uttermost. Having behind us the producing masses of this nation and the world, supported by the commercial interests, the laboring interests, and the toilers everywhere, we will answer their demand for a gold standard by saying to them: You shall not press down upon the brow of labor this crown of thorns, you shall not crucify mankind upon a cross of gold.

FURTHER READING

Argersinger, Peter H. *The Limits of Agrarian Radicalism: Western Populism and American Politics*. Lawrence: University Press of Kansas, 1995.

Goodwyn, Lawrence. *Democratic Promise: The Populist Moment in America*. New York: Oxford University Press, 1976.

Johnston, Robert D. *The Radical Middle Class: Populist Democracy and the Question of Capitalism in Progressive Era Portland, Oregon*. Princeton, NJ: Princeton University Press, 2002.

Kazin, Michael. *A Godly Hero: The Life of William Jennings Bryan*. New York: Knopf, 2006.

Larson, Robert W. *New Mexico Populism: A Study of Radical Protest in a Western Territory*. Boulder: Colorado Associated University Press, 1974.

McMath, Robert C. *American Populism: A Social History, 1877–1898*. New York: Hill and Wang, 1993.

Nugent, Walter. *The Tolerant Populists: Kansas, Populism and Nativism*. Chicago: University of Chicago Press, 1963.

Ostler, Jeffrey. *Prairie Populism: The Fate of Agrarian Radicalism in Kansas, Nebraska, and Iowa, 1880–1892*. Lawrence: University Press of Kansas, 1993.

Pollack, Norman. *The Populist Response to Industrial America*. Cambridge, MA: Harvard University Press, 1962.

Postel, Charles. *The Populist Vision*. Oxford and New York: Oxford University Press, 2007.

Sanders, Elizabeth. *Roots of Reform: Farmers, Workers, and the American State, 1877–1917*. Chicago: University of Chicago Press, 1999.

Stoll, Steven. *The Fruits of Natural Advantage: Making the Industrial Countryside in California*. Berkeley: University of California Press, 1998.

Vaught, David. *Cultivating California: Growers, Specialty Crops, and Labor, 1875–1920*. Baltimore: Johns Hopkins University Press, 1999.

Wright, James Edward. *The Politics of Populism: Dissent in Colorado*. New Haven, CT: Yale University Press, 1974.

Detail from a union broadside, ca. 1907. Industrial expansion all across America came at a price: violence and social upheaval. No region of the nation expressed these tensions more glaringly than the mining communities of the American West, as striking miners faced off against their employers and, often, state and federal soldiers. This graphic image, designed in 1907 by William "Big Bill" Haywood, founder of the Western Federation of Miners, expresses the radical union's opposition to martial law imposed in the mining camps of some Rocky Mountain towns. In questioning the legality of certain acts by authorities—including the chaining of strikers to trees and their imprisonment in corrals (or "bull-pens")—the Western Federation asks, "Is Colorado in America?" How might this image have been used in the battle for public opinion?

Labor Unrest in the West

As we saw in previous chapters addressing politics and the interconnected phenomena of urbanization, industrialization, and immigration, huge social forces changed America in the late nineteenth and early twentieth centuries. Such change was uneven, wrenching, and hardly of proportional benefit to those affected by it. Nor was all this change confined to the swelling neighborhoods and byways of the cities and their burgeoning and belching factories. Change, and the anxieties and troubles it brought with it, seeped everywhere in American life, even into the dark and dangerous places below the earth's surface.

Perhaps more than any other region in America, the mining zones of the Rocky Mountains and the Southwest, which saw bitter and protracted labor strife at the end of the nineteenth century and the dawn of the twentieth, epitomized the contested process of mass industrialization. Not that the West and Southwest were alone in terms of troubles. Mill towns in the South, rail yards in Chicago, and steel mills in Pennsylvania reverberated with tension and violence, too. But the distress seemed particularly acute in the mining and industrial sites in places such as Idaho, Colorado, New Mexico, and Arizona. Having flirted with Populism's promises of reform, even revolutionary reform, by way of ballot-box victories, miners and their employers squared off in battles more ferocious in the wake of Populism's decline and fall.

Indeed, if one were to look for "classic" displays of western violence, they would more likely be expressed in the clashes between workers and employers in western mines and mining towns than in the cinematic six-gun disputes on the Main Streets of the West's cattle towns. With the advantage granted us by more than a century's worth of hindsight and scholarship, we can argue that the American West was in the midst of a protracted labor war from the 1870s until the early decades of the twentieth century, so common and so endemic were the clashes. These were not episodes with little in common; they were, instead, chapters in a long and violent book about labor, politics, and industrial capitalism. The places and the details changed from town to town, from mine to mine, but so much stayed the same. From Bisbee to Cripple Creek, Boise to Sacramento, labor troubles seemed a part of the landscape every bit as much as the coal, silver, gold, copper, or lead within it. No western region was left untouched or unscarred, by either the mines themselves or what happened in and around them.

The labor disputes were often grim and extremely violent, but they defy simple generalizations, or at least those that go beyond "power struggles between bosses and workers." It is important to remember that western mining was varied and diverse, in terms of both the valuable thing the miners sought and how they went after it. A western mine might be small, worked by an individual prospector or two, but by the last decades of the nineteenth century, this would be the exception rather than the rule. By then, most western miners worked for wages, and they worked for a company or a corporation. This was also true for the tens of thousands of others who made up the post–Civil War industrial workforce. Railroad workers operated in conditions nearly as dangerous and uncertain as any miner. So, too, with the workers who built the West's cities and began to lift them toward the sky.

Workers organized for rights and better wages and safer conditions. Trade unions were tolerated, if not encouraged, in many industries, but they struggled to find footholds of either power or permanence. Matters grew especially tense in the 1890s, once the effects of a national depression worsened already-tense relations between miners and owners across the Rockies. In Colorado, Cripple Creek miners faced off against US troops over mine conditions and pay, and the same was true at about the same time with striking railroad workers in California. Idaho's panhandle and the mining regions of Coeur d'Alene exploded in one violent episode after another. Miners knew how to use guns and explosives, and they—and their opponents—did not hesitate to do so. Striking miners in Idaho found themselves locked up by authorities, if not by the law, in fenced-off "bull pens." In 1905 the former governor of Idaho, a supporter of mine owners in their disputes with workers, walked out of his house in Caldwell one morning, opened his front gate, and got blown up by a bomb wired to the latch. In 1917 authorities in Bisbee, Arizona, working closely with heavily armed vigilantes, rounded up as many as twelve hundred people suspected of radical pro-labor activities and put them on railcars leaving copper country.

This chapter focuses on the Western Federation of Miners (WFM). Founded in the midst of Rocky Mountain labor strike, the WFM was dedicated to a radical reorganization of American industrial capitalism. Led by the charismatic and ambitious William "Big Bill" Haywood (who would later be instrumental to the founding of the Industrial Workers of the World, known as the Wobblies), the WFM was a powerful force of socialist opposition to mine owners throughout the West and south into Mexico. The WFM's concerted, violent critique not only of mining corporations but of the whole fabric of American capitalism set it apart from less radical (and more narrowly focused) unions. Vehemently and violently opposed to the WFM, for obvious reasons, mine owners banded together and looked to the federal government for military, legal, and other support, which they received. Victories for radical labor, by contrast, were few and far between—a dynamited mine here and there, a few protracted, expensive strikes, and, most prominently, Haywood's acquittal in the conspiracy trial that tried to link him to the bombing murder of Frank Steunenberg, the former Idaho governor killed in 1905.

Here we look at documents examining various conflicts from multiple perspectives. Jack London, as famous a writer as one could find in the early twentieth century, penned a pro-labor, pro-worker piece set in Idaho right after the Steunenberg murder. His sentiments were echoed in a WFM rejoinder regarding conditions and positions in Colorado. "Mother Jones" offers her own defense of workers in questioning the legality of Colorado's anti-labor practices. Other pieces move the argument to the middle of the road. John D. Rockefeller takes a somewhat conciliatory, if defensive, position in a speech about regarding conditions in the vast mining enterprise he owned in southern Colorado.

AS YOU READ: Think about the various points of view that each author adopts. How do they marshal facts in their arguments? How do legal protections and rights get invoked for one reason or another, one side or another? In the case of Colorado and its strife and dissent, what other sources would you like to see to get a fuller view of the situation there in the early twentieth century? Where would you look for them?

25. THE "WHITE CAPS" OF NEW MEXICO MAKE THEIR DEMANDS KNOWN

The expansion of absentee ranching and mining interests in the Southwest in the last third of the nineteenth century destabilized the pastoral folkways and lives of the region's Hispano peoples. Racial and ethnic tensions, long simmering in the aftermath of the 1846–48 Mexican War, worsened as landed Anglo elites—both present and absentee—gobbled up land and the water and mineral rights attached to it. In the wake of such change and turmoil, a grassroots protest movement coalesced around the Gorras Blancas, or White Caps. Hispano farmers and subsistence ranchers, for the most part, the Gorras Blancas pushed a platform of resistance to political and economic dominance by outside interests and occasionally performed acts of violence, including destruction of new railroad lines into the region. Strongest in New Mexico's San Miguel County, the Gorras Blancas anonymously posted their platform of positions and demands in and around the county seat of Las Vegas in March 1890. As you read this document, think of the various themes and points it raises. What changes provoked this grassroots protest?

"The White Caps 1,500 Strong and Gaining Daily"
Nuestra Platforma
1890[1]

Our purpose is to protect the rights and interests of the people in general and especially those of the helpless classes.

We want the Las Vegas Grant settled to the benefit of all concerned, and this we hold is the entire community within the Grant.

We want no "land grabbers" or obstructionists of any sort to interfere. We will watch them.

We are not down on lawyers as a class, but the usual knavery and unfair treatment of the people must be stopped.

Our judiciary hereafter must understand that we will sustain it only when "Justice" is its watchword.

We are down on race issues, and will watch race agitators.

We favor irrigation enterprises, but will fight any scheme that tends to monopolize the supply of water sources to the detriment of residents living on lands watered by the same streams.

The people are suffering from the effects of partisan "bossism" and these bosses had better quickly hold their peace. The people have been persecuted and hauled about in every which way to satisfy their caprices.

We must have a free ballot and fair court and the will of the Majority shall be respected.

We have no grudge against any person in particular, but we are the enemies of bulldozers and tyrants.

---

1. David J. Weber, ed., *Foreigners in Their Native Land: Historical Roots of the Mexican Americans* (Albuquerque: University of New Mexico Press, 1973). Originally published in the *Las Vegas Daily Optic*, March 12, 1890.

If the old system shall continue, death would be a relief to our suffering. And for our rights, our lives are the least we can pledge.

If the fact that we are law-abiding citizens is questioned, come out to our houses and see the hunger and desolation we are suffering; and *this* is the result of the deceitful and corrupt methods of "bossism."

26. UNREST IN IDAHO

In addition to short stories and novels such as The Call of the Wild *(1903) and* White Fang *(1906), Jack London wrote newspaper articles and essays for the socialist press, which had a large readership, especially in the nation's cities. Many of London's writings, fictional as well as journalistic, have strong pro-labor and pro-worker perspectives; his political positions and his outspokenness helped make him an unpopular figure in the eyes of mine owners and big-business interests. This brief piece, published in the* Chicago Daily Socialist, *pertains to the trial of "Big Bill" Haywood and other WFM officials who were charged with assassinating Frank Steunenberg, the former governor of Idaho. What evidence does London use to bolster his argument that there is "something rotten" in the justice system in Idaho? How does this essay compare with the point-by-point argument put forward by the Western Federation of Miners (see Document 27 on p. 96)? Would London's essay be convincing to union opponents?*

Jack London
"Something Rotten in Idaho"
1906[1]

Up in the State of Idaho, at the present moment, are three men lying in jail. Their names are Moyer, Haywood and Pettibone.[2] They are charged with the murder of Governor Steunenberg. Incidentally they are charged with thirty, sixty or seventy other atrocious murders. Not alone are they labor leaders and murderers, but they are anarchists. They are guilty, and they should be swiftly and immediately executed. It is to be regretted that no severer and more painful punishment than hanging awaits them. At any rate there is consolation in the knowledge that these men will surely be hanged.

The foregoing epitomises the information and beliefs possessed by the average farmer, lawyer, professor, clergyman and businessman in the United States. His belief is based upon the information he has gained by reading the

---

1. Philip S. Foner, ed., *Jack London, American Rebel* (New York: Citadel, 1947), 407–10.
2. **Moyer, Haywood and Pettibone:** Charles Moyer, William Haywood, and George Pettibone, officials of the Western Federation of Miners, were charged with complicity in the murder of former governor Steunenberg of Idaho. All were acquitted.

newspapers. Did he possess different information, he might possibly believe differently. It is the purpose of this article to try to furnish information such as is not furnished by 99 percent of the newspapers of the United States.

In the first place, Moyer, Haywood and Pettibone were not even in the State of Idaho at the time the crime with which they are charged was committed. In the second place, they are at present in jail in the State of Idaho because of the perpetration of lawless acts by officers of the law, from the chief of the state executives down to the petty deputy chiefs—and this in collusion with mine owners' associations and railroad companies.

Here is conspiracy self-confessed and openly flaunted. And it is conspiracy and violation of law on the part of the very men who claim that they are trying to bring punishment for conspiracy and violation of law. This is inconsistency, to say the least. It may be added that it is criminal inconsistency. . . .

The evidence against these labor leaders is contained in the confession of one Harry Orchard. It looks bad, in the face of it, when a man confesses that at the instigation of another, and for money received from that other, he had committed murder. . . .

But this is not the first time that these same labor leaders have been charged with murder; and this is not the first confession implicating them. Colorado is a fertile soil for confessions. Moyer, in particular, has been in jail many times charged with other murders. At least five men have solemnly sworn that at his instigation they have committed murder. Now it is a matter of history that when the tool confesses, the principal swings.

Moyer gives the lie to history. In spite of the many confessions he has never been convicted. This would make it look bad for the confessions. Not only does it make the confession look rotten, but the confessions, in turn, cast a doubt on the sweetness and purity of the present confession of Harry Orchard. In a region noted for the rottenness of its confession-fruit, it would be indeed remarkable to find this latest sample clean and wholesome.

When a man comes into court to give testimony, it is well to know what his character is, what his previous acts are, and whether or not self-interest enters into the case. Comes the mine owners' association of Colorado and Idaho to testify against Moyer, Haywood and Pettibone. Well, then, what sort of men are the mine owners? What have they done in the past?

That the mine owners have violated the laws countless times, there is no discussion. That they have robbed thousands of voters of their suffrage is common knowledge. That they have legalized lawlessness is history. But these things have only a general bearing on the matter at issue.

In particular, during and since the labor war that began in Colorado in 1903, the mine owners have charged the members of the Western Federation of Miners with all manner of crimes. There have been many trials, and in every trial the verdict has been acquittal. The testimony in these trials has been given by hired Pinkertons[3] and spies. Yet the Pinkertons and spies, masters in the art of gathering evidence, have always failed to convict in the courts. This looks bad for the sort of evidence that grows in the fertile Colorado soil.

But it is worse than that. While the Pinkertons and spies have proved poor evidence-farmers, they have demonstrated they are good criminals. Many of them have been convicted by the courts and sent to jail for the commission of crimes ranging from theft to manslaughter.

Are the mine owners law abiding citizens? Do they believe in law? Do they uphold the law? "To hell with the Constitution" was their clearly enunciated statement in Colorado in 1903. Their military agent, General Sherman Bell, said: "To hell with habeas corpus! We will give them post-mortems instead!" Governor Gooding, the present governor of Idaho, has recently said: "To hell with the people."

Now it is but natural to question the good citizenship of an organization of men that continuously and consistently consigns to hell the process of habeas corpus, the people and the Constitution. In Chicago a few years ago some men were hanged for uttering incendiary language not half so violent as this. But they were workingmen. The mine owners of Colorado and Idaho are the chief executives, or capitalists. They will not be hanged. On the contrary, they have their full liberty, such liberty they are exercising in an effort to hang some other men whom they do not like.

Why do some mine owners dislike Moyer, Haywood and Pettibone? Because these men stand between the mine owners and a pot of money. These men are leaders of organized labor. They plan and direct the efforts of the workingmen to get better wages and shorter hours. The operation of their mines will be more expensive. The higher the running expenses, the smaller the profits. If the mine owners could disrupt the Western Federation of Miners, they would increase the hours of labor, lower wages, and thereby gain millions of dollars. . . .

. . . Judas betrayed Christ to crucifixion for thirty pieces of silver. Human nature has not changed since that day, and it is conceivable that Moyer, Haywood and Pettibone may be hanged for the sake of a few millions of dollars. . . .

In brief, the situation at present in Idaho is as follows: following a long struggle between capital and labor, the capitalist organization has jailed the leaders of the labor organization. The capitalist organization is trying to hang the labor leaders. It has tried to do this before, but its evidence and its "confessions" were always too rotten and corrupt. Its hired spies and Pinkertons have themselves been sent to prison for the commission of all manner of crimes, while they have never succeeded in sending one labor leader to prison.

---

3. **Pinkertons:** private detectives of the Pinkerton Detective Agency.

The capitalist organization has been incendiary in speech, and by unlawful acts has lived up to its speech. It will profit by exterminating the labor organization. The capitalist organization has a bad character. It has never hesitated at anything to attain its ends. By sentiment and act it has behaved unlawfully, as have its agents whom it hired. The situation in Idaho? There can be but one conclusion—THERE IS SOMETHING ROTTEN IN IDAHO!

27. THE MINERS REPLY

The WFM answered some of the charges made against it by Colorado mine owners and property owners in this statement, printed as an official document of the US Senate. The WFM outlines the goals and principles established at the organization's founding in 1893. In language rooted in the American Revolution, it casts itself as the protector of the rights of the American worker. According to the WFM, the owners of western mines, many of whom are foreign-born, are guilty of operating their companies and their mines under outrageously dangerous conditions. They are the true criminals in the mining districts of the West. How does this WFM statement compare with Ray Stannard Baker's views in the document that follows this one? What are the WFM's major points defending the activities it has been involved in? How would John D. Rockefeller Jr. (see Document 30 on p. 107) have viewed these political expressions?

Western Federation of Miners
Statement in Answer and Rebuttal
1904[1]

STATEMENT: In support of the resolution introduced by Senator Patterson, of Colorado, the Western Federation of Miners desires to submit a reply to the lengthy statement introduced by Senator Scott, of West Virginia, in rebuttal of the fabricated and unsupported assertions contained in said statement. The document introduced by Senator Scott to the United States Senate brands the Western Federation of Miners as a criminal organization and has been introduced for the sole purpose of poisoning the public mind. In order that the honorable body which compose the Senate of the United States may have a clear conception of the objects and aims of the Western Federation of Miners we hereby present the preamble of our organization:

---

1. "Statement of the Western Federation of Miners," 58th Congress, 2nd session, 1904, S. Doc. 163, 1–6, 39–41.

PREAMBLE: We hold that all men are created to be free and should have equal access and opportunity to the enjoyment of all benefits to be derived from their exertions in dealing with the natural resources of the earth, and that free access and equal opportunity thereto are absolutely necessary to man's existence and the upward progress of the human race. Since it is self-evident that civilization has, during centuries, made progress in proportion to the production and utilization of minerals and metals, both precious and base, and that most of the material prosperity and comforts enjoyed by mankind are due to this progress, it is highly fitting and proper that the men who are engaged in the hazardous and unhealthy occupation of mining, milling, smelting, and the reduction of ores should receive a just compensation for their labors, which shall be proportionate to the dangers connected therewith, and such protection from law as will remove needless risk to life or health, and for the purpose of bringing about and promoting these and other proper and lawful ends, and for the general welfare of ourselves, families, and dependent ones we deem it necessary to organize and maintain the Western Federation of Miners, and, among our lawful purposes, we declare more especially our objects to be:

First. To secure compensation fully commensurate with the dangers of our employment and the right to use our earnings free from the dictation of any person whomsoever.

Second. To establish as speedily as possible, and so that it may be enduring, our right to receive pay for labor performed, in lawful money, and to rid ourselves of the iniquitous and unfair system of spending our earnings where and how our employers or their agent or officers may designate.

Third. To strive to procure the introduction and use of any and all suitable, efficient appliances for the preservation of life, limb, and health of all employees, and thereby preserve to society the lives and usefulness of a large number of wealth producers.

Fourth. To labor for the enactment of suitable laws and the proper enforcement thereof.

Fifth. To provide for the education of our children and to prohibit the employment of all children until they shall have reached at least the age of sixteen years.

Sixth. To prevent by law any mine owner, mining company, or corporation, or the agents thereof, from employing detectives, or armed forces, and to provide that only the lawfully elected or appointed officers of the county, State, or province, who shall be bona fide citizens thereof, shall act in any capacity in the enforcement of the law.

Seventh. To use all honorable means to maintain and promote friendly relations between ourselves and our employers, and endeavor by arbitration and conciliation, or other pacific means, to settle any difficulties which may arise between us, and thus strive to make contention and strikes unnecessary.

Eighth. To use all lawful and honorable means to abolish and prevent the system of convict labor from coming into competition with free labor and to demand the enforcement of the foreign contract-labor law against the importation of pauper labor from any foreign country, and also to use our efforts to make it unlawful to bring persons from another State, Territory or province to take the places of workingmen on a strike, or who may be locked out, by means of false representation, advertisements, or other misleading means.

Ninth. To demand the repeal of conspiracy laws that in any way abridge the right of labor organizations to promote the general welfare of their membership, and also to use our influence to bring about legislation which will prevent government by injunction by either Federal, State, or provincial courts. To procure employment for our members in preference to non-union men, and in all lawful ways cooperate with one another for the purpose of procuring a just share of the product of our toil and mutual advancement in order that the general welfare of the membership and their families may be steadily advanced and promoted.

Tenth. To use our united efforts to discourage the contract-labor system, and, as soon as practicable, to abolish the same, believing the said system to be detrimental to the best interests of organized labor.

For the further enlightenment of the members of the United States Senate, and in order to show that our organization is a legitimate body, we quote the following from the constitution:

> SEC. 2. The objects of this organization shall be to unite the various persons working in and around the mines, mills, and smelters into one central body, to practice those virtues that adorn society, and remind man of his duty to his fellow man, the elevation of his position, and the maintenance of the rights of the workers.

Previous to an applicant being initiated to membership in the Western Federation of Miners or taking the obligation, the following assurance is made:

> This body exacts no pledge or obligation which in any way conflicts with the duty you owe to your God, your country, or your fellow-man.

The Western Federation of Miners was organized in Butte, Montana, on May 15, 1893, and for ten years the organization has kept inviolate the principles enunciated in the preamble and constitution.

Because of the success, growth, and strength of the organization, and because of its progressive spirit in defending the humblest of its members from the tyranny of corporate oppression, the Federation has been assailed, not only by the federated might of the smelting trust and the various mine-owners' associations, but corporation journals owned and controlled by magnates in the mining and smelting industries have loaded their editorial columns with slander and vituperation in obedience to the mandates of the moneyed fraternity that molded the convictions of mortgaged editors. The Western

Federation of Miners has never waged a battle except in self-defense. All strikes that have arisen can be traced to the encroachments of corporations, whose managers received their orders and instructions from a foreign source.[2] . . .

Permit us to call the attention of the United States Senate to the reckless slaughter of human life that may be laid at the door of the mine operators.

In Scofield, Utah, some three or four years ago, nearly three hundred miners were killed by an explosion, which resulted on account of the failure of the mine owners to comply with the law governing ventilation. In May, 1901, a disaster occurred in Fernie, British Columbia, where 137 men lost their lives and a coroner's jury brought in a verdict of culpable negligence against the company, and this "criminal" organization, the Western Federation of Miners, immediately sent a representative with $3,000 for the relief of the widows and orphans. Before all of the bodies were removed from the mine, Manager Tonkin reduced the wages of those who survived this blood-curdling disaster.

It should be fresh to the memory of the members of the United States Senate concerning the appalling disasters which have taken place in Tennessee, Wyoming, and Pennsylvania, and all of which could have been averted if the mine operators had placed a higher value upon human life than dividends and complied with the laws of the respective States. . . .

In Park City, Utah, at the Daly-West mine, thirty-five miners were killed by an explosion of giant powder that was stored in the mine by the company contrary to every safeguard which common sense should suggest.

In November, 1901, twenty-two miners lost their lives by being suffocated on account of a fire which destroyed a boarding house that was connected with the tunnel of the Smuggler Union mine, a property that was then under the management of Arthur L. Collins. The law had not been complied with, for the doors of the tunnel were not so adjusted as to prevent the flames and smoke from entering the mine. The mine operators shed no tears for the sacrifice of these twenty-two miners who were smothered to death, but when some unknown assassin pulled the trigger and ended the life of one man, Arthur L. Collins, a mighty wail went up and the finger of suspicion was pointed at the Western Federation of Miners.

It is only but a few days ago when fifteen men were hurled into eternity at the Independence mine, in the Cripple Creek district, through defective machinery and an incompetent engineer who was imported by the Mine Owners' Association as a strike breaker, and in whose ignorant keeping, for mercenary reasons, was placed the lives of all the men in the mine. . . .

The people of this nation for a century and a quarter have celebrated the anniversary of that great epoch in American history, and dedicated with

---

2. **from a foreign source:** a reference to non-American, often British, ownership of many Western mining operations.

parade and speech the memorable 4th day of July in commemoration of the notes of liberty that rang from the old casting suspended in the tower of Faneuil Hall, signalizing the birth of a Republic whose people had groaned beneath the yoke of king rule. Each succeeding year the people have gathered in city, town, and hamlet and boasted of the justice and freedom contained in the Declaration of Independence. The eloquent tongue and the poetic pen have paid tributes to our liberty and made us feel that here in this land where Columbus planted the Cross—the emblem of Christianity—men were kings and women were queens, armored and shielded with a panoply of sovereignty that proclaimed defiance to every species of despotism. . . .

Upon the industrial battlefield for a quarter of a century in this nation has been heard the dying wails and groans of labor's victim. The pistol of the hired corporate murderer and the rifle of the uniformed soldier have poured their missiles of death into the ranks of labor, and moneyed nobility has applauded with cheers the wanton slaughter. The soil of every State of our Union has been wet with the blood of labor's martyrs to appease the thirst of soulless greed. The commandment "Thou shalt not kill" has found no place in the lexicon of commercial avarice. The "government of the people, by the people, and for the people" has become the government of trusts and corporations, and citizenship without property has no protection under the constitution of State or nation. . . .

A civilization that demands the implements of war to protect it is doomed, and the great mass whom plutocracy has destined to bear the brunt of conflict will not be carried off its feet by a patriotism that establishes commercial supremacy at the expense of human life. That nation is only strong whose yeomanry bask in the sunlight of a liberty that is free from the noxious effluvia of an atmosphere that breeds in the human heart the germs of murder. Wrong was never righted by the bullet or the sword. The savage and the barbarian who use the club and spear have as high a conception of justice as so-called civilized society that slakes its thirst in blood through the polished steel of Gatling gun and cannon.

Wrong maintained and perpetuated by all the modern machinery of war may have a temporary triumph, and right may be put in prison, but the spirit of justice that will be as eternal as humanity itself shall repeat its demands until the thundering voice of the mighty millions shall shake the pillars of a system that has molded and invented the machines of blood and carnage. The poverty of the world born in greed shall weld together the links of a chain that shall circle the globe, and the plebeian disinherited mass shall come together in a fraternity whose brotherhood will sweep from the face of our planet the last vestige of that tinseled pageantry that marked the era of war.

Western Federation of Miners
Charles Moyer, President
Wm. D. Haywood, Secretary-Treasurer

28. A MUCKRAKER CHARTS A MIDDLE COURSE

Ray Stannard Baker was one of the best known of the "muckrakers" (a term supposedly coined by President Theodore Roosevelt), the investigative journalists of their day. Through their essays and stories in popular national magazines and in novels, the muckrakers went after big-business interests. Sometimes they attacked corporations for unfair or noncompetitive business practices; sometimes they tried to expose dangerous working conditions. At the height of their influence, in the early decades of the twentieth century, the muckrakers exercised a great deal of political influence. This article for a popular national magazine takes a middle-of-the-road approach to events in the western mining regions by using Colorado as a case study. Baker points out that the strife between workers, management, and the vigilante Citizen's Alliance had been exacerbated by violent lawlessness on all sides. What prescriptions does Baker offer for solving industrial unrest? How does he establish a neutral position as someone able to make an objective assessment of affairs in the mining camps? Does it work?

Ray Stannard Baker
"The Reign of Lawlessness: Anarchy and Despotism in Colorado"
1904[1]

During much of the past year, and continuing until the present moment, certain parts of the state of Colorado have been governed by military law. Governor Peabody, a banker himself, closely identified with the conservative business interests of the state, and therefore unlikely to make exaggerated statements, has proclaimed the existence of a condition of "insurrection and rebellion."

And martial law has been neither gentle nor forbearing; when accused of violating the Constitution, Judge Advocate McClelland remarked:

"To hell with the Constitution; we are not following the Constitution."

Colonel Verdeckberg, commanding officer in the Cripple Creek district, declared:

"We are under orders only from God and Governor Peabody."

But, if military rule has been despotic, many citizens have been lawless, and civil government ineffective. The miners' union has broken the law, there have been dynamiting and assassination; the corporations have broken the law, there have been bribery and corruption; the citizens' organizations, representing in some degree the great third party—the public—have broken the law; even the Legislature itself, wherein the law is made, has been lawless. We have

---

1. *McClure's Magazine* 23 (May 1904): 43–47.

to-day, indeed, in certain parts of Colorado, a breakdown of democracy and, through anarchy, a reversion to military despotism.

What are the causes of these appalling conditions?

Insurrection and Rebellion Proclaimed

Martial law was declared in the Cripple Creek district on December 4th, and a month later in Telluride. The Cripple Creek proclamation was read in the city of Victor by a cavalry major guarded by fifty troopers, the citizens of the town gathered about, silent. After proclaiming that a condition of anarchy there existed, that civil government had become abortive, that life was in peril, and property unsafe, the Governor pronounced judgment upon this common-wealth:

> Now, therefore, I, James H. Peabody, Governor of the State of Colorado, by virtue of the authority in me vested, do hereby proclaim and declare the said County of Teller, in the State of Colorado, to be in a state of insurrection and rebellion.

Rebellion, then, must be stamped out! The silent citizens return to their homes. The Major, well backed by his troopers, seizes for military headquarters a building owned by a private citizen. He marches to the seat of government and informs the mayor and the chief of police that unless they obey military orders he, the Major, will seize the City Hall. He visits the office of the Victor *Record* and establishes a military censorship. The editor is forbidden to print an editorial concerning these military doings, and the next morning, or maybe the morning after, the paper appears with a black-bordered column, significantly blank, as it happens in Russia.

Having violated the rights of private property, overturned the people's government, suppressed free speech and a free press, the Major left armed men to patrol the city streets, and clattered away up the hill with his troop.

But the Proclamation of the Fourth of December was only the formal dramatic declaration on the part of the Governor of a condition long existent. For some two months prior to this time the military forces had been practically in control. And it had not been pleasant—martial rule. Soldiers are not that way.

Character of Cripple Creek Miners

Cripple Creek and Victor are American towns. Most of the citizens are miners, long resident in Colorado. They have played no unimportant part in making this district, among the tops of the Rocky Mountains, the greatest gold producing camp in the world. In 1902 they dug $25,000,000 from the hills. This is their home; they have here bought land and built houses; have here raised their children. . . .

Arrests without Warrants

Well, some of these men were arrested by the military forces, arrested without warrants and without charges, locked up in an unsavory place called the Bull-Pen,[2] and kept incommunicado, often for weeks. Just at this place I am not discussing the reasons for these arrests, nor asserting that the men were not guilty; the point is: every right of the individual citizen was here trodden upon and disregarded.

Friends of the men arrested had immediate recourse to the civil courts. They began habeas corpus proceedings before District Judge Seeds, of Cripple Creek.

As every one knows, the writ of habeas corpus is one of the most precious rights of the Anglo-Saxon, called by Blackstone the "second Magna Charta." It has for its object the protection of the precious personal liberty of the free citizen—it provides that he shall not be held a prisoner without due process of law. Judge Seeds ordered that the Bull-Pen prisoners be brought into court, that an orderly inquiry might be made as to whether any innocent man was deprived of his liberty. General Chase and General Bell, then in command, obeyed the writ in their own significant way. They surrounded the court house with armed men; they planted sharpshooters on the roofs of the buildings roundabout; they set a Gatling gun in the street outside, and then they marched into court with an overawing force of troopers which they planted squarely in front of the judge's bench. When the judge approached his own court he was halted with a bayonet brought to his breast, and kept waiting the pleasure of an officer from Denver! After the bailiff rapped for order, Eugene Engley, former attorney-general of the state of Colorado, one of the attorneys for the prisoners, declaring that no real justice could be administered in a court intimidated by armed men, left the room. "The constitutional guarantee that courts shall be open and free has been invaded and overthrown," he said. But the judge finally decided that the prisoners, whatever their offense, must not be deprived of their liberty without charges, and ordered that they be surrendered to the civil court.

Writ of Habeas Corpus Suspended

The generals deliberately violated the court order, and marched the prisoners back to the Bull-Pen, with the sharpshooters and the Gatling gun. They were subsequently released by special order of the Governor, but others were arrested repeatedly and held for considerable periods. And finally the Governor himself took the gravest step which any executive officer in this country can take, a step forbidden, except under the most stringent safeguards, by the constitution of practically every state in the Union, including that of

---

2. **Bull-Pen:** stockade or jail patrolled by military authorities.

Colorado—suspended the writ of habeas corpus in the case of one Victor Poole, keeping him locked up without due process of law, for weeks.

Censorship of the Press

Nor was this all. I have already spoken of the censorship of the Victor *Record*. Some weeks before this occurred, a company of cavalry, under the command of General Chase himself, appeared one night after eleven o'clock, surrounded the *Record* office, arrested the entire force, and marched them off to the Bull-Pen, without warrant and without charges, although it was understood that Mr. Kyner, the editor, had criticized the methods of the soldiery. Here they were kept without proper food for twenty-four hours. It so happened that the plucky wife of one of the linotype operators, herself an operator, Mrs. Emma F. Langdon, hurried to the office after the force was arrested, and she and the office boy and the business manager, aroused from his bed, barricaded the doors, refused to admit a military guard which demanded entrance, and at three o'clock in the morning got out the paper. At the head of the first page there was this line: "Somewhat Disfigured, but Still in the Ring."

And in the gray of the next morning she stuffed her sleeves with damp copies of the paper, and climbed the hill to the Bull-Pen, there to be halted by the guard and not allowed to see the editor and his force, among whom was her own husband.

Small boys, and even women, one the wife of a merchant, were actually arrested for speaking disparagingly of the soldiers and sent to the Bull-Pen. Private homes, the castles of the citizens, were entered and searched without warrant. A squad of soldiers visited the home of Sherman Parker in the night, while Parker himself was away, aroused his wife from bed, forced her, in her night-clothes, in the presence of these men, to hold the lamp while they searched the house—and found no arms.

In Cripple Creek, on December 28th, John M. Glover, former United States Congressman from Missouri, who stood upon his constitutional right to own and keep arms (with undue truculency, it may be, though this does not alter the facts of the case), was attacked in his law office by a squad of soldiers. He barricaded the door, and, when the troops attempted to force an entrance, he opened fire through the panels. The soldiers replied with a volley through the door and walls. Glover, shot through the arm, finally surrendered. His revolvers were seized and he himself detained a prisoner.

Doings not dissimilar to these also took place at Telluride. Citizens, some of whom owned property and had been long residents of the town, were arrested for vagrancy. Most of them were strikers; strikers by right, if they wished to strike, neither beggars nor vagrants, and having no specific charges of crime against them. Some of them were put to work like criminals in a chain gang on the streets. . . .

Democracy and Despotism

And, finally, as a result of all this long-continued brazen law-breaking, we see the privileges of free government taken from the people and placed in the hands of an outside despot who rules by powder and shot. In the long run, the law gets itself executed, inevitably, mercilessly; if not by the ordinary machinery of the civil officials, then by the extraordinary machinery of martial rule.

Getting down at last to fundamental principles, this is the condition in Colorado: the people have broken the law and they are being punished. Not part of the people, but every person in Colorado; not only he who bludgeoned or bribed, but he who, greedily, in the pursuit of his private business, has forgotten his civic duties, who has not, himself obedient to the law, *demanded* the election of men who will enforce the law, not union men, nor corporation men, but Americans.

There is no better evidence of the responsibility of every voter in Colorado than that every voter has suffered—if not directly in the strike, then in loss of business, in increased cost of coal and other commodities, in rising taxes. Colorado will long bend under the burden of paying for its troops, now for many months in the field, and for the endless lawsuits arising out of these disturbances. It is not cheap—lawlessness.

Perhaps just this appalling punishment was necessary to shake the people of Colorado—and of the country—from their indolent indifference. The white-hot anger of the people of Colorado, though it may be directed at the wrong thing—at the union, at the citizens' alliance, at the trust, when it should be directed at lawlessness—is a sign of hope: through the passion of this anger changes may be wrought.

29. PROTESTING CONDITIONS IN COLORADO

Mary Harris Jones, known throughout the nation as Mother Jones, was for decades an active and provocative friend of the industrial laborer. At the time she wrote this letter from southern Colorado, where she had been jailed by military authorities, Mother Jones was probably in her late seventies (or perhaps as old as she claims to be in the letter). Regardless of her age, she was without doubt an important American labor leader; her activities on behalf of miners, from West Virginia to the Rocky Mountains, earned her the enmity of mine owners as well as police and the military. Here she casts herself as a victim of the heavy-handed power of men like John D. Rockefeller. How does Mother Jones link events of the period to a greater struggle? What claims does she make about the legitimacy of the miners' actions in Colorado?

Mother Jones
"To My Friends and the Public Generally"
1914[1]

Walsenburg, Colo.
Military Bastile
March 31, 1914.

To My Friends and the Public Generally:

I am being held a prisoner incommunicado in a damp, underground cell, in the basement of a military bullpen at Walsenburg, Colorado. Have been here since 5:30 a.m. of the 23rd of March, when I was taken from the train by armed soldiers as I was passing through Walsenburg. I have discovered what appears to be an opportunity to smuggle a letter out of prison, and shall attempt to get this communication by the armed guards which day and night surround me (me, a white-haired old woman eighty-two years of age).

I want to say to the public that I am an American citizen. I have never broken a law in my life, and I claim the right of an American citizen to go where I please so long as I do not violate the law. The courts of Las Animas and Huerfano are open and unobstructed in the transaction of business, yet Governor Ammons and his Peabody appointee, General Chase, refuse to carry me before any court, and refuse to make any charge against me. I ask the press to let the nation know of my treatment, and to say to my friends, whom, thank God, I number by the thousands, throughout the United States and Mexico, that not even my incarceration in a damp, underground dungeon will make me give up the fight in which I am engaged for liberty and for the rights of the working people. Of course, I long to be out of prison. To be shut from the sunlight is not pleasant, but John Bunyan, John Brown and others were kept in jail quite a while, and I shall stand firm. To be in prison is no disgrace. In all my strike experiences I have seen no horrors equal to those perpetrated by General Chase and his corps of Baldwin-Feltz detectives that are now enlisted in the militia. My God—when is it to stop? I have only to close my eyes to see the hot tears of the orphans and widows of working men, and hear the mourning of the broken hearts and the wailing of the funeral dirge, while the cringing politicians whose sworn duty it is to protect the lives and liberty of the people crawl subserviently before the national burglars of Wall Street who are today plundering and devastating the State of Colorado economically, financially, politically and morally.

Let the nation know, and especially let my friend General Francisco Villa[2] know, that the great United States of America, which is demanding of him that

---

1. Edward M. Steel, ed., *The Correspondence of Mother Jones* (Pittsburgh: University of Pittsburgh Press, 1985), 125–26.
2. **General Francisco Villa:** Francisco "Pancho" Villa, Mexican revolutionary.

he release the traitors he has placed under arrest, is now holding Mother Jones incommunicado in an underground cell surrounded with sewer rats, tinhorn soldiers and other vermin.

Mother Jones

30. SUPPORT FOR THE MINE OWNERS

No single family symbolized mine ownership in the American West more than the Rockefellers. At the turn of the century, the Anaconda Mine in Montana, controlled by the Rockefellers' Standard Oil Company, employed an astonishing 75 percent of the wage earners in the whole state. This made Montana, for all intents and purposes, a "company state." The Rockefellers' Colorado Fuel and Iron (CF&I) was no small operation, either; the largest industrial enterprise in Colorado, it employed more than ten thousand workers to pump out Rocky Mountain coal and steel. The following address to company officials and worker representatives highlights a perspective common to mine owners like Rockefeller: if everyone just understood his place at the "table" of labor relations, all would be fine. In the spring of 1914, CF&I's coal fields became the site of a disastrous encounter between national guardsmen and striking members of the United Mine Workers of America. The guardsmen and strikebreakers set fires that ignited the tents where people had sought protection from gunfire. The resulting conflagration—the "Ludlow Massacre"—killed dozens of strikers and many women and children. The shadow of this event hovers over Rockefeller's October 2, 1915, address. How would you characterize Rockefeller's position toward industrial labor? What major points does he make before the group? How would Jack London (see Document 26 on p. 93) have responded to Rockefeller's assumptions?

John D. Rockefeller Jr.

Address to Colorado Fuel and Iron Officials and
Employee Representatives
1915[1]

Mr. President, and Fellow Members of The Colorado Fuel & Iron Company:

This is a red-letter day in my life. It is the first time I have ever had the good fortune to meet the representatives of the employees of this great company, its officers and mine superintendents, together, and I can assure you that I am proud to be here, and that I shall remember this gathering as long as I live. Had this meeting been held two weeks ago, I should have stood here as a stranger to

---

1. *Address by John D. Rockefeller Jr. Delivered at Pueblo Colorado* (Denver: W. H. Kistler Stationery Co., 1915), 3–6, 9–11.

many of you, recognizing few faces. Having had the opportunity last week of visiting all of the camps in the southern coal fields and of talking individually with practically all of the representatives, except those who were away; having visited in your homes, met many of your wives and children, we meet here not as strangers but as friends, and it is in that spirit of mutual friendship that I am glad to have this opportunity to discuss with you men our common interests. Since this is a meeting of the officers of the Company and the representatives of the employees, it is only by your courtesy that I am here, for I am not so fortunate as to be either one or the other; and yet I feel that I am intimately associated with you men, for in a sense I represent both the stockholders and the directors. Before speaking of the plan of industrial cooperation to which our President has referred, I want to say just a few words outlining my view as to what different interests constitute a company or corporation.

Every corporation is composed of four parties. First, there are the stockholders; they put up the money which pays the wages, builds the plants, operates the business, and they appoint the directors to represent their interests in the corporation. We have, secondly, the directors, whose business it is to see that the chief executive officers of the Company are carefully and wisely selected, to plan out its larger and more important policies, particularly its financial policies, and generally to see to it that the company is wisely administered. And, thirdly, we have the officers of the company, whose duty it is to conduct the current operation of the business. While last, but by no means least—for I might just as well have started at the other end—we come to the employees, who contribute their skill and their work.

Now the interest of these four parties is a common one. An effort to advance one interest at the expense of any other, means loss to all, and when any one of the four parties in this corporation selfishly considers his own interest alone, and is disregardful of the interests of the other three parties, sooner or later disaster must follow. This little table [*exhibiting a square table with four legs*] illustrates my conception of a corporation; and there are several points in regard to the table to which I want to call your attention. First, you see that it would not be complete unless it had all four sides. Each side is necessary; each side has its own part to play. Now, if you imagine this table cut into quarters, and each quarter separated from the others, what would happen? All of them would fall down, for no one could stand alone, and you would have no table. But when you put the four sides together, you have a useful piece of furniture; you have a table.

Then, secondly, I call your attention to the fact that these four sides are all perfectly joined together; that is why we have a perfect table. Likewise, if the parties interested in a corporation are not perfectly joined together, harmoniously working together, you have a discordant and unsuccessful corporation. . . .

When you have a level table, or a corporation that is on the level, you can pile up earnings on it [*piling coins on the table*]. Now, who gets the first crack at the earnings? You know that we in New York don't. Here come along the employees, and first of all they get their wages [*removing some of the coins*], every two weeks like clock-work, just what has been agreed on; they get the first chance at the pile. You men come ahead of the President, the officers, the stockholders and directors. You are the first to put a hand into the pile and take out what is agreed shall belong to you. You don't have to wait for your share; you don't have to take any chances about getting it. You know that there has never been a two-weeks period that you have worked when you have not been able to get your pay from this company; whatever happens, so long as the company is running, you get your pay.

And then the officers and superintendents come along, and they get theirs, they don't get it until after you have gotten yours [*removing more coins*].

Then come the directors, and they get their directors' fees [*removing the balance of the coins*] for doing their work in the company.

And, Hello! There is nothing left! This must be the Colorado Fuel & Iron Company. For never, men, since my father and I became interested in this company as stockholders, some twelve or fourteen years ago—never has there been one cent for the common stock. For fourteen years the common stockholder has seen your wages paid to you workers; has seen your salaries paid to you officers; has seen the directors draw their fees, and has not had one cent of return for the money that he has put into this company in order that you men might work and get your wages and salaries. How many men in this room ever heard that fact stated before? Is there a man among you? Well, there are mighty few among the workers who have heard it. What you have been told, what has been heralded from the Atlantic to the Pacific, is that those Rockefeller men in New York, the biggest scoundrels that ever lived, have taken millions of dollars out of this company on account of their stock ownership, have oppressed you men, have cheated you out of your wages, and "done" you in every way they could. That is the kind of "dope" you have been getting, and that is what has been spread all over this country. And when that kind of talk was going on, and there were disturbances in this part of the country because the four sides of this table were not square and the table was not level, there were those who in the streets of New York and in public gatherings, were inciting the crowd to "shoot John D. Rockefeller, Jr., down like a dog." That is the way they talked. . . .

This meeting has been called today for the purpose of seeing whether we can work out and agree upon, among ourselves here, some plan which will accomplish what I feel sure we all want to accomplish. I have been asked to explain the plan which is up for our consideration. I may say, men, that for years this great problem of labor and capital and of corporate relationships has engaged my earnest attention and study, while for the last eighteen months I have spent more of my time on the particular problems which confront this company than I have put on any other one interest with which I am related. I have talked with all of the men whom I could get in touch with who have had experience with or have studied these vital questions. I have conferred with experts, and I have tried in every way to get the best information I could looking toward the working out of some plan which would accomplish the result we are all striving to attain. Nearly a year ago the officers of the company, after having studied this question with us in New York, introduced, as you know, the beginning of such a plan, namely, the selection by the men at each camp of duly chosen representatives, to confer with the officers of the company in regard to matters of common interest. . . . I have visited every camp, with the exception of those on the western slope, and lack of time alone has prevented my getting over there to see you men. I have gone, as you know, to every camp in the southern fields, have talked privately with every superintendent, except one who was away, and with all of the representatives at each camp with the exception of some two or three who were not available at the time; I have gone into scores of your homes and met your wives and children, and have seen how you live; I have looked at your gardens, and in camps where fences were only recently built have seen how eagerly you have planted gardens the moment opportunity was afforded, and how quickly you have gotten the grass to grow, also flowers and vegetables, and how the interest in your homes has thereby been increased. I inquired specifically about the water supply at each camp; I went down into several of the mines and talked with hundreds of the miners; I looked into the schools, talked with the teachers, inquired what educational advantages your children were getting. I asked what opportunities you men, my partners, had for getting together socially, and I visited some of your club-houses and saw plans for others. I went into your wash-houses and talked with the men before and after bathing. As you know, we have pretty nearly slept together—it has been reported that I slept in one of your nightshirts—I would have been proud had the report been true. If any man could have gone more carefully, more thoroughly, into the working and living conditions that affect you, my partners, I should be glad to have had him make me suggestions as to what further I might have done. . . .

I want to stay in Colorado until we have worked out some plan that we all agree is the best thing for us all, because there is just one thing that no man in this company can ever afford to have happen again, be he stockholder, officer, or employee, or whatever his position, and that is, another strike. I know we are all agreed about that, every last man of us, and I propose to stay here if it takes a year, until we have worked out among ourselves, right in our own family, some plan that we all believe is going to prevent any more disturbances, any more interruption of the successful operation of this great company in which we are all interested. . . .

FURTHER READING

Andrews, Thomas G. *Killing for Coal: America's Deadliest Labor War*. Cambridge, MA: Harvard University Press, 2008.
Berman, David R. *Radicalism in the Mountain West, 1890–1920: Socialists, Populists, Miners, and Wobblies*. Boulder: University Press of Colorado, 2007.

Byrkit, James. *Forging the Copper Collar: Arizona's Labor-Management War of 1901–1921*. Tucson: University of Arizona Press, 1982.

Clements, Eric L. *After the Boom in Tombstone and Jerome, Arizona: Decline in Western Resource Towns*. Reno: University of Nevada Press, 2003.

Dubofsky, Melvyn. *We Shall Be All: A History of the Industrial Workers of the World*. Chicago: Quadrangle Books, 1969.

Igler, David. *Industrial Cowboys: Miller and Lux and the Transformation of the Far West, 1850–1920*. Berkeley: University of California Press, 2001.

Isenberg, Andrew. *Mining California: An Ecological History*. New York: Hill and Wang, 2005.

Katherine, Benton-Cohen. *Borderline Americans: Racial Division and Labor War in the Arizona Borderlands*. Cambridge, MA: Harvard University Press, 2009.

Lingenfelter, Richard E. *The Hardrock Miners: A History of the Mining Labor Movement in the American West, 1863–1893*. Berkeley: University of California Press, 1974.

Lukas, J. Anthony. *Big Trouble: A Murder in a Small Western Town Sets Off a Struggle for the Soul of America*. New York: Simon and Schuster, 1997.

Montgomery, David. *The Fall of the House of Labor: The Workplace, the State, and American Labor Activism, 1865–1925*. Cambridge, England: Cambridge University Press, 1987.

Perales, Monica. *Smeltertown: Making and Remembering a Southwest Border Community*. Chapel Hill: University of North Carolina Press, 2010.

Peterson, Richard. *The Bonanza Kings: The Social Origins and Business Behavior of Western Mining Entrepreneurs, 1870–1900*. Lincoln: University of Nebraska Press, 1977.

Schwantes, Carlos. *Radical Heritage: Labor, Socialism, and Reform in Washington and British Columbia, 1885–1917*. Seattle: University of Washington Press, 1979.

Sullivan, Marianne. *Tainted Earth: Smelters, Public Health, and the Environment*. New Brunswick, NJ: Rutgers University Press, 2014.

Wolff, David A. *Industrializing the Rockies: Growth, Competition, and Turmoil in the Coalfields of Colorado and Wyoming, 1868–1914*. Boulder: University Press of Colorado, 2003.

Wyman, Mark. *Hard Rock Epic: Western Miners and the Industrial Revolution, 1860–1910*. Berkeley: University of California Press, 1979.

Los Angeles River and Lincoln Heights from Elysian Park, 1909. This amazing photograph was taken from a balloon or some other conveyance. Convinced that the new century would bring great prosperity and population growth to the would-be metropolis in Southern California, residents and newcomers alike championed Los Angeles as an exceptional city—a place of unrivaled natural promise, beauty, and potential. At work within all that exuberant praise, though, were strident contradictions and challenges. Was it a place for everyone? Was it indeed a place of natural harmony, as so often claimed, or did the upstart city depend on dangerous processes of pushing nature around to suit the present's vision of the future?

Los Angeles Comes of Age

From its origins as a tiny pueblo nestled against the little Los Angeles River, late nineteenth-century Los Angeles grew at a pace and with an exuberance that startled even its residents. By the end of the century, a growth machine driven by frenzied boosterism, rising worldwide awareness of the region's salubrious Mediterranean climate, and opportunities in everything from agriculture to oil, industry to real estate, had proven that Los Angeles was on the rise. Before long it would become the West's most important city and the capital of a far-flung region that stretched south into Mexico, north toward San Francisco, and farther west to the shores of Asia and the Pacific Rim.

By the first few decades of the twentieth century, further energized by the infant motion picture industry's claim on Southern California as the center of American moviemaking, Los Angeles became an example of metropolitan growth the likes of which had never happened in the history of the nation. The city was championed as a place of harmonious urban interactions with beneficent nature, even as engineers and political leaders proved all too willing to attempt dominance over that supposedly "friendly" nature (such hubris often eventually brought dire and unintended consequences). Seen as the playground of American youth—many drawn as moths to the flame of motion picture fame—Los Angeles also drew the elderly, the weary, and the sick. These people figured at least they would be warm in the sunshine of Southern California, if not happy, if not cared for, if not renewed, if not healed.

One thing was for sure: expanding Los Angeles needed water and lots of it. The Los Angeles River—temperamental, as prone to wintertime floods as to summertime disappearance—adequately provided for the modest water needs of Los Angeles up until about 1900. With the new century, and Los Angeles booster aims to eclipse San Francisco and even Chicago in size and influence, it became abundantly clear that the place would need to find new sources to quench its thirst.

The grasping city, and gargantuan Los Angeles County surrounding it, simply added water acquisition to the checklist that launched the juggernaut of growth. Before long, it had grabbed a big Sierra Nevada river made of snow and snowmelt in the form of the Los Angeles Aqueduct (1913), which moved the Owens River a couple of hundred miles all the way to Los Angeles. And when even that audacious project proved (quickly) not bold enough, not watery enough, Southern California, with Los Angeles playing a leading role, reached its grasp and its aqueducts to the biggest watershed of the entire western slope of the Rockies: the mighty Colorado River.

Los Angeles was both very much like other western cities of the era, and nothing like them. Like its peers and competitors, it was an ambitious place: gobbling up terrain, muscling nature around as it could and would (if temporarily), and selling itself to the world for jobs, health, new beginnings, renewal in the West, fame, wealth, and everything else that could be made into a slogan or a poster or a come-on. But Los Angeles stood out, too: bolder, bigger, riding a bucking bronco of growth, all the while boisterously claiming to grab the brass ring of the future.

AS YOU READ: Think of the ingredients of western urban growth as exemplified by the case of Los Angeles. What had to be in place? What challenges to growth did geography or other factors pose? How does the case of Los Angeles look and feel different than that of other western cities, some of which we have already visited in earlier chapters and documents?

31. THE (PRESUMED) CONTROL OF NATURE: LOS ANGELES PLANS TO CONCRETIZE ITS RIVER

The Los Angeles River simply refused to behave. In the wintertime, flooding every decade or so destroyed valuable cropland and infrastructure. Aridity made the river go away in the summertime. By the early twentieth century, emboldened by runaway metropolitan growth (and the taxes that arrived on top of it), Los

Angeles decided that it had had enough. A river running through the very heart of Southern California's population centers had to stay put, had to flow where the city dictated that it must flow; no more flooding. And thus, beginning with plans laid out here, Southern California embarked on a near century-long project to wrap its river in nearly fifty miles of concrete straitjacket, holding it in place and rushing its water, when it had water, out to sea. It took an astonishing amount of money, labor, and expertise to do it, but in a sense it worked. Only in recent years have different ideas surfaced—ideas that, with energy, attention, and money, promise to reenvision the river and its place in the imagined and real Southern California landscape.

Los Angeles Times

"First Long Step Made toward Flood Control"

1915[1]

"The First Long Step Made toward Flood Control: County Board of Engineers Submits Exhaustive Plans Calling for Five Years' Work at Cost of Sixteen and a Half Millions—Next Move Is to Form District, Vote Bonds, Hire a Boss and Start"

Estimating the cost of adequate flood control for Los Angeles County at $16,508,900, the Board of Engineers, Flood Control, submitted collective and individual reports to the Board of Supervisors yesterday, and the body was dissolved, after spending $100,000 in investigations and drafting plans.

The estimate includes an item of $1,827,000 for work in connection with the harbor. This expenditure will probably be borne by the government, thus reducing the county's estimated outlay to $14,681,900, or $5,000,000 in excess of the preliminary estimate, made shortly after the board was organized.

Further reductions in the county's outlay through State aid is expected. In this connection it is recommended that steps be immediately taken looking towards co-operation by the State and Federal governments in the work, which it is estimated will take about five years to complete. . . .

. . . All five of the engineers agree that the diversion of flood waters from the harbor is the major desideratum of the whole plan, it being set forth in axiomlike form in the main report that the harbor is the county's greatest asset. In this connection the proposed visits [in] the coming month of both the Rivers and Harbors Committee of the United States House of Representatives and the Board of Engineers for Rivers and Harbors, War Department, is considered as recognition that the harbor is a government asset to be safeguarded.

---

1. *Los Angeles Times*, July 28, 1915.

The Next Step

Dissolution of the Board of Engineers, Flood Control, means simply that one unit of the great work of "removing the risk" from 215,300 acres of land, valued conservatively at more than $50,000,000, has been completed. The second step, under the terms of a bill passed by the last Legislature, at the solicitation of the Los Angeles County Flood Control Association, is to create a flood control district, issue bonds and appoint an engineer to supervise the work. To give the electorate an opportunity to study the subject, before initiatory steps are taken, the Board of Supervisors authorized the printing of the full text of the engineers' report in the following words: "At a meeting looking to relief from flood damage recently held in Topeka, Kan., it was estimated that flood damage in the State of Kansas during the present year, 1913, amounted to $15,000,000. The State of Kansas has an area of 82,158 square miles. Los Angeles County has 4067 square miles. If the relative economic interests are directly proportional to the amount of damage and inversely as to the area, then Los Angeles has an incentive about twenty times as great as that of Kansas to accomplish flood control."

In general, the plan of both the majority and minority of the Board of Engineers for adequate flood control contemplates . . . "conservation, retardation, reforestation, spreading of the waters of some streams, diversion of those of others, and channel rectification and improvements." . . .

. . . Hundreds of other recommendations are made, affecting all parts of the county, and calculated to make all land area from the mountains to the sea immune from flood.

32. THE SOCIALIST PARTY IN LOS ANGELES SUPPORTS THE L.A. AQUEDUCT

At virtually the same time as it sought to tame the Los Angeles River, Los Angeles embarked on a bold plan to seize the Owens River, some 250 miles away, and bring it by gravity and an aqueduct system to the city. Controversial even at the time, although supported by enthusiastic Angelenos who paid for it with bonds and taxes, the Owens River Aqueduct project became a political hot potato in the 1911 municipal elections. Socialist Party candidates— the party was a powerful political player at the time—pledged to complete the project, while condemning those who would seek to profit by way of land speculation (buying up cheap, dry land on the almost certain faith that it would rise in value once watered by the new aqueduct). In that year's mayoral primary, attorney Job Harriman, a Socialist Party stalwart, came very close to winning, an outcome that probably would have changed the course of modern Los Angeles.

"Municipal Platform: Socialist Party of Los Angeles"
August 6, 1911[1]

Our Water Supply

We favor hastening the work of completing the Owens River Aqueduct, for which the people of Los Angeles have devoted $23,000,000 under the belief that the water and the electric energy to be derived therefrom was to be delivered to the people, and used for their benefit.

We demand that this electric power be held by the people to their use and not delivered now or at any time in the future to any corporation of avaricious and exploiting capitalists.

We pledge ourselves to take immediate steps towards bringing the Owens River water to Los Angeles. We view with utmost abhorrence plans which have been secretly carried out for years and which, if allowed to be consummated, would result in flowing the waters of the aqueduct upon lands held by some of the most infamous exploiters of land and labor in America.

We condemn the present city administration for permitting and causing the workers on the aqueduct to be fed upon and forced to eat a short allowance of spoiled and unhealthful food in order to increase the profit of private contractors, and we pledge ourselves to remedy this evil if placed in power.

---

1. John R. Haynes Papers, Department of Special Collections, UCLA.

33. WATER FOR THE THIRSTY METROPOLIS *(SEE P. 118)*

When it opened in 1913, only five years after construction began, the Los Angeles Aqueduct, also known as the Owens River Aqueduct, seemed as if it would solve the city's water shortage problems for decades, if not longer. At the opening ceremony to cheer the coming of the water from 250 miles to the northeast, the project's chief engineer, the famed William Mulholland, gestured to the aqueduct he built and said, famously, "There it is. Take it."

34. THE OCEAN BECKONS *(SEE P. 118)*

At almost the same time that Los Angeles leaders, engineers, and even everyday residents and visitors were thinking more about fresh water and how to get more of it, they felt increasingly pulled to the salt water of the Pacific Ocean at the western edge of Southern California. Migration to the ocean—to see it, to play in it, to try to live alongside it—was a process. Earlier generations had seen the ocean as more a threat than an attraction (remember that most people in the

The Los Angeles Aqueduct, ca. 1919
Courtesy the Huntington Library, San Marino, California.

Bathers on the beach, Southern California, ca. 1915
Courtesy the Huntington Library, San Marino, California.

nineteenth century did not swim), and cultural proscriptions meant that "sun-bathing" looked and felt a lot different. But as the twentieth century arrived, the beach became inviting to wider cross sections of the population. People ventured westward to the ocean, and began to spend more time in it. As they did, they—even more gradually—allowed their bodies to be more uncovered. And as all that began to happen, the beach and beachfront living rose up the ladders of class: in less than a century, the Southern California beach would become both a place for the masses to recreate and a restricted residential enclave of the very wealthy whose mansions rose as sentinels looking west toward the vast sea.

Here, in this early twentieth-century photograph, all that is still far in the future. Because we know more about what happened as the century deepened, we might be tempted to see this picture as an especially nostalgic, even romantic, glow about an earlier time in the coastal history of Southern California. While that might be at least somewhat reasonable or understandable, we have to remember as well that beaches in this era—like virtually every other public and certainly most private places and spaces, in L.A. and across the nation—were strictly segregated. The image looks less quaint when we register its unanimous whiteness.

FURTHER READING

Beauchamp, Cari. *Without Lying Down: Frances Marion and the Powerful Women of Early Hollywood.* Berkeley: University of California Press, 1998.

Davis, Clark. *Company Men: White-Collar Life and Corporate Cultures in Los Angeles, 1892–1941.* Baltimore: Johns Hopkins University Press, 2000.

Davis, Mike. *City of Quartz.* London: Verso, 1990.

Deverell, William. *Whitewashed Adobe: The Rise of Los Angeles and the Remaking of Its Mexican Past.* Berkeley: University of California Press, 2005.

Deverell, William, and Greg Hise, eds. *Companion to Los Angeles.* Malden, MA: Wiley-Blackwell, 2010.

———. *Land of Sunshine: An Environmental History of Los Angeles.* Pittsburgh: University of Pittsburgh Press, 2005.

Flamming, Douglas. *Bound for Freedom: Black Los Angeles in Jim Crow America.* Berkeley: University of California Press, 2005.

Fulton, William. *Reluctant Metropolis: The Politics of Urban Growth in Los Angeles.* Baltimore: Johns Hopkins University Press, 1997.

de Graaf, Lawrence B., Kevin Mulroy, and Quintard Taylor. *Seeking El Dorado: African Americans in California.* Los Angeles: Autry Museum of Western Heritage, 2001.

Hise, Greg, and William Deverell. *Eden by Design: The 1930 Olmsted-Bartholomew Plan for the Los Angeles Region.* Berkeley: University of California Press, 2000.

Hundley, Norris, and Donald C. Jackson. *Heavy Ground: William Mulholland and the St. Francis Dam Disaster.* Berkeley: University of California Press, 2016.

Jefferson, Alison Rose. "African American Leisure Space in Santa Monica: The Beach Sometimes Known as the 'Inkwell.'" *Southern California Quarterly* 91 (2009): 155–89.

Molina, Natalia. *Fit to Be Citizens? Public Health and Race in Los Angeles, 1879–1939.* Berkeley: University of California Press, 2006.

Mulholland, Catherine. *William Mulholland and the Rise of Los Angeles.* Berkeley: University of California Press, 2000.

Nicolaides, Becky. *My Blue Heaven: Life and Politics in the Working-Class Suburbs of Los Angeles, 1920–1965.* Chicago: University of Chicago Press, 2002.

Schrank Sarah. *Art and the City: Civic Imagination and Cultural Authority in Los Angeles.* Philadelphia: University of Pennsylvania Press, 2009.

Sitton Tom. *John Randolph Haynes, California Progressive.* Stanford, CA: Stanford University Press, 1992.

Sitton, Tom, and William Deverell. *Metropolis in the Making: Los Angeles in the 1920s.* Berkeley: University of California Press, 2001.

Soldiers boarding a train in Southern California, 1917. This image of World War I soldiers leaving for training camp is in many ways familiar: young American men have gone off to fight many times in the last eighty years. But World War I, the "Great War," was not one America entered willingly; on the contrary, the nation stayed out of the conflict until it was nearly over. Yet to say that the United States was not affected by it would be wrong. Even before the formal declaration of war against Germany and its allies in 1919, it touched the lives of Americans everywhere. After all, millions of Americans traced their roots to those very European nations caught up in the crisis. Wartime troop mobilization changed the lives of those who suddenly found themselves fighting in the trenches of Europe. Wartime fears and national prejudices erupted in towns large and small. How do you think the experiences of soldiers like these mirrored those of other soldiers in other wars? What might their thoughts be at this moment?

World War I and the West

World War I jolted America out of an optimism that, as Europe devolved into mass killing, very quickly began to look naive or worse. When hostilities broke out in 1914, Americans looked beyond them, claiming that European squabbles, even as they threatened to overwhelm entire cultures and countries, ought to be of little concern to the United States and its other-side-of-the-world isolation. President Woodrow Wilson, backed by a diverse coalition of pacifists, labor leaders, and political allies on the right and the left, urged American neutrality.

But this would prove a difficult, even impossible, stance to maintain. Despite geography, Americans maintained long and important ties to Europe. It was where many Americans traced their origins; people still had family members in every European region; and Americans watched the deepening war with rising concerns. Some who had Eastern European or German ancestry rallied in support of the Central Powers, finding allies among Irish Americans who harbored deep antipathies toward England. Other Americans who traced their roots to Britain, Russia, and France generally supported those nations. America might not go to the war, but the war—its passions, fears, and enmities—certainly came to America. It would be hard to stay neutral, hard to stay out of it.

But if the United States entered the war, which side would it choose? The answer was not so clear. Americans of all walks of life and all national origins had their opinions, and these often were at odds with one another. Of critical importance was the escalation of German submarine attacks on civilian and military vessels sailing the Atlantic. When a German U-boat (the name given German submarines) torpedoed and sank the luxury liner *Lusitania* in the spring of 1915, many Americans were convinced that the United States could no longer stay on the sidelines. President Wilson, for a time, withstood such pressures, and fragile neutrality was maintained.

It did not last. Germany stepped up submarine warfare against British and American ships. Then, in early 1917, Britain intercepted a coded telegram sent by German foreign secretary Arthur Zimmermann to the German ambassador in Mexico. In it, he urged Mexico to side with the Central Powers in the war; in exchange, Germany would help Mexico regain Texas, New Mexico, and Arizona, territory ceded to the United States in the aftermath of the Mexican War in 1848. Outraged by the "Zimmermann Telegram" and the continued sub attacks, President Wilson went before Congress in April 1917 to seek a formal declaration of war. He got it, and before long, American troops were drilling on hastily established bases across the country and heading out to the trenches of European battlefields.

The Zimmermann Telegram and US relations with Mexico played key roles in the decision to enter the war. This helped to focus a great deal of attention, and tension, upon the entirety of the American Southwest and the borderlands region with Mexico. The Zimmermann controversy was just one of several border provocations preceding the US declaration of war on Germany and its allies. In fact, parts of the American West were first to mobilize for war.

President Wilson harbored strong feelings about Mexico and its future. Beginning back in 1911, the year in which Mexican dictator Porfirio Díaz was overthrown, Mexico experienced a tumultuous cycle of political revolution. Wilson proved increasingly willing to involve the United States in Mexican political and economic affairs, believing that American democracy could be exported, even if by force, to other regions around the world. This perspective would also play a significant role in America's involvement in World War I, seeing as Wilson believed in a US obligation to make the world "safe for democracy."

In 1914, a year after Mexican leader Francisco Madero was assassinated, Wilson ordered US troops to occupy the Mexican port city of Veracruz. When the revolutionary Francisco "Pancho" Villa destroyed the little town of Columbus, Mexico, in 1916 (killing more than a dozen US civilians in the process), Wilson sent General John J. Pershing on a punitive expedition into Mexico to capture Villa. Mexican authorities angrily demanded that Pershing and his thousands of troops pull back to the US side of the border, which they did only after a fruitless chase that lasted many months. For a time, it looked as though the United States might go to war in and with Mexico, a possibility that at least briefly looked more likely than war in Europe. When the Zimmermann Telegram came to light, it only reignited tensions at the border that had not gone away. Eventually, General Pershing assumed command of the American Expeditionary Force to Europe in 1917.

Support for US involvement in Europe varied in the cities, towns, and countrysides of the West. Across the Great Plains, into the Rockies, and on to cities like San Francisco, groups of Irish and German Americans believed that the country should stay out of the war. Or, once the decision had been made, they believed that Wilson and Congress had picked the wrong side to support. Some of these people, especially the German Americans, were attacked as anti-American, and waves of anti-German thought and deed swept across the country. Labor organizations such as the Western Federation of Miners and the Industrial Workers of the World, which took a hard line against US foreign and economic policies, were hit with heavy-handed government reprisals. In the northern Rockies, Congresswoman Jeannette Rankin of Montana, the first woman in US history to be elected to Congress, voted against the declaration of war. Western Populist and former presidential candidate William Jennings Bryan of Nebraska resigned as Wilson's secretary of state because he disagreed so vehemently with the administration's policies.

Once the nation committed to the war, however, the West mobilized rapidly. The selections in this chapter illuminate the region's response to war, as well as the West's simultaneous contributions to the advancement of aviation (which would aid the war effort from the skies in Europe). From the firestorm over the Zimmermann Telegram to newspaper editorializing, from supposedly patriotic German-bashing speechmaking in Wyoming to a young soldier's reactions to training camp in Texas, these documents provide a glimpse of the impact of wartime preparations and wartime fever on everyday life.

AS YOU READ: Think about the ways in which the US preparation for war may have differed from region to region. How do you think people imagined the role of aviation in the coming war, or in life in general? What special circumstances existed in the West such that the *Los Angeles Times* could make the pronouncements it did in the excerpt printed below? Why did events in Mexico provoke particular responses in the West? How might things have worked out differently?

35. LOS ANGELES WELCOMES LIGHTER-THAN-AIR MACHINES

In 1910, Southern California hosted the world's second international air meet (the first had been in Paris the year before). Though these "lighter than air" machines may look impossibly fragile to our eyes, this image (which isn't real, but a collage) shows that the aviation revolution had arrived. Clear skies, brave and inventive pilots, investment capital, and lots of open space: Southern California proved an ideal and idyllic spot to push flying and technological innovations

Los Angeles hosts the world's second-ever international air meet, 1910. In 1910, Los Angeles hosted the world's second-ever (after Paris) international air meet for lighter-than-air flight. This event, which drew as many as one hundred thousand spectators, signaled Southern California's attraction to—some would say obsession with—aviation, aviators, and the ways in which the future of the ambitious metropolis was linked with machines that fly in the air.

Courtesy the Huntington Library, San Marino, California.

forward. All did not always work out well—the historical record is full of images of daring pilots standing next to their machines one moment and being pulled, injured or worse, from the wreckage of a crashed airplane the next. But the die had been cast; from this moment forward, the West, and especially Southern California, would be closely associated with commercial and military aviation.

36. AVIATORS PUSH THE BOUNDARIES OF FLIGHT AND DISTANCE *(SEE P. 125)*

Just at the moment when women and their suffrage-minded male allies attempted to bring voting freedom to half the population of this or that western state (and the nation), others sought very different forms of freedom. Calbraith "Cal" Perry Rodgers, the grandson of Admiral Matthew Perry, became the first aviator to fly coast

Aviator Calbraith "Cal" Perry Rodgers, 1911
Courtesy the Library of Congress Prints and Photographs Division.

to coast across the United States in 1912. He and a few other intrepid pilots were trying to win a $50,000 prize offered up by California publishing titan William Randolph Hearst for the first thirty-day airplane flight across the country.

Rodgers lined up a sponsor, the Armour meat-packing company of Chicago, and agreed to promote Armour's new soft drink, "Vin Fiz," which quickly became the name of his airplane. Two competitors began before Rodgers—one flew east from California, but could not get over the Sierra Nevada mountains, and one flew west from New York, but crashed so often that he quit. Avoiding the mountains entirely, Rodgers flew toward the Southwest and from there toward Southern California; with the wind at his back, he could go about sixty miles an hour, often using railroad tracks as his guide. Rodgers flew, crashed, flew, and crashed (nearly twenty crashes in total) all the way across the country. On November 5, well past the deadline for the prize but remarkable nonetheless, he brought the Vin Fiz to a stop at a park that is now part of the California Institute of Technology in Pasadena. Christened the "King of the Air," he tried to fly to the Pacific Ocean a week later but crashed badly, breaking both of his legs. A month after that, still on crutches, he successfully made the short flight to the edge of the Pacific in Long Beach. At nearly that same spot, a few months later, Rodgers flew into a flock of seagulls, crashed into the ocean, and was killed.

The era of long-distance flight, however dangerous, had arrived. Before long, and because of innovations at least in part pushed forward in the far West, airplanes would become potent weapons of war.

37. MEXICO INVITED TO JOIN THE CENTRAL POWERS

Intercepted by the British in early 1917, the Zimmermann Telegram immediately prompted a rallying call for American preparedness. By suggesting a possible Mexican reconquest of the Southwest with German help—the details of which were conveniently left vague—the document incited a strong response in the border states. Army troops and tens of thousands of National Guardsmen were soon patrolling the border, as politicians and military leaders organized in anticipation of German or Mexican attacks on American soil. Would a German alliance with Mexico have produced a wartime front in, for instance, Arizona or New Mexico? Why would German officials expect Mexican authorities to give the Zimmermann Telegram any attention?

The Zimmermann Telegram
1917[1]

We intend to begin on the first of February unrestricted submarine warfare. We shall endeavor in spite of this to keep the United States of America neutral. In the event of this not succeeding, we make Mexico a proposal of alliance on the following basis: make war together, generous financial support and an understanding on our part that Mexico is to reconquer the lost territory in Texas, New Mexico, and Arizona. The settlement in detail is left to you. You will inform the President [of Mexico] of the above most secretly as soon as the outbreak of war with the United States of America is certain and add the suggestion that he should, on his own initiative, invite Japan to immediate adherence and at the same time mediate between Japan and ourselves. Please call the President's attention to the fact that the ruthless employment of our submarines now offers the prospect of compelling England in a few months to make peace.

Zimmermann

---

1. Samuel Spencer Jr., ed., *Decision for War, 1917* (Rindge, NH: Richard R. Smith, 1953), 61–62.

38. PREPARING FOR WAR

The following sharply worded editorial appeared in response to the disclosure of the captured Zimmermann Telegram. In it the editors of the Los Angeles Times *declare that there "is no longer any doubt of the desire of Germany to make war upon us" and suggest that Germany's alliance with Japan and Mexico is a fore-*

gone conclusion. "Get together and get ready," the paper urges Californians, for the war is coming. The newspaper suggests, however, that "the greatest danger" is not from foreign nations but from "treason and sedition within our own gates." Sentiments such as these encouraged hostility toward Americans of German heritage. The excesses of patriotic fervor also led to repression of groups considered un-American, and members of political and labor organizations found their patriotism and loyalty to the nation in question. If you compared this editorial with those in other American newspapers of the period, would you expect the response to be the same? How would you compare the language here to that in the Wyoming speech in Document 39, p. 128?

Los Angeles Times

Editorial

1917[1]

Get Together and Get Ready!

The people of no American city have shown more patriotic zeal for military preparedness than the citizens of Los Angeles. The need of this government has met with a response from Los Angeles that has rung with enthusiasm and sturdy eagerness to serve. On every hand patriotic societies are springing up, pledged to the furtherance of our belated military activity. . . .

Out of their zeal, these societies and movements have created one complication; the danger is that these activities may not follow the same path—that they may scatter their strength.

Working in concert, these patriotic organizations might be able to do a great deal of good. Working along their scattered lines, they may still do much good, but they will always be in danger of crossing one another's paths.

It would appear to be the practical thing to first ascertain just what the government wants from its citizens in the way of practical help. The War College and the General Staff have very definite plans. In working along the lines of our own enthusiastic efforts, it is most important that we should do nothing to embarrass these plans in any remote way.

There surely is a way, however, for us to get behind these war plans and to do what we can toward forcing them through to completion in a way that seems best to the army officers who have made a special study of these matters.

The first step toward this end would seem to be the formation of a sort of central Los Angeles war board made up of representatives from the different movements. They could take stock of their various resources and see that a complete co-operation existed between the different bodies and patriotic movements.

---

1. *Los Angeles Times*, March 1, 1917, 4.

It would then be possible to bring the entire patriotic movement into close communication with the War College and General Staff in order to help these army officers bring about the necessary legislation.

Let us find out how we can help the army; then get together in one big organized movement to do the work.

We must bestir ourselves—for the sky is full of portents. There is no longer any doubt of the desire of Germany to make war upon us—and the proposed alliance with Mexico and Japan is no dream. The thing long dreaded has come. We are virtually at war today. AND THE GREATEST DANGER IS FROM TREASON AND SEDITION WITHIN OUR OWN GATES!

39. SUPPORT FOR THE WAR IN WYOMING

Harrison Dale, a political science professor at the University of Wyoming, delivered this address before the Laramie One Hundred Per Cent American Club on Lincoln's birthday in 1918. Like other exhortations of its kind, the speech distinguishes between good Americans and bad, between "one hundred per cent Americans" and those whose loyalties could be called into question. Dale's discussion of those he calls "hyphenated" Americans is typical of this period of hyper-patriotism. According to this line of thought, America had no place for people who hyphenated their origins and thus, it was thought, their loyalties. The war years proved especially intolerant of ethnic diversity in the American population. How would Professor Dale identify a "one hundred per cent American"? How do the sentiments in this speech compare with those in the Los Angeles Times *newspaper editorial of a year earlier?*

Harrison Clifford Dale
"What We Are Fighting For"
1918[1]

It is altogether fitting that, on the anniversary of the birth of the man whom I think we can safely describe as the most American American that ever lived, we should consider, as he considered in the masterful language of the Gettysburg Address, the things for which we are fighting. President Wilson has sketched these objects, these principles, in his historic message to Congress before the outbreak of the war, later in his reply to the Pope's peace proposals, more recently in his address before the opening session of the present Congress, and finally in his remarks of yesterday. In looking over these statements of principles and of policy one might be inclined to think that our objects are manifold. So they are. But in last analysis it strikes me that they boil down to

1. Harrison Clifford Dale, *What We Are Fighting For: An Address Given before the Laramie One Hundred Per Cent American Club* (Laramie, WY: n.p., 1918), 1–4.

three main purposes: (1) an American America, not a German-America or a hyphenated America of any sort or description, but an American America; (2) the preservation of the Monroe Doctrine,[2] or, to put it more generally, the preservation of all America north and south for Americans; and (3) the attainment through democracy of the peace of the world, so that just as death overcame death so war may overcome war and not only the world be made safe for democracy, but the world made *safe* by making it democratic!

First, then, to make of this splendid country of ours an American America. I put this object first because, it seems to me, it is one of the aims, one of the purposes in which we here in Laramie, we the members of the One Hundred Per Cent American Club, can most surely and most helpfully assist. We are not ninety-nine and nine-tenths per cent Americans; we are one hundred per cent Americans. Now did you ever realize what it means to be an American citizen?[3] "A Frenchman may reside for years in England, or Germany, or Russia, but he will always remain a foreigner, no matter how many papers of citizenship he may secure. An Englishman may spend a lifetime in Italy, and catch, as Browning[4] caught, the poetry of her soul; but he will die an alien. A Russian may rear his family in Holland, but they will never become Dutch. But let this same Frenchman or Englishman or Russian come and dwell on our shores, and this great moving force of Americanism transforms him into a true American. A nation so composed cannot stand upon a narrow platform of provincial patriotism. Its fundamentals of citizenship must transcend race, and its ideals must be so high that ancient animosities and hereditary loyalties cannot compete with them, or divide the allegiance which they demand. Had our President called for a rally 'round the banner of the Anglo-Saxon, millions would have answered: 'We are not ready to die for Anglo-Saxon traditions.' Had he raised the cry of Teutonic loyalty, other millions would have answered: 'We do not acknowledge the divine right of the Hohenzollerns.'"[5] The only call which can command the support of the American nation is the call of America.

Now it is undeniably true, it is regrettably true, alas! the evidence is all too overwhelming, that the hyphen has been cultivated in this country for the benefit of that natural foe to liberty, the Imperial German Government. I say regrettably true because, thank God, not all Americans of German antecedents have allied themselves with this effort to create in our midst a separate nationality, and a separate culture, whose allegiance lay not here, but across the seas in the realm of the Hohenzollerns. Certainly it is a gratifying thing that we can

---

2. **Monroe Doctrine:** In 1823, President James Monroe warned European nations not to meddle in political affairs of the Western Hemisphere. This aggressive diplomatic stance became known as the Monroe Doctrine.
3. **[Quote marks]:** The unattributed quotes in this text, like the one that follows, appeared in the original text and have been reproduced here.
4. **Browning:** Elizabeth Barrett Browning (1806–1861), English poet of the Victorian era.
5. **Hohenzollerns:** members of the German royal family.

count as members of this One Hundred Per Cent American Club, as loyal and true members, a number of Americans of more or less remote German origin. Not all Germans in this country are hyphenated Americans. Isn't it a heartening thing, ladies and gentlemen, that practically all of those who breathe our pure mountain air—and somehow all through history mountain air has been called the air of freedom—isn't it a splendid and a heartening thing, I say, that practically all those of German or Austrian origin who live in our county, and our city, are able in their heart of hearts to sign our constitution and by-laws as one hundred per cent Americans!

But, alas! this has not been the case in all parts of the United States. There has been a concerted effort to keep alive German culture, German traditions, and the spirit of German nationality in the United States, not with the real object of enriching *American* life, but with the aim and purpose of fostering the ambitions of a foreign and at present an enemy state.

For example, there are a great number of German organizations in this country which are bound together for a common purpose in the German-American National Alliance. One of the aims of this Alliance has been, so it is stated, to promote friendly political relations between the United States and the German Empire. That those societies which make up the German-American National Alliance have done much to promote friendly political relations between Germany and the United States is doubtless correct. But, true to the hopes and expectations of their leaders here and in Germany, they have acted in this work as members of the German nationality and not as Americans. "They have sought to keep the peace by trying to force the United States during the past three years to endure such a series of insults, affronts, and injuries at the hands of Germany as were never before inflicted by one nation on another with which it was at peace." The statement that the German-Americans could give complete devotion to their adopted country and yet cultivate the German language would be accepted by most Americans as harmless and as true, were it not for the assertion of Dr. Julius Goebel, a German-American college professor, that the German language and German culture are the best means of preserving German nationality and that "the possession of them alone is sufficient to prevent the process of Americanization." This same Professor Goebel urges "that all the teachers of the German language and literature in American Universities, the teachers of German in the lower schools, the German clergy of all confessions, and all educated Germans in America should co-operate in spreading the German language and German ideas, for these will prevent citizens of German descent from becoming Americans in spirit." Thank Heaven, this is not true to the degree that Professor Goebel and others of his ilk believe.

After declaring that the Alliance will always be loyal to its adopted country and promote its welfare, the constitution continues: "The Alliance has no particularistic interests in view, it does not intend to found a state within a state, but sees in the centralization of people of German origin the shortest way and the best security for the ends laid down in this constitution." "The statement that the Alliance does not intend to found a state within a state is doubtless true, because such an enterprise is obviously impossible to carry out in the United States. It does aim, however, to assist in founding a *nation within a nation*, to establish amidst the American nation another national unit whose members shall be bound together by the ties of a common race, a common language, a common spirit, a common civilization, in a word, by all those bonds which consolidate nationalities everywhere." The members of the German nationality resident in the United States are, according to the repeated assertions of its creators both here and in Germany, to be distinct in all these fundamental characteristics from the American nationality. And more than that, they are to feel a special attachment for an alien and at present an enemy state. "Of all the outrages which Germany has inflicted on the United States, none is more infamous than this subtle and insidious effort to undermine the national life of the American people. For if the effort is successful, and there are numberless proofs that it has succeeded all too well, it will destroy the unity of national sentiment in this country. What greater danger could the nation face?"

"What will be the results in the United States if the comprehensive and energetic effort is successful to weld the German-Americans into a separate national unit? The greatest result of all can be stated with certainty, because it is already upon us. This effort has produced a schism in the *American nation* along the line of race cleavage. Many thousands of people of German blood have acted on the doctrine, long inculcated, that they belong together and apart from the rest of the American people. If this German principle were followed by the members of other nationalities here, it would result in disaster for America. For its population would disintegrate into racial groups, each with its program of a separatist and particularistic aims, as the German group now has. There would be a Russian, a Hungarian, an Italian, a Swedish, a Greek, and a south Slav group. The United States would find itself in a racial and political condition resembling in some important particulars that of the Austro-Hungarian Empire or the Balkan peninsula. The racial division throughout the nation would be reflected in Congress and questions of national policy would become race issues." They have already become such in part, for, before we entered the war, there was a German party acting in the interests of Germany both in the Senate and the House of Representatives of the United States of America.

"*Germanism in the United States is a destructive and disintegrating force.* In just so far as it grows strong, the United States grows weak, nationally and internationally. Its unity of national sentiment is destroyed and its patriotism undermined. Its power to act as a unified nation is crippled. Internationally it grows weak because the members of an alien nation within its borders make impossible freedom of action in dealing with foreign states."

What can the people of the United States do about it? They can at least exert against the nationalistic German societies here the force of a justly angered public opinion. For these societies are a detriment to America. Our national life will be stronger, sounder, and healthier without them. "There is no place in any state for a press and for organizations which aim to consolidate a foreign nationality, to propagate a foreign civilization and to serve a foreign state. What would the German government do under similar circumstances?"

One of the results of this war, one of the results of the work of this One Hundred Per Cent American Club, must be to create a newer, a more vigorous sense of American nationality. We are a nation; we must think, feel, and act as a nation, as ONE nation, one and indivisible.

And then, in the second place, we are fighting for the Monroe Doctrine, and Cuba, and Panama, and Brazil are fighting with us for the Monroe Doctrine. This is no selfish motive. We are not fighting to grab the trade of Latin America under the guise of the Monroe Doctrine. In the noble words of President Wilson, "We have no selfish ends to serve. We desire no conquest, no dominion. We seek no indemnities for ourselves, no material compensation for the sacrifices we shall freely make." For the last ten years we have been enjoying increasingly friendly relations with our Latin neighbors in the other American continent. At times it has been pretty up-hill work to convince them of the sincerity of our friendship. Do you know why this is so? It is because German propaganda in Latin America has sedulously endeavored to prevent those democracies from becoming friends with our own great republic of the north. The Zimmermann note with its slimy scheme of stirring up Mexico against us is only one effort of this kind. . . .

40. CAMP LIFE IN TEXAS

This selection from a soldier's description of his World War I experience details life in one of the wartime camps designed to turn young American men into soldiers. Camp Bowie, outside the town of Fort Worth, Texas, became an important military training camp for US soldiers and civilians called up by the wartime draft. Private Harlow's account of the drills, the routines, and the military tedium of camp life stands in stark contrast to the horrors of trench warfare some of these young men would soon face in Europe. How did the surrounding community respond to the soldiers stationed at Camp Bowie? Why were the draftees treated so differently from the people from the surrounding countryside, towns, and cities? What role did the experiences of some soldiers on the Mexican border play in their preparation for war?

Rex F. Harlow
"Camp Bowie"
1919[1]

. . . All of the organizations that were used in the development of the 61st were
made up of National Guard troops, who were gathered from all parts of Texas
and Oklahoma and sent to Camp Bowie, Fort Worth. Upon arriving at Fort
Worth they detrained and proceeded immediately to the Clark farm, so called
because it was owned by Mrs. Clark. It was covered by Johnson grass about
knee high and showed nothing of the great camp that was later built, except
that a few piles of lumber lay scattered at random over the place. The men put
up tents the first afternoon, immediately after their arrival, but slept that night
on Johnson grass, which bed, in fact, served them for several nights thereafter.

The first duty of the newly arrived troops was that of acting as camp guards,
for each day brought in vast amounts of government property, especially building material. Not all of the men were used as guards, however, and just as rapidly as time permitted and men could be spared for the purpose, the camp was
put into shape. Grass was cut, troop streets were laid out and graded, ditches
were dug and a thousand and one things incident to the building of a new camp
were done by the men. There were no quiet hours, for the soldiers realized that
they were engaging in the biggest piece of work of their lives and that they must
enter into this work with energy and spirit if they were to become properly
trained for overseas. Moreover, most of them believed that their stay in Camp
Bowie would be short and that they would rapidly be trained to the point where
they could leave for France; and this belief caused them to lose no time in
putting themselves into condition.

As the cavalry troops were the first soldiers to occupy Camp Bowie, they
were forced not only to do guard duty over government stores, but also to furnish military police for Fort Worth, where troops were coming and going and
over-patriotic citizens were being imposed upon. Work of this kind occupied
about three months of time, after which other troops arrived and the cavalry
units were transferred to the artillery service.

But most of the work during the early months of their stay in Camp Bowie
was pleasing to the men because of the generous manner in which the towns-
people of Fort Worth proved their appreciation of the soldiers and gave of their
bounteous hospitality. Nothing was too good for the newly arrived soldiers; no
opportunity was overlooked to give them automobile rides or to treat them to
candy, ice cream and cold drinks; and it early became an established policy on
the part of families of Fort Worth to invite soldiers to their homes for Sunday
dinners and for other forms of entertainment. No city could have shown a

---

1. Rex F. Harlow, *Trail of the 61st: A History of the 61st Field Artillery Brigade during the World
War, 1917–1919* (Oklahoma City: Barlow, 1919), 13–17, 19–20, 22–25.

warmer attitude of helpfulness and kindly interest toward its soldiers than Fort Worth did during the first few months after Camp Bowie was opened.

So many people called at the camp to take the boys for automobile rides that the soldiers soon learned to accept this kindness as a matter of course and thought nothing more of it than they did of receiving food free of charge from the government. It is a sad fact that this attitude grew to such proportions that carelessness in their treatment of the citizens of Fort Worth became common among the soldiers, and the city in self-protection, practically shut its doors to the camp. . . .

To the majority of soldiers who first came to Bowie, camp life was not new, for they had passed several months on the Mexican border and had grown accustomed to soldier life. They felt with reason that since they had served their apprenticeship on the border they would not be compelled to remain long in an American camp, but would soon be developed into efficient fighting men competent to meet the best troops of the German army and to successfully cope with them. . . .

Shortly after the various units of the National Guard had gotten properly settled in camp a training schedule was established by the Commanding General and the men were soon engaged in executing such squad movements as were required on the parade grounds or in the field. This training was made difficult by the fact that the drills were held over ground which was badly broken and cut by ravines and literally covered with rocks, which had to be removed with hands or shovels. Camp Bowie is located on seven hills to the west of Fort Worth and these hills are separated by small valleys over which the men had to work in their maneuvering and training. . . .

The Y.M.C.A. provided interesting and educative entertainments practically every evening and these entertainments were usually attended by large audiences, the soldiers eagerly accepting an opportunity to get away from their quarters for a while. Any number of first-class moving pictures were offered at the "Y." . . .

Likewise, the entertainments furnished by the Liberty Theater, were welcome to the majority of the soldiers, for at nominal expense good bills could be seen there practically any evening. Thousands of soldiers were entertained at the Liberty Theater by Theda Bara, Douglas Fairbanks and other noted movie stars. . . .

Other amusements supported freely and enjoyed greatly, were boxing and wrestling matches. Frequent bouts were held and the men were given the opportunity of seeing the country's best fighters and wrestlers in action. . . .

Moreover, many of the national singers and entertainers found their way to Camp Bowie during the time the 61st was in training there and it was largely the fault of the soldiers themselves if they didn't have pleasant times. . . .

On October 15, 1917, the 61st Field Artillery Brigade was formed from the Oklahoma and Texas Guards, but as these organizations did not contain a sufficient number of men to fill the brigade to full war strength a large number of drafted men from the first national army draft were secured on October 22, 1917 from the 165th Depot Brigade at Camp Travis; and the first week in June, 1918, a second contingent of draft men were brought to Camp Bowie from Texas and Oklahoma, though chiefly from Camp Travis. The life of these newly drafted soldiers was entirely different from that of the National Guardsmen at the time the latter entered camp. The drafted men were taken to detention camp immediately upon arrival, where they were given bed-clothing and cots and were assigned to tents. The detention camp, which was constructed to accommodate about 5,000 troops, was surrounded by ten-foot woven wire, at the top of which were stretched several strands of barbed-wire. The entrances were kept heavily guarded and it was seen that none of the new men were allowed to leave detention camp during their stay there.

The theory upon which the detention camp was established was that men coming from all parts of the country were likely to carry diseases with them. . . . It was here that the authorities carefully examined every man, vaccinated him for small-pox and typhoid, and saw to it that he was made into a perfectly sanitary being before being allowed in the camp proper.

The tents, occupied by the new-comers, accommodated from six to eight men and were practically a replica of the tents in the main camp. The men were taught to prepare their bunks, to answer reveille, and to police their quarters each day—experiences entirely novel to them. They were arranged into companies, having their own company streets, latrines and mess halls, and were placed under the immediate command of sergeants who had been selected for this purpose from the trained units in the main camp.

To these civilians, life in the detention camp was "one damn thing right after another." They were rudely awakened each morning by the shrill whistle of the "Top Cutter" and, in case they didn't fall out promptly, were more rudely ousted from their bunks by some unsympathetic, curt orderly who was sent to their tents with the gruff admonition to "get those rookies to hell up in line; what do they think this is—their birthday?" . . .

After having "fallen in" and dressed their lines they were given orders for the day and were likely divided into groups to take exercises. This exercise business proved to be quite an interesting affair to these soft men, who had come to camp from offices and indoor work. Some fat fellows, especially, found it difficult to execute all of the movements, their grunts and pantings often keeping time to the commands of their leaders. With the perspiration bursting forth from their round cheeks and their flesh forming in great remonstrating rolls, the only indication they gave of ever becoming soldiers was the earnest manner in which they entered into their work. . . .

The morning meal was usually followed by general policing of quarters and preparations for the day's drill. The men were placed in groups of from eight to fifty, according to the number of men available to train them and usually each group contained several men who had had some previous military training, these men being always in demand by the sergeants in charge. . . .

The vaccinations were the most unpopular experiences in the detention camp, for not only did sore arms develop from the small-pox vaccinations, but fever and racking headaches also resulted from the injection of anti-typhoid serum. Sometimes as many as half of the men in a company of three or four hundred were too sick to drill or to go on hikes and marches. The men dreaded each trip to the infirmary, for they never knew when they were going to be examined or made to take some kind of medicine. Salts, especially, seemed to be quite popular with the medical officers, the men being lined up quite often to "pass in review" before a large tub of strong salts, each man receiving from a half pint to a pint of this pleasant drink. The results of such kindly attention on the part of the medical officers always resulted in great camp activity, the men often living up to the reputation of sprinters while engaged in the proper execution of their pressing military duties. . . .

An order in detention camp which will long live in the memory of the men who were affected by it was that calling for the cutting of all hair to a shortness of one-half inch. When this order was read to the troops it created much consternation, many lads fondly passing their fingers through their endangered locks, with the prayer that they might escape. But the ruthless mule clippers found their way to the heads of even the most beautiful hair and each man was turned out a freshly sheared sacrifice to the god of military efficiency, bearing witness that lice and Uncle Sam had declared war on each other. Many of the Indians refused to credit the order when it was first read to them and, upon being approached about having their braids of hair removed, were emphatic in their refusals to be subjected to such indignity. But the sergeants, firm in their duty, marched forth with a host of assistants to impress upon these wayward nephews of Uncle Sam that all individual religious customs and rights must be waived when Uncle Sam issued orders. The Indians were seized by enough men to hold them securely and rough hands applied the mule shears to the quivering indignant heads of these embryonic war chiefs, leaving them in a badly shorn condition. In several instances they bellowed and roared, threatening to subject all sergeants and "Uncles" to the deepest and hottest depths of perdition, but their vitriolic upheavals always subsided into stoic moroseness, from which they were again aroused with difficulty.

Most of the men enjoyed the opportunity of going on hikes, even though the weather was tremendously hot and the marches were several miles in length and over rough roads. . . . The trips to Lake Komo were especially pleasing to them because they were allowed to take swims there on numerous occasions. The change from the stuffy hot camp to the freedom of this nice cool lake was a Godsend and they enjoyed it accordingly. . . .

FURTHER READING

Bilstein, Roger E. *Flight in America: From the Wrights to the Astronauts*. Baltimore: Johns Hopkins University Press, 2001.

Boghardt, Thomas. *The Zimmermann Telegram: Intelligence, Diplomacy, and America's Entry into World War I*. Annapolis, MD: Naval Institute, 2012.

Bristow, Nancy K. *Making Men Moral: Social Engineering during the Great War*. New York: New York University Press, 1996.

Doenecke, Justus D. *Nothing Less Than War: A New History of America's Entry into World War I*. Lexington: University Press of Kentucky, 2011.

Hall, Linda B. *Revolution on the Border: The United States and Mexico, 1910–1920*. Albuquerque: University of New Mexico Press, 1988.

Katz, Friedrich. *The Life and Times of Pancho Villa*. Stanford, CA: Stanford University Press, 1998.

Kennedy, David M. *Over Here: The First World War and American Society*. Oxford and New York: Oxford University Press, 1982.

Lotchin, Roger W. *Fortress California, 1910–1961: From Warfare to Welfare*. New York: Oxford University Press, 1992.

Luebke, Frederick C. *Bonds of Loyalty: German-Americans and World War I*. Dekalb: Northern Illinois University Press, 1974.

Pisano, Dominick A., ed. *The Airplane in American Culture*. Ann Arbor: University of Michigan Press, 2003.

Truett, Samuel. *Fugitive Landscapes: The Forgotten History of the US-Mexico Borderlands*. New Haven, CT: Yale University Press, 2006.

Tuchman, Barbara W. *The Zimmermann Telegram*. New York: Viking, 1958.

Van Vleck, Jenifer. *Empire of the Air: Aviation and the American Ascendancy*. Cambridge, MA: Harvard University Press, 2013.

Westwick, Peter J., ed. *Blue Sky Metropolis: The Aerospace Century in Southern California*. Berkeley: University of California Press, 2012.

Wild, Mark. *Street Meeting: Multiethnic Neighborhoods in Early Twentieth-Century Los Angeles*. Berkeley: University of California Press, 2005.

California Campaign Edition

THE WESTERN WOMAN VOTER

VOL. 1   SEATTLE, WASHINGTON, SEPTEMBER, 1911   NO. 9

COLLEGE GIRLS PUTTING UP SUFFRAGE POSTERS

WASHINGTON, last November, gave women the ballot by 20,000 majority---the largest majority ever given a suffrage amendment in the history of the world. Here's to a bigger majority in California on October 10!

California Next ! !

The women's suffrage movement, 1911. This front page of the *Western Woman Voter*, a suffragette newspaper in Seattle, rallies Californians with a photograph of young women plastering a wall with posters. Women toiled for many decades to achieve the right to vote, and they succeeded first in Wyoming in 1869. Other western states soon followed suit, paving the way for the rest of the nation. As their posters indicate, these Washington women promoted suffrage by allying their 1910 campaign to such public figures as Theodore Roosevelt, Abraham Lincoln, and even Mark Twain. Why do you think they invoked these famous men in support of their cause?

Courtesy the Huntington Library, San Marino, California.

Progressives, Progressivism, and the American West

Historians look to the first two decades of the twentieth century as constituting the Progressive Era. It is complex and difficult to describe, but one of its chief components was certainly a sense of optimism—at times an urgent optimism—about the future. The twenty or so years assigned to the period saw marked public effort on the part of progressives, a loose collection of people trying to find solutions to social, political, and other problems. Reformers of one or another political party or persuasion, they were generally urban professionals who saw the twentieth century as their own—who imagined, by way of their laws and reforms and technologies, that the future, near and far, could be improved, if not perfected. This faith could be an ugly one, tied as it often was to perceptions of racial, national, or cultural hierarchies. At its most humane, though, it bespoke a faith in the better angels of individuals, institutions, and nations. Often, the progressives believed that the tools of government—local, state, and federal mechanisms of policy and law—would offer the leverage required to solve vexing challenges.

The Progressive Era witnessed critical changes in American political and economic systems, from President Theodore Roosevelt's legislative and public relations attempts to limit corporate power, to prohibitions against child labor, to the passage in 1920 of the Nineteenth

Amendment granting women the right to vote. Countless other political developments occurred at the state and local levels, usually as a result of progressives' attempts to rein in the power of special interests—which they believed corrupted politics and made it harder for democracy to function. Progressive innovations included important changes in the ways voters could express their preferences (or their anger) and new methods of organizing municipal political leadership within cities and towns. It was during the Progressive period that a number of American cities opted to abolish the office of an elected mayor (too political, too vulnerable to graft) in favor of the supposedly more "efficient" appointed city manager. This innovation had particular sway in the West.

Reform-minded change had a long tradition in the West. Reformers tackled the political and social problems of western cities and tried to curtail the reach and entrenched power of corporations, especially the big railroad corporations. Other issues, too, had a truly western feel and cast to them. Environmental innovations—political and legal efforts to address environmental degradation and exploitation—had western roots. The first national parks arose in the West in the last third of the nineteenth century, and, with the coming of the Progressive Era and the twentieth century, progressives built the government agencies and operations designed to protect those places and spaces. Conservation became, by the 1910s, a national issue, and westerners like the environmentalist John Muir (and the western Sierra Club) played key roles on the regional and national stages in that regard.

Sometimes, however, reformist innovation, even fervor, cut across progress. For all their claims about expanding democracy, progressives also had a hand in limiting the political rights of ethnic and racial minorities, in the West and across the nation. The embrace of "Americanization" efforts designed to turn new immigrant arrivals into model citizens is a case in point. These programs—after-school language classes, cooking classes for immigrant women, playground and recreation programs for children, public health provision in poor neighborhoods—could look as if the goal was to turn immigrants into white, middle-class, and often Christian Americans. Humane regard and xenophobic concerns could, in the intricate ways in which Progressive reform worked, exist together in thoughts and practice. In this, the West had history to draw upon: much of the Progressive effort to Americanize the immigrants in homes, schools, and neighborhoods looked like earlier (and ongoing) attempts to "civilize" indigenous men, women, and children on western reservations and in "Indian schools."

During the Progressive Era, the nation—by way of the progressive champions—began to see technology and science as a source of positive change. Many progressives believed that where politics had failed to make society just, efficient, and productive, science and technology could be brought to the task. This is not to say that progressives uniformly embraced technological innovation; some wanted early twentieth-century technology kept in check. This was particularly true if it meant that big business could be spared the seductions of politics, especially dirty politics. For instance one of the period's most successful politicians, California's Hiram Johnson, won that state's gubernatorial election in 1910 by insisting that the Southern Pacific Railroad's long history of throwing its political clout around the state had come to an end. The time had come, Johnson said in speech after speech, to kick the railroad out of state politics once and for all.

Successful progressives like Johnson knew that they had to enlarge their voter bases, but such efforts faced limitations, often of the progressives' own making. Many western politicians, like their counterparts elsewhere, did not believe in racial equality, at the polls or otherwise. They sometimes used racist issues and planks to win votes. Johnson, for instance, was only too happy to support anti-Asian legislation that added further restrictions to those already placed on Asian and Asian Americans by such measures as the Chinese Exclusion Act of 1882 (and those that followed; see Document 15 on p. 43).

As a way to think about the era, remember that progressives believed in hygiene of all kinds: they wanted clean government, clean cities, clean food, clean water, even clean bloodstreams and gene pools (which tied many a progressive to eugenic ambitions and programs). With the right laws, the right science, the right political systems in place, progressives thought to get the new century off on the right track. As with any movement of often unwieldy and even contradictory impulses, the Progressive Era both succeeded and failed, and it has left us with a complex legacy of forward-thinking and retrograde ideas and programs. The outbreak of World War I, and America's eventual involvement in the conflict, dampened the fire of many progressive efforts. The legacy of Progressivism is, in a word, mixed.

The selections here focus on different forms of, or themes within, the larger Progressive movement in western settings. Men had to be convinced women deserved the vote, since they would be the ones voting on women's suffrage, and not all of them shared a belief in equality and citizenship rights regardless of gender. The essay by George Patton addresses the topic from the ideas and mindset of one such opposed man. We see the other side through the passionate efforts and labors of someone like Charlotte Anita Whitney. An account of how Oregon utilized the recall tool as a democratizing lever attests to the ability of voters to affect local or state politics well after they cast election ballots. A selection on Americanization serves as a reminder that although access to voting might have increased during the Progressive Era, age-old tensions about "the right kind" of voter continued to surface. And last, a poignant image of a family of itinerant beet pickers in northern Colorado early in the twentieth century indicates the era's need to create and apply child labor laws beyond the harsh working environments of the West's mines, mills, and factories.

41. A CALIFORNIAN ARGUES AGAINST WOMEN'S SUFFRAGE

The father of the famed World War II general of the same name, George Patton was a Virginian who moved to Southern California in the late nineteenth century. A political mover and shaker in and around Los Angeles (he served as a kind of right hand to railroad magnate Henry Huntington), Patton vehemently opposed women's suffrage. This excerpt from an essay originally published in West Coast Magazine, *a monthly literary and political journal from Los Angeles, is a strongly worded statement of his ideas—ideas that appealed to many Americans (men and women alike) who believed that equal suffrage was a mistake. Their traditional views generally put them at odds with progressive reforms. Patton reveals his assumptions about the role of women in society as well as his fears about the racial future of the Pacific coast. Why does Patton oppose suffrage? What evidence does he marshal to show that equal suffrage would be ill advised? How would women like those in the photograph on page 138 respond to Patton's arguments?*

George S. Patton

"Why Women Should Not Be Given the Vote"
1911[1]

. . . You will observe that I do not state the problem as the suffragists do. I do not state that the question is whether or not women shall enjoy a right now denied them, or whether we shall confer upon women a privilege not now enjoyed by them,—but shall we or shall we not impose upon them a burden, a duty, an obligation, from which they are at present free. . . .

I submit . . . that the electoral franchise, by which men in our modern civilization . . . carry on the functions of such government, is . . . a duty and an obligation, and not a privilege at all; that politics, through and by means of which the electoral franchise is utilized as an effectual means of human government is in its final analysis, a struggle, a contest, a combat; is, in fact, merely modified war,— and that it necessarily follows that its carrying out rests upon that half of the human race, upon which from its very birth, through all its evolution, has rested the warlike and combative obligation, to the exclusion of the other half of the race. That the electoral obligation now rests, as it should rest, exclusively upon men.

. . . In the prolongation of the human period of infancy some have seen the direct hand of an overruling Providence, thereby compelling a division and specialization of the duties of the man and of the woman. Thus prior to the birth of the human young, and for a long period thereafter, and repeated over and over again during the whole period of child-bearing, the mother was not only help-

---

1. *West Coast Magazine* (Los Angeles), September 1911, 3–16.

lessly unfitted to the man's task, but her special duties and obligations were so heavy, and of such an absorbing nature that she could not if she would, perform, or share in, his special duties. . . . There was no question here between the primeval pair, of superiority or inferiority. Each was superior in his exclusive sphere, and between them there was perfect equality, perfect unity of purpose. . . .

. . . In these communities, the men necessarily continued to be the physical defenders and providers.

In these primitive communities it necessarily early became essential that some means should be devised by which, from time to time, questions of tribal or community policy should be settled. These we now call questions of public policy. Such questions then, as now, gave occasion for radical differences of opinion, or a selfish and powerful individual or group of individuals attempted, then as now, to seize and enjoy some special privilege or immunity.

Such controversies could only be settled by an appeal to arms, to force. . . .

As tribes grew into peoples, and nations, by the orderly process of evolution, stable governments were evolved, based upon the rule of the majority of the force and power of the nation. Today, in every civilized government it is in its last analysis, force and force only, fighting physical brute force, if you will, that stands behind and gives efficacy to the verdict of the majority cast at the polls. . . .

From all participation in this ultimate appeal to force women are necessarily excluded, and the reasons for such exclusion are as compelling and immutable in this day as they were in that earlier day when she relied for protection from stalking dangers in forest shadows, upon the strong arm of her mate. . . .

Between the nations of the world there exists an armed truce. Never since the creation of man has he so feverishly and madly prepared for war.

Here in California we occupy the position of the vanguard of Aryan civilization, and before our very eyes the Asiatic Titan stretches his giant limbs after the sleep of centuries.

Every great invasion in times past, when the hordes overran Europe, came when some prolific people were pressed for land to live upon. Such a condition now confronts such a people beyond the Pacific. The men of our race, as if by some instinct, are preparing to hold by force the vantage ground we have gained. Hence the Panama canal, the fortifications at Guam and Pearl Harbor, and new Dreadnaughts[2] and guns.

The possibilities that led to the recent mobilization of army and navy are patent and known to all men; and yet in the face of all these things suffragists vaguely tell us, "When women vote there will be no more war—we will not allow it."

When asked the direct question, "How will you accomplish this laudable result?" they become both dumb and indignant. . . .

---

2. **Dreadnaughts:** battleships.

The argument of those suffragists who claim and declaim that women have a "right" to the ballot, and that this "right" is denied them by men, is wholly fallacious. The truth is, the voting function is not a "right" and cannot become a right until it has been granted by law.

. . . Another fallacious "argument," often heard from suffragist women, is that man and man-made laws treat women as though they were inferior beings. Nothing could be further from the truth. Men do not treat women as inferior beings—rather they treat them as superior beings—and it is only from women's lips that we hear of woman's inferiority to man. . . .

Another argument frequently heard—that withholding the franchise from women is a similar case to that of Great Britain in the levying of the stamp tax, and is "taxation without representation"—will not bear a moment's analysis and betrays an ignorance both of logic and of the plain facts of history. The cry of "taxation without representation" arose in the Revolutionary period of our history and was founded upon substantial reason. Between England and the American colonies, it was practically the case of a foreign tyrant imposing laws upon the subject colonies which were not imposed upon the home people. . . . If men, therefore, should impose upon women or their property, a tax which men and their property did not bear, there would be just and grievous cause of complaint. But certainly it is not tyrannous if men say "my property" as well as "your property," shall be subject to the same uniform law. . . .

. . . What worthy cause is now being injured or jeopardized by delay? What are women going to do when they get the ballot? Do they know themselves? Have they, or has a single one of them outlined a policy in government and its origin and evolution, that indicates real thought or study of our governmental structure, or pointed out where woman suffrage will advance a single reform, not now as readily or more readily attainable? . . . Then why this clamorous demand for change? Does it not really spring from the misconception of the nature of the voting function, the erroneous idea that it is a privilege and therefore something to be desired, which is denied and forbidden to women?

. . . I most solemnly warn all women against entertaining the belief that the ballot in their hands will have the slightest effect upon ameliorating their economical conditions. Such amelioration and betterment, and no woman desires it more than men do, can never come through statute laws, but can and must come only from the education and enlightenment of public sentiment, coupled with the organization of labor, working for its own betterment. . . .

In other respects and wherever the law thinks it wise so to do, an absolute equality is established, not only between the sexes, but between husband and wife. Thus, the husband has absolutely no control over his wife's property, and the wife is as free as the husband to contract with him or with anybody else, not only as to property but as to any other matter which is the subject of contract.... An unmarried woman may as freely engage in business or trade as may a man and under no restrictions. Even a married woman may engage in trade entirely apart from her husband's control.... Could women armed with the ballot and divided as they say they will be into hostile and contending political factions—as men are,—have secured these or any of these valuable privileges and immunities which men have freely accorded them upon their own motion or upon the request of women—as women—without the ballot?

In all of those great rights of modern life, the right to own, control and dispose of property and the right to contract, it will be seen that in this state, women not only stand upon an equality with men, but, if anything, are favored over men by laws designed for their protection. There is but one class of property over which a husband exercises a dominion superior to that of a wife. That class of property is known to the law as community property. Over this class of property the husband is given the dominion and control within certain limitations, and this must be so because in our modern civilization, wherever the married state exists, it is usually the husband that is the bread winner; it is usually the husband who transacts what we call business.... But even upon his right of control and notwithstanding the fact that this property has been acquired wholly by his own endeavor ... he may not give it away nor part with it except for value. If he proposes to make any gift, it cannot be done unless the wife assents thereto and joins therein, and upon the husband's death she takes, beyond his power to dispose of it by will, one-half of all the community property so accumulated during their married life....

What are the great advantages which it may be said men take to themselves under their laws? They grow almost entirely out of the obligations which men take upon themselves to the state by the exercise of the franchise. Men alone vote and men alone, with certain limitations not necessary here to consider, fill the offices of state. Women or rather the suffragist minority of women are seeking to enter upon this domain upon terms of equality with men. I have before pointed out that it can never in the nature of things be that they enter upon these duties upon terms of equality. You cannot have an army of women. You cannot have the city of Los Angeles policed by women. You cannot have any law which may be placed upon the statute books by women enforced, unless it meets the approbation of men, because, as I have said, in the last analysis it is the physical force of men which executes the law.

Ask yourselves, therefore, my suffragist friends, what laws you would put upon the books, if you had the suffrage, which men have not put upon the books, and whenever you can think of such a law I will make answer that if it be a reasonable law, one for the betterment of women, the men themselves will be swift, not only to put it upon the books but to see that it is enforced. "This means, of course," you answer, "that the law must appear to be reasonable to the men or it will not be placed upon the books." But to this I reply, that if it does not appear reasonable to the men, even if the women placed it upon the books, it would never be executed. . . .

And here let me repeat that few things are more destructive of the well-being of the state than indifference to or disrespect for the law. . . . Disrespect and disregard for the law mean the swift destruction of any form of government. . . .

But I now propose to speak briefly of what I conceive to be the threatened evils of woman suffrage—evils to women themselves, evils to the state; particular and specific dangers, as against the vague general expressions that the ballot in the hands of women will do so much good.

Women, even the highly intelligent ones, are prone to compare themselves with men of much inferior education and ability. They say: "You give the ballot to this ignorant day laborer, do I not know more than he?" They say: "My coachman or chauffeur whom I pay can vote. Does he know more than the woman who pays his wages?" But this is not the true consideration. One answer to it is that the same chauffeur and the same day laborer can bear arms and may be called upon to bear arms in defense of the laws which they have made. But when women discuss the question of universal suffrage they must not select individuals of their sex. They must treat their sex as a mass. They must bear in mind that the ballot to them does not mean the ballot to the most intelligent of them, but it means the ballot to the day laborer's wife, who, if anything, is more ignorant of public affairs than is her husband—who, by the way, is actually frequently one of the most intelligent of voters. . . .

The very best that can be said upon this topic is that suffrage for women means a doubling of the present vote without in any material sense changing the character of that vote for the better. . . .

. . . Women now have full suffrage in five states; the State of Washington having recently joined Colorado, Utah, Wyoming and Idaho in the experiment.

In the four last named states it has been in operation for a number of years.

If a tithe of the great benefits which suffragists declare will follow the granting of the franchise to women are to be realized—some indication must surely by this time have been given toward that result in these states.

Instead, the history of legislation in the states named without exception dicates the very reverse, and demonstrates a pitiable failure to achieve any of the benefits so freely predicted. Recently the editor of the *Ladies' Home Journal* sent Mr. Richard Barry as a special commissioner to investigate the workings of suffrage in the then four suffrage states. The *Journal* published his report, which now, in pamphlet form, is being distributed by the Woman's League opposed to suffrage.

It is a most complete and damning arraignment of suffrage, a most amazing demonstration of failure and folly.

It is too long to reproduce here—but a few extracts will prove enlightening. Says Mr. Barry, speaking of Colorado:

... The chief of police of Denver told me that juvenile crime is on an alarming increase in that city. . . .

The chief of police of Denver joins with the chief of police of Salt Lake City (the only two towns of any size in the woman-suffrage country) as my authority for the statement that prostitution is largely on the increase both in Colorado and in Utah. Idaho and Wyoming, being rural communities, can show a better record, but still no better than similar communities elsewhere. . . .

... Supplementing Mr. Barry's report, here is what a prominent Colorado woman, Mrs. Francis W. Goddard, President of the Colonial Dames of Colorado, has to say as recently as December last:

... For years I believed in woman suffrage and have worked day in and day out for it. I now see my mistake and would abolish it tomorrow if I could.

No law has been put on the statute book of Colorado for the benefit of women and children that has been put there by the women. The child labor law went through independently of the women's vote. The hours of working women have not been shortened; the wages of schoolteachers have not been raised; the type of men that got into office has not improved a bit.

Frankly, the experiment is a failure. It has done Colorado no good. It has done woman no good. The best thing for both would be if tomorrow the ballot for women could be abolished.

... In view of all these objections theoretical and practical, I say with deep earnestness that the men of California whose votes will determine the question on October 10, have never had presented to them a political question more fraught with potency of evil to the cause of good government, or government by responsible voters, enacting wise and enforcible laws. . . . The dictates of simple prudence should impel the thoughtful men of the state to smother under an overwhelming adverse verdict the attempt of a handful of mistaken enthusiasts to place upon the unwilling shoulders of our good women a responsibility and a burden which they are constitutionally unable to assume.

42. SUFFRAGIST STRATEGY IN CALIFORNIA

This document was written by the president of the College Equal Suffrage League of Northern California, Charlotte Anita Whitney, in 1911, just after California voted in favor of women's suffrage. In this foreword to a book published by the league, Whitney discusses various strategies for keeping the suffrage juggernaut moving across the nation's political landscape. The movement demands strong organizational leadership, she declares, as well as clear-cut goals and aims so that others will join the cause. Whitney's insistence that the suffrage movement is an educational, even spiritual endeavor is very much at odds with the perspective of an opponent like George Patton. In terms of political strategies, what suggestions look familiar, even these many years later? How would Whitney respond to Patton's declaration that equality between men and women already existed in many areas? How do Whitney's strategies for cooperative organization contrast with Patton's notions of "rule by force"?

Charlotte Anita Whitney

"Suggestions for Successful Organization"
1911[1]

In making an active campaign for equal suffrage, no matter how vital other reforms may appear, let equal suffrage and equal suffrage alone be the issue of your organization. If your association allows itself to become identified with Socialism, Women's Christian Temperance work, Prohibition, reforms for working women, or any other measure, it will be at the expense of alienating the interest of some of the friends of your own cause. . . .

The planning of a campaign is the first work of a president and her board, but as the actual work must be carried out in committee a president should put her best effort into building up strong committees and in discovering fit chairmen. In this the president should insist on the advice and coöperation of her board. A committee once formed should be held responsible for the work for which it was created, and though the presiding officer may have to spend much time in keeping the committee up to its business, it is far more advantageous, on all accounts, that she should do this than that she should perform any part of its work, since the assumption of a committee's duties destroys its interest and usefulness. A committee may be reorganized and should be strengthened and refreshed by new members, as its work unfolds.

Whenever it is possible, volunteers should be placed at once upon some committee, because real work should be supplied for everyone. Experience in our campaign convinced us that when a woman was set actively to work her interest kindled and her neutrality warmed into partisanship. Sometimes a single errand to the printer's or a trip to arrange for a permit from the Chief of Police, was enough to draw in a new enthusiast, who, from that hour, felt that the work of the League was her own intimate concern. The vigor of a league may be measured by the number of its healthy and well-sustained enterprises, and this demands a body of ardent and intelligent workers, constantly reinforced by new members. . . .

---

1. College Equal Suffrage League of Northern California, *Winning Equal Suffrage in California* (San Francisco: National College Equal Suffrage League, 1913), 13–16.

One of the gravest puzzles of organizations is involved in the effort to attain a thorough coöperation between all the different suffrage societies of a State or city. How much time and effort can be wisely expended in harmonizing the work and plans of all? In an effort to attain such coöperation we had an Inter-league Conference, formed of representatives from all of the societies for equal suffrage in San Francisco, and we found that this body of eighteen was much too large for swift decisions, on a variety of complex activities. It is inevitable that the most conservative, or the most obstructive, members of such a group must either be converted, or swept along protesting, by the more enterprising majority. A small body of strong representatives should gain much by a short weekly conference, and if the chairman insists that no new plan can be submitted, except in writing, and that no member may speak more than once to a motion—until all have spoken—it is possible to control the waste of time to some extent. Perhaps the best plan is to coöperate on matters that show an unmistakable gain from large concerted action, such a plan as election day work at the polls, and to leave separate plans to be handled by each group, reporting upon them, in a very general way, at the weekly conference, to prevent any unfortunate interference of dates or engagements. With frankness and forethought there need not be the least rivalry between people who are all working for one end, and something is certainly gained by the experience of special groups in planning for the sort of people whose needs and interests they know best.

In all of the work, it should be borne in mind that a suffrage campaign is an educational campaign and must be kept clear-cut, clean and open. Invite interested members of the society, from time to time, to the meetings of your board, or executive committee. Every campaign will develop workers of good judgment and enthusiasm who will be invaluable assets in the work, and though such a worker may not become a voting member of the directorate, she should be made so welcome a guest at your councils that you can avail yourself of her experience and suggestions. No chairman of an important committee should ever be excluded from the board. Unity of aim and method, harmonious progress of plan and development can be attained only in this way. An intelligent visitor, who is present during the discussion of an important policy, who hears the pros and cons as they are advanced, gains a comprehension of a situation which is apt to bring both herself, and, eventually, the group to which she belongs, into harmony with the board's carefully worked out policy. Full and accurate information about any of the plans of the organization should be easily accessible to all members, and they should be encouraged to get a working knowledge of the progress of the work.

The president should remember that she is, first of all, presiding officer of the board, and that her chief duty is to see that the business of the board is conducted as quickly and efficiently as possible. She should not hesitate to use her gavel, nor to hold members of the board to business methods of debate and procedure. But she will weaken her board as a whole, and, therefore, her organization, if she assumes duties and responsibilities and makes decisions that rightfully devolve upon the board. She should never be drawn into any conference or correspondence that is not known to her directors, and that may not be freely told to any member. In this way, only, can she command the respect and confidence of her follow-workers, and upon this depends the position of her organization in the outside world. She must remember that no one person can develop a strong organization, and that her function is to bring out in her board and in her membership the spirit of good team-work. She must bring as many members as possible to the front—giving them as far as possible opportunities to carry out plans that enlist their special capabilities, and accord to them due credit for all such work. Let her not be afraid to put responsibility on others.

The president may well consider herself an understudy to every committee chairman and should stand ready to fill in gaps and avert failures in any work that has been undertaken, always bearing in mind that the committee should, when it is possible, be made to do its own work. It is more essential that a president sees that no piece of work, to which her league has put its hand or its name, fails, than that she inaugurate many new enterprises.

Above all, every worker for equal suffrage must believe in equal suffrage as a great, world-wide movement—an essential part of a moral and spiritual awakening; believe in it so firmly that faith begets courage and enthusiasm; and never forget that because it is a great, educational movement the foundation of work must be laid with all sincerity and truth.

43. LEGISLATIVE REFORM IN OREGON

Women's suffrage doubled the number of voters in one stroke, but additional electoral reforms, such as the recall, the ballot initiative, and the referendum, were necessary to enable voters to take action more quickly and (at least theoretically) efficiently. As tools for expressing voter preference and voter frustration, these innovations began popping up in states like Oregon and California not long after the turn of the century, and along with equal suffrage, they changed American voting. These excerpts from a volume addressing the Oregon reforms explain the basic tenets of direct government and give readers examples of how they operate. The recall, for instance, allowed voters to gather signatures on a petition declaring their dissatisfaction with an elected official. If they gathered enough signatures, a special election would be held to determine whether the official could continue in office. The initiative and the referendum allowed voters to take similar action over specific laws. It is interesting to note, as this document attests, that Oregon's recall law came about through an initiative movement of the state's voters. How would George Patton respond to these innovations? Would he be likely to claim that women would use innovations like the initiative or the recall differently from men? How does the Klamath County judge challenge the recall petition aimed at removing him from office?

Gilbert L. Hedges

From *Where the People Rule*
1914[1]

Enactment

The recall amendment to the Constitution was submitted by initiative petition to the vote of the electors at the regular election held in the State of Oregon on June 1, 1908. There were 58,381 votes cast for the amendment and 31,002 votes cast against it. By virtue of the proclamation of the Governor, the amendment became effective June 23, 1908. . . .

The Recall in Klamath County

The recall was invoked against William S. Worden, county judge of Klamath County. The petitions containing the required number of names were regularly filed and the county clerk called the election for June 2, 1913. Two candidates were placed in the field against the judge. One of these polled few votes and his part in the campaign was negligible. The principal reason for resorting to the recall was the court's decision to build a new court house upon a site some distance from the old building in the town of Klamath Falls, the county seat. Some of the older residents who were opposed to the change were instrumental in instituting and promoting the recall. Other charges were made and the campaign against the recall was conducted by Judge Worden with vigor and energy. He stumped the county and everywhere awakened the people to a full realization of the meaning of the election. The charges brought against the judge as set forth in the petition and on the sample ballot are as follows:

> Unlawful, unwise and inefficient management of county finances; the incurring of a large amount of unlawful indebtedness; unnecessarily increased taxation; waste of money in county expenses; favoritism in contracting with and employing relatives of members of the county court and certain firms and corporations at a financial loss to the county; unlawful issuing and selling warrants of the county at a discount; carelessness and inefficiency in auditing bills against the county; accepting employment from corporations whose interests are opposed to the public interests and at far greater salaries than that paid by the county; inefficient and unsatisfactory service as a county judge; failure to get value received for money spent for roads, though petitioners are not opposed to good roads; lack of ability, as shown in the past, to expend future levies for roads; inability to construct a new courthouse with

---

1. Gilbert L. Hedges, *Where the People Rule, or, The Initiative and Referendum, Direct Primary Law and the Recall in Use in the State of Oregon* (San Francisco: Bender-Moss, 1914), 93, 97–98, 107–10.

economy and a due regard for cost, though petitioners are not opposed to the new courthouse and are indifferent as to its location, but only insist that it shall be built economically and that the cost shall not be excessive, which the past actions of said officer indicate that he will not be able to do.

To these charges, the judge replied on the sample ballot as follows:

> This is not a regular election. It is an attempt to remove me from office in the middle of my term.
>
> Two years ago you elected me on a basis of Good Roads and the building of a new courthouse on the Hot Springs site. I have kept my promises. The work has been done well and as cheaply as consistent with permanency. What has been done will not have to be done over again.
>
> The new courthouse has been built economically and well. We have saved money for you in our plan.
>
> I deny the accusations of the opposition on the ground that they are gross misrepresentations and intended to cloud the issue and fool the voter. No other county in the state has accomplished so much in the way of good roads. The men who are behind this recall have threatened me ever since my term of office began unless I would submit to their dictation.
>
> The Grand Jury report was not correct and has been so proven relative to culvert, harness and other matters. If wrong in some, wrong in others. All I want is a square deal. The opposition will not give it.

With the exception of one paper, the press of the county was against the recall. This one paper was acquired by friends of Judge Worden before the campaign closed. The election was held pursuant to notice on June 2, 1913. The vote stood as follows: J. R. Ritter 56, Frank Ira Wade 974, and Wm. S. Worden 2286. By their votes, the people sustained the county judge and registered an emphatic protest against the recall movement. . . .

The Recall in the City of Medford

Medford is a thriving town of about 9,000 inhabitants, situated in the southern part of the State of Oregon. The progress made by this city during the past decade has been remarkable. The temper of the people is essentially progressive. The official acts of two of the city's councilmen were strongly disapproved by many of the leading citizens. This feeling against the two councilmen increased until it crystallized into a recall movement against them. The regular city election was held January 13, 1914, and prior to this date recall petitions had been circulated, signed and filed, and a recall election called for the date of the city election. The councilmen whose official acts were condemned were: G. H. Millar, councilman from the Third Ward, and J. E. Stewart, councilman from the Second Ward. To oppose G. H. Millar, the organization carrying on the recall campaign nominated Dr. H. P. Hargrave. To run against Councilman J. E. Stewart, the organization nominated Mr. V. J. Emerick.

Of all the recall elections held in the State of Oregon, this one in the city of Medford was probably the most exciting. Every voter within the corporate limits of the city was thoroughly alive to the issues involved. The newly enfranchised women played a prominent part in this election and the result may be ascribed, in great part, to their participation in the election.

The reason for demanding the recall of G. H. Millar as set forth on the sample ballot was:

> That the said G. H. Millar does not truly represent the residents of said (Third) Ward and because of his general incompetence and extravagance in office.

To this charge, Councilman Millar replied upon the sample ballot as follows:

> The recall charges of general incompetence, extravagance and not truly representing the residents of the Third ward, are both untrue and ridiculous, as a just investigation of the city records will prove.

The charge of general incompetence and extravagance in office was also made against Councilman J. E. Stewart and given as the reason for demanding his recall. To this charge J. E. Stewart replied as follows upon the sample ballot:

> One year ago the electors of my ward elected me to the office of council-man and I assumed the duties of that office in entire good faith and with a purpose on my part to perform those duties to the best of my ability and with a due regard to the welfare of my City. This purpose, I have performed; many accusations have been made as to misconduct in my official position, but no official act of mine has been pointed to as being a violation of my duties, or of my oath of office.
>
> If I have erred, it is an error of judgment; no person is infallible. If I should be recalled by the citizens of my ward, there can be no certainty of perfection of official conduct in my successor. He, too, may be fallible as myself.
>
> Should a man be recalled from an official position he occupies because somebody is piqued by his conduct or differs in judgment from him? Such a result is substantially a conviction, without trial, and a judgment without a preferred charge.
>
> I ask the suffrages[2] of my fellow citizens in my behalf.

The recall was successful and both councilmen were recalled. The vote by which Mr. Millar was deposed stood as follows: Millar 244, Hargrave 283. Councilman Steward received 300 and his opponent 368 votes.

The Recall Generally

In the preceding paragraphs specific instances of the use of the recall have been set forth. It will be noted that the highest office involved in these various elections has been that of county judge. . . . It is a difficult position to fill without making enemies. The county judges, who have run the gauntlet of the

---

2. **suffrages:** votes.

recall, have been attacked for their acts performed while sitting as a member of the board of county commissioners.

The recall has been used at times without sufficient reason. Since its enactment it has been used frequently, and with the lapse of time it will be invoked more often. Different officials have been threatened with the recall. A circuit judge was threatened with the recall because of his charge in a murder trial; a sheriff was threatened with the recall because of his vigorous suppression of a street speaking nuisance; an assessor has been threatened with the recall because he dared to do his duty and list property for taxation which many thought exempt.

The recall can not take the place of impeachment trials. Charges are preferred against an official under the recall amendment, but the campaign is a general campaign to defeat the incumbent by the use of any political device or charge. Quite often the charges preferred are ignored and title to office is tried with the people as judges by the introduction of any evidence which might be urged in an unrestricted political campaign.

To give those against whom the recall is invoked a fair trial, all of the people should be compelled to vote. A man's right to hold office should not be determined by a minority. It is not enough that the opportunity to pass upon a man's official acts should be given. He is entitled to have his right to hold office passed upon by the entire jury of qualified voters.

44. NEW VOTERS AND THE AMERICANIZATION MOVEMENT

Progressives expressed qualms about the ability of immigrants to participate in American politics, and this was true in the West no less than in other regions of the country. Progressives often latched onto "Americanization" as a way of allaying their own concerns about the effect of immigrants on American culture and American institutions. At heart, the effort was motivated by humanitarianism, but Americanization also imposed a set of ideas about citizenship determined by mainstream values on class, religion, and other concerns. In other words, while progressive reforms were broadening the voting base of the American polity, progressive reformers were working to Americanize new voters or the parents of American-born citizens along acceptable lines of behavior and culture. This selection illustrates some of the organizational strategies of the California Americanization effort spearheaded by the state's Commission of Immigration and Housing. How would you define "true democracy" as used in this selection? How would George Patton define the term? Charlotte Anita Whitney? Why do you think Americanization is seen as a problem?

California Commission of Immigration and Housing

From *Americanization*

1918[1]

Out of an actual experience in the field of Americanization extending over five years, the Commission of Immigration and Housing of California has evolved certain lessons which it has the honor of presenting to the attention of those interested in the subject.

᯾ First, the commission has come to a realization of the seriousness of the situation. . . . A nation made up, as is America, of diverse elements must be unified to be safe.

Then the commission's experience has brought out the fact that Americanization should take within its scope the native born as well as the immigrant. Not all antipatriots are foreign born. Furthermore, the attitude of the alien toward this country, in great part, is a reflection of the attitude of our own citizens towards him. Americanization should undertake to teach the duty of the host, not less than the duty of the guest.

Again, the commission has discovered that Americanization means infinitely more than teaching English to foreigners. That is of great importance, for many reasons, but there is much which can not wait for a new language, and which it is vitally important, both to the foreigner and to the country, that he should know. It must never be forgotten that these people are being transplanted, and "in transplanting it is fatal to destroy the roots." If while the roots are fresh and vital they are to find the subsoil of American ideals, of an intelligent conception of liberty and of a new loyalty, the foreigner must be reached in a language which he understands, and through media with which he is familiar.

Further, the commission has learned very definitely that to succeed in this task of Americanization, an organization must be thoroughly and sincerely democratic. All committees should carry representation of the foreign born and of labor. . . .

As the result of its successful pioneering efforts, the commission presents the following outline of a working program of Americanization, and offers its very hearty service to any and all counties of the state.

True democracy is the goal of Americanization.

Upon true democracy, then, must the Americanization movement itself be based and the spirit of that democracy must direct every aspect of the organization of such a movement.

---

1. State Commission of Immigration and Housing, *Americanization: The California Program* (Sacramento: California State Printing Office, 1918), 5, 7–8, 13.

The program of Americanization of the Commission of Immigration and Housing of California is built on this conviction. On this conviction also is built its method of procedure in organizing the state for this work.

The rapid awakening of our foreign-born element to the desirability of Americanization justifies our seeking their large co-operation. No program, however excellent, can have its best success when handed down ready-made from above. Only when it is built on the needs of the people, which they themselves best understand, and when they themselves have had a hand in its making, can it be a living and working thing.

And it is right that the foreign born and native born should share the responsibility of choice as to what is for the good of all.

Experience is showing that leaders in the foreign-born groups are ready and eager to enter upon this work, and to co-operate cordially with their American neighbors.

There is, in the working out of a program such as this, the greatest possible amount of unity and good feeling. There is, from the start, a sense of co-operation and friendliness. The pride of organization and the feeling of responsibility go far toward adjusting any possibility of disagreement at any point in the program, for that program must be recognized as an elastic thing, subject to modification by advancing experience. New problems will arise at every step and the greatest care will have to be given to each one of these. And only if throughout we are governed by the spirit of true democracy can we hope to keep our way.

The Commission of Immigration and Housing has been given charge of the entire subject of immigration in California. Upon the commission, therefore, rests the responsibility of definite plans for the solution of the problem of Americanization. . . .

In each county the commission is appointing a chairman of Americanization—an American-born man or woman, who can attract a more general following than a member of any foreign group.

The county chairman will seek out the leaders of various foreign groups, and invite them, with well informed representatives of the native born, to a meeting for organization, where these Americans, born here and abroad, will determine their plans. At this time the committees and subcommittees should be chosen, including men and women representing—

(*a*) Foreign born.
(*b*) Labor.
(*c*) Employers.
(*d*) Americanization organizations.
(*e*) Education authorities.

The county chairman should use the organized machinery of all existing agencies in carrying out the program. . . .

The county committee, including men and women representing the foreign born, labor, employers, Americanization organizations and educational authorities, should first *determine upon the exact task to be undertaken.*

To reach this determination definite information as to the foreign population must be gathered swiftly, by temporary committees, which may be appointed throughout the county, on

Nationality.

Education.

Social agencies.

The Committee on Nationality should secure careful estimates on

The number,

The nationality,

The location,

of the foreign-born people of the country. It should find whether these people live in groups or scattered throughout the community; whether they speak English, read foreign newspapers, attend foreign-speaking churches, have American standards of living and have contact with wholesome American living. . . .

45. CHILDREN IN THE FIELDS *(SEE P. 158)*

(SEE P. 158)

The Progressive Era saw real gains in the eradication of child labor across industrial America. Thanks to new and vigorously enforced laws, poor and working-class children, whose childhoods and bodies (and even lives) had been so commonly threatened in years past, were less and less likely to fill the ranks of those doing the most dangerous work in mines, factories, and sweatshops. But agricultural work still featured the labor of American children. Itinerant, and thus hard to track, working families went from farm to farm, harvest to harvest, and prohibitions against child labor often did not travel with them. Either because of enforcement challenges, or because reformers were less aggressive in policing farm and family labor than factories and assembly lines, planting and picking remained jobs in which kids shouldered a lot of the work. The father of these beet worker children, pictured on a farm in Colorado in 1915, said, "The children can thin the beets better than grown-ups. We all work fourteen hours a day at times because when the beets is ready they has to be done. About twelve weeks is about all the children can work on thinning and topping. Some of them hoe a little." Progressives may have patted themselves on the back for the work they did in cities and factories, but the wide-open spaces of the West's farms and ranches could tell a different story.

Attributed to Lewis Hine, *A Family Working on a Sugar Beet Farm in Northern Colorado*, 1915
Courtesy the Library of Congress Prints and Photographs Division.

FURTHER READING

Atkinson, Diane. *Votes for Women*. Cambridge, England: Cambridge University Press, 1988.

Beeton, Beverly. *Women Vote in the West: The Woman Suffrage Movement, 1869–1896*. New York: Garland, 1986.

Cherny, Robert. *Populism, Progressivism, and the Transformation of Nebraska Politics, 1885–1915*. Lincoln: University of Nebraska Press, 1981.

Cowan, Geoffrey. *Let the People Rule: Theodore Roosevelt and the Birth of the Presidential Primary*. New York: Norton, 2016.

———. *The People v. Clarence Darrow: The Bribery Trial of America's Greatest Lawyer*. New York: Times Books, 1993.

Deverell, William, and Tom Sitton, eds. *California Progressivism Revisited*. Berkeley: University of California Press, 1994.

Feinman, Ronald. *Twilight of Progressivism: The Western Republican Senators and the New Deal*. Baltimore: Johns Hopkins University Press, 1981.

Fitzpatrick, Ellen. *Endless Crusade: Women Social Scientists and Progressive Reform*. New York: Oxford University Press, 1990.

Gould, Lewis. *Reform and Regulation: American Politics, 1900–1916*. New York: Wiley, 1978.

Hays, Samuel P. *The Gospel of Efficiency: The Progressive Conservation Movement, 1890–1920*. Cambridge, MA: Harvard University Press, 1959.

Hofstadter, Richard. *The Age of Reform*. New York: Vintage, 1955.

Lehan, Richard Daniel. *Quest West: American Intellectual and Cultural Transformations*. Baton Rouge: Louisiana State University Press, 2014.

Lower, Richard. *A Bloc of One: The Political Career of Hiram Johnson*. Stanford, CA: Stanford University Press, 1993.

Mead, Rebecca. *How the Vote Was Won: Woman Suffrage in the United States, 1868–1914*. New York: New York University Press, 2004.

Olin, Spencer. *California's Prodigal Sons: Hiram Johnson and the Progressives*. Berkeley: University of California Press, 1968.

Sitton, Tom. *John Randolph Haynes, California Progressive*. Stanford, CA: Stanford University Press, 1992.

White, Richard, and John Findlay, eds. *Power and Place in the North American West*. Seattle: University of Washington Press, 1999.

Speakeasy in Oakland, California, 1929. The Eighteenth Amendment to the US Constitution outlawing "the manufacture, sale, or transportation" of alcoholic beverages went into effect in January 1920. Prohibition, long an issue of fierce debate in American politics and society, had become federal law. This police photograph of a speakeasy in Oakland captures the obvious discomfort of the illegal bar's patrons. Notice that they do not want their faces seen—some try to stay out of the picture altogether, but the mirror catches their reflections. Their reaction hints at the social and legal complexities of the era. Are they ashamed of breaking the law, or ashamed of the drinking? What does the photograph suggest about how western saloons changed after Prohibition became law?

The 1920s

10

Prohibition and the West

The 1920s stand out as one of the most contradictory periods in American history. The decade was characterized by creativity and economic exuberance on the one hand, and conservative repression on the other. A strong national economy led Americans to spend money on a vast array of consumer goods: cars, household appliances, radios, and thousands of other things. The 1920s also ushered in greater freedoms for women, marked most notably by the passage of the Nineteenth Amendment in 1920, which granted them the right to vote. Popular culture grew as radio and motion picture entertainment reached wider audiences, and Americans began listening to jazz, an innovative new form of music. African American artists, musicians, and writers came together in New York in the renowned artistic movement known as the Harlem Renaissance. The energy of the times inspired the decade's nickname: the Roaring Twenties.

But not everything was so rosy. Throughout the decade individuals and groups squared off in ferocious cultural battles all across the nation. Americans disagreed, often vehemently, over such issues as the role of science in schools, the place of immigrants in the country's future, and the morality (or immorality) promoted by urban culture. These clashes often pitted the modern values of city dwellers against the traditional values of country folk.

These tensions were mirrored in the Prohibition movement's efforts to outlaw the consumption of alcohol. Opposition to alcohol was inextricably intertwined with deeply held cultural traditions and religious beliefs. The Prohibition effort of the 1920s was only the latest stage in America's long-standing temperance crusade.

More than any other region, the American West propelled the Prohibition issue toward its final destination in 1919: the ratification of the Eighteenth Amendment forbidding the manufacture, distribution, or sale of alcoholic beverages. For years prior to this victory, the West promoted the issue, sometimes quietly but occasionally with considerable fanfare. Carrie Nation, a reformer of fearless religious conviction, became famous for her anti-saloon exploits in Kansas. She would barge into saloons swinging a club or a hatchet, smashing everything in sight.

On the less explosive side of the issue, the West acted as a proving ground for national legislation, much as it did for women's suffrage. Town after town "went dry" in the nineteenth century. In many cases they had started out that way when they were founded as Protestant, Mormon, or other alcohol-free communities. Local measures rapidly grew into statewide laws prohibiting liquor sales. Kansas outlawed the sale of liquor in 1878, and North Dakota and South Dakota by the end of the nineteenth century. Oklahoma entered the union as a dry state in 1907. Arizona, Colorado, Washington, and Oregon also adopted antiliquor laws. During World War I anti-German sentiment helped push Prohibition forward: breweries came under attack because the industry was dominated by German Americans, and many argued that a nation at war needed to turn grain into bread, not beer. By the time the Eighteenth Amendment went into effect, more than thirty states had already embraced Prohibition, the bulk of them in the West and the South.

Women's suffrage, an issue that, as we have seen, also had powerful western roots, likewise influenced Prohibition. Through the 1910s women campaigned for both suffrage and Prohibition, especially through such groups as the Woman's Christian Temperance Union. Historians recognize a connection between those western states that offered women the vote and those that embraced temperance legislation ahead of the rest of the nation. Even as far back as the 1850s women helped raise temperance before the eyes of the nation, and their activism in the West made the region, in the words of historian Richard White, "a bastion of prohibition."

Prohibition laid bare the tensions in American society. In the West as elsewhere, support and opposition were likely to break along religious and class lines with Protestants, Mormons, and the middle class more likely to be in favor of the ban on alcohol, and Catholics and the working class more likely opposed. Prohibitionists called the liquor interest a conspiracy against moral reform. Prohibition opponents fought the measure every bit as energetically. Brewery workers opposed Prohibition because it cost them their jobs. Catholics fought Prohibition because they felt the measure, supported by Protestants and anti-Catholic groups like the Ku Klux Klan, unfairly attacked their religion and culture. Others simply resented the measure as an intrusion into private life. In many ways, the Prohibition movement's moralistic overtones reflected other Progressive Era efforts, such as Americanization. The arrival of millions of eastern Europeans, the bulk of them Catholic and working class, exacerbated the conflict over Prohibition in the 1920s. The revival of the white supremacist Ku Klux Klan can in part be explained by the Klan's support for Prohibition and "traditional American values." The Klan also gained popularity by championing other supposedly "old-fashioned" values, such as anti-Catholicism and immigration restriction. In the mid-1920s the Klan briefly dominated the state governments of Colorado and Oregon. The West also added a further dimension to Prohibition squabbles with its long-standing history of liquor laws aimed at Native Americans.

Despite the passage of the Eighteenth Amendment and its enforcement legislation, the Volstead Act, Americans did not stop drinking (though statistics from the early 1920s suggest that they cut back). By the middle of the decade, however, rampant drinking and the rise of violent organized crime syndicates to control alcohol sales indicated that Prohibition had gone awry. Secret drinking establishments called speakeasies flourished. By the early 1930s, as the nation became preoccupied by the disaster of the Great Depression, Prohibition looked like a large-scale blunder. The Eighteenth Amendment was finally repealed in 1933.

The 1920s showed the growing pains of America's headlong rush into modernity. This chapter's selections provide a glimpse of America's struggle with modernity as it played out in the West. Pre-Prohibition subtleties from the legal code of Montana reveal the West as the vanguard of the nationwide move toward dunning alcohol. Accounts of public opinion and Prohibition enforcement—one focused on the Northwest and another on the Rockies—offer insight into the difficulties of making Prohibition stick. In the final selection, a physician offers reasons why Prohibition should be enforced.

AS YOU READ: Think of the ways in which the American West led the nation in the Prohibition movement. Why do you think it played this role? If, as historians argue, Prohibition was a reaction of the rural against the urban, of the native-born against the immigrant, of traditional America against modernism, how did these themes play out in the West?

46. MONTANA TAKES A STAND ON ALCOHOL

Laws about the consumption of liquor reveal a great deal about social attitudes. This is true even for the years preceding national Prohibition, as states and territories in the West experimented with various forms of legal temperance. This selection of the Montana legal code covering liquor laws prior to the Eighteenth Amendment is no exception. Note the special prohibitions aimed at women selling liquor and the sale of liquor to the state's Native American population, the latter a common feature of western liquor laws. It is curious, though, that the compiler of the pamphlet Liquor Laws of Montana *was one C. N. Kessler, a brewery owner and beer distributor. Can you construct a list of the events, issues, and people these laws are designed to control? In other words, what is at stake here besides the sale, purchase, or consumption of alcohol? What attitudes are being described and promoted by this kind of legislation? Why would someone in the alcohol business compile liquor statutes? What would he achieve by doing so?*

C. N. Kessler

From *Liquor Laws of Montana*
1915[1]

Sales to Drunkards, Minors and Indians Prohibited . . .

Section 8380. Every person who sells or gives intoxicating liquors to persons who are in the habit of getting drunk or intoxicated, or of drinking intoxicating liquors to excess, *after being notified in writing of such habit*, or who sells or gives intoxicating liquors to persons at the time in a state of intoxication, or visibly affected by intoxicating liquors, or who sells or gives intoxicating liquors to a minor or to an Indian, is liable in damage to any person who is injured thereby in money, property or means of support. In a suit for recovering damages named in this section, a married woman may sue in her own name and a minor by guardian.

Section 8380 (a). A violation of any of the provisions of this act shall be deemed a misdemeanor, and upon conviction the offender shall be punished by a fine of not less than Fifty Dollars and not exceeding Two Hundred and Fifty Dollars, and persons acting as servants, employees or agents shall be liable in the same manner as their employers or principals.

Section 8380 (b). Any person convicted a second time for a violation of the provisions of this act, in addition to the penalty above named, if he be engaged in the business of selling intoxicating liquors, shall be prohibited from the conduct of such business for a period of three months from the date of such conviction and any such person convicted a third time for a violation of the provisions of the act shall, in addition to the penalty prescribed in Section 8380 (a)

---

1. C. N. Kessler, *Liquor Laws of Montana* (Helena: Montana State Brewer's Association, 1915), 16–19.

hereof, be barred from obtaining a retail liquor license for a period of six months to three years within said county.

Section 2. Any minor who shall misstate his age shall be guilty of a misdemeanor, and any person who shall send a minor to any person to purchase any such intoxicating liquors shall be equally guilty with the person who shall give or sell such intoxicating liquor as provided in Section 1 of this act.

Section 8373. Sale of Liquors and Employing Women to Sell Liquors. Every person who sells or furnishes any malt, vinous or spirituous liquor to any person in the auditorium, boxes or lobbies of any theater, melodeon, variety show, museum, circus or caravan, or any place where any farce, comedy, tragedy, ballet, opera or play is being performed, or any exhibition of dancing, juggling, wax-work figures and the like is being given for public amusement, and every person who employs or procures or causes to be employed or procured any female to sell or furnish any malt, vinous or spirituous liquors at such place is guilty of a misdemeanor.

Section 8374. Selling Liquors at Camp Meeting. Every person who erects or keeps a booth, tent, stall or other contrivance for the purpose of selling or otherwise disposing of any wine, spirituous or intoxicating liquors or any drink of which wines, spirituous or intoxicating liquors form a part, or for selling or otherwise disposing of any article of merchandise, or who peddles or hawks about any such drink or article within one mile of any camp or field meeting for religious worship during the time of holding such meeting is punishable by a fine of not less than five nor more than five hundred dollars. . . .

Section 8376. Females Exhibited in Public Places. Every person who causes, procures or employs any female for hire, drink or gain to play upon any musical instrument or to dance, wait, promenade or otherwise exhibit herself in any drinking saloon, dance-cellar, ball-room, public garden, public highway, common park or street, or in any steamboat or railroad car, or in any place whatsoever, if in such place there is connected therewith the sale or use as a beverage of any intoxicating, spirituous, vinous or malt liquors, or who shall allow the same in any premises under his control where intoxicating, spirituous, vinous or malt liquors are sold or used, when two or more persons are present, is punishable by a fine of not less than fifty nor more than five hundred dollars or by imprisonment in the county jail not exceeding three months, or both; and every female so playing upon any musical instrument or dancing, waiting, promenading or exhibiting herself, as herein aforesaid, is punishable by a fine not exceeding one hundred dollars or by imprisonment in the county jail not exceeding one month, or both.

Section 8382. Prohibition against Use of Screens and Other Obstructions in Saloons. During the time or hours when, by the provisions of any statute of the State of Montana saloons must close, all curtains, screens, movable blinds, shutters, paint, frost, dirt, or other things that obstruct the view from the outside of the bar or place in any saloon where liquors are sold, or kept for sale, shall be removed. It shall be the duty of every owner, licensee, proprietor or employee in charge of any saloon to remove any and all movable obstruction or obstructions at the hour that the saloon is by law required to close, or within fifteen minutes after said hour.

Section 8383. Wine Rooms or Private Apartments in Saloon Must Be Kept Open to Public View. It shall be unlawful to erect or maintain or allow to remain in existence in, or in connection with any saloon, either as a part thereof or as an adjunct thereto, or on any floor, or in any basement of any saloon, any wine room, or private apartment, with any door, curtain or screen of any kind, or any room or private apartment unless the interior thereof is left open to public view, and unless there be an opening from such rooms or apartments of at least three feet in width and six feet in height, without any curtains or screens whatsoever in, or in front of, or inside of such opening or in any passageway connected therewith or adjacent thereto. And every day during which any such prohibited apartment or room is maintained or allowed to remain in existence shall be deemed a separate offense.

Section 8384. Prohibition against Female Persons Entering Saloons. It shall be unlawful for any owner, licensee, proprietor or manager of any saloon, or his clerk, agent, servant or bar tender, to have with, or as a part of, any saloon any room or apartment, with or without door or doors, curtain or curtains, or screen of any kind, in which any female persons shall be permitted to enter from the outside or from such saloon.

Section 8385. Same (as above). It shall be unlawful for any owner, licensee, manager, clerk, agent, bar tender, or other employee, having for the time being charge or control of any saloon, or any place connected therewith, either by doors or otherwise, to suffer or permit any female person to be or remain in such saloon, or place connected therewith, for the purpose of being there supplied with any kind of liquor whatsoever. Provided, that when a bar-room is maintained in any hotel, this act shall not be construed to apply to the parts of the building where the other business of the hotel is transacted.

Section 8386. Prohibiting Display of Certain Signs. It shall be unlawful for any owner, proprietor, licensee, manager or other person owning, running or conducting any saloon, to put up, maintain or allow to remain in place over or near any door, or in or near any passageway, opening or leading into such saloon the words "ladies' entrance," or "women's entrance," or "private entrance," or any words of like import on any wall, door, sign board or otherwise.

Section 8387. Loitering of Female around Saloon Prima Facie Evidence of Guilt. If it shall appear that any female shall at any time be allowed loiter in any saloon, or to be or remain in any room, apartment or place in or connected with such saloon, such fact shall be prima facie evidence or presumptive evidence that such female was permitted to be or remain in said saloon or place connected therewith for the purpose of being supplied with liquor, and shall be prima facie or presumptive evidence in favor of the guilt of the accused party or parties. *Provided*, that when a bar-room is maintained in any hotel, this act shall not be construed to apply to the parts of the building where the other business of the hotel is transacted. . . .

47. WET AND DRY IN THE FAR WEST

The historian George Fort Milton traveled through the West in 1926 trying to track the region's sentiments on Prohibition for the important national journal Century Magazine. *He found that while western "wets," those who favored repeal of Prohibition, appeared to have great influence, the dry forces could count on getting more people to vote to keep Prohibition going. His descriptions here, especially those of the Pacific coast and Montana, hint at the complexity of the issue. What western groups would you expect to be vociferous wets? Which would you expect to be dry? Why do you think the wets were unable to muster strength at the ballot box, despite their outspokenness? How does Milton's account of Prohibition support and enforcement in the West compare with the findings of Martha Bensley Bruere or August Kuhlmann in the selections that follow?*

George Fort Milton
"The Wets and the West"
1926[1]

Not even the most ardent dry will contend that Rudyard Kipling had prohibition in mind when he made his famous assertion regarding East and West and the improbability of their ever meeting.[2] Yet despite the modification demands of the Eastern wets, the facts are that the "heart of America"—to use Woodrow Wilson's characterization of the country west of the Mississippi—is becoming more and more convinced of the value and necessity of prohibition.

. . . From my observations, conversations, and experiences, I should say, speaking broadly, that the wet drive has failed in the West. . . .

Several well intentioned newspaper gentlemen recently devised the idea of a series of nation-wide polls that they might ascertain the general feeling toward prohibition. The result of these polls was received by the dripping wets, the moists, and even the merely humids as evidence of a vast overturn of public sentiment, and as foreshadowing the doom of the Volstead Act.

---

1. *Century Magazine* 112 (July 1926): 344–47.
2. **meeting:** This reference is to a line in "The Ballad of East and West," a poem by the English author and poet Rudyard Kipling (1865–1936), that reads, "Oh, East is East, and West is West, and never the twain shall meet."

Such a poll was stirring up the citizens of the hospitable city of Seattle during the week of my visit there. Pretty constantly it ran about seven wet to one dry. The totals were rather amazing. Not only were polls conducted, but one of the city's newspapers, not in the poll-conducting group, was so conscious of its lack that it opened a letter-writing contest offering large cash prizes for the best arguments for and against prohibition. The wets proved to be the readier letter writers, although the difference was not nearly so great as in the coupon-clipping polls of the other papers.

At the same time Seattle was quarreling her way through a city election campaign, and as usual there was a variety of alleged issues. One of the candidates was Mayor Edwin J. Brown, an ex-socialist, dentist, lawyer, and would-be successor to himself. He had gained considerable national reputation by forceful handling of some I.W.W.[3] disturbances in Seattle; he had a powerful political organization; and even his enemies conceded him an eccentric and appealing career, as well as a strong and vote-getting personality.

Now Dr. Brown had been mayor of Seattle for a number of years. He had all the prestige and the power that the office always gives. Incidentally—no, not incidentally, but by intention and most vigorously—Dr. Brown was wet. One of his pungent campaign phrases was, "You can't run a seaport town like a church bazaar."

His opponent was a woman, Mrs. Bertha K. Landes, the wife of a professor at the University of Washington. She was not unknown in Seattle's public life, as she had once been president of the city council and had clashed with the mayor a number of times. . . .

Mrs. Landes is a dry. She believes in the enforcement of the prohibition law, both State and national. One of her campaign planks was for cleaning up and drying up Seattle. Of course there were other issues on which the candidates were divided; as, for example, Mrs. Landes favored the city manager form of government, while Brown frowned on it. Both were supposed to be friendly to continued municipal ownership and operation of Seattle's amazing power project. But the dominant issue between them was defined by most local observers as "wide open" against law enforcement.

Mrs. Landes won. The total votes were: Landes, 48,700; Brown, 42,802. Out of 91,502 votes, she had a majority of 5898.

So there can be seen, side by side, the seven-to-one wet straw vote in Seattle newspapers, and the eight-to-seven prohibition enforcement vote in Seattle ballot-boxes. . . .

A San Franciscan's pithy comment on the situation in California perhaps indicates the general Western trend:

"Never depend on the wet vote. It talks big and votes little. The straw polls are a joke. The wets vote in the newspapers. The drys vote in the elections."

---

3. **I.W.W.:** Industrial Workers of the World, a radical labor organization, prominent in the timber belt of the Northwest in the early twentieth century.

A wet himself, he was disgusted with the people on whose support he felt he should have been able to count in a recent election.

"California to-day would go a hundred and fifty thousand or more dry," he went on. . . .

"Why, look at it! When the country and the State were wet, we had all the wet influences organized and active to keep us wet: the brewers, and the distillers—organized, financed, and politically powerful; the property-owners who rented to saloons; the saloons themselves—the 'poor man's club'; the dives and speak-easies; the men who loved to drink and who wanted to be able to keep on drinking. And then last, but not least, the theoretical wet who believed in 'personal liberty.' And don't forget the grape and hop growers, the brewery unions, and all of their ties and connections.

"And still the country went dry, and the State voted for the enforcement act. Where can the wets get to-day? They had it then and couldn't keep it. Anybody that tells you California is wet is stringing you."

The California grape-grower was generally conceded to be on friendly terms with the wine-cup. But he is so no longer. For curiously enough, he is making more money under Volstead than he did in the good old days.

Before prohibition the wine-grape grower often was paid as low as $8 a ton and seldom higher than $30 a ton for his grapes. Since prohibition he has been getting from $60 to $140 a ton. Perhaps many of his grapes go into home-made wine. But a limited quantity of home-made wine for home consumption is not a violation of the Volstead Act. Raisins have had a tremendously increased sale, while grape-juice is in demand where its existence was not even recognized before. . . .

Montana is to have another test of strength this fall. Having easily secured the small percentage of registered voters necessary to a referendum, the wets have put on the November ballot a drink or dry query. They are conducting a well financed and highly organized campaign.

But during my trip through Montana Governor John Erickson and ex-Governor Sam V. Stewart assured me that in their opinion the referendum would show Montana quite as dry as ever. Butte and Helena, they thought, might go wet, as both have a large foreign mining element. But the dry farmers of the State are expected to overwhelm these wet city ballots.

As against this opinion, a prominent Butte lawyer believes that the reverse will happen, that the Butte-Helena vote will overcome the farmer. Only the election will tell.

In none of the Western States could I learn of any definite tendency toward modification. In Nebraska some of the associates of former Senator Gilbert M. Hitchcock, who has been an anti-prohibition champion, privately admitted that they thought Nebraska drier than ever. Nowhere could I find a friend of the swinging door and the brass rail, the unsung and unhonored American saloon.

The States in which prohibition sentiment seemed to be gaining, chiefly because of economic conditions, are, I should say, California, Wisconsin, Iowa, and Nebraska. The States in which the increasing support is due to moral convictions would include the two Dakotas, Montana, Idaho, Washington, Oregon, Utah, Colorado, and the other intermountain States. . . .

The Western drys did not seem to understand that the Eastern wets are as resolute in their wetness as they themselves are determined in their dryness. . . . As the sides line up it really begins to look—and unfortunately—as if the East is East and the West is West.

48. PROHIBITION IN THE MOUNTAIN WEST

From the very moment that it became law, Prohibition came under intense scrutiny. Did it work? In this selection, Martha Bensley Bruere, a social worker and writer, examines Prohibition in the mountain states of the West. Working with a small team, she distributed a detailed questionnaire on Prohibition to social workers. They asked respondents about local declines in alcoholism, any rise in crime and delinquency rates, and such things as "the political significance of the present disregard of the amendment." Her findings about Prohibition and the legacies of earlier antiliquor legislation, published as Does Prohibition Work?, *reveal the differences in opinion in places like Colorado compared to Nevada. What specific social or political realities in the mountain West made enforcement or support of Prohibition so complex? How would you compare the findings of Bruere with those of George Fort Milton in the Northwest and C. N. Kessler in Montana? How would you explain regional differences?*

Martha Bensley Bruere
From *Does Prohibition Work?*
1927[1]

South of the Inland Empire the high Sierras cross and crisscross. They divide populations from one another, interests and occupations. Mountains, deserts and tablelands know both solitary prospectors and city populations. Here lies a wilderness tamed by religious devotion; there is a wilderness not yet tracked except by wild creatures. Here is a man's world and men's work. Can prohibition be enforced under these physical and psychological conditions?

Colorado, in a revolt against the saloon, went dry in 1914. The dry votes came largely from the small towns and cities with a Nordic population, from the agricultural districts and financial centers. Labor generally and the mining

---

1. Martha Bensley Bruere, *Does Prohibition Work?* (New York: Harper and Brothers, 1927), 31–37.

camps of southern Colorado were wet. Here are populations from the south and east of Europe and from Mexico. It was believed by many that the elimination of the saloon would diminish labor troubles, which at times, in the Colorado Fuel and Iron mines, had developed into veritable warfare.

Today, reports from the social workers show the old lines of cleavage. The press of the cities and rural districts is dry and for enforcement. The mining camps are relatively wet and the rank and file of labor is for modification. Labor's leaders tend to copy the bosses—to speak "dry." Denver's local enforcement problem is complicated by the fact that the city is a Mecca for conventions, for great hordes of summer vacationists, for a transient population which brings in a personal interpretation of the law. There is further complication by the winter hibernation of hundreds of Mexican beet-field workers in the city. To them boot-legging is not a serious crime.

"We believe," writes Mrs. Anna G. Williams of the Denver Social Service Bureau, "that while rum was a great disturber of domestic peace, it was but a minor cause of poverty. Prisoners in making application for parole used to state that they were intoxicated at the time they committed their crimes. Among the poorer families statistics show greater savings and a higher standard of living."

The report from a social worker of Boulder is enthusiastic. Here is the state college and here there has always been local option.[2]

"In a recent election, Colorado overwhelmingly defeated the attempt to change the Volstead Act. Colorado may not be entirely satisfied with prohibition enforcement, but it is not entirely satisfied with the divorce laws, either. Burglary still goes on, but we do not repeal the laws against it because they do not operate. Boulder has no recent comparisons to make, for it refused to consider saloons for years, but the surrounding towns, particularly mining camps, were hotbeds of drinking and vice. Boulder escaped the delirium tremens, poverty, crime, undernourished children, and dirt of the surrounding mining camps where saloons flourished."

"The only noticeable effect of state prohibition, which came in 1914, was the decrease in the number of homeless men," writes Mr. Justin L. Hills of the Colorado Springs Associated Charities. "And we felt that in all probability this was because the men who were making their transcontinental tours[3] followed the southern route through Wyoming, which had remained wet, or the southern route through wet New Mexico."

Colorado Springs, since its founding in 1871, has always had a clause in all deeds that no intoxicating liquors shall be manufactured, sold, or otherwise disposed of in any public place or upon any premises within the city of Colorado Springs. An infraction of this law causes the property to revert to the original owner.

---

2. **local option:** when voters declare a particular jurisdiction—a town or a county—dry.
3. **transcontinental tours:** often by stowing away on railroad cars.

"Therefore," Mr. Hills writes, "with the enactment of national prohibition there was no noticeable change in the family problem. Probably the amendment has had no effect one way or the other in the amount and nature of crime and disorder in this distinctly American town, where public conviction is wholly on the side of law enforcement."

Just as Colorado is made sectional by its geography, so is it made sectional by religion, by industry, by race. It is natural that the enforcement of prohibition should also show sectional differences. The Klan, Protestant and dry, has fought the Catholics, fought "wets," fought "foreigners." Issues have become confused by the injection of extraneous factors. A "dry" foreign miner is driven into the camp of the "wets" to protect himself from junker Americanism.[4] An American with sentiments for a modification of the Volstead Act is driven into the camp of the "drys" because of the attack on his religion. This confusing of interests, the blending of hatreds, has divided the state in factional allegiances and complicated considerably law enforcement.

In southern Colorado, among the coal and metal miners, and in the beet fields among the Mexicans, there is widespread feeling that prohibition was imposed upon the workingman by the mine-owning class and large employers who thought thereby the better to control and further to exploit him. They see the law unequally applied; the homes of the workingmen unlawfully entered, judges holding that if liquor is found the entry was justified. They know the homes of the financially powerful are safe against such raiding. With the knowledge that the interests which they have so long fought in their struggle for wages and protection are publicly dry and often privately wet, labor has always been antagonistic to dry laws, and officers without the backing of public sentiment find enforcement in mining camps extremely difficult. Lonely gulches and isolated ravines furnish places, as in the mountains of Kentucky, for the manufacture of "moonshine," and people used to hard liquor as well as to drudging labor are resistant to the Eighteenth Amendment.

Enforcement officers in Colorado have geographical barriers on their side. Colorado is as isolated as an island from the mainland of bootleggers. North of the state are mountains and barren plains; east of it are driest Kansas and sparsely settled Oklahoma; south is New Mexico with its deserts and sandstorms; west is Utah, dry Mormon territory. With the militant Klan, with newspapers, with great financial interests, with a large Nordic-American population, with an arid boundary, all on the side of the Eighteenth Amendment, Colorado's enforcement problem should not be so difficult as that of other mountain states. . . .

What of Nevada's attitude toward the Eighteenth Amendment? In November, 1926, Nevada, in a vote of 12,500 as opposed to 3,290, demanded that a

---

4. **junker Americanism:** a reference to the charged anti-German patriotism of World War I.

constitutional convention be called for amending the Volstead Act. Nevada further said, in a vote of 11,840 as against 3,350, that "experience has demonstrated that the attempt to abolish recognized abuses of the liquor traffic by the radical means of constitutional prohibition has generally failed of its purpose."

This is the conclusion of the desert state with a surplus male population after eight years of national prohibition.

According to Mrs. F. E. Humphrey of Reno, a former social worker, the net gain of prohibition is that the saloon is done away and with it the treating habit. Alcohol was only a minor cause of poverty and many of the social and economic troubles of other states "are not real troubles here."

As regards youth, Mrs. Humphrey says that "the situation is much worse than before prohibition. It is now the smart thing to carry a flask. Nobody respects a law that cannot be enforced. The danger of blindness is a menace. There are 'rings' everywhere and anybody can get liquor." Mrs. Humphrey, herself a club woman, says that many mothers' clubs feel a grave mistake has been made and the majority of people who voted "dry" want the law amended to governmental control. . . .

Other social workers give a different picture. Mrs. M. L. Macauley, executive secretary of the American Red Cross, says: "I do know that many families who knew no comfort under the saloon conditions, whose earners spent every dollar obtainable drinking and left their dependents to be fed, clothed, and cared for by charitable organizations or kind neighbors, now are independent. They buy food, clothing and small luxuries, enjoy the movies, go into the higher grades in school, and are generally progressive.

"While we hear of the cases of bootlegging all too often to suit law-abiding people, they are really not numerous when compared with the great bulk of our people who are going along, without a thought of stepping backward after the big move forward.

"The poverty we are meeting in our work here in Reno is largely due to the restless spirit bred by unemployment. Many unsuccessful people, believing that another locality will afford better opportunity, buy cheap cars and start out. Result: greater poverty and need for help elsewhere. Drink does not enter into our cases. Of old it was the great trouble. All of the causes contributing to poverty cannot begin to furnish the trouble that was due of old to drink alone."

The principal of the Reno high school, Mr. E. Otis Vaughn, says: "I know from my experience, dating back to 1907, that there is very much less habit-forming drinking. I believe that prohibition has been very successful, when we consider the slight hold that the liquor habit has on our young people today."

With this conclusion, Mr. J. A. Fulton, director of the Mackay School of Mines, connected with the University of Nevada, agrees: "At our meeting of deans of the different departments here in the University last Monday, I asked the assembled deans what their opinion was as regards the beneficial results of prohibition here in the University among the student body. The replies were all of a uniform nature, namely that the student body was much more orderly, that there was much less evidence of drinking at dances and at other gatherings, and that the opinion of the deans was that there was no question that Eighteenth Amendment had been very beneficial to this student body."

Nevada, in the orderly way provided by democratic government, in a vote over three to one, says prohibition has failed—Colorado by the same test says it is a success.

49. A PHYSICIAN SUPPORTS PROHIBITION

Both before and after it became law, Prohibition kept printers busy as each side of the debate hustled out pamphlets and booklets to support or protest the ban on alcohol. In this typical Prohibitionist tract, August Kuhlmann, a physician, suggests that Prohibition is good for both the human body and the body politic. He traces the impact of Prohibition legislation by studying the groups and individuals who operate in violation of the law. Prohibition's supporters, in the West as well as elsewhere, sought the endorsement of physicians like Kuhlmann, believing that publicity on the health benefits of an alcohol-free society would only help their cause. In this passage, however, the writer makes much of Prohibition's tendency to create a criminal underclass, which would be quick to take advantage of the situation. How could an experiment often couched in tones of moral reform possibly countenance the high levels of lawbreaking—from illegal cocktail parties to large-scale rum-running—that immediately followed adoption of the Eighteenth Amendment? What are the major points in Kuhlmann's essay? How does he characterize the impact of Prohibition? What comparisons does he make between the health of individuals and the health of the nation? Why does Kuhlmann argue that Prohibition ought to be obeyed?

August Kuhlmann

From *Prohibition as It Is in Some Parts of the West*
1928[1]

. . . Liquor in a moderate form in the proper quantity would hardly hurt anybody. It is a mild stimulant and appetizer, and creates a little pep, but, most all of us who do some observing realize it sometimes creates an awful undesirable habit.

Some of the most sincere arguments that prohibition reduces crime, empties our jails, and changes the people to a more noble and higher level have all

---

1. August Kuhlmann, MD, *Prohibition as It Is in Some Parts of the West* (n.p., 1928).

been (apparently) shattered so far; because there evidently is more crime now, than there was before prohibition.

In spite of all the above arguments we can live just as happy without booze as with booze. It is a luxury and sometimes worse than that. In fact if a young man would ask me about certain points, for success in life, one point I would emphasize in my advice would be, "keep away from booze." If we all would do that, it would settle the whole prohibition problem at once. But we know people think differently. We have to abide by the happy majority, otherwise we would live in a state of continuous warfare. To conquer ourselves is the greatest victory. Let us enjoy liberty, but we must not infringe upon the liberty of others. These are all wise sayings which mean we should always consider our neighbor. If the money involved in the liquor traffic would be taken out, it would quickly die a natural death.

That there is too much brewing in some parts of the country is unquestionably true, and it is a big factor to destroy the morale of our youth and land. Since moon-shining is here and is a big business, so let us discuss it as follows: There are four main types or classes involved in order of their importance.

1. Hijackers.
2. Active distillers, cookers, bootleggers, and dispensaries.
3. The army of soaks—or losers.
4. The irreconcilables and defenders of personal liberty.

The hi-jackers are the real brains of the moonshine business. They are a class of people of the intelligent type. They are in the business only and solely for making easy money quickly. They are working in the dark. They are fully conscious of the penalty attached. Therefore hire their underlings to do the active work. They furnish the money for the equipment, stills, etc., and take over the finished product. They like to shine in society and make propaganda for their business. They organize and facilitate transportation and attend to the wholesale work. They see to it that something is furnished at parties, dances, etc. They sometimes out-wit the clergy at church parties.

You see them often sitting at special tables at church parties, gambling or playing for money in a conspicuous place. They have the moon in a coal bin or automobile attended to by an underling. They like to have prominent people with them to advertise through them to make an impression. In smaller towns or villages they like to get a mayor or president elected who is under obligation to them and who is willing to hire an extra policeman to look out for the federal agents.

They are a very clever bunch and have a conscience like a rubber bag, that will stretch as long as a dollar is in sight. They like to pose and have their tools sitting on a wagon box or grandstand on public occasions for public adoration in order to make an impression. They are smooth-tongued artists and inspire their force under them as if they were heroes.

They work on the ignorant and superstitious—trying to make them believe it is all right to make moon because Christ made wine and that Eve ate from the forbidden apple. They try to make people believe that moon is a cure for many ills. They usually have a roll of cash with them that staggers almost some federal agents and paralyzes them. Some like to act as a double—a law-breaker and a law-enforcer. If you are siding with them they are jake, but if you do not pull with them, then they are dirty fighters—fabricate false stories and slander for punishment. They try to get a person mixed up with them in order to stick.

They enjoy holding high offices in lodges where the ritual is against booze in order to make it look absurd and hypocritical. They are a polished class trying to brush everything aside that is not working with them in order to make clear sailing for their underlings. So you see they are a dirty set and hypocrites destroying the public morale and decency. In this class we find the pistol shoot-ers, safe-crackers and love artists.

The second class includes the active distiller, cooker, the bootlegger and dis-penser. They are not so hard and rotten as class number one—the hi-jackers. They are also mainly in the business because it is easy money, and for other rea-sons. Some say, "I am in this business because it is easy money to make a living. It means bread and butter for me and my family." Some say, "I want to make a few thousand in order to get a start in something else then I'll get out." Some are out of a job and class number one offers them a great inducement. Some young fellows want to shine and get a car because they are furnished by class number one. Some have lost money in banks, etc., and think it is all right to get it back in some way or another.

Of late many farmers have fallen victims and have been induced by the hi-jackers, because it has been told them, that it is an easy way to pay off their mortgage and make money. In fact they are outwitted by class number one because they want to have a place where they can put their stills, get their raw supply easily and feel secure. It is surprising to find some good farmers where you least expect it.

It has been a very good winter for the cookers on account of the abundance of snow. Many of the roads were impassable and they felt secure. There are thousands and thousands of gallons hidden and stored up. There is such a sup-ply on hand by the subs, who are not in with class number one, that a gallon of liquor has gone down to three dollars. A sign of over-production—an index of trade, of supply and demand. Some of these moonshiners drive fine cars, thereby creating the admiration of the youth and the envy of some ladies. Some think a person cannot be sociable unless you dish out some booze to their friends. They look upon you with scorn and disdain if you refuse a drink. Most of these farmers who dabbled in this business have lost more by not attending to their farms than they have made. Some are making soaks out of themselves and their children and spoiling the neighbor's children.

What they call a good bootlegger, is usually a bold and a confirmed liar. They seem to have a certain admiration or fear of class number one—the hi-jackers.

The third class includes the "army of soaks"—because they like the stuff. It seems they are not happy unless they have a few under their belts. They sacrifice everything in order to get booze. One of their most fervent prayers seems to be: "I and my stomach—my stomach and myself—have mercy on me, amen." This class are always the losers; but they do not seem to have the moral and physical stamina to hang on to themselves. Some claim they have to take a shot before they go to church and think they can pray better and take another afterwards so it soaks in. Some claim they can work better. Some get drunk when they have a quarrel with their wife and seek consolation in a saloon, because a good saloon-keeper never contradicts his patrons.

The fourth class constitute the irreconcilables and defenders of personal liberty. These are otherwise a well-balanced crowd. They can afford to take a drink and know how to handle themselves. They have been accustomed to take a drink before and stay within the psychological limit.

They insist that prohibition is an infringement of their personal liberty. They take a drink and make nothing of it. They are indifferent until it strikes home, until their sons or daughters are meshed in what they know is not very honorable.

Now what is the solution for a right-minded citizen, hearing all these pros and cons; some say, "it almost makes a person crazy." Some think "the world is coming to an end," etc. Nothing to it! The solution is a simple one. Since it is the law of the land we as citizens have to obey the law for the sake of our country, until we change the law to a different form in an election. Those who think they can defy the United States government are sadly mistaken.

FURTHER READING

Bader, Robert S. *Prohibition in Kansas*. Lawrence: University Press of Kansas, 1986.

Blocker, Jack S. *Retreat from Reform: The Prohibition Movement in the United States, 1890–1913*. Westport, CT: Greenwood, 1976.

Clark, Norman H. *The Dry Year: Prohibition and Social Change in Washington*. Seattle: University of Washington Press, 1965.

Dumenil, Lynn. *The Modern Temper: American Culture and Society in the 1920s*. New York: Hill and Wang, 1995.

Goldberg, Robert. *Hooded Empire: The Ku Klux Klan in Colorado*. Urbana: University of Illinois Press, 1981.

Gould, Lewis L. *Progressives and Prohibitionists: Texas Democrats in the Wilson Era*. Austin: University of Texas Press, 1973.

Kerr, K. Austin. *Organized for Prohibition: A New History of the Anti-Saloon League*. New Haven, CT: Yale University Press, 1985.

McGirr, Lisa. *The War on Alcohol: Prohibition and the Rise of the American State*. New York: W. W. Norton, 2016.

Noel, Thomas J. *The City and the Saloon: Denver, 1858–1916*. Lincoln: University of Nebraska Press, 1982.

CCC workers in Coeur d'Alene National Forest, 1934. This photograph shows young men planting trees in an Idaho forest following a forest fire. They are members of the Civilian Conservation Corps (CCC), one of dozens of federal programs created by the Roosevelt administration to put people to work during the Great Depression. CCC workers, mostly young men, spread out across the West planting trees, fighting fires, and building trails. Their projects, many of which are still visible and in use today, helped refashion and reshape vast stretches of the western landscape. The CCC owed much of its organizational ethos to the US military. What clues about its military orientation can you identify in this photograph? Are you aware of any CCC projects near where you live?

Courtesy the US Forest Service.

The Great Depression

The New Deal and the Western Landscape

Few periods in American history have demonstrated the transformative power of the Great Depression. For comparison, we would probably have to point to the establishment of the nation, coming out of the era of the American Revolution, and the fighting and aftermath of the Civil War. The years between 1930 and the coming of US involvement in World War II in 1941 were punctuated by national and international events: the stock market crash in the fall of 1929; the introduction of President Franklin D. Roosevelt's array of New Deal programs; and the Japanese attack on Pearl Harbor in 1941. The Depression itself was not limited in any way to the United States and was every bit as much of a global crisis as the war that followed. Even so, the Depression's impacts and effects varied from region to region across the United States; what it meant, what it felt like, and what was done to mitigate its worst aspects took on particular aspects in and across the West, and it is those specific aspects that we examine in the documents below.

The roots of the Great Depression stretch back far earlier than 1929. Much of the difficulty can be assigned to overconfidence. As world markets for natural resources (many of them coming out of the West, such as timber, coal, oil, and all kinds of farming commodities) began to dry up in the late 1920s, Americans were slow to recognize signs of impending trouble. For the most part, people continued with life and business as usual, and they also continued to speculate in an overheated stock market.

This was a big mistake. Along with millions of Americans who failed to heed the signs of economic distress, the president of the United States missed all the signs. A mining engineer born poor on an Iowa farm, raised in Oregon, and educated at Stanford University in Northern California, Herbert Hoover had risen to worldwide acclaim during World War I through his relief work in war-torn Europe. In 1928 he became the first US president to be elected from the American West. Nine months later, the stock market collapsed, and the Great Depression arrived.

President Hoover was convinced that the nation could weather the storm, and he placed the blame for the Depression on crashing European economies. He thought that little could be done, and that it was only a matter of time before the US economy righted itself. In his thinking, federal intervention was both unwise and unwarranted. But Hoover was wrong. His inability to grasp the magnitude of the economic crisis doomed him politically and has tarnished his legacy ever since. By the early 1930s, homeless Americans—many of whom had never before faced such trouble—mocked the president by naming their shantytown communities "Hoovervilles" or "Hoovertowns." They were hardly alone in their antipathy toward the president. Unemployment continued to rise, and before long, 25 percent of the workforce was out of work. Across the nation, charitable groups as well as social service providers at the local, state, and federal levels buckled under the pressure of having to respond to so many people in need and distress. Families tried to make do with less; people began to grow more of their own food; and family members moved in with one another to wait out the crisis as best they could.

By 1932 political dissent and anger was on the rise, with particular power in the West. In some places and in some circumstances, people and groups threatened violence unless the government stepped in to help alleviate at least some of the misery. By that summer, thousands of World War I veterans, a great many of them coming from the West, banded together in a great march on Washington, DC, hoping to pressure Congress to authorize early payment of their military pensions. Farmers throughout the West, fearful of losing homes and farms, banded together in ways that looked at least a little bit like Populism of yore, and tried to force the government to do something about farm commodity prices, which had fallen through the floor. When President Hoover ran for reelection in 1932, even though he had some powerful western support, he could not succeed. The Depression was too severe, and his response to it had been too tepid. On election day, Hoover did not carry a single western state, even though he was closely aligned with the region by way of his attachment to Stanford and to California more generally. Voters instead pinned their hopes on Franklin D. Roosevelt, whom they swept into office as the nation's thirty-second president.

Roosevelt, or FDR, as he was known to millions, got immediately to work. Within just months of taking office he launched a dizzying array of federal programs, known collectively as the New Deal, designed to alleviate the worst aspects of the Great Depression: combat suffering, get people back to work, prop up the economy, get prices to rise.

The New Deal operated mostly through programs run through what were often referred to, with good reason, as the "alphabet agencies." In very short order, Congress created the Federal Emergency Relief Administration (FERA), the Agricultural Adjustment Administration (AAA), the Home Owners Loan Corporation (HOLC), the Works Progress Administration (WPA), the Civil Works Administration (CWA), and the National Recovery Administration (NRA). These and other federal programs and agencies offered employment (and no small amount of hope to the desperate) and provided federal funding to relieve and to remake depressed areas, especially in the West. The New Deal reshaped the western landscape in astonishing ways and, in the process, the lives of millions.

Federal money came to the rescue of the young men like those in the image that leads off this chapter, working hard and long on projects in the backwoods, mountains, and plains of the West. The workers of the Civilian Conservation Corps (CCC) fought fires, worked on flood control projects, and built thousands upon thousands of miles of hiking trails all over the West which are largely extant to this day. The Roosevelt administration's dam-building projects reshaped western watersheds to supply the region's hydroelectric, irrigation, and aqueduct systems. The WPA carried out projects all over the West: construction workers built federal buildings, roads, schools, and bridges, and agency artists filled them with inspiring and powerful murals and other works of art. Through the Agricultural Department, New Deal workers helped cattle ranchers whose lives and livelihoods had been decimated by the dust storms that turned huge swaths of the southern plains into the Dust Bowl.

The New Deal's many programs were felt *everywhere* in the West, and its effects can still be seen *everywhere*, from shored-up trails in the Rockies to massive aqueducts in California and giant dams in the Northwest. New Deal canals and other water systems still carry water through the far West; people still drive on New Deal roads and bridges; and schoolchildren still study in schools graced by New Deal murals. The selections below illustrate just some of this impact on the lives of people in the West, as well as on their surroundings.

AS YOU READ: Think of the legacies, built and otherwise, of the New Deal in your region, maybe even in your own life. Think of some of the ways in which the federal government's policies and programs affected the West. Imagine the issues and challenges that even New Deal money and New Deal programs could not address.

50. WHAT TO EXPECT IN THE CIVILIAN CONSERVATION CORPS

Franklin Roosevelt established the Civilian Conservation Corps in the first months of his presidency. Immensely popular and successful, the CCC put nearly three million young men, often teenagers and often from the cities, to work outdoors on flood control, forestry, and soil conservation projects throughout the United States. Because the CCC was a federal agency, such entities as the National Park Service, the Forest Service, the Department of Agriculture, and the Soil Conservation Service directed various CCC projects. The CCC concentrated its efforts on federal land, and the US government owned more land in the West than in any other region of the country. One CCC contingent employed tens of thousands of Native Americans to work on the West's Indian reservations. Although the impact was not nearly as dramatic as Boulder Dam, we can argue that it was as lasting and certainly as important. The agency's work is still evident all over the West. This document is a mock question-and-answer pamphlet designed to inform the parents of CCC workers in California about what their sons would be doing for the agency. What questions or responses strike you as specific to this period? Which are more timeless? How would you compare CCC work to the Boulder Dam project as described in the documents that follow? What parallels can you find between the CCC and the US military?

California State Relief Administration
"Typical Questions and Answers"
ca. 1936[1]

Q[uestion]. Can my son be assigned to a camp near here so that he can come home now and then?

A[nswer]. The Army recruiting units and those in charge of the acceptance stations assign the boys to the camps where they are needed. We do not know the camp to which your son will be assigned and can give you no assurance that he will be sent to any particular camp.

Q. Will my son have to fight forest fire[s]?

A. Yes, if a fire breaks out in the vicinity of the camp to which he is assigned. However, it may ease your mind to know that with the modern, efficient methods of combating forest fires there is very little danger. The camp officers and forestry officials directing a forest fire are cognizant of the inexperience of the average youth in fighting forest fires and do not allow them to get into difficulties. In addition the fire loss in California has been reduced since the advent of the CCC to just about 20% of the average annual loss suffered in years before 1933.

---

1. California State Relief Administration, Civilian Conservation Corps, "Typical Questions and Answers" (Sacramento: State Relief Administration, ca. 1936), 1–4.

Q. In the event of war, will my son be subject to immediate draft by the Army?

A. No more so than he would be if he remains at home. The Civilian Conservation Corps is not a military organization. There is neither military training nor discipline. The clothing issued is not a military uniform. The fact should be known that because he goes to an Army acceptance station for enrollment, it does not mean that he joins the Army. He remains a civilian from beginning to end. The Army is in the picture because they have trained officers, equipment and systems available to handle the examinations, enrollments, and transportation in the most efficient manner possible. However, the training received by young men in the CCC from a standpoint of learning to carry out orders properly and efficiently would stand them in good stead and greatly increase their chances of survival in the event of foreign conflict at any time, but they are in no way any more subject to military draft in a CCC camp than they would be right at home.

Q. Do the men have adequate medical attention?

A. Yes, there is a doctor, usually an Army Reserve Officer, on duty in each camp to whom the youth can apply at any time for medical treatment. In addition, a periodical, compulsory examination is given that insures your son being well cared for. In cases of serious illness the ailing youth is removed to the nearest Government hospital, such as Letterman Hospital in San Francisco, where some of the finest physicians and surgeons in the country are on duty and if the youth is too ill to travel, or requires an immediate operation, he is taken to the nearest local hospital and his care paid for out of Government funds.

Q. Do the men have adequate supervision in camp and on leave?

A. The youths are, in most instances, under far more rigid and close supervision in camp and on leave than they would receive in their home town. An officer or responsible man is placed in a supervisory capacity covering each group that goes on leave in an adjacent town or city and the enrollee's actions, if not of the best, are reported to his Commanding Officer. . . .

Q. How is the food in the camps? I have heard contradictory stories about it—some good and some—not so good.

A. The food must pass Government inspection and measure up to standards prescribed by the War Department. It is of good wholesome quality and your son may have all of it he can eat. The food is not fancy, but it is solid, substantial food, fresh and clean and provided in a balanced diet. There is a proper ratio of salads, entrees, vegetables, desserts and beverages. The fact that recent statistics show an average gain per man of ten pounds during a six-month's enrollment is more eloquent than words in proof of the quality and abundance of the food served in camp.

Q. How will my son attend church?

A. Regular, non-sectarian services are held in camp. In addition, enrollees are granted liberty regularly to attend the church of their own denomination if they so desire where the camp is adjacent to a town or city.

Q. If a better position for the youth than the one in camp develops is there any difficulty in obtaining his immediate discharge?

A. None whatsoever. Upon submission to the camp commander of proof of an available position the youth will be immediately honorably discharged and furnished transportation home, or to the point of selection, at the discretion of the Army.

Q. Is it permissible for me to return to my son part of the allotment check?

A. Return of all or part of the allotment check[2] to the enrollee is against the basic principles of this program and is cause for immediate discharge of the enrollee receiving it.

Q. My son overstayed his leave and has been discharged for desertion. How may he be reinstated?

A. He cannot be reinstated except on the filing of an appeal to the Corps Area Commander through his Commanding Officer, stating the circumstances. If the enrollee can prove illness to himself, member of his family, or transportation delays, etc. beyond his control, the Corps Area Commander would be inclined to look favorably upon his appeal. Otherwise, the enrollee could not be reinstated.

Q. What opportunity does a youth have for improving himself while in camp other than the out-door life he naturally spends at work and play?

A. Each camp has an Educational Advisor. Regular classes are conducted in camp covering many subjects. Over 100 valuable correspondence courses are available and a certificate awarded to those satisfactorily completing any course or courses. In addition, a very complete library of proper and acceptable books and current magazines of intelligent selection is maintained in each camp.

Q. What opportunities are there for promotion?

A. There are a limited number of promotions available in each camp for youths who show marked ability and application. These ratings are known as "Leaders" and "Assistant Leaders." A leader receives an additional $15 per month allowance and an assistant leader an additional allowance of $6.00 per month over the basic $30. The basic allotment of leaders and assistant leaders may be increased but it is not mandatory.

Q. What opportunities are available in camp for private employment?

A. The President authorized, some time ago, that the Technical Services (that is, the Forestry units supervising the work projects) should select from the ranks of their youths in camp a certain percentage of the foreman and supervi-

---

2. **allotment check:** In this program, the family of the CCC worker received a check from the government. Workers drew an allowance while in camp.

Los Angeles Hoovervilles, 1930s
Courtesy the Huntington Library, San Marino, California.

sory personnel. During the past year over 100 young California Juniors have been given positions as Camp Foremen, Fire Lookouts and Assistant Wardens at salaries ranging from $80 to $120 per month.

Q. What insurance does an enrollee have while in the CCC?

A. The enrollee is protected under the Federal compensation laws which provide compensation for injury or illness sustained while in the CCC and only excepts cases where the injury or illness is contracted by wilful misconduct or intent to bring injury upon himself or others. . . .

51. DESTITUTION AND HOMELESSNESS *(SEE PHOTO ABOVE)*

As the Great Depression deepened across the nation, more and more Americans struggled to meet their basic needs of food and shelter. Some resorted to building shacks, tents, and lean-tos out of whatever they could scavenge, or began to live out of their cars. Small villages of the homeless popped up in cities across the United States, and residents often called these places "Hoovervilles" or "Hoovertowns" in stinging reference to former President Herbert Hoover, who many thought had done little to address the Depression's depredations.

52. A THIRTEEN-YEAR-OLD BOY WRITES TO ELEANOR ROOSEVELT

Children felt the impact and challenges of the Great Depression acutely. Many hundreds of them reached out to President Franklin Roosevelt or his wife, Eleanor, to seek help or simply make contact with someone who might pay attention to the troubles that they and their families faced. Here is one such letter, from the plains of Kansas, written to Eleanor Roosevelt.[1]

Nov. 3, 1937

Dear Mrs. Rosevelt:

I am 13 years old and will be 14 the 27 of this month. I am a victim of a shut in. I have been sick ever since the 12 of July. And have a very lonely place to stay. My parence's are very poor people. I cant even go to school yet with the other kids. And doubt if I can this year. I have nothing I can do but set around and I get so lonely I don't know what to do. And if you want to cheer me up and make me one of the happies boys in the world just send me some money to get a cheap raido. I have got proof by the neighbors that I am sick and have nothing to do. My parence names is Mr. + Mrs. A. J. M. My name is F. M. I live at Kismet. Many, many thanks if you would cheer me up that way I wouldn't spend it for nothing but a radio. It would pass my lonely time a way so much faster. I only ask for a cheep one.

F. M.
Kismet, Kansas

P.S. If I had any thing to do I wouldent ask you of it. It will be highly appreached.

I am in the dust bowl. We didn't raise any crop this year. And we have to live off of the releif and theres no injoyment out of that. But were thankful for it. My mother is sick and under the doctor's care most of the time and my Grandma that lives with me is very poorly. And that keeps my heart broken all the time. And nothing to amuse myself with.
thanks a lot.

---

1. Richard M. Wyman, *America's History through Young Voices: Using Primary Sources in the K–12 Social Studies Classroom* (Boston: Pearson, Allyn and Bacon, 2005): 137–38.

53. WORKERS ON BOULDER DAM

Although it was begun during the administration of President Herbert Hoover, Boulder Dam, on the Colorado River, was the quintessential New Deal project. The dam was built with government funds at a site just outside Las Vegas, Nevada, by a consortium of engineering and construction firms called the Six

Companies. It was the first giant project completed during the New Deal, fittingly in the American West. Like other New Deal projects of similar magnitude, Boulder Dam accomplished a number of things at once. It completely changed the natural landscape, in this case the Colorado River and large swaths of the Southwest. It emboldened and empowered federal agencies, especially the Bureau of Reclamation, which would become the West's most active dam-building entity. It enriched those private companies large enough to benefit from New Deal partnerships with the federal government (the Six Companies made millions of dollars on the project). It also put people to work, employing more than five thousand men. Boulder City, the project headquarters, was built from scratch to house the workers. The following oral histories, collected in the 1970s, describe the labor involved in an undertaking of this magnitude and some of the social realities that workers, especially minority workers, faced in the overnight communities that housed and entertained them in their off hours. How would you describe the working conditions on this New Deal project? How would you describe the racial climate? Did the project help change these attitudes in any way? How would you compare the actual work described here with the comments made by President Roosevelt at the dam's dedication in 1935 (see Document 55 on p. 196)?

Oral Histories of the Boulder Dam Project

1931–35[1]

Joe Kine

. . . They was hiring men, and I was working down there. They just had to have men. They just took you over, and you was a high scaler if you wanted it or not. I had worked in the mines, but I had never done any high scaling. It was all brand-new to me. Then it wasn't all that bad of a job once you got it going, got on to it.

My first job high scaling was over the Nevada valve house, cutting down to put the valve house in. That was the steepest canyon wall of all. We had a crew of men, and they came and went together all the time. I'd have a buddy that worked with me, and we'd be together all the time unless he took a day off or something. We tied our rope to a steel in the ground at the top of the canyon wall. We tied our safety belts and our bos'n chair on that. We had inch ropes. We had good ropes. They didn't break. That was never any worry. And then as they got frayed and unraveled out, they'd drop them down on the ground and burn them. We had an extra rope to tie the jackhammer on, and we tied our steel on, too.

---

1. Andrew J. Dunar and Dennis McBride, *Building Hoover Dam: An Oral History of the Great Depression* (New York: Twayne, 1993), 145, 147–50, 159, 184, 140, 142, 144.

We dropped ourselves over. Then we slid down to where we wanted to work, whether it was close or way down. We could move back and forth pretty good with our ropes. Then if you had to go up a little bit, you put a twist around your foot with the rope and slid up. We could sneak up pretty slow with that, but we very seldom had to go up. We used to climb out before the cableways were put up. Once the cableways got up, they'd go back and forth, and they could pick us up and move up and down and all ways. Then we had a big cable ladder too that we could go out on.

We didn't have expert powdermen. We done the whole business ourselves: drilled, loaded the holes and shot, barred down. Whatever was loose, we'd stick a bar behind it and pry it off and let it drop down. The engineers would mark it how far back we wanted to go. They'd take their transits and shoot and check it and tell you whether you had enough off or didn't have enough off. They had that all figured out. They'd mark it. Then we'd drill some more and go ahead.

There was never a dull moment on that high-scaling job. Something was going on all the time. . . .

Jake Dieleman

They hired anyone who didn't have brains enough to be scared. You was 900 feet up in the air. It took a lot of guts.

Tommy Nelson

We had some Marion electric shovels down there. When I think about it today, guys dragging that 2,300-volt cable around in that water and the foreman saying, "It won't hurt you"—oh boy. It would just scare you to death.

I was assigned to the excavation of the riverbed as a flagman. The purpose of this flagman was to . . . keep the trucks busy, and the shovels busy.

There was quite a number of dump trucks down there during this excavation, hauling this debris, this rock out of there: the International, the Mack, the Boreman, the White, and the GMC. The workhorse was the old International, the corn binder. As she went up the hill with a load, she'd belch fire up the river. Many of these trucks that we had down there were hard tails. I better explain what a hard tail is, because the younger generation wouldn't know. A hard-tail truck was a truck that had hard rubber [tires] on the back, solid rubber. We had quite a few of those down there on the job. Now, a person had to be very careful where he set that truck, because if you got him back in there where he was going to get mired down, you were in for a chewin'. You might have quite a job to get him out. Now this driver who piloted that truck, he was in reverse about as much as he was forward. There was a little canopy built right over the steering wheel. That would keep the rocks from falling on him.

Curley Francis

After my dad died in 1933, I rustled around and got a job up at the high mix. I was the extra man there, running the gas locomotives and flatbed trucks. My job was to haul concrete to the cableways. I ran locomotives from the high mix mostly.

When you went into the high mix, you'd come out the outside track and come to a spring switch. Then you'd come underneath the mix, get your load.

Then you'd start out, and you'd have a red light. I worked graveyard shift. It was kind of challenging, because you'd run into a red light on the track, by golly, and you'd sit there and you'd get two or three minutes' sleep. You always kept a water bag outside the window. Whenever you didn't wake up good, you'd just put it on top of your head and shake it around.

If it was green, of course, you went around the turn. You might go on the inside; you might go on the outside. You didn't know where you was going, except when you got your assignment with the train, they'd say, "You're on Number 8 Cableway." Or Number 10 Cableway. You didn't care where they was pouring; it was just the fact that you had to go to that cableway with the bucket.

Oh, I'll tell you, that was a complicated system. . . .

Tommy Nelson

I was running a jackhammer at the side of the cliff. This was during the dam construction, after the concrete had started being poured. I was running a jackhammer in there to put an anchor bolt in. It was just shaking the daylights out of me. An old construction stiff came by, and he said, "Hey, kid. Why don't you get a Mexican to hold up that hammer?" I looked up at him, and I said, "We haven't got any Mexicans around here." "Oh," he said, "you don't know what I mean." He grabbed a piece of reinforcement steel and he came over with it, stood it up alongside the jackhammer, put a little haywire around it. "There, let it hold you up, kid." And it did. So that was a little trick, you know. You learned a lot of them. That was kind of humorous, when I think about it.

Agnes Lockette

The people that I know usually think of Boulder as a town—it's an all-white community, most of them think it is. This is based on the fact that many [black] people have relatives who came to Boulder to seek employment in the time that the dam was being built and were turned away. Historically they think of Boulder as being an all-white community.

Bud Bodell

Right at the beginning there wasn't [any blacks], but by the time I'd been there a month, there were Negroes, 13 or 14. One was killed. I went down to the funeral, and I found out there were 14, including him, down there. All laborers.

Erma Godbey

There weren't hardly any Negroes in this area anyhow until they started Basic Magnesium.[2] Then they brought a lot of Negroes to work at Basic Magnesium. There were a few over in West Las Vegas, but not many. And, of course, we hadn't started all the hotels and all those things, so there wasn't any reason for them to be here.

Bob Parker

There were a lot of them that worked on the dam. I say a lot; I'd say a maximum probably of 50 or 100. But they all lived in Las Vegas.

Claude Dumas was a big black man. In the old days they thought that any scale or rust on reinforcing steel or concrete wouldn't cause the concrete to bond to it. So they brushed all the scale off the steel they took down there, and any rust. They had it all there in the steelyard over where the Park Service Building [warehouse] is, down through there and over below Lakeview now. They unloaded all that steel over in there. These black men, several of them, were out there brushing this steel. Black people do everything with a rhythm. Brushing steel, they'd be going this way, and the rear end would be going the other, back and forth. They developed a rhythm brushing steel, [and] they were singing hymns.

Charlie Rose had the colored crew down at the dam, the colored crew that built the parapet walls along the highway there and around the spillways, around the canyon wall there, all that rockwork. That's as beautiful a piece of rockwork as you'll see anywhere in the country. He was a white man, Charlie was. When Charlie would take a day off, they'd put someone else down there to run the colored crew, and the colored crew wouldn't work. Most of them [would] take the day off too. Charlie Rose knew how to treat them. They would work for him. Anybody else they wouldn't work for.

But there was another deal down there. We had a [Bureau of Reclamation] regional director here. I'm not going to mention any names, because I don't know whether they're all gone or not. I know that the man that put the winged figures in, and the safety island down there and all of that terrazzo work, out-lined the center of the flagpole—I know that Hansen, Oskar J. W. Hansen, was the sculptor on that. He was out there one day, and one or two of the colored men asked him something about that terrazzo work there. He was explaining it

---

2. **Basic Magnesium:** industrial firm that processed magnesium, a silvery metal that burns with an intense white light.

to them. This project manager, he was actually—was over there and heard it. He went over there, and he really chewed Oskar Hansen out about associating with those colored men out there in the public. Of course, the tourists and everybody else heard him. Old Oskar flipped his lid. He really told that project manager off. He told him he wasn't fit to have those men working for him. He really read him off. Two weeks later that project manager was running an engineering chain gang in Redding, California, at Shasta Dam. He wasn't here a month after that happened down on top of the dam. . . .

Madeline Knighten

I remember one time [at the Green Hut]. It could have developed into a free-for-all. In those days, you know, the Negroes weren't welcomed into any café. The Green Hut did have a very wonderful Negro cook. He was a very fine man, and he was a marvelous cook. But so far as serving was concerned, back in those days it was not common.

I was back in the kitchen visiting with my husband one of these dance evenings when we were expecting a dance crowd in any moment. The waiter rushed back to the window just all in a tizzy. He said, "There's a great big Negro out here." The waiter was a southern boy, Johnny Whittingham. He rushed back all in a tizzy and said, "There's a big Negro out here wanting to eat. What will I do with him?"

Howard, my husband, looked out and saw him. Fortunately, we had lived on the Apache reservation in Arizona and we knew the Apache people. Instantly he knew that he wasn't a Negro; he was an Apache Indian. He thought he probably was one of the high scalers. He said, "I want to talk to him anyhow." So he went out and talked to him, and he was one of the high scalers. They had at least two Apaches high scaling.

It was all eventually diverted. He ordered what he wanted to eat. They prepared it back in the kitchen, the other cooks back there. The waiter brought it out to him. My husband talked to him for a few minutes about things we knew. So he ate and left. But if he had realized that they were not ready to serve him, no telling what he might have done. He might have had a rage right there. He could have. But he didn't.

54. DEATH ON BOULDER DAM

Construction of Boulder Dam lasted for four years. At completion, it was easily the biggest dam in the world, and its sheer massiveness overwhelms the modest engineering description of it as "a storage reservoir." But it came at a high human price. This tabulation, drawn from government records and those of the Six Companies consortium, records the deaths that occurred on the project. First and last killed were a father and son: J. G. Tierney worked for the US Bureau of Reclamation, the agency that superintended the dam and oversaw federal water projects across the West. His son, killed not long after Franklin Roosevelt dedicated the dam, also worked for the Bureau of Reclamation. The consortium of construction and engineering firms that made up the Six Companies had a huge workforce, but it also had the highest casualty rate during dam construction. This tabulation contains some fascinating information about the human costs of massive engineering projects. What can you deduce from these statistics and from the oral accounts in the last selection about the dangers the dam workers encountered? How did these dangers change over the duration of the project?

Boulder Canyon Project Fatalities
1922–35[1]

	1922	
12/20	J. G. Tierney, US Bureau of Reclamation (USBR)	Drowned
	1931	
5/17	Harry Large, Six Co.	Rock Slide
5/17	Andrew Lane, Six Co.	Rock Slide
5/18	Fred Olsen, Lewis Const. Co.	Premature Explosion
6/20	William Bryant, Six Co.	Explosion
6/20	J. P. Sweezy, Six Co.	Explosion
6/26	Ray Hapland, Six Co.	Heat Prostration
6/27	Pat Shannon, Six Co.	Heat Prostration
6/28	Mike Madzia, Six Co.	Heat Prostration
7/5	Joe Rolland, Six Co.	Drowned
7/5	Martin Puluski, visitor	Drowned
7/8	Robert Core, Newberry Elec.	Heat Prostration
7/10	A. E. Meridith, Lewis Const.	Heat Prostration
7/11	Joe Lyons, Anderson Bros.	Heat Prostration
7/13	Earl Parker, Six Co.	Heat Prostration
7/15	John Swenson, Six Co.	Heat Prostration

1. Andrew J. Dunar and Dennis McBride, *Building Hoover Dam: An Oral History of the Great Depression* (New York: Twayne, 1993), 317–20.

7/20	Chase Allen, Six Co.	Heat Prostration
7/22	A. A. McClurg, Int'l. Truck Co.	Heat Prostration
7/23	Tom Noonal, Six Co.	Heat Prostration
7/24	Joe Ganz, Anderson Bros.	Heat Prostration
7/26	Lew Starnes, Anderson Bros.	Heat Prostration
9/11	H. H. Kidd, Six Co.	Falling Rock
9/29	Jack Seitz, Six Co.	Fell 400 feet
10/2	Lauri Lehto, Six Co.	Falling Rock
10/17	Ralph Henderson, Six Co.	Falling Rock
10/17	M. C. Stuckey, Six Co.	Falling Rock
11/7	D. R. Elston, Six Co.	Struck by Truck
12/15	M. J. Sidmore, Six Co.	Premature Explosion
12/15	Frank Manning, Six Co.	Premature Explosion

1932

1/7	S. A. McDaniel, Six Co.	Fell
2/11	Joe Talbert, Six Co.	Power Shovel
2/25	Ben Johnson, Six Co.	Drowned in Tank
3/11	O. A. George, Six Co.	Crushed—Trucks
3/30	Frank Brady, Six Co.	Falling Rock
4/14	Carl Bennett, Six Co.	Explosion
4/21	H. H. Nightingale, Six Co.	Shovel—Crushed
4/26	L. N. McBride, Six Co.	Struck by Skip Line
4/27	Bert Lynch, Six Co.	Falling Rock
4/28	V. R. Moore, Six Co.	Struck—Concrete Skip
5/11	John Abercrombie, Six Co.	Transport Collision
5/20	B. S. Joyce, Six Co.	Falling Rock
5/30	H. A. Willis, Six Co.	Electrocuted
6/17	H. L. Scothern, Six Co.	Struck by Cable
7/25	Walter Hardesty, Six Co.	Struck by Crane
7/27	E. A. Bishop, Six Co.	Truck Went Overboard
7/29	Alexander Girardi, Six Co.	Fell from Wall
8/24	A. E. Wooden, Six Co.	Crushed by Form
8/31	E. H. Gammill, Six Co.	Premature Explosion
9/24	V. I. Kemnitz, Six Co.	Rock Fall

9/25	P. B. Hicks, Six Co.	Fell from Wall
9/28	James C. Roberts, Six Co.	Falling Rock
11/9	Louie Goss, Six Co.	Fell from Wall
11/16	Carl Soderstrom, Six Co.	Drowned
12/12	Dan Shovlin, Six Co.	Struck by Truck
12/23	Walter Hamer, Six Co.	Fell from Valve House

1933

1/1	F. C. Palmer, Six Co.	Fell from Valve House
1/10	Gus Enberg, Six Co.	Explosion
1/11	Howard Cornelius, Six Co.	Explosion
2/1	V. H. Blair, Six Co.	Fell from Truck
2/7	J. H. Powers, Six Co.	Truck Fell on Him
2/7	M. H. Kaighn, Six Co.	Rock Slide
3/12	Tome Markey, Six Co.	Fell
3/16	William Koontz, Six Co.	Run Over by Truck
4/8	Dan Kalal, Six Co.	Gravel Slide
5/20	H. D. Bluhm, Six Co.	Struck by Shovel
5/22	Pete Savoff, Six Co.	Fell
6/23	Mike Landers, Six Co.	Falling Rock
6/26	L. W. Steele, Six Co.	Run Over by Truck
7/1	F. B. Kassell, Six Co.	Premature Explosion
7/13	George Falkner, Six Co.	Falling Timber
7/19	J. M. Nelson, Six Co.	Fell from Form
9/15	V. O. Lee, Six Co.	Electrocuted
10/1	James Jackman, Six Co.	Falling Concrete Bucket
11/8	W. A. Jameson, Six Co.	Concrete Slide
11/8	James Tocci, Six Co.	Run Over by Truck
12/6	L. E. Roach, Six Co.	Fell from Jumbo
12/29	P. A. Malan, Six Co.	Fell from Form

1934

1/22	George Good, Six Co.	Falling Material
2/1	Rosyn Grant, Six Co.	Fell

2/6	Kenneth Walden, Six Co.	Crushed by Concrete Bucket
2/26	Eugene Buckner, Six Co.	Falling Timber
3/10	George R. Robinson, Six Co.	Elevator Accident
3/23	Harry Morgan, Six Co.	Fell
4/14	Allen Jackson, Six Co.	Fell
5/16	G. D. McIsaac, Six Co.	Electrocuted
5/20	Howard Bently, Six Co.	Falling Rock
5/26	Samuel L. Carter, Six Co.	Hit by Concrete Dinky
5/26	Fred Deckmann, Babcock & Wilcox (B&W)	Fell
6/11	Grant Miles, Six Co.	Fell 60 feet walking thru drain. Not considered industrial by Six Co. as he did not accept furnished mode of transportation
6/24	Victor K. Auchard, Six Co.	Crushed under Jumbo
8/27	Harris Lange, B&W	Objects from Broken Sling
9/16	Frank A. Fritz, Six Co.	Electrocuted
9/26	John W. Rawls, Six Co.	Fell from Form
11/1	Paul L. Jordan, B&W	Fell from 30 Foot Pipe
11/1	Richard M. Whelan, B&W	Penstock Car Ran Wild
11/1	Martin L. Hempel, B&W	Penstock Car Ran Wild
11/4	Alfred E. Foreman, B&W	Penstock Car Ran Wild
11/14	K. H. Rankin, USBR	Struck by Concrete Bucket

1935

1/3	J. W. Pitts, Six Co.	Struck by Concrete Bucket
2/19	Kenneth L. Wilson, Six Co.	Line Broke—Fell 200 Feet
2/21	B. R. Reaves, Six Co.	Fell into Tunnel; Drown
5/15	David C. Nixon, Six Co.	Crushed: Concrete Bucket
5/17	Verne Matson, B&W	Falling Pipe
6/21	Harold Koile, B&W	Falling Casting
8/14	William R. Skaloud, B&W	Fell
11/17	Albert G. Loper, Six Co.	Fell
11/24	Roy Stevens, Six Co.	Struck by Flying Object
12/20	Patrick W. Tierney, USBR	Fell: Intake Tower, Lake

Summary	
Company Name	*Total Fatalities*
Anderson Brothers	4
Newberry Electric	1
International Truck Co.	1
Babcock & Wilcox	9
Lewis Construction Company	2
Six Companies	91
US Bureau of Reclamation	3
Visitors	1
Total Deaths	112

55. DEDICATION OF BOULDER DAM

It may seem ironic that a project paid for and completed during the Roosevelt administration is now named after Roosevelt's predecessor. But the Hoover administration had initiated the Boulder Dam project in the 1920s, and through accidents of timing as much as anything else, it became a New Deal challenge. To get the dam built in just four years, the US government joined with the Six Companies consortium of construction firms: the Morrison-Knudson Corporation of Boise, MacDonald & Kahn and Bechtel & Kaiser of San Francisco, the Pacific Bridge Corporation and J. F. Shea Company of Portland, and the Utah Construction Company in Salt Lake City. Following Boulder Dam, these firms went on to build other giant projects throughout the American West, the nation, and the world. Boulder Dam embodied the New Deal approach to the western landscape: through partnerships with firms like the Six Companies, the government would employ people hard hit by the Depression and, at the same time, sponsor projects producing huge environmental changes. This is the text of President Franklin D. Roosevelt's dedication of the dam in the fall of 1935. He praises it as a triumph: of engineering, of human over nature, of the New Deal. Does the president view the dam as a political opportunity? What does he mean by an "unregulated river"? How does he characterize the work of building Boulder Dam, and the dam's workers? In what ways does he claim the project for the New Deal?

Franklin D. Roosevelt

Address at Boulder Dam
1935[1]

. . . Ten years ago the place where we are gathered was an unpeopled, forbidding desert. In the bottom of a gloomy canyon, whose precipitous walls rose to a height of more than a thousand feet, flowed a turbulent, dangerous river. The mountains on either side of the canyon were difficult of access with neither road nor trail, and their rocks were protected by neither trees nor grass from the blazing heat of the sun. The site of Boulder City was a cactus-covered waste. The transformation wrought here in these years is a twentieth-century marvel.

We are here to celebrate the completion of the greatest dam in the world, rising 726 feet above the bed-rock of the river and altering the geography of a whole region; we are here to see the creation of the largest artificial lake in the world—115 miles long, holding enough water, for example, to cover the State of Connecticut to a depth of ten feet; and we are here to see nearing completion a power house which will contain the largest generators and turbines yet installed in this country, machinery that can continuously supply nearly two million horsepower of electric energy.

All these dimensions are superlative. They represent and embody the accumulated engineering knowledge and experience of centuries; and when we behold them it is fitting that we pay tribute to the genius of their designers. We recognize also the energy, resourcefulness and zeal of the builders, who, under the greatest physical obstacles, have pushed this work forward to completion two years in advance of the contract requirements. But especially, we express our gratitude to the thousands of workers who gave brain and brawn to this great work of construction.

Beautiful and great as this structure is, it must also be considered in its relationship to the agricultural and industrial development and in its contribution to the health and comfort of the people of America who live in the Southwest.

To divert and distribute the waters of an arid region, so that there shall be security of rights and efficiency in service, is one of the greatest problems of law and of administration to be found in any Government. The farms, the cities, the people who live along the many thousands of miles of this river and its tributaries—all of them depend upon the conservation, the regulation, and the equitable division of its ever-changing water supply.

What has been accomplished on the Colorado in working out such a scheme of distribution is inspiring to the whole country. Through the cooperation of the States whose people depend upon this river, and of the Federal Government

---

1. Andrew J. Dunar and Dennis McBride, *Building Hoover Dam: An Oral History of the Great Depression* (New York: Twayne, 1993), 311–15.

which is concerned in the general welfare, there is being constructed a system of distributive works and of laws and practices which will insure to the millions of people who now dwell in this basin, and the millions of others who will come to dwell here in future generations, a just, safe and permanent system of water rights. In devising these policies and the means for putting them into practice the Bureau of Reclamation of the Federal Government has taken, and is destined to take in the future, a leading and helpful part. The Bureau has been the instrument which gave effect to the legislation introduced in Congress by Senator Hiram Johnson and Congressman Phil Swing.

As an unregulated river, the Colorado added little of value to the region this dam serves. When in flood the river was a threatening torrent. In the dry months of the year it shrank to a trickling stream. For a generation the people of the Imperial Valley had lived in the shadow of disaster from this river which provided their livelihood, and which is the foundation of their hopes for themselves and their children. Every spring they awaited with dread the coming of a flood, and at the end of nearly every summer they feared a shortage of water would destroy their crops.

The gates of these great diversion tunnels were closed here at Boulder Dam last February. In June a great flood came down the river. It came roaring down the canyons of the Colorado, was caught and safely held behind Boulder Dam.

Last year a drought of unprecedented severity was visited upon the West. The watershed of this Colorado River did not escape. In July the canals of the Imperial Valley went dry. Crop losses in that Valley alone totaled $10,000,000 that summer. Had Boulder Dam been completed one year earlier, this loss would have been prevented, because the spring flood would have been stored to furnish a steady water supply for the long dry summer and fall.

Across the San Jacinto Mountains southwest of Boulder Dam, the cities of Southern California are constructing an aqueduct to cost $220,000,000, which they have raised, for the purpose of carrying the regulated waters of the Colorado River to the Pacific coast 259 miles away.

Across the desert and mountains to the west and south run great electric transmission lines by which factory motors, street and household lights and irrigation pumps will be operated in Southern Arizona and California. Part of this power will be used in pumping the water through the aqueduct to supplement the domestic supplies of Los Angeles and surrounding cities.

Navigation of the river from Boulder Dam to the Grand Canyon has been made possible, a 115-mile stretch that has been traversed less than half a dozen times in history. An immense new park has been created for the enjoyment of all our people.

At what cost was this done? Boulder Dam and the power houses together cost a total of $108,000,000, all of which will be repaid with interest in fifty years under the contracts for sale of the power. Under these contracts, already completed, not only will the cost be repaid, but the way is opened for the provision of needed light and power to the consumer at reduced rates. In the expenditure of the price of Boulder Dam during the depression years work was provided for 4,000 men, most of them heads of families, and many thousands more were enabled to earn a livelihood through manufacture of materials and machinery.

And this is true in regard to the thousands of projects undertaken by the Federal Government, by the States and by the counties and municipalities in recent years. The overwhelming majority of them are of definite and permanent usefulness.

Throughout our national history we have had a great program of public improvements, and in these past two years all that we have done has been to accelerate that program. We know, too, that the reason for this speeding up was the need of giving relief to several million men and women whose earning capacity had been destroyed by the complexities and lack of thought of the economic system of the past generation.

No sensible person is foolish enough to draw hard and fast classifications as to usefulness or need. Obviously, for instance, this great Boulder Dam warrants universal approval because it will prevent floods and flood damage, because it will irrigate thousands of acres of tillable land and because it will generate electricity to turn the wheels of many factories and illuminate countless homes.

But can we say that a five-foot brushwood dam across the head waters of an arroyo, and costing only a millionth part of Boulder Dam, is an undesirable project or a waste of money? Can we say that the great brick high school, costing $2,000,000, is a useful expenditure but that a little wooden school house project, costing five or ten thousand dollars, is a wasteful extravagance? Is it fair to approve a huge city boulevard and, at the same time, disapprove the improvement of a muddy farm-to-market road?

While we do all of this, we give actual work to the unemployed and at the same time we add to the wealth of the Nation. These efforts meet with the approval of the people of the Nation.

In a little over two years this work has accomplished much. We have helped mankind by the works themselves and, at the same time, we have created the necessary purchasing power to throw in the clutch to start the wheels of what we call private industry. Such expenditures on all of these works, great and small, flow out to many beneficiaries. They revive other and more remote industries and businesses. Money is put in circulation. Credit is expanded and the financial and industrial mechanism of America is stimulated to more and more activity.

Labor makes wealth. The use of materials makes wealth. To employ workers and materials when private employment has failed is to translate into great national possessions the energy that otherwise would be wasted. Boulder Dam is a splendid symbol of that principle. The mighty waters of the Colorado were running unused to the sea. Today we translate them into a great national possession.

I might go further and suggest to you that use begets use. Such works as this serve as a means of making useful other national possessions. Vast deposits of precious metals are scattered within a short distance of where we stand today. They await the development of cheap power.

These great Government power projects will affect not only the development of agriculture and industry and mining in the sections that they serve, but they will also prove useful yardsticks to measure the cost of power throughout the United States. It is my belief that the Government should proceed to lay down the first yardstick from this great power plant in the form of a State power line, assisted in its financing by the Government, and tapping the wonderful natural resources of Southern Nevada. Doubtless the same policy of financial assistance to State authorities can be followed in the development of Nevada's sister State, Arizona, on the other side of the River.

With it all, with work proceeding in every one of the more than three thousand counties in the United States, and of a vastly greater number of local divisions of Government, the actual credit of Government agencies is on a stronger and safer basis than at any time in the past six years. Many States have actually improved their financial position in the past two years. Municipal tax receipts are being paid when the taxes fall due, and tax arrearages are steadily declining.

It is a simple fact that Government spending is already beginning to show definite signs of its effect on consumer spending; that the putting of people to work by the Government has put other people to work through private employment, and that in two years and a half we have come to the point today where private industry must bear the principal responsibility of keeping the processes of greater employment moving forward with accelerated speed.

The people of the United States are proud of Boulder Dam. With the exception of the few who are narrow visioned, people everywhere on the Atlantic Seaboard, people in the Middle West and the Northwest, people in the South, must surely recognize that the national benefits which will be derived from the completion of this project will make themselves felt in every one of the forty-eight States. They know that poverty or distress in a community two thousand miles away may affect them, and equally that prosperity and higher standards of living across a whole continent will help them back home. . . .

That is why I have the right once more to congratulate you who have built Boulder Dam and on behalf of the Nation to say to you, "Well done."

FURTHER READING

Cohen, Robert, ed. *Dear Mrs. Roosevelt: Letters from Children of the Great Depression.* Chapel Hill: University of North Carolina Press, 2002.

Dewing, Rolland. *Regions in Transition: The Northern Great Plains and the Pacific Northwest in the Great Depression.* Lanham, MD: University Press of America, 2006.

Dunar, Andrew J., and Dennis McBride. *Building Hoover Dam: An Oral History of the Great Depression.* New York: Twayne, 1993.

Gordon, Linda. *Dorothea Lange: A Life beyond Limits*. London and New York: W. W. Norton, 2009.

Grant, Michael Johnston. *Down and Out on the Family Farm: Rural Rehabilitation in the Great Plains, 1929–1945*. Lincoln: University of Nebraska Press, 2002.

Gregory, James. *American Exodus: The Dust Bowl Migration and Okie Culture in California*. New York: Oxford University Press, 1989.

Hill, Edwin G. *In the Shadow of the Mountain: The Spirit of the CCC*. Pullman: Washington State University Press, 1990.

Hiltzik, Michael. *Colossus: Hoover Dam and the Making of the American Century*. New York: Free Press, 2010.

Kennedy, David. *Freedom from Fear: The American People in Depression and War, 1929–1945*. New York: Oxford University Press, 1999.

Lowitt, Richard. *The New Deal and the West*. Bloomington: Indiana University Press, 1984.

Maher, Neil M. *Nature's New Deal: The Civilian Conservation Corps and the Roots of the American Environmental Movement*. Oxford and New York: Oxford University Press, 2008.

Mullins, William H. *The Depression and the Urban West Coast, 1929–1933: Los Angeles, San Francisco, Seattle, and Portland*. Bloomington: Indiana University Press, 1991.

Nash, Gerald D. *The Federal Landscape: An Economic History of the Twentieth-Century West*. Tucson: University of Arizona Press, 1999.

Phillips, Sarah T. *This Land, This Nation: Conservation, Rural America, and the New Deal*. Cambridge, England: Cambridge University Press, 2007.

Starr, Kevin. *Endangered Dreams: The Great Depression in California*. New York: Oxford University Press, 1996.

Terkel, Studs. *Hard Times: An Oral History of the Great Depression*. New York: Avon, 1971.

Worster, Donald. *Dust Bowl: The Southern Plains in the 1930s*. New York: Oxford University Press, 2004.

Wyman, Richard M. *America's History through Young Voices: Using Primary Sources in the K–12 Social Studies Classroom*. Boston: Pearson, Allyn and Bacon, 2005.

Camouflaging the internment staging ground at Santa Anita Racetrack in Southern California, 1942. In the aftermath of the Japanese attack on Pearl Harbor in December 1941, the United States immediately declared war; any pretense of waiting out the war on the far side of the globe evaporated. What took more time, as the nation and its leaders adjusted to the new reality of war and the shock of Pearl Harbor, was how best to protect the nation from the nations and peoples it now called enemies. In a tragic spasm of anger and fear, racism and anxiety, the federal government opted for a brutal move: everyone of Japanese descent living on the Pacific coast had to move inland or to the Eastern seaboard, or else be forcibly removed to hastily built or refurbished internment camps.

How could these people—more than one hundred thousand of them, mostly US citizens—respond? Where were they supposed to go? Their lives and families, and their individual and collective American histories, were rooted in the far West. Go they did, though, and by force, to camps where they held their lives and families together as best they could. It was a wholesale violation of their constitutional rights. This picture shows workers disguising the Santa Anita Racetrack in Southern California—a site where local "internees" went before they were assigned to a camp elsewhere. Fears that the Japanese might attack the US mainland motivated actions like this. Camouflage worked well to cover buildings and roofs—but not so well at covering up egregious attacks on civil rights.

Courtesy the Library of Congress, Prints and Photographs Division.

Domestic Turmoil and Intolerance in a Time of War

I t would be difficult to overestimate the shock Americans felt on December 7, 1941, when a Japanese air attack came close to wiping out the United States fleet at Pearl Harbor in Hawaii. Americans everywhere knew that there was a war on and that the Roosevelt administration was playing a critical role, mostly through the lifeline of supplies sent to Allied forces in Europe. But the mayhem, destruction, and death at Pearl Harbor were a new experience. It became clear that the United States could not stand idly by while the conflict threatened to engulf the whole world. The attack provoked the United States to declare war.

Like the Great Depression, World War II transformed the West in remarkable ways. People still came West, and for many of the same reasons, such as searching for work, but now the wartime economy promised a better chance of finding a job. African Americans migrated from the South to take jobs in the labor-starved defense industry. In California, many of the same Dust Bowl migrants who had poured into the rural flats of the huge Central Valley now found work in the defense plants or shipyards of the Bay Area and Southern California. And many came west during the war years because they were newly enlisted or drafted into the armed forces. The military presence in the West, increasing through the late 1930s by presidential order, grew at blinding speed in the months following

Pearl Harbor. Millions of young men and women in uniform found themselves at the airfields and shipyards that seemed to pop up almost overnight.

But movement in the West during World War II was not only due to opportunity or wartime military service. The forced internment of Japanese aliens and Japanese Americans in camps in the West and South was an outgrowth of the wartime paranoia and hysteria that followed the attack on Pearl Harbor. Not long after, President Roosevelt signed Executive Order 9066, which allowed the rounding up of everyone of Japanese descent, citizen or noncitizen, along the entire Pacific coast, from the Canadian border to San Diego. More than one hundred thousand people, most of them American-born, were evacuated from their homes, their jobs, and their communities, ostensibly because they constituted a potential threat to the internal security of the United States. Once the order to evacuate was given, people had two days to arrange their affairs, pack a few belongings, and say goodbye. Most believed that wartime hysteria would soon subside and they would be allowed to resume their normal lives. And while some Americans bravely spoke out against internment, public opinion supported the president's action.

The government moved internees away from the Pacific coast, believing that the coastline was vulnerable to enemy attack. German and Italian aliens living in or near San Francisco also found their civil liberties curtailed, if only briefly, but it was the Japanese community that bore the brunt of this policy. Many viewed the presence of so many of Japanese descent as an invitation to treachery and treason, although no Japanese American was ever charged with wartime espionage. A special government agency called the War Relocation Authority was set up to deal with the problem of imprisoning tens of thousands who had broken no laws. Internees first faced processing and paperwork, their introduction to a dehumanizing process. Then they were sent to one of the internment camps that dotted the deserts and interior of the West (and locations as far away as Arkansas). Internees were housed in these isolated outposts for an average of two and a half years.

The internment camps were usually hastily constructed barracks enclosed by barbed wire. The movements of internees were heavily restricted. Because of the fear of espionage, they were not allowed to own or use camera equipment (at least at first), and their access to the outside world was limited. Like prisons, the camps were communities within communities, with separate facilities, schools, and social activities. Certain people could come in—schoolteachers, government officials, journalists—but internees could not leave except under tightly controlled and temporary circumstances. Serving in the US armed forces was the only means to avoid incarceration. The federal government evidently trusted young Japanese American men to fight for their country, but it did not trust the families that had raised those same loyal soldiers. This irony was not lost on internees or their families. While Japanese American military units served with distinction—the 100th Battalion and the 442nd Regimental Combat Team remain the most decorated units in US history—many in the community resisted wartime service precisely because they recognized the stark inconsistency in the government's stance. Most internees struggled through the humiliating years of confinement without overt protest, however, believing that resistance to the government's policies would only make things worse.

As if troubled by a nagging conscience, the War Relocation Authority gradually relaxed its supervision of the camps during the later stages of the war. Some student internees were allowed to leave to attend college and then, gradually, all were set free to try to pick up the pieces of their lives. Most had very little to return to. Many had lost their homes and their businesses when ordered to the camps in early 1942. Some estimate that the interned Americans sold off, often at ridiculously low prices, upward of $500 million worth of farmland, homes, and other property. The US Supreme Court upheld internment in 1944, though one member of the court declared the government's actions the "legalization of racism." Only recently did the government recognize the moral and constitutional lapses of internment; in 1988, Congress voted to pay reparations and apologize to those the federal government had robbed of their freedom.

The selections in this chapter cover various facets of the internment issue. Two eyewitness accounts of the internment process—one an excerpt from a memoir, the other a series of captioned drawings—capture the fear of those considered so dangerous, they had to be removed from their homes and jobs. The executive order authorizing internment attempts to justify it on the grounds of internal security. In the final selection, the government director of internment argues that somehow, in the midst of the wholesale violation of the civil liberties of tens of thousands of Americans, democracy might be preserved.

AS YOU READ: Think of the social and racial situation in the wartime West that made internment possible. What do these documents reveal about the West's role in the federal internment effort? What fears and biases are reflected in these documents? From what you know, do you see any similarities between internment and the Native American reservation system in the West?

56. INTERNMENT IN WASHINGTON

This passage from her memoir describes the impact of Pearl Harbor and the internment order on the lives of Monica Sone and her family, friends, and neighbors in Seattle. Wrenched from a peaceful life in the Pacific Northwest, where her father ran a small hotel, Sone and her family spent several years in an internment camp in Puyallup, Washington. Her description of how rumor and hearsay played into local fears of espionage and treason are particularly revealing. She also records local racism directed at Japanese people, which only increased in the wake of the Pearl Harbor attack. How do Sone and her family react to Executive Order 9066? How do her responses compare to those of Miné

Okubo (see Document 58 on p. 209)? How would you describe Sone's fears as the internment rumors became a reality? Would things have been any different if Sone and her family had lived in the Midwest or the South?

Monica Sone

From *Nisei Daughter*
1953[1]

On a peaceful Sunday morning, December 7, 1941, Henry, Sumi and I were at choir rehearsal singing ourselves hoarse in preparation for the annual Christmas recital of Handel's "Messiah." Suddenly Chuck Mizuno, a young University of Washington student, burst into the chapel, gasping as if he had sprinted all the way up the stairs.

"Listen, everybody!" he shouted. "Japan just bombed Pearl Harbor . . . in Hawaii! It's war!"

The terrible words hit like a blockbuster, paralyzing us. . . . I knew instinctively that the fact that I was an American by birthright was not going to help me escape the consequences of this unhappy war.

One girl mumbled over and over again, "It can't be, God, it can't be!" Someone else was saying, "What a spot to be in! Do you think we'll be considered Japanese or Americans?"

A boy replied quietly, "We'll be Japs, same as always. But our parents are enemy aliens[2] now, you know." . . .

The pressure of war moved in on our little community. The Chinese consul announced that all the Chinese would carry identification cards and wear "China" badges to distinguish them from the Japanese. Then I really felt left standing out in the cold. The government ordered the bank funds of all Japanese nationals frozen. . . .

In the afternoon President Roosevelt's formal declaration of war against Japan was broadcast throughout the nation. In grave, measured words, he described the attack on Pearl Harbor as shameful, infamous. I writhed involuntarily. I could no more have escaped the stab of self-consciousness than I could have changed my Oriental features. . . .

We had a family conference to discuss the possibility of Father and Mother's internment. Henry was in graduate school and I was beginning my second year at the university. We agreed to drop out should they be taken and we would manage the hotel during our parents' absence. Every week end Henry and I accompanied Father to the hotel and learned how to keep the hotel books, how to open the office safe, and what kind of linen, paper towels, and soap to order.

---

1. Monica Sone, *Nisei Daughter* (Boston: Little, Brown, 1953), 145–46, 149–50, 157–61.
2. **enemy aliens:** *Issei* refers to those Japanese in America who were born in Japan and thus not US citizens. *Nisei* are the American-born children of *issei* parents, and thus US citizens.

Then a new menace appeared on the scene. Cries began to sound up and down the coast that everyone of Japanese ancestry should be taken into custody. For years the professional guardians of the Golden West had wanted to rid their land of the Yellow Peril, and the war provided an opportunity for them to push their program through. As the chain of Pacific islands fell to the Japanese, patriots shrieked for protection from us. A Californian sounded the alarm: "The Japanese are dangerous and they must leave. Remember the destruction and the sabotage perpetrated at Pearl Harbor. Notice how they have infiltrated into the harbor towns and taken our best land." . . .

In February, Executive Order No. 9066 came out, authorizing the War Department to remove the Japanese from such military areas as it saw fit, aliens and citizens alike. Even if a person had a fraction of Japanese blood in him, he must leave on demand.

A pall of gloom settled upon our home. We couldn't believe that the government meant that the Japanese-Americans must go, too. We had heard the clamoring of superpatriots who insisted loudly, "Throw the whole kaboodle out. A Jap's a Jap, no matter how you slice him. You can't make an American out of little Jap Junior just by handing him an American birth certificate." But we had dismissed these remarks as just hot blasts of air from an overheated patriot. We were quite sure that our rights as American citizens would not be violated, and we would not be marched out of our homes on the same basis as enemy aliens. . . .

Once more I felt like a despised, pathetic two-headed freak, a Japanese and an American, neither of which seemed to be doing me any good. . . .

Events moved rapidly. General DeWitt[3] marked off Western Washington, Oregon, and all of California, and the southern half of Arizona as Military Area No. 1, hallowed ground from which we must remove ourselves as rapidly as possible. Unfortunately we could not simply vanish into thin air, and we had no place to go. We had no relatives in the east we could move in on. All our relatives were sitting with us in the forbidden area, themselves wondering where to go. The neighboring states in the line of exit for the Japanese protested violently at the prospect of any mass invasion. They said, very sensibly, that if the Coast didn't want the Japanese hanging around, they didn't either. . . .

The orders were simple:

> Dispose of your homes and property. Wind up your business. Register the family. One seabag of bedding, two suitcases of clothing allowed per person. People in District #1 must report at 8th and Lane Street, 8 p.m. on April 28.

. . . We were advised to pack warm, durable clothes. In my mind, I saw our permanent camp sprawled out somewhere deep in a snow-bound forest, an American Siberia. I saw myself plunging chest deep in the snow, hunting for small game

---

3. **General DeWitt:** General J. L. DeWitt of the US Army Western Defense Command, who convinced President Roosevelt to issue Executive Order 9066 authorizing internment.

to keep us alive. I decided that one of my suitcases was going to hold nothing but vitamins from A to Z. I thought of sewing fur-lined hoods and parkas for the family. I was certain this was going to be a case of sheer animal survival. . . .

57. INTERNMENT ORDERS FROM THE PRESIDENT

In this executive order, issued shortly after the December 1941 attack on Pearl Harbor, President Franklin D. Roosevelt outlines the distribution of authority to those military bodies charged with interning people deemed dangerous to the US war effort. Roosevelt had been persuaded by the US Army that the presence of so many people of Japanese descent along the Pacific coast could lead to possible foreign attack or sabotage. More than one hundred thousand people were immediately transferred to one of ten internment camps scattered throughout the West or to one of two camps in Arkansas. Note that the document does not specifically mention people of Japanese descent. How does the executive order describe the threat posed by the Japanese and Japanese Americans? How are the various military commanders supposed to recognize such threats? What provisions does the executive order make for returning to peacetime existence?

Franklin D. Roosevelt
Executive Order 9066
1942[1]

Whereas the successful prosecution of the war requires every possible protection against espionage and against sabotage to national-defense material, national-defense premises, and national-defense utilities as defined in Section 4, Act of April 20, 1918, 40 Stat. 533, as amended by the Act of November 30, 1940, 54 Stat. 1220, and the Act of August 21, 1941, 55 Stat. 655 (U.S.C., Title 50, Sec. 104):

Now, therefore, by virtue of the authority vested in me as President of the United States, and Commander in Chief of the Army and Navy, I hereby authorize and direct the Secretary of War, and the Military Commanders whom he may from time to time designate, whenever he or any designated Commander deems such action necessary or desirable, to prescribe military areas in such places and of such extent as he or the appropriate Military Commander may determine, from which any or all persons may be excluded, and with respect to which, the right of any person to enter, remain in, or leave shall be subject to whatever restrictions the Secretary of War or the appropriate Military Commander may impose in his discretion. The Secretary of War is hereby authorized to provide for residents of any such area who are excluded therefrom, such transportation, food, shelter, and

---

1. Office of the Federal Register, National Archives and Records Service, *Code of Federal Regulations, Title 3—The President 1938–1943 Compilation* (Washington, DC: General Services Administration), 1092–93.

other accommodations as may be necessary, in the judgment of the Secretary of War or the said Military Commander, and until other arrangements are made, to accomplish the purpose of this order. The designation of military areas in any region or locality shall supersede designations of prohibited and restricted areas by the Attorney General under the Proclamations of December 7 and 8, 1941, and shall supersede the responsibility and authority of the Attorney General under the said Proclamations in respect of such prohibited and restricted areas.

I hereby further authorize and direct the Secretary of War and the said Military Commanders to take such other steps as he or the appropriate Military Commander may deem advisable to enforce compliance with the restrictions applicable to each Military area hereinabove authorized to be designated, including the use of Federal troops and other Federal Agencies, with authority to accept assistance of state and local agencies.

I hereby further authorize and direct all Executive Departments, independent establishments and other Federal Agencies, to assist the Secretary of War or the said Military Commanders in carrying out this Executive Order, including the furnishing of medical aid, hospitalization, food, clothing, transportation, use of land, shelter, and other supplies, equipment, utilities, facilities, and services.

This order shall not be construed as modifying or limiting in any way the authority heretofore granted under Executive Order No. 8972, dated December 12, 1941, nor shall it be construed as limiting or modifying the duty and responsibility of the Federal Bureau of Investigation, with respect to the investigation of alleged acts of sabotage or the duty and responsibility of the Attorney General and the Department of Justice under the Proclamations of December 7 and 8, 1941, prescribing regulations for the conduct and control of alien enemies, except as such duty and responsibility is superseded by the designation of military areas hereunder.

Franklin D. Roosevelt
The White House
February 19, 1942

58. PICTURES FROM INTERNMENT

These captioned sketches are from a book written by Miné Okubo, a young Japanese American woman from Southern California who was a promising art student at the University of California at Berkeley when the internment order was issued. First sent to the Tanforan Assembly Center, a racetrack near San Francisco, for processing and incarceration, Okubo was then sent to the Central Utah Relocation Camp known as Topaz. Her sketches and captions capture the surreal quality of the entire internment process: everyday life went on. People in the camps went to school, held community meetings and elections, and maintained social and religious rituals. These drawings portray the early stages of internment at the

Tanforan racetrack. What attitudes toward the internment process can you discern from Okubo's sketches and captions? What parallels can you draw between this account and that of Monica Sone? How do these drawings compare with the statements of the internment director, Dillon S. Myer, in the following selection?

Miné Okubo
Citizen 13660
1946

"Civil Control Stations were established by the Wartime Civil Control Administration in each of the designated areas. One member of each family was asked to register for the family; people without families registered individuals. On Sunday, April 26, 1942, I reported to Pilgrim Hall of the First Congregational Church in Berkeley to register for my brother and myself—a family unit of two Soldiers were standing guard at the entrance and around the buildings."

Miné Okubo, *Citizen 13660* (New York: Columbia University Press, 1946), 18–21, 35.

"A woman seated near the entrance gave me a card with No. 7 printed on it and told me to go inside and wait. I read the 'funnies' until my number was called and I was interviewed. The woman in charge asked me many questions and filled in several printed forms as I answered. As a result of the interview, my family name was reduced to No. 13660. I was given several tags bearing the family member, and was then dismissed. At another desk I made the necessary arrangements to have my household property stored by the government."

"On Tuesday when I returned to the Civil Control Station, I found our names posted on the board along with the family number. My family unit of two was scheduled to leave with the next to the last group at 11:30 a.m. on Friday, May 1, 1942. Our destination was Tanforan Assembly Center, which was at the Tanforan Race Track in San Bruno, a few miles south of San Francisco."

"We had three days and three nights to pack and get ready. My brother was excused from the University with a promise that he would receive his B.A. degree in June. Our friends came to cheer us up and to wish us luck. It was like old home week but we were exhausted from work and worry. On the last morning the main part of the packing was finished but there was still plenty to be done. I asked different friends to take care of some of my cherished possessions. In the last hour I dashed to the bank to get some money, picked up my laundry, and paid my household bills."

"[At Tanforan, a] guide left us at the door of Stall 50. We walked in and dropped our things inside the entrance. The place was in semidarkness; light barely came through the dirty window on either side of the entrance. A swinging half-door divided the 20 by 9 ft. stall into two rooms. The roof sloped down from a height of twelve feet in the rear room to seven feet in the front room; below the rafters an open space extended the full length of the stable. The rear room had housed the horse and the front room the fodder. Both rooms showed signs of a hurried whitewashing. Spider webs, horse hair, and hay had been whitewashed with the walls. Huge spikes and nails stuck out all over the walls. A two-inch layer of dust covered the floor, but on removing it we discovered that linoleum the color of redwood had been placed over the rough manure-covered boards."

59. THE DIRECTOR OF RELOCATION ADDRESSES INTERNMENT

When he was tapped to head up the internment camps in June 1942, Dillon S. Myer had been a longtime federal and civil service employee. In this fascinating essay published in a well-known civil rights journal, Myer does not exactly attempt to justify internment. Instead, he tries to show how democratic principles might be preserved in the program, suggesting that the internment process is a referendum on the American commitment to democratic ideals. If he believes that internment of Japanese Americans is an indictment of the nation's democratic claims, he wishes that the careful way in which the program is run might mitigate the worst of the offenses. In many ways, as this essay makes clear, Myer wished the internment camps to be miniature versions of small-town American life. While this might be partly true—internees worked hard to maintain some semblance of normal routine—the fact was that they spent each day behind barbed wire. How would you characterize Myer's view of internment? How does he attempt to envision democracy within internment? How might Monica Sone or Miné Okubo react to his views? What do you think motivated Myer to write this essay? Could democracy exist within internment?

Dillon S. Myer
"Democracy in Relocation"
1943[1]

The greatest involuntary migration in the history of the United States has been completed. Within the space of a few months, some 110,000 men, women, and children of Japanese ancestry, about two-thirds of them American citizens, have been moved from their homes in the western portions of the country. After temporary residence in assembly centers, they now are living in ten relocation centers between the Mississippi River and the high Sierras.

This mass evacuation shatters all precedent so far as this nation is concerned.

But evacuation was a step which seemed necessary to help insure the safety of our western shore against an enemy who looked like these people and who had taken advantage of the situation to infiltrate the Japanese population of our West Coast with his agents. Even the people of Japanese ancestry who were loyal to the United States could not always detect the enemy agents in their midst. . . .

The exclusion order, which called for all persons of Japanese ancestry to leave the western portions of Washington, Oregon, California, and the southern part of Arizona (later all of California was included in the area to be evacuated), was issued on March second of this year. The evacuated persons might leave when they liked and go to any place outside the area to be evacuated. As might have been anticipated, they were slow to move. Most of the Japanese and their American-born children and grandchildren always had lived in the coastal states and were at a loss to know where to go. It took time to make arrangements for disposing of businesses, farms, and homes. Many made no effort to move. So it became apparent that voluntary evacuation within a short period of time was doomed to failure, not only because of reluctance to go but because the movement of more than 100,000 people into new communities was bound to cause trouble. . . .

On March 29, just twenty-seven days after evacuation was begun, voluntary evacuation was halted, and planned and systematic evacuation began. Area by area, evacuees left their homes when they were ordered by authorities to do so. Temporary quarters were provided hurriedly by the military, while a search

---

1. *Common Ground* 3, no. 2 (Winter 1943), 43–48.

was made for other places where evacuees might live and work until such time as they might be reabsorbed into society. The temporary quarters, provided by the Wartime Civil Control Administration, were called assembly centers, fourteen in number, all located in the area to be evacuated. In a few weeks 10 other sites were chosen for relocation centers into which the evacuated persons would be moved as soon as accommodations could be provided. These are in eastern California, Arizona, Utah, Idaho, Wyoming, Colorado, and Arkansas, for the most part on publicly owned land which has possibilities of development for agriculture and other enterprises.

The War Relocation Authority has responsibility for the welfare of the evacuees after they have been removed from the assembly centers to these relocation centers. This is a responsibility not to be taken lightly, for on the conduct of the relocation program as a whole rest the future attitudes of some 110,000 persons, including about 70,000 American citizens.

If the evacuees are permitted to live in a manner as nearly normal as possible, with responsibility for the management of the communities in which they live, with educational opportunities, with a chance to develop initiative, and with reason to look forward to a better day, then there is a probability that they may retained as contributing members of a democratic society.

II

. . . In certain respects, life in relocation centers is not unlike life in any other community. In other respects, for reasons of economy and efficiency of administration and because of the temporary nature of the centers, conditions are necessarily different.

Housing is on the pattern of Army "Theatre of Operations" type of construction: barrack-type buildings, 100 feet long by 20 feet wide, usually divided into four compartments, 20 by 25 feet. Some of the single men live in barracks without the compartment divisions. The buildings are arranged in blocks, with a dining hall, bath house, and recreation hall to each block, to serve the needs of 275 to 300 people. The feeding problem, purchasing, distribution, and preparation of food is handled much like Army mess. Everyone eats in dining halls, and the menus are planned as a compromise between the tastes of the aliens, who have a preference for Oriental dishes, and their American-born children and grandchildren who prefer American-type foods. Families live together, but it is not feasible at present to provide for individual family feeding.

Almost all the families, of course, had household goods. Put in storage at government expense at the time of evacuation, it is now being sent to the owners at relocation centers as rapidly as possible, so that each family may have its own furniture.

Clothing is provided within certain maximum limits. It is up to each family to determine what clothing will be bought within the limits of the allowance.

The community stores are to be operated as co-operative enterprises, by an association to which any evacuee resident of the community may belong. The cooperative association chooses its own officers who determine what kinds of shops, stores, and other enterprises will be undertaken, and how the profits will be distributed, in accordance with the laws of the state in which it is incorporated. The staff of the War Relocation Authority audits the books at intervals, but the management is entirely in the hands of the evacuees themselves, and of course there is an abundance of merchandising experience and skills upon which they may draw. In most centers, whose population ranges from 7,000 to 18,000, the cooperative association elects to establish one or more "general stores" which sell soft drinks, ice cream, usually a few items of groceries, clothing, shoes, tobacco, candy, toilet articles, and other items not supplied to the evacuees by the administration of the center, and a shoe repair shop, barber shop, and beauty parlor. A newspaper is also a standard enterprise to meet the needs of the community.

The newspaper stands as one of the notable evidences of democracy in the center. Once the paper has been established as a community enterprise under evacuee management and control, the editorial staff has complete freedom of expression except for the restrictions against libel and personal attack which limit the activities of the press anywhere.

Organizations of many kinds are permitted. Since the Issei, or Japanese-born people, usually do not speak English well, their meetings are held in the Japanese tongue, if they desire.

There is freedom of worship. Services are conducted regularly by members of Buddhist, Catholic, and most of the Protestant faiths. Many of the ministers are evacuees, though Caucasian ministers come in from outside, representing their national church organizations.

In each relocation center schools have been established, with curricula which meet the standards of the state in which the center is located. The regular school system within the community covers the range from kindergarten through high school; other educational activities go beyond the usual school age limits, with day nurseries for the tiny ones, and an extensive program of adult education for persons beyond ordinary school age. Evacuee teachers are used to the fullest available extent, but approximately two-thirds of the teachers are Caucasians. The one major respect in which the curriculum in a relocation center school varies from other schools in the state is that more opportunity is provided for vocational education. The work activities provide laboratories for youngsters, particularly in high school, so they may obtain more than the usual amount of supervised experience in agriculture, carpentry, sewing, and other vocational activities.

The extent to which democracy is practiced in the relocation centers is represented best, perhaps, by the community government. While the administrative staff of necessity must have responsibility for such things as food, housing, employment, and agricultural production, the supervision of life in the community is left largely up to the evacuees themselves. The legislative body is a Council, with representatives chosen from each block. All residents of the center eighteen years of age and above may vote, but only American citizens twenty-one and older may hold elective office. Anyone of voting age, however, may serve on committees or in appointive positions.

The regulations and laws of the community are established by the Community Council, and the "court" is a Judicial Commission, usually consisting of three persons, which sits in judgment on cases of violation of the community laws. Major offenses, such as felonies, are turned over to officials and courts outside.

Each relocation center has its own fire department and its own police, or "wardens" as the evacuees prefer to call them. The wardens are not armed, and their job for the most part is one of helping, rather than restricting, the residents of the community.

III

With the nation fighting for its life and needing the productive effort of every man and woman, it is unthinkable that the available manpower in the relocation centers should not be employed in productive effort of some kind. True, the Geneva Convention, governing treatment of enemy aliens, prevents the use of citizens of Japan in direct war work, but there are other ways in which their skills may be used. A fundamental objective of the administration of the relocation centers is to see that work opportunities are provided for everyone. During the early days of each center, this was rather difficult, but as time passes, more and more things are developed which mean jobs for more people.

One of the basic considerations in selecting sites for the relocation centers was the possibility of agricultural production. In some instances, part of the available land already was in production; other land had to be cleared, or leveled; water had to be brought onto the land, or drained off. But with potentially productive soil, and with about half the population composed of farm people, agriculture is one of the great possibilities. About 2,700 acres of crops were planted and harvested in 1942 and several hundred acres of winter vegetables now are growing. Before the close of the production season in 1943, it seems likely that the relocation centers will produce all their own vegetables, all their eggs and poultry, and about half their meat requirements, largely in the form of pork and pork products. This, of course, will help reduce the public expense of operating the relocation centers. In addition to subsistence production, there are some agricultural commodities which can be produced to meet the needs of the nation as a whole: one of the centers is in the heart of the long-staple cotton area of Arizona; others are well suited to the production of sugar beet seed and vegetable seeds, and some of the evacuated farmers are skilled in seed production.

Opportunities for the establishment of industries in which evacuees may work are being explored, and hold considerable promise. It is planned to establish some types of industries to manufacture goods needed by the evacuees themselves. Clothing and school furniture are two things which appear to be likely objects of manufacture at the present time. Early in the evacuation program, American citizens among the evacuees went to work weaving colored burlap into nets, to make camouflage screens for the Army. The long lists of materials needed by the Army and the Navy suggest other items which might be manufactured in relocation centers.

As this is written, one manufacturer who has a war contract is breaking ground for a factory building at one of the relocation centers. At first, about 120 evacuees will be employed and trained in a trade completely new to all of them. If the experiment is successful, the factory may be expanded to employ several times as many persons.

All evacuees at relocation centers are provided with food, lodging, and medical care. In addition, those who perform services for the community as a whole, such as the cooks, stenographers, farm workers, truck drivers, and time-keepers, receive nominal wages, or "cash advances" from the War Relocation Authority and clothing allowances for themselves and their dependents. The cash advances are $12 for beginning workers, $16 monthly for the majority of the workers, and $19 monthly for those performing difficult, responsible, or professional tasks.

Those employed in enterprises run by the co-operative association receive wages and clothing allowances on the same scale, paid out of funds of the cooperative association. However, industries under private management established at or near the relocation centers to employ evacuee workers will pay the wages prevailing in the industry. Workers in these industries will reimburse the administration for the cost of subsistence for themselves and their families. It will be left to the evacuee community to determine whether those workers will keep all the remaining money, or whether everything above $16 or $19 monthly will be put into a general fund to be divided among all workers, those employed in community services as well as those who earn the higher wages. Thus far, there has been no opportunity for an evacuee community to cast a vote on the matter, but the first decision of this sort will be watched with a great deal of interest.

During the summer months, there was a serious shortage of labor in many parts of the country, and sugar beet growers asked that groups of evacuees be permitted to leave the assembly and relocation centers to care for the growing beet crop. About 1,700 workers left the centers to work in the sugar beet fields. The locations in which they worked all were outside the evacuated area and within limits, they traveled, lived, and worked without guard, just as any other group might have done. About 1,200 stayed outside the centers though the harvest season. When harvest time for sugar beets came, the demand for labor was even greater, and several thousand were permitted to leave the centers for this work. At the close of the season, they will return to the relocation centers. Several hundred other evacuees picked long-staple cotton in Arizona, living in the relocation center and going to and from the cotton fields daily. The total employment of evacuees in the harvesting of farm crops at this writing is over 7,600.

Before the workers went out of the centers to the sugar beet fields, there were certain conditions which had to be met: the employer agreed to provide satisfactory housing; and an official of the state or county agreed to be responsible for loss and order. There were no serious incidents of any kind, and the workers met with the general approbation of their employers.

The success of this large-scale experiment suggests that as the supply of manpower in the nation grows smaller and the demand grows stronger, employers of many different kinds may request that persons now living in relocation centers be permitted to leave to take jobs. If that should become the case, the policies of the War Relocation Authority will permit such employment of individuals or groups. The evacuees now living in the relocation centers may leave the centers if certain conditions prevail: (a) if they have a definite place to go and means of support, outside of designated military areas; (b) if they agree to report any change of address; (c) if there is reasonable assurance of their acceptability in the community where they plan to go; and (d) if nothing in their records with official investigative agencies indicates they would constitute a danger to the security of the nation. The great majority of the 110,000 residents of the relocation centers will be able to meet these requirements, and so will be available for employment if needed and desired.

The success of this permanent, dispersed phase of relocation will be dependent on the sentiment of the public in general, and the sentiment of the evacuees. If evacuated persons will be accepted by the public, and if the evacuees themselves are willing to try to establish themselves in communities outside the relocation centers, then genuine progress can be made in permanent relocation. The principles underlying public acceptance of the evacuees as individuals would seem to be closely allied to the things we are fighting for.

60. RACIAL PROFILING IN WARTIME

As we have learned in both volumes of this book, the American West has a distinctly troubling history of discrimination and violence aimed at Asians and Asian Americans. Think back to the discussion in chapter 3 of this volume that detailed the exclusionary and violent response to the Chinese in the nineteenth-century West. Following the Japanese attack on Pearl Harbor, Americans suddenly found themselves militarily and otherwise aligned with China, which Japan had previously invaded. In this excerpt from the pages of Life *magazine,*

Americans are supposedly taught how to distinguish ally Asians (the Chinese) from enemy Asians (the Japanese). The blatant racism is stunning, and, in recognizing this, we must also note that the 1940s were really not that long ago at all.

Life Magazine
"How to Tell Japs from the Chinese"
December 1941[1]

In the first discharge of emotions touched off by the Japanese assaults on their nation, U.S. citizens have been demonstrating a distressing ignorance on the delicate question of how to tell a Chinese from a Jap. Innocent victims in cities all over the country are many of the 75,000 U.S. Chinese, whose homeland is our stanch ally. So serious were the consequences threatened, that the Chinese consulates last week prepared to tag their nationals with identification buttons. To dispel some of this confusion, LIFE here adduces a rule-of-thumb from the anthropometric conformations that distinguish friendly Chinese from enemy alien Japs.

To physical anthropologists, devoted debunkers of race myths, the difference between Chinese and Japs is measurable in millimeters. Both are related to the Eskimo and North American Indian. The modern Jap is the descendant of Mongoloids who invaded the Japanese archipelago back in the mists of prehistory, and of the native aborigines who possessed the islands before them. Physical anthropology, in consequence, finds Japs and Chinese as closely related as Germans and English. It can, however, set apart the special types of each national group.

The typical Northern Chinese . . . is relatively tall and slenderly built. His complexion is parchment yellow, his face long and delicately boned, his nose more finely bridged. [A representative] of the Japanese people . . . betrays aboriginal antecedents in a squat, long-torsoed build, a broader, more massively boned head and face, flat, often pug, nose, yellow-ocher skin and heavier beard. From this average type, aristocratic Japs, who claim kinship to the Imperial Household, diverge sharply. They are proud to approximate the patrician lines of the Northern Chinese.

---

1. *Life*, December 22, 1941, 81–82.

61. RACIAL AND ETHNIC TENSIONS IN SOUTHERN CALIFORNIA: THE ZOOT SUIT RIOTS OF 1943 *(SEE P. 219)*

In the summer of 1943, servicemen and police in Los Angeles and neighboring communities went on a series of nighttime attacks aimed at young men wearing "zoot suits," a stylish outfit of loose pants and jacket with wide lapels, often adorned with fobs and chains, worn by Mexican Americans, Filipinos, and

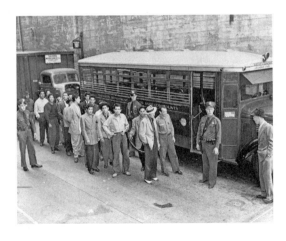

Zoot suiters lined up outside Los Angeles jail en route to court after feud with sailors, ca. 1943

Courtesy the Library of Congress, Prints and Photographs Division.

African Americans (and some whites as well). The military and police person-nel, acting out on racial tensions of the times and claiming that they were per-forming a patriotic duty in opposing indiscriminate use of fabric in times that demanded rationing, set upon and beat young zoot suiters across several nights of violence. Men and teens had their clothes ripped away, and they were beaten with fists and clubs. Often, as we see here, those attacked were the ones arrested and sent off to jail and court.

Tensions cooled after a week or two, but not before the Los Angeles City Council adopted a resolution outlawing the wearing of zoot suits within city lim-its. The claim that the violence had been sparked, and legitimated, as a patri-otic response to non-rationing fell apart after a series of investigations found the root cause of the "Zoot Suit Riots" to be plain and simple racism.

FURTHER READING

Avila, Eric. *Popular Culture in the Age of White Flight.* Berkeley: University of California Press, 2004.

Crost, Lyn. *Honor by Fire: Japanese Americans at War in Europe and the Pacific.* Novato, CA: Presidio Press, 1994.

Escobedo, Elizabeth. *From Coveralls to Zoot Suits: The Lives of Mexican American Women in Los Angeles on the World War II Home Front.* Chapel Hill: University of North Carolina Press, 2013.

Himes, Chester B. *If He Hollers Let Him Go.* Garden City, NY: Doubleday, Doran, 1945.

Hirabayashi, Lane Ryo, James A. Hirabayashi, Brian Niiya, and Wakako Yamauchi. *The View from Within: Japanese American Art from the Internment Camps, 1942–1945.* Los Angeles and Seattle: Japanese American National Museum and the University of Washington Press, 1994.

Houston, Jeanne Wakatsuki. *Farewell to Manzanar: A True Story of Japanese American Experience during and after World War II Internment.* New York: Bantam, 1995.

Johnson, Marilynn S. *The Second Gold Rush: Oakland and the East Bay in World War II.* Berkeley: University of California Press, 1993.

Leonard, Kevin Allen. "Federal Power and Racial Politics in Los Angeles during World War II." In *Power and Place in the North American West,* edited by Richard White and John M. Findlay, 87–116. Seattle: University of Washington Press, 1999.

Lotchin, Roger. *Fortress California, 1910–1961: From Warfare to Welfare*. New York: Oxford University Press, 1992.

McWilliams, Carey. *Southern California Country: An Island on the Land*. New York: Duell, Sloan and Pearce, 1946.

Nash, Gerald. *The American West Transformed: The Impact of the Second World War*. Lincoln: University of Nebraska Press, 1990.

Pagán, Eduardo Obregón. *Murder at the Sleepy Lagoon: Zoot Suits, Race, and Riot in Wartime L.A.* Chapel Hill: University of North Carolina Press, 2003.

Reeves, Richard. *Infamy: The Shocking Story of the Japanese American Internment in World War II*. New York: Henry Holt, 2015.

Robinson, Greg, and Elena Tajima Creef, eds. *Miné Okubo: Following Her Own Road*. Seattle: University of Washington Press, 2008.

Smith, R. J. *The Great Black Way: L.A. in the 1940s and the Lost African-American Renaissance*. New York: PublicAffairs, 2006.

Taylor, Sandra C. *Jewel in the Desert: Japanese American Internment at Topaz*. Berkeley: University of California Press, 1993.

Observing an atomic blast, 1958. This photograph shows reporters on "News Knob," covering nuclear experiments at the Nevada desert proving grounds. Ten miles away, a mushroom cloud forms over ground zero. The intimate contact with atomic explosions illustrated here was not uncommon in the 1950s West: soldiers, journalists, government officials, and even local residents often joined scientists at the test sites to observe atomic "bursts." Many eyewitnesses described the explosions and resulting clouds as beautiful. How do you think the American public of the late 1950s reacted to images like this? Would public opinion today likely be the same, or different, and why?

CORBIS/Bettmann.

The Cold War and the Atomic West

13

There is little doubt that the anxieties and the stresses of the Cold War made and remade the modern American West. The West, more than in any other region of the nation, is still living with the revolutionary changes ushered in by the deepening antagonism between the United States and the Soviet Union in the aftermath of World War II. It is most evident in the ways in which the Cold War reshaped the American armaments industry, from the astonishing buildups of World War II to the equally remarkable response to the Cold War. The West armed America anew in the 1950s and 1960s: advances in aerospace technology launched project after project, company after company, as the nation raced to build an arsenal of weaponry the likes of which the world had never before seen.

In 1953 the United States exploded its first hydrogen bomb, which upped the ante in the global arms race for ever more powerful nuclear weapons. When the Soviet Union launched Sputnik, the world's first satellite (small in size, huge in global impact) in the fall of 1957, the United States responded by making good on what President Dwight Eisenhower would later call the "military-industrial complex."

Fueled by defense dollars, armies of military veterans, young engineers, shop-floor workers, mom and pop fabrication outfits, and all manner of other technological and logistical supporters rolled into western cities and the western landscape. They made rockets and jets and missiles and bombs, and they experimented with them in the wide-open spaces of western deserts. The Sun Belt boomed: Denver, Colorado Springs, Tucson, Albuquerque, Seattle, and others like them shot up, embraced the Cold War with a mixture of exuberance and fear, and would never be the same.

Despite the economic juggernaut, though, the Cold War definitely cast a shadow over the nation, and the West in particular. People feared imminent nuclear attack. Out-of-the-way western towns and villages built civilian sentry shacks in which locals sat and scanned the skies for incoming missiles or bombs. Schoolchildren practiced sliding under their desks, as if that would offer any protection whatsoever from the fiery destruction of an atomic blast. Families across the West and the nation dug fallout shelters in their backyards: vaults stocked with canned goods and other supplies that would supposedly help them survive the attack that many imagined was imminent. It may seem comical to us now, these flimsy and odd precautions, but we would be wrong to discount the sheer anxiety they expressed.

The Cold War transformed western nature into a guinea pig of nuclear testing—tests that made the atomic bombs dropped on Japan in 1945 look positively puny in comparison. The landscape and atmosphere of the West has been rocked by more nuclear blasts than anyplace else on the Earth. It remains unclear exactly what the long-term effects of the tests will be on human and nonhuman life, and on western soils and waters, although the relatively short-term consequences were unquestionably deleterious.

President Harry Truman established the Nevada Test Site on a vast desert landscape whose ecological fragility was either not recognized or not regarded as important by the agencies and individuals who proceeded to explode things on, under, and above it. As newer and more powerful weapons emerged, the hydrogen bomb being the most destructive example, more than one thousand nuclear tests were performed there. Soldiers were ordered to watch detonations of this or that weapon and then engage in mock "atomic warfare" battles. Mock towns, looking very much like movie sets hastily erected in desert sands, complete with mannequin people, were bombed and burned and blown over by nuclear winds so that scientists and military officials might gain some understanding of the consequences of such weapons. Journalists flocked to these places, poorly protected themselves, and wrote about, photographed, and filmed what was going on.

People living near the Nevada Test Site (later called "downwinders" to indicate their vulnerability to airborne radiation) grew accustomed to the bombs going off nearby. "Oh, go back to sleep," a wife might tell a husband who had been awaken at night by a ferocious "BOOM!" "It's only an atomic bomb." People such as these, including the Navaho and other Native Americans living nearby, had no idea that their proximity was so dangerous. They would learn it soon, however, as they and their animals sickened and died of cancer at rates far and away higher than populations in other regions.

The 1950s scared Americans. The documents we've assembled here tell the stories of those fears through the lives, words, and experiences of westerners. Read them with an appreciation of their worries and with empathy for the mysteries they wondered about. Would war come? Would the West and its many weapons installations of corporate or military origin be the first to be attacked? Where exactly would such attacks happen first, and how would they be carried out?

62. OBSERVER'S REPORT OF ATOMIC TEST

This eyewitness report was prepared by Frank P. Zeidler, the mayor of Milwaukee. Along with Atomic Energy Commission officials, Department of Defense employees, and others, he watched an atomic test in spring 1952 at the Nevada Test Site, a federal facility outside Las Vegas that was the nation's major atomic testing site for more than a decade. Zeidler describes the use of troops in the exercise: the soldiers not only watched the blast, they were ordered into mock battle shortly after the bomb was detonated. Only in recent years, with the release of formerly secret Atomic Energy Commission documents, has the full extent of radiation testing on individuals during the 1940s and 1950s come to light. What does this eyewitness account suggest about the era's faith in science? Why do you think the mayor of a city like Milwaukee would make the journey to Nevada to witness a test?

Frank P. Zeidler
"Observer's Report of Atomic Test"
1952[1]

PROVING GROUNDS ...   For a city dweller accustomed to narrowly constricted views, it is important to remember the large distances of the proving grounds. When one sees the floor of a desert ten miles across boiling from the force of a single burst, it becomes easier to translate this effect on a center of population.

An elaborate system of security is maintained. Forty-two miles from Las Vegas is Indian Springs Air Force Base which gives the air support to atomic experiments; 17 miles farther is Camp Desert Rock, the army support base; and 3 miles up a special road is Mercury, Nevada, a construction camp where

---

1. Frank P. Zeidler, "Observer's Report of Atomic Test at Nevada Proving Ground, April 2, 1952," typescript (Milwaukee, WI: Milwaukee Public Library).

construction companies engaged in numerous works for the Atomic Energy Commission have their field offices. Nineteen miles farther are the main control buildings for Frenchmen Flat and Yucca Flat experiments. It is here, near these two flats, that observations are made. . . .

INSPECTION TOUR: On April 20th, a caravan of invitees inspected Indian Springs Air Force Base, Camp Desert Rock, and the proving grounds.

At Indian Springs, Brigadier General John Mills described the support work of his planes including transport devices, atomic cloud gathering devices, atomic cloud tracing planes, "drop" planes and helicopter services.

At Camp Desert Rock, General Stork described the use of soldiers in this exercise. The bomb was to be dropped from an airplane on a target, theoretically an enemy strong point, surrounded by two hills, back of which were masses of material.

Troops would advance from the front and cross ground zero to take the objective while the airborne troops would drop at the rear of the objective and cross to the front to join forces.

From Camp Desert Rock, the inspection party proceeded to Mercury, Nevada, construction camp for a respite. Upon another security check, the caravan then drove past Frenchmen Flat to the main observation point of A.E.C.[2]

At this point, the party was shown a broad view across the desert to the approximate location of ground zero in Yucca Flat which lay below at a much lower elevation. The party also got a brief review of the control room with its intricate timing devices and recording devices.

Some of the staff described the location. Many of the staff members were young persons in their early twenties and thirties. These are among the "atomic scientists." I was told by Gordon Dean, head of the Atomic Energy Commission, that the average age of persons at the Los Alamos project was 33 years. These young persons with their ingenuity and powers of reasoning, invented and designed many of the devices to create the ultimate effects of a massive explosion of nuclear energy.

From the control house, the inspection party was taken to Yucca Flat where it saw certain installations. These included two towers for further explosions, one bunker for housing recording devices one-half mile from one of the towers, and other installations which were not identified. . . .

Beneath the towers where future explosions were to take place were instruments and cables to collect data and to transmit it in millionths of a second before the instruments themselves were vaporized.

The bunkers were of massive construction with lead doors, baffled entrances, thick concrete walls and roofs, mounded with earth. Whether such

---

2. **A.E.C.:** the United States Atomic Energy Commission.

a shelter could withstand a direct burst overhead of say 2000 feet, I do not know.

The inspection party was then taken to the point where it was expected to observe the burst, 10 miles or 11 miles on a large rock outcropping in the desert near the main A.E.C. observation point.

After inspecting the site, the party returned to Las Vegas.

The effect of this inspection tour was to tend to ease uncertainties about hazards which might be encountered in the actual test.

SECOND BRIEFING: On Monday, April 21st, before the test the group was briefed both in the morning and afternoon. Speakers included Gordon Dean of the Atomic Energy Commission who pointed out that the explosion was the largest anticipated for the continental United States. Dean stressed the necessity of carrying out these experiments because of the tremendous growth in the nature and diversity of present weapons.

Governor Millard Caldwell, Director of Federal Civil Defense Administration, pointed out the vital nature of this program for civil defense and the millions of lives that would be lost if atomic warfare started. He cited statistics showing the enlargement of civil defense functions in Europe and Russia and the actual construction of shelters in Scandinavian countries. . . .

BURST DAY: Photographers left Las Vegas on April 22, 1952, at 4:00 A.M. The main party followed at 5 A.M. A general tension gripped everyone, even those with extensive front line experience in World War II and Korea.

Just before reaching Camp Desert Rock, the troops who were to participate in the exercise pulled out in convoy and proceeded ahead. At the main observation point the troops proceeded in their trucks to the trenches about six miles ahead of the main party of observers on the rocky outledge called "News Knob."

It had been announced in the briefing that the bomb drop would occur at 9:30 A.M. on April 22nd if the weather permitted, and if the wind was blowing right. The forecast made the night before indicated the program would proceed.

Announcements from the loud speakers kept the observers posted. A half million dollars worth of cameras and radio and television equipment had been assembled. A TV expert named Klaus Landsberg made television possible by finding an unnamed peak near Charleston Peak from which he could transmit a beam to another peak in California and then by various stages to Los Angeles.

Observers were given "4.1" goggles to allow them to look at the burst which was a hundred times brighter than that of the bright desert sun. The sun through these goggles appeared merely as a glowing orb.

H hour–2 was announced. At about H–1 the drop plane from Kirtland, New Mexico airbase appeared. High above, the observers saw vapor trails of the various planes. At H–1 a ton of high explosive was detonated to get blast characteristics and other data.

H hour–30 minutes and H hour–15 minutes were announced. Repeated warning were given not to look at burst except through goggles, not to take goggles off until after the count of three, not to look at burst through binoculars and to brace oneself for any massive shock.

It was announced that the bomb would be dropped from a height near 33,000 feet to explode at a height of between 3,000 to 3,500 feet. The bomb would drop in 42 seconds. A great tenseness held the audience.

The minutes were counted. At H–1 goggles were put on. An announcement was made that the bomb was away. The seconds were counted and the explosion occurred with a few seconds of scheduled time within 200 feet of ground zero.

THE EXPLOSION: An indescribably brilliant flash occurred. Those without glasses who turned away saw the desert become blinding with light. After a few seconds goggles were removed, and an expanding ball of fire, turning over and over was seen. The ball rose rapidly and turned to pink and white and other colors.

Almost simultaneously with the burst came the blast of heat. Many seconds later came a hard crack of the burst followed by the blast wave.

The ground boiled with dust for miles across the desert.

So many phenomena occurred in so short a time that no one could see all of them. Some persons observing the rising ball, missed the stem of the mushroom, enormous as it is, until completely formed. Others failed to see the boiling dust. Still others failed to see the changes going on in the cap of the mushroom itself.

People were gripped by the awe of the tremendous spectacle, fascinated by a sort of hypnotism. Constant exclamations were heard that "This is the most beautiful thing I have ever seen." The colors are not readily described since they range through the spectrum.

Some persons, including myself, heard two distinct bursts, although others heard only the one. The blast wave itself was not as strong as anticipated since it was not focussed where the observers were.

No one, who has not seen this phenomenon, can appreciate its beauty and its horrifying power.

MILITARY EXERCISE: Planes circled the atomic cloud at a respectful distance. After some time a helicopter went into the dust cloud and came out. Far away on the desert, trucks to convey troops started to move to ground zero. Planes flew in and out of the area on tests. Finally paratroopers, picked up by planes on the far end of Yucca Flat, flew to the site and the paratroopers jumped.

After about an hour, a commanding general of the 6th Army flew into the dust zone to talk to the men in the trenches and shortly after three men, a captain, a sergeant, and a private, were flown out of the area in a helicopter to describe what the first radiological team did in the area.

The captain was a school teacher, called up as a reservist; one of the privates was a Ph.D. in nuclear physics. The men described their apprehension at the announcement that the bomb was dropped. They were ordered to crouch in their trenches and look down. After the burst, a loud speaker system ordered them to look up and see the ball of fire. The ball, however, was quickly obscured by the dust wave and blast which slapped them back against the trench and then forward.

The men were four miles from the burst. Fires were burning at what I judged to be two and one-half miles away from the burst. After twenty minutes, the men came out of the trenches. After an hour they walked to their objective which took another hour. The dust however had not completely settled at the time the main party left three hours later.

OBSERVATIONS ON THE BOMB: Discussion between observers and officials of the Army and the Atomic Energy Commission brought out interesting effects.

1. The bomb itself was close to the largest, if not the largest exploded in the United States. Data taken will later reveal what rank this explosion holds.

2. The flash was seen 400 miles away in Idaho on the ground. The blast was felt at St. George, Utah, 120 miles away, although observers close at hand said the blast effect was somewhat disappointing. However, this probably was due to focusing of blast waves.

3. There have been larger balls of fire than in this blast.

4. The bomb was bigger than the Hiroshima, Nagasaki, and Bikini bombs, but much larger ones have been exploded at Eniwetok. I guess that this bomb might be described as a "11/2x" or 30,000 kiloton bomb.

5. Fires were started by bomb. Several shacks burnt, and troops reported fire damage 21/2 miles out.

6. The same target was used 6 times before.

7. Troops could have gone into ground zero much sooner than they did.

8. The radioactive cloud dispersed after several hours and by six o'clock P.M. search planes could not find it.

9. A.E.C. personnel went into ground zero and found only 1/10 roentgens[3] per hour. Since 3 roentgens per hour are permissible for a time, the area was considered safe for a man to stay for about 30 hours.

10. Atomic clouds did go higher than this one.

11. Army observers said trenches fairly close up were destroyed if not well revetted. Sandbags were burnt or scorched. Bunkers of army type probably would have been squashed flat.

---

3. **roentgens:** a unit of radiation measurement.

12. The atomic bomb is not yet considered an artillery weapon.

13. Anesthetized pigs and conscious mice were in the zone. . . .

14. Soldiers were apprehensive at the distance of 4 miles. The psychological effect of the bomb is going to be studied. Practically all observers were impressed by the beauty of the spectacle and those close up expressed a desire to see it again. . . .

63. CIVIL DEFENSE IN THE NUCLEAR AGE

This excerpt from a booklet prepared by the North Dakota Civil Defense Agency discusses how to respond to the threat of nuclear attack. During the 1950s and 1960s, across the West and the nation as a whole, civil defense operations published literature instructing Americans on what to do in case of nuclear war. This booklet may seem naive or silly to us today, but the outdated ideas and instructions should not obscure people's real fear of a possible attack. What aspects of this booklet strike you as particularly dated? What specific fears does it address? Do you think this civil defense information would have allayed the anxieties of North Dakotans?

North Dakota Civil Defense Agency
"How You Will Survive"
ca. 1960[1]

Yes, We Can Be Attacked

Long range jet bombers are presently in the hands of many nations, friendly and hostile. The intercontinental missile that can be sent almost anywhere in the world is being rapidly developed. Both the jet bombers and the missiles will be able to bring deadly weapons down on the United States. Military planners admit that even the best defense system will not be able to stop all enemy planes or missiles.

The weapon most likely to be used in an all out war is the hydrogen bomb which now has 1000 times the explosive force of the atomic bombs dropped on Japan in World War II. The North Dakota Survival Plan anticipates the use of bacteriological and chemical mixtures to further cripple the nation.

HEAT: Since the hydrogen bomb is expected to be the most dangerous weapon, we must know what this bomb can do. Its explosion will generate heat that comes close to that actually on the sun. With an expected temperature of sev-

---

1. North Dakota Civil Defense Agency, *The North Dakota Plan: How You Will Survive* (Bismarck, ND, ca. 1960).

eral million degrees Fahrenheit at the point of the blast, the heat will melt metal and destroy all life within the immediate area.

BLAST: The concussion created by the explosion will turn skyscrapers into shambles. Humans or animals caught in the immediate area will die from rupture of lungs and blood vessels due to the sudden changes in pressure.

RADIOACTIVITY: The explosion of a hydrogen bomb will create deadly rays which can pass through flesh and destroy it. The radiation intensity from residual fallout will be so great near the target area that people won't be able to live there for days, weeks, months, and possibly years. As the bomb bursts, it will throw radioactive particles into the air where the winds will pick them up and spread them throughout the country. As a result, the effects of hydrogen warfare can reach several hundred miles from the target.

TARGETS: North Dakota is presumed to have four possible targets which the enemy may strike. They are the air force bases at Minot and Grand Forks, Hector Airport at Fargo and the State Capitol in Bismarck.

The largest hydrogen bomb presently anticipated in our plans is equal to 20 million tons of TNT. This would create damage 20 miles from the point of explosion, creating a damage area 40 miles across. Destruction would be absolute at the burst site but would gradually diminish outward.

What Will Happen

Four Major Cities May Be Destroyed

Communications Will Be Gone

Evacuation of Endangered Areas

Radioactivity Will Be a Hazard

Government Will Have to Be Reorganized

Volunteers Will Be Needed

Families Will Be Separated

Economy Must Be Rebuilt

Everyone Must Plan for Survival

The Plan of Defense

INTERCEPTION: The major portion of the American defense system is military. This includes the mobilization of the armed forces for repelling an attack and proceeding to defeat the enemy. We can expect rapid interception of enemy planes but even the best of the military planners concede that some enemy planes are bound to get through.

WARNING: As soon as enemy planes are sighted or enemy action is definite, the national warning point at Colorado Springs, Colorado will relay the warning to four points in North Dakota. All four points are the police station at Bismarck, Minot, Fargo and Grand Forks where there is a 24-hour watch.

WARNING POINT: As soon as the warning point receives the alert, it will send the alert to the entire State Civil Defense organization through the police radio system. On this system are the highway patrolmen, the state game wardens, all sheriffs and city police departments. The state points as well as the local points will immediately warn the Civil Defense organizations, the governing officials and civilians.

YOU WILL BE ALERTED!:   Every city and county will have a warning system to reach the public, according to the North Dakota Survival Plan. The system must be finely developed in the four target areas as evacuation or shelter are the only practical defenses against hydrogen weapons. Alert systems are necessary outside of the target areas since radioactivity may endanger lives and the Civil Defense forces must be mobilized to help meet the demands for housing and supplies. In target areas, a steady siren blast will mean evacuate; a wailing sound will mean to take cover. Battery radios will be important for receiving the official Civil Defense broadcasts on CONELRAD, which will be on 1240 and 640 only.

Evacuation

GOVERNMENT: One of the most critical responsibilities during an attack is the preservation of our government—and law and order. Since we know that destruction of democracy is one of the objectives of communism, we can be assured that they shall seek to destroy our organized society. All officials of government in each target area must evacuate as a group and re-establish themselves at a new site.

CIVIL DEFENSE: Local Civil Defense organizations will have the responsibility of supervising the evacuation of equipment and supplies from the target areas. This will include rescue trucks, fire trucks, radio equipment, foodstuffs, heavy equipment and a mass of usable items that will be needed for recovery.

CIVILIANS: The people must be prepared to leave the target areas as well as stand by for possible movement out of fallout patterns. Civilians must take all supplies possible so they can maintain themselves until they can be taken care of outside of the target areas.

You Must Follow Traffic

We can expect congested traffic in a full-scale evacuation of the target areas. Everyone must be prepared to follow the emergency traffic rules:

1. Know your evacuation plan. Each city has one.
2. Outbound highways will be for one direction only—OUT.
3. Follow directions given by police and auxiliary police.
4. Do not try to travel into a possible target area when an alert has been given.

You Will Be Assigned Shelter

Evacuees coming from the target areas will be cared for in the outlying areas, with Civil Defense organizations in the "support" area being responsible for housing and feeding. In most cases, housing will be in private homes and farms. Evacuees will remain in private dwellings until the alert is over or the economy can be rebuilt.

You Must Be Self-Reliant

PROVIDE YOUR OWN TRAVEL: Every family should arrange for its own travel. Vehicles should always be kept in good running condition. The tank should always be half full of gasoline. A reserve supply should be kept in the trunk for emergencies. Every family should make arrangements for travel under all circumstance[s]. In addition to providing its own transportation, families should pick up others who may be stranded.

PROVIDE YOUR OWN NEEDS FOR SEVEN DAYS: In the initial attack, you will be unable to depend on others. So be prepared to survive by yourself for one week.

1. Stock basic foods for immediate packing.
2. Take a good supply of fresh, clean water.
3. Take blankets and clothing for cold weather.

SHELTER IN TARGET AREA: If you are caught in the target area when the "Take Cover" signal (a wailing signal on the siren) is given, you must get into the deepest possible location. Perhaps the handiest will be your house basement. Shut off all power, gas and water lines leading into your house.

SHELTER YOURSELF FROM FALLOUT: Once in the reception area, your main concern will be radiation from fallout. Fallout is the radioactive particles falling from the sky which can be fatal if you are exposed over [a] period of time. Fallout will be carried by the wind in an oval pattern away from the target. The Civil

Defense organization will attempt to constantly monitor the fallout intensity so you can be alerted when it becomes critical.

ROOT CELLARS: In the rural parts of North Dakota, farmers and residents of smaller communities have built root cellars to store foodstuff and as shelter from tornadoes. Whether constructed of concrete or sod, these root cellars are excellent protection against heavy radioactivity. The ideal covering is two or three feet of sod or concrete. Such a shelter should be equipped for living for two weeks and should have carefully controlled ventilation.

BASEMENTS AND INTERIORS: If a root cellar is not available, the next best shelter is the home itself, and more particularly the basement, if you have one. An ordinary house without [a] basement probably would cut the radiation in half, if you stay on the first floor near the center of the house. Staying in a house basement will reduce your exposure to about 1/10 the outside exposure rate. If you should elect to build a shelter in a corner of your basement, you may reduce the exposure to 1/500 or more. The State Civil Defense Office in Bismarck has plans and specifications for several types of fallout shelters. These plans are designed to aid the home-owner who desires to build his own shelter at a minimum cost and graduate in scale to a more expensive shelter located underground adjacent to the home.

SHELTER SUPPLIES: Whether you evacuate or take shelter in an emergency, one of the basic necessities is an adequate food supply for your family. You should assemble a two-week food supply in your home shelter area, and a three-day evacuation survival kit in your family automobile. The North Dakota Civil Defense Office in Bismarck has a suggested list of these supplies available in pamphlet form, or you may obtain this information from your local Civil Defense Director.

SHELTER LIVESTOCK: If you have livestock of any kind, you should get it under cover. A barn or cattleshed will prevent material damage to your animals. If you have no enclosed area for them, even a roof shelter will help prevent the particles from settling on their bodies. You should also get their feed under cover.

CLEANING THE CONTAMINATED: As soon as possible, the people who have been in radioactive areas must wash thoroughly in purified water to wash off any particles that may have fallen on them. Everything exposed should also be washed in clean water, such as clothing, blankets, and household goods. Radioactivity cannot be cleansed but it can be washed away with the particles emitting it. . . .

64. CONDITIONS IN BOMBED AREAS

This magazine article describes the sections of Nevada most affected by atomic testing, which by the time the story appeared had been going on for several years. Many Americans had probably never heard of the places mentioned, but nuclear testing and the effects of radiation were big news stories in the era. What makes this story unusual is that it puts atomic testing and Cold War fears together with grassroots interviews done with people near (sometimes very near) the test sites. In this way, readers would be reminded that the Cold War was both an international and a very local phenomenon. In what ways is this account similar to or different from Frank Zeidler's eyewitness account? Are there any hints about the long-term environmental costs of such testing? Does the article suggest that the government is concerned about the effects of radiation?

U.S. News & World Report
"What It's Like to Live in Earth's Most A-Bombed Area"
1957[1]

Out of sixty-eight atomic explosions set off by the United States, forty-nine have taken place at the Nevada test site near here. More A-bombs have been exploded in Nevada than in any other part of the world.

What has been the result? Are people living near the test area panicked? Have cattle in nearby ranching areas become radioactive? Is the food supply contaminated?

If anybody in the world, outside of Hiroshima and Nagasaki, should be alarmed by fall-out and other effects of bomb tests, the people in this region should be. A sampling of sentiment, however, fails to uncover general alarm— or any convincing evidence that things are much different than they were before tests began.

MARGIN OF SAFETY: Scientists making regular checks for the Atomic Energy Commission report officially that radiation has not reached danger levels anywhere in this test-site region that includes parts of Nevada, Utah and Arizona.

The maximum recorded for any one community, during the entire six-year period since nuclear tests began in Nevada, is 4.3 roentgens. . . . That compares with the AEC's recommendation that 23.4 roentgens could safely be permitted for the period.

In one freak case, near Bunkerville, Nevada, a cloud dumped an extra-heavy dose of fall-out on a motel occupied by fifteen people, who might have

---

1. *U.S. News & World Report*, June 28, 1957, 79–82.

accumulated up to 13 roentgens if they had continued to live there. The motel has since been deserted.

And yet, here and there in this desert region surrounding the test site, you do find people wondering—and, in some cases, worrying—over possible effects of the atom tests. This is clear in soundings made throughout this three-State area by a Regional Editor of "U.S. News & World Report."

LOCAL EVENTS: Several local happenings in recent years are blamed by some people on fall-out or bomb shock. For example, there are the cases of Mrs. Gerald Sharp, of Nyala, Nevada, 80 miles north of the test area, and Dewey A. Hortt, of Mesquite, 110 miles to the west. Both have lost all the hair on their heads.

Martin Bardoli, a seven-year-old, has died of leukemia, as has Robert Howe, four and a half. Some cattle belonging to the Fallini Ranch, near Warm Springs, have developed "cancer eye." Sheep have died after tests, as have ducks and chickens in their eggs.

The people affected admit that all this is nothing new, nor is it limited to the area surrounding the major tests. Hereford cattle had "cancer eye" long before the atomic age began. People in other places, at other times, have died of leukemia or suddenly lost their hair.

Another man admits that "the thing is you don't know, so you begin to wonder when you have aches and pains, if the tests could be to blame." Dr. D. D. Carr, Clark County's health director, explains, "There's a psychological effect on people to find reasons for what they have."

CLAIMS FOR DAMAGE: The AEC investigates all claims made against it. These claims for alleged damage, injury or illness caused by nuclear tests have reached a total of 640 since 1951. So far, payments totaling $53,624 have been made for 384 claims—for damage only, and mostly blast damage.

The AEC, in reviewing its investigations into these claims, says this: "No claim has ever been settled on the basis of alleged biological injury to humans, although the AEC compensated the owners of some horses which were grazing very near the test site."

GENERAL ACCEPTANCE: By and large, despite claims and complaints, most people in this desert region seem to agree that living here appears to be just about as safe as living anywhere else. This feeling is summed up by J. C. Adams, a retired ranch hand at Glendale Junction, Nevada.

Mr. Adams says: "Those AEC people are pretty accurate about how much has fallen and how much it takes to do you harm. We don't pay any attention any more."

R. L. Hickman, sales manager for the Arden Meadowgold Dairy in Cedar City, Utah, declares: "I think people are more concerned about smog in California than about fall-out in Cedar City."

Just about the only outward reminder that people here are living close to the world's main atomic test site is the badges that some of them wear, each containing a test strip of film to record exposure to fall-out.

These badges permit local AEC offices in seventeen different zones to check up regularly on the levels of radiation—in towns, on ranches and in different occupations. The badges are not compulsory for ordinary citizens, but some two thousand people wear them.

LINGERING FEARS: While there are no signs of general alarm over fall-out, you do find some people wondering more than others about how the unseen and largely unknown cumulative hazards of radiation might affect them.

One worry that some hold is expressed by Robert A. Crandall, editor of the *Times-Bonanza* in Tonopah, Nevada, some 100 miles north of the test site. In an editorial, Mr. Crandall puts it this way: "Tests have been delayed because of the possibility of 'light but unacceptable fall-out' over Las Vegas, says the AEC. But we're in the 'virtually uninhabited area,' so we get it."

That is denied by AEC, and refuted also by an AEC map showing the amounts of radiation recorded in various places around the test site. This shows that there is no set pattern of fall-out favoring certain areas over others. Towns lying side by side vary greatly in the amount of radiation received.

EXTRA PRECAUTIONS: The AEC has stepped up its safety measures for the current series of nuclear tests. Some bombs are being detonated from balloons and even underground to cut the danger of local fall-out caused by the metal used in the steel towers.

Then there is the weather to reckon with. If clouds are too low or conditions otherwise might unduly concentrate what fall-out there is in local areas, a nuclear test is postponed. So far this year, more than 80 such postponements have been caused by weather.

Local health authorities are running their own checks all the time to safeguard against food or water contamination. Marvin T. Skodje, public-health-service monitor at Mesquite, says: "There's more danger to Mesquite's water supply from natural causes than from fall-out."

SHORT-LIVED JITTERS: Six years of living practically side by side with the A-bomb has made little change in the lives of most people. A young mother in Hurricane, Utah, shrugs and says: "It kinda gives you the jitters when it goes off, but then you forget." Most everyone seems to be agreed that it would be nice if further tests did not have to be held—but there's no sign of any public protest against them.

Instead, most people here seem to agree with Morris Dannelly, a tractor driver who works near Cedar City.

As Mr. Dannelly puts it: "It might be dangerous—this fall-out and all—but I'd rather have us find out all about this atomic business so the Russians won't be the only ones."

What the Folks Say in "Fall-Out City"

[*These remarks originally appeared in a photo essay next to each resident's picture.*]

Jeter C. Snow, mayor and manager of a chain store, recalls that, during the 1955 tests, "some people came to us to see if they couldn't stop them." Uranium prospectors said the tests "messed up" the Geiger counter readings. A farmer blamed tests for the death of a new-born calf. Nowadays, however, Mayor Snow says: "I've not noticed any real concern," though "people here wish it could be some other way."

Dr. M. K. McGregor, who assists his father at the McGregor private clinic, finds that some people are inclined to put the blame on atom tests—wrongly— for all sorts of ills and mishaps. The young doctor says: "There's a lot of spotty baldness, but it's all due to anxiety—not to any fall-out I know of." He recalls hearing that one man, just back from a trip, claimed that marks on his arm were caused by fall-out. The marks turned out to be fingernail scratches. Dr. McGregor concludes: "It's important to know more about fall-out."

Mrs. Kate Empey, secretary of the town information office, once was dead set against the atom tests. Last year she visited an AEC exhibit, heard that radiation can affect the body, came back to town ready to circulate a petition to stop the tests. But she never did. She says she is still concerned with the health hazard, but "I've never felt any ill effects."

Wayne Whitehead, of Whitehead's Dairy, says: "The tests don't worry me. I think that the guys who are doing it are competent. If they weren't, they wouldn't be doing it."

Rex Frei, cattleman who helps work some thousand head on a public range, says: "I don't see how that little flash down at Vegas could affect us. I had my wife operated on for cancer and they gave her tremendous doses [of radiation] over months. She's still alive, so this can't be too bad."

Mrs. Margie Bowler, waitress and cashier at Dick's Cafe, confesses that she once had been "quite alarmed" about atom tests—but no more. She says: "We've got pretty used to the tests; this year they are pretty small. Our relations back East have asked us about living so close, but we told them we were not concerned."

Ellis Everett, instructor in physics and mathematics at Dixie College, says he knows of some people who have written to their Congressmen to try to get the tests stopped. As for him, "I take the AEC's word on how much people can stand. I'm not worried about it. Our big problem here is finding a physics teacher."

65. PLEDGING PATRIOTISM, OR ELSE

The anxieties and tensions of the Cold War left a great deal of damage in their wake. Americans were frightened by what the Soviet Union represented, frightened by the idea that infiltration, spying, and even subliminal brainwashing could all be taking place inside the United States by disloyal Americans. These people were understood to be "hiding in open space" in such fields as the military, government, the film community, and other areas of the arts, and Cold War warriors in national security, law enforcement, and all levels of government went after them with urgency and abandon. One sector hit especially hard were educators, given the belief that unpatriotic or even communistic ideas could be planted inside the hearts and minds of the nation's young people, perhaps even without them realizing it. In California, and elsewhere in the West and the nation, government officials and education boards insisted that public educators sign loyalty oaths declaring their allegiance to the United States and their animosity to Communist ideas, ideals, and teachings. This move proved exceedingly controversial, as academics and university administrators pushed back, claiming that such oaths violated their rights of free expression and/or academic freedom.

University of California Loyalty Oath

1950s

Constitutional Oath (Constitution of the State of California, Article 20, Section 3)

"I do solemnly swear (or affirm, as the case may be) that I will support the Constitution of the United States and the Constitution of the State of California, and that I will faithfully discharge the duties of my office according to the best of my ability."

As Passed by the Regents, April 12, 1950

"Having taken the constitutional oath of the office required by the State of California, I hereby formally acknowledge my acceptance of the position and salary named, and also state that I am not a member of the Communist Party or any other organization which advocates the overthrow of the Government by force or violence, and that I have no commitments in conflict with my responsibilities with respect to impartial scholarship and free pursuit of truth. I understand that the foregoing statement is a condition of my employment and a consideration of payment of my salary."

Current State Oath of Allegiance

"I do solemnly swear (or affirm) that I will support and defend the Constitution of the United States and the Constitution of California against all enemies, foreign and domestic; that I will bear true faith and allegiance to the Constitution of the United States and the Constitution of California; that I take this obligation freely, without any mental reservation or purpose of evasion; and that I will well and faithfully discharge the duties upon which I am about to enter."

FURTHER READING

Ackland, Len. *Making a Real Killing: Rocky Flats and the Nuclear West.* Albuquerque: University of New Mexico Press, 1999.

Amundson, Michael A. *Yellowcake Towns: Uranium Mining Communities in the American West.* Boulder: University Press of Colorado, 2002.

Boyer, Paul. *By The Bomb's Early Light: American Thought and Culture at the Dawn of the Atomic Age.* Chapel Hill: University of North Carolina Press, 1994.

Brugge, Doug, Timothy Benally, and Esther Yazzie-Lewis, eds. *The Navajo People and Uranium Mining.* Albuquerque: University of New Mexico Press, 2006.

Edgington, Ryan H. *Range Wars: The Environmental Contest for White Sands Missile Range.* Lincoln: University of Nebraska Press, 2014.

Fernlund, Kevin J., ed. *The Cold War American West, 1945–1989.* Albuquerque: University of New Mexico Press, 1998.

Fuller, John G. *The Day We Bombed Utah: America's Most Lethal Secret.* New York: New American Library, 1984.

Heefner, Gretchen. *The Missile Next Door: The Minuteman in the American Heartland.* Cambridge, MA: Harvard University Press, 2012.

Hevly, Bruce, and John M. Findlay, eds. *The Atomic West.* Seattle: University of Washington Press, 1998.

May, Elaine Tyler. *Homeward Bound: American Families in the Cold War Era.* New York: Basic Books, 1988.

Misrach, Richard. *Bravo 20: The Bombing of the American West.* Baltimore: Johns Hopkins University Press, 1990.

Pasternak, Judy. *Yellow Dirt: An American Story of a Poisoned Land and a People Betrayed.* New York: Free Press, 2010.

Price, V. B. *The Orphaned Land: New Mexico's Environment since the Manhattan Project.* Albuquerque: University of New Mexico Press, 2011.

Pugh O'Mara, Margaret. *Cities of Knowledge: Cold War Science and the Search for the Next Silicon Valley.* Princeton, NJ: Princeton University Press, 2005.

Szasz, Ferenc Morton. *The Day The Sun Rose Twice: The Story of the Trinity Site Nuclear Explosion, July 16, 1945.* Albuquerque: University of New Mexico Press, 1995.

Titus, A. Costandina. *Bombs in the Backyard: Atomic Testing and American Politics.* Reno: University of Nevada Press, 1986.

United States Congress, Senate Committee on Labor and Human Resources. *Health Effects of Radiation Exposure.* Washington, DC: Government Printing Office, 1990.

Voyles, Traci Brynne. *Wastelanding: Legacies of Uranium Mining in Navajo Country.* Minneapolis: University of Minnesota Press, 2015.

Westwick, Peter, ed. *Blue Sky Metropolis: The Aerospace Century in Southern California.* Berkeley: University of California Press, 2012.

Wills, John. "'Welcome to the Atomic Park': American Nuclear Landscapes and the 'Unnaturally Natural.'" *Environment and History* 7, no. 4 (November 2001): 449–72.

Free Speech Movement, University of California at Berkeley, ca. 1965. In the fall of 1964, officials at the University of California at Berkeley banned political activity at a popular gathering spot at the edge of campus. Before long, students organized to protest the action, banding together in what they called the Free Speech Movement (FSM). Many of them had been active in the civil rights movement in the South, working on issues such as voting rights for African Americans, and back home they resumed implementing the same techniques and organizing practices that they had learned in places like Mississippi. With the rise of civil rights activism across the nation in the 1960s, American students, like Berkeley's FSM participants pictured here, joined with others working toward greater civil rights for millions of Americans, inaugurating an era of student civil rights activism on campuses across the nation. How would you describe the scene pictured here? Why do you think the FSM protestors are dressed as they are?

Bancroft Library, University of California at Berkeley.

Generation and Other Gaps

Historians, students, and those who lived through it see the 1960s as a decade of great turmoil in American history. Vast social and cultural changes rocked the status quo, and divides between people, their leaders, and their visions of America deepened. It has also been looked to as, amid such turmoil, a period of far-reaching reform in the extension of civil and other rights. Of course important strides forward in the extension of rights were not bounded by the decade of the 1960s. Nor can we any longer suggest that the American South, that region with arguably the most distance to travel in regard to human rights for all, is the only beacon in the long-standing struggle for equality among Americans of all backgrounds. The West played a role—it still does—and we begin to unpack that role with the documents chosen for this chapter.

As in the South, civil rights activism in the American West traces its roots back further than we usually attest or suggest. In the anti-Communist and Cold War hysteria of the 1950s (as we saw in the loyalty oath stories of the previous chapter), many westerners took courageous stands for civil rights and free speech protections. The infamous "Hollywood Ten" episode, which destroyed the lives and careers of creative individuals in the film industry who were deemed radical threats to the nation, is one such case, as several individuals refused to go along with the oppression and the attacks. College campuses, too, had their share of episodes in which students, faculty, and staff refused to support the intervention of those who wished to test the patriotic loyalties of people deemed not quite American enough for this or that investigatory body or grandstanding superpatriot.

By the fall of 1964, student interest in free speech, and especially the protection of it, developed into the famous Free Speech Movement growing out of the campus at the University of California, Berkeley. The magnitude of that effort, and its growing significance as a touchstone of youthful political protest and activism, stunned the nation (and probably the students themselves). Free Speech at Berkeley marked the beginning of an association between western colleges and universities and the era's civil rights struggles, and the West had its own stories to tell and battles to fight.

By the 1960s, the fight for African American civil rights had turned to examples of radical protest and radical acts across the nation. In 1966, two men from Oakland, California, Bobby Seale and Huey Newton, founded the militant African American group the Black Panthers. The Panthers carried automatic weapons, dressed in military garb, and espoused the violent defense of African American civil rights. Although their stance undoubtedly frightened white America, the Panthers expressed the concerns of many African Americans who had not grabbed a gun or donned fatigues. Thousands of African Americans—tens of thousands, hundreds of thousands—believed, with good reason and plenty of evidence, that the prosperity of the Cold War and the 1950s had bypassed them.

Many Mexican Americans felt similarly. A potent political force, if not yet activated in the ways it eventually would be, this population also took part in the civil rights struggles of the era. In doing so, like the African American community, Latinos built upon important political mobilization and some notable successes from the recent past. In the 1940s, for example, Mexican American Edward Roybal was elected to the Los Angeles City Council. He was the first Latino to be on this body in the modern era—a success that went far beyond symbol, as it signaled an awakening of Mexican American political activism and rising clout. By the 1960s Mexican Americans had begun capitalizing on the radicalizing possibilities of cultural and ethnic heritage across the greater Southwest and into Mexico. Using a single ethnic identifier—that of Chicano— people of diverse Latin descent forged a powerful cultural and historical identity attached to place. From this, they began to leverage political and cultural authority, which they used to battle discrimination in the arenas of civil and economic rights. In the fields of California, for example, Mexican and Mexican American farmworkers—laborers who had the fewest rights (if, in some respects, any at all) of any in the entire American West—rallied around the charismatic leadership of Cesar Chavez. Co-creator of the United Farm Workers, Chavez organized strikes against the entrenched, autocratic power of

California's giant fruit and vegetable corporations to gain worker rights of contract, labor conditions, and pay.

We might be tempted to see Native American efforts at gaining civil and political rights in a brighter 1960s light. We would probably be wrong in that, however, especially if we realize how beaten and battered the nation's indigenous peoples and communities were to begin with. The country did pass the Indian Civil Rights Act of 1968, a step forward, if late. But violence and frustration also colored the efforts to gain ground for Indians. For two years, radicals occupied Alcatraz Island in San Francisco Bay, using the former prison site as a theatrical home base to broadcast anger over issues of Native sovereignty, land rights, political expression, free speech, and broken treaties. This kind of dramatic activism took a darker turn in the early 1970s, when federal law enforcement personnel engaged in regular gunfire with members of the American Indian Movement (AIM), who had held the town of Wounded Knee on the Pine Ridge Reservation in South Dakota for a two-month protest of ineffectual Indian policy reform.

The civil rights challenges of minority and marginalized groups did not go unanswered. On the contrary, the efforts of African Americans, Mexican Americans, women, LGBT, and Native American groups and individuals to remedy patterns (and laws) of discrimination sometimes triggered social unrest and retaliatory violence. Some of the worst episodes occurred in the West. A tense confrontation between police and the African American residents of the South Los Angeles neighborhood of Watts erupted in violence and rebellion in the summer of 1965. Similar incidents followed in cities across America, as "the Watts Riots" became the unfortunate spark to others in other cities and other states. There might be some angle at which we could look at these events, in which a lot of people died, as at least a little productive: the nation's enlightened leaders tried to rouse Americans to wrestle with the deeply troubled state of race relations across the North, South, East, and West. If anything, Watts proved that boxing off the American South as "the region with racial problems" made no sense.

The 1960s were filled with protests large and small, individual and collective. The selections below are meant to give meaning and language to some of them. You will read a now-famous speech given in the Free Speech Movement at Berkeley (we recommend you read this one aloud). Martin Luther King Jr. can be heard in the telegram he sends in support of striking Mexican farmworkers in California, seeing as he did that the freedom struggles of African Americans and Mexican Americans had much in common. Oral histories of Black Panthers bring you inside that group's mission and ideals. Other documents point to other struggles, other fights. These stories won't inspire romantic views of civil rights fights of yore; on the contrary, read (and listen) to these beliefs, claims, and objectives knowing just how seriously these actors regarded them.

66. FIGHTING FOR EQUALITY AND VOICE

Founded in Los Angeles by activist Harry Hay and friends shortly after the end of World War II, the Mattachine Society was an early and critical gay rights organization. Largely secret and anonymous in order to protect members from harassment or reprisal, the organization lobbied to raise awareness of rampant anti-gay discrimination and violence, and to link gay rights with the rights of other minority groups, all of which felt Cold War pressures, tensions, and fears. In this "Call to Arms," distributed as a leaflet around Los Angeles, the group made explicit its alliance with other oppressed racial or ethnic groups. The modern gay rights movement of the later twentieth and early twenty-first centuries owes much to the example and bravery of this early movement in the far West.

Mattachine Society
Call to Arms
ca. 1952[1]

So long as there is one group whose members, *as citizens*, are prey to blackmail, intimidations both social and physical in nature, shakedown, entrapments, search and seizure without warrant, incarceration without charge, denial of right to summon counsel or bail, and even subject to arraignments without being informed of specific charges,—SO LONG AS ONE MINORITY GROUP (regardless of the justice or the injustice of the prejudice against them)—IS THUS HARRIED AND HOUNDED,—NO MINORITY GROUP OR COMMUNITY GROUP IS SAFE. . . . [W]e urge you to realize that if the Homosexual does NOT have equal citizenship guarantees, privileges, and dignities, under the law,—THEN NEITHER DO YOU.

---

1. From Mattachine Society Project Collection, ONE National Gay and Lesbian Archives, University of Southern California.

67. STUDENT MOBILIZATION FOR FREE SPEECH

The Free Speech Movement (FSM) proved to be a turning point for student activism in the West in the early 1960s. It galvanized student leaders who would play prominent roles in protest movements in later years; it reminded the West, and the nation, that students in places like Northern California might have something important to say about civil rights; and it helped make Berkeley a national symbol for civil rights protests. In the following impromptu exhortation, graduate student Mario Savio urges his fellow students to fight for civil rights, and cautions against the impersonal politics and institutions that he fears are gaining power over the hearts and minds of the American people. Before long, the FSM had inspired thousands of students at Berkeley. They performed acts of civil disobedience, seized a number of campus buildings, and held large rallies in support of free political expression. FSM activists infuriated the administration and may have horrified their parents, but in the end the university relented and allowed the free distribution of political literature on university property. Do you think there are particular reasons why the Free Speech Movement began at a place like the University of California? How would you describe Savio's impression of the modern university? What words or phrases mark the speech as a product of the 1960s?

Mario Savio
Address to the Free Speech Movement
1964[1]

Well. This started out as a completely spontaneous response of students at this University against arbitrary action taken by the dean's office here against certain students who thought they had the right to free expression at this University. Well, free expression, for the University, means that you can talk about lots of things, but as we just heard in the statement from Chancellor Strong, those things you can't do are the taking of action on various ideas that you discuss. Now I'd like to connect that, right here, very, very clearly, with statements that have been made by President Kerr in his book on the multiversity. President Kerr has referred to the University as a factory; a knowledge factory—that's his words—engaged in the knowledge industry. And just like any factory, in any industry—again his words—you have a certain product. The product is you. Well, not really you. And not really me. The products are those people who wouldn't join in our protest. They go in one side, as kind of rough-cut adolescents, and they come out the other side pretty smooth. When they enter the University, they're dependent upon their parents. That kind of dependency is the sort of thing that characterizes childhood and adolescence. When they're in school, before they enter the University, part of that dependency is shifted to the various schools that they're in. Then they come to the University. And now, instead of suckling at their mother's or at the breast of their schools, they suckle at the breast of Holy Mother University. So here they are. Now, they're dependent upon the University. They're product. And they're prepared to leave the University, to go out and become members of other organizations—various businesses, usually—and I hope I'm not offending anyone in this, but I'm speaking *my* mind—which they are then dependent upon in the same way. And never, at any point, is provision made for their taking their places as free men!

---

1. David Lance Goines, *The Free Speech Movement: Coming of Age in the 1960s* (Berkeley: Ten Speed, 1993), 151–53.

Never at any point is provision made—you know, someplace in society, some things you can do which in some ways can be expressive of your individuality. You just can't do that unless you have no intention of making it in this society. You can be poor and have dignity, but if you have any intention of making it in any way, you're out of it, you're just completely out of it! You've gotta be a part; part of a machine.

Now, every now and then, the machine doesn't work. One of the parts breaks down. And in the case of a normal, regular machine, you throw that part out; throw it out, and you replace it. Well, this machine, this factory here, this multiversity, its parts are human beings. And, sometimes, when *they* go out of commission, they don't simply break down, but they really gum up the whole works! [*Scattered laughter*] That's what we're all doing here. We've kind of gone out of commission. We won't operate according to the way the parts of this machine should operate, and the machine started to go out of commission. But the remedy is the same! In the case of a regular machine, in the case of *this* machine, you throw the parts out! And that's what they decided to do. That's what the statement says. They're on indefinite suspension—I presume that's close to the words he used—of those students who went out of commission; those students who weren't good enough parts, who didn't function well enough. For one brief moment, there were lots of people, lots of students, whose imaginations were fired. Maybe we would not have to likewise be parts. Maybe somehow we could take our place as free men also! So those students said, "We're with you! We stand right with you! Not behind you. We're next to you! We're brothers!" They signed that sheet! That sheet said, "We want you to treat us *all the same way.*" Now, you know it was an unreasonable demand. It was unreasonable in this regard: it's not a demand the University could have met without completely dropping any kind of disciplinary action against anyone. And they knew it! And . . . we knew it.

Well, they've decided, instead, to disregard your protest, and to assume that you had never come in here, nothing like that had happened, that instead what it is—the eight students, they refused to speak with the proper authorities, and they've been axed.

We can do various things. I suppose that's really what we want to talk about. We can do various things. We can—and this is what I would hope the group here would want to do—we can make as the issue of our continued protest three things: First, whatever action has been taken against these particular individuals singled out by the administration, this action be dropped, completely! [*Thunderous applause and cheers*]

Are there any abstentions? [*Laughter*]

The second thing is that we here, all of us, the committee of the whole, we demand those particular demands I read to you from that yellow sheet earlier today concerning freedom of expression on this campus. We are putting our weight behind those demands. [*Applause*]

In particular, our protest is demanding a meeting with Chancellor Strong—none of these little guys, we're done with that. [*Laughter and applause*] We're demanding a meeting with Chancellor Strong to discuss those demands!

Third, we demand that, at least until that meeting has taken place, if there are any groups on campus who exercise what they believe to be their rights of free expression, there will be no disciplinary action taken against them, at any time! [*Cheers and applause*]

I presume that, from the basis of the response, in the name of all the people assembled here, and hopefully in the name of the University of California, we can make these demands public, and make them to the administration; to the chancellor. Is this something we can do? [*"Yes! Yes!" Great applause*]

68. SUPPORT FOR CALIFORNIA FARM WORKERS

This remarkable telegram ties together two of the nation's greatest civil rights leaders—Cesar Chavez, a leader of Mexican Americans, and Martin Luther King Jr., the critical figure in the African American civil rights movement. Under the leadership of men like Chavez, the National Farm Workers Association, and Larry Itliong of the Agricultural Workers Organizing Committee, fieldworkers went on strike in the agricultural region around the small California town of Delano. Chavez and the others were protesting the working conditions imposed upon the multiethnic migratory workforce by the area's growers; they called their struggle for greater civil rights and economic power La Causa, *or* The Cause. *The strike lasted five years and resulted in greater recognition of union labor by the state's large agricultural growers. The Delano strike, out of which grew the United Farm Workers, helped make Chavez into a recognized leader in the civil rights efforts of poor migrant workers of the West, regardless of their race or ethnicity. In this telegram, King expresses his solidarity with Chavez and the striking Mexican, Filipino, and other workers. What does King see as common ground between the African American and Mexican American civil rights movements? Why do you think King expressed his interest and support in a civil rights struggle in the American West?*

Martin Luther King Jr.

Telegram to Cesar Chavez Regarding the Delano Strike
1965[1]

As brothers in the fight for equality, I extend the hand of fellowship and good will and wish continuing success to you and your members. The fight for

---

1. Jacques E. Levy, *César Chávez: Autobiography of La Causa* (New York: W.W. Norton, 1975), 246.

equality must be fought on many fronts—in the urban slums, in the sweat shops of the factories and fields. Our separate struggles are really one—a struggle for freedom, for dignity, and for humanity. You and your valiant fellow workers have demonstrated your commitment to righting grievous wrongs forced upon exploited people. We are together with you in spirit and in determination that our dreams for a better tomorrow will be realized.

69. THE RISE OF THE BLACK PANTHERS

The oral histories that follow recount the origins of the militant Black Panthers, the African American civil rights organization founded in Oakland, California, in the late 1960s. From Oakland the Panthers spread outward, but their influence was always greater than the group's numbers would suggest until government and police crackdowns at the end of the decade crushed them. Through their aggressive organizing, public displays of guns and force, and effective propaganda, the Black Panthers struck a particularly harsh chord in 1960s America. To many, they seemed to symbolize everything wrong with the country: lawlessness, racial combativeness, urban struggle. To others the Panthers represented hope, or at least concerted action in the face of crisis in American cities. The selections here reflect some of these hopes and fears. From these brief excerpts, how would you describe the program of the Black Panthers? Why do you think the Panthers originated on the Pacific coast and not elsewhere? Do these oral histories suggest that the particular circumstances of a place like Oakland might have contributed to the birth of the Black Panthers?

Various Oral Histories
1990[1]

Huey Newton

It was in 1953, I think, that Oakland had its first black policeman, who was a friend of my father's. His name was Kinner. My father broke friendship with Kinner because of his membership in the Oakland police. Not because he was a policeman, but because at the time the policy was that Kinner could only arrest black people. He could detain a white, but he would have to call a white officer. And my father thought that this was degrading. It was no change from what was happening in the South.

---

1. Henry Hampton and Steve Fayer, *Voices of Freedom: An Oral History of the Civil Rights Movement from the 1950s through the 1980s* (New York: Bantam, 1990), 351–54.

The police, not only in the Oakland community but throughout the black communities in the country, were really the government. We had more contact with the police than we did the city council. The police were universally disliked. In Oakland, in October '66, when the party was founded, there was about one percent blacks on the police department. The police were impolite and they were very fast to kill a black for minor offenses, such as black youth stealing automobiles. They would shoot them in the back and so forth.

Bobby Seale

In 1966, numerous acts of police brutality had sparked a lot of spontaneous riots—something that Huey and I were against, these spontaneous riots. And Huey and I began to try to figure out how could we organize youthful black folks into some kind of political, electoral, *power* movement. Stokely Carmichael was on the scene with Black Power.

Huey and I had been involved for some time, off and on, studying black history—what Malcolm had done, where Martin Luther King came from. I was highly influenced by Martin Luther King at first and then later by Malcolm X. Largely, the Black Panther party came out of a lot of readings, Huey and I putting scrutiny to everything going on in the United States of America. Like we must have subscribed to twenty-some-odd different periodicals, offbeat periodicals like *The Liberator, Freedomways*, what have you, even some periodicals out of Africa. We had digested Frantz Fanon's *Wretched of the Earth*. We knew Lerone Bennett's *Before the Mayflower*. I knew about the two hundred and fifty slave revolts that included Gabriel Prosser and Nat Turner and Denmark Vesey. I mean, Frederick Douglass, the Nation of Islam, what had happened in the 1930s, what have you and so on. And there we were with all this knowledge about our history, our struggle against racism.

At that time, Huey and I were working with the North Oakland Neighborhood [Anti-Poverty] Center on the advisory board. We got five thousand signatures for them to go to the city council, to get the city council to try to set up a police review board to deal with complaints of police brutality. Well, the city council ignored us. So that phenomenon was that the city council was just a racist structure which could care less about the forty-eight percent black and Chicano people who lived in the city of Oakland. So there we are, trying to figure out what to do. We finally concluded through those months that we had to start a new organization.

Huey Newton

Bobby Seale and I used the North Oakland service center as the original work spot to put together our program. They had all the machinery—mimeograph machines and typewriters. The North Oakland service center was a part of the poverty program. The service centers collected names of people on welfare, elderly people who needed aid. We used those lists to go around and canvass the community in order to find out the desires of the community. So we would go from house to house and explain to people our program. We printed up the first program at the North Oakland service center.

Our program was structured after the Black Muslim program—minus the religion. I was very impressed with Malcolm X, with the program that Malcolm X followed. I think that I became disillusioned with the Muslims after Malcolm X was assassinated. I think that I was following not Elijah Muhammad or the Muslims, but Malcolm X himself.

Bobby Seale

We sat down and began to write out this ten-point platform and program: We want power to determine our own destiny in our own black community. We want organized political electoral power. Full employment. Decent housing. Decent education to tell us about our true selves. Not to have to fight in Vietnam. An immediate end to police brutality and murder of black people. The right to have juries of our peers in the courts.

We summed it up: We wanted land, bread, housing, education, clothing, justice, and peace. Then we flipped a coin to see who would be chairman. I was chairman.

Bobby Seale

We had written the Ten-Point Platform and Program of the organization but yet didn't have a name. A couple of days later, Huey Newton and I was trying to figure out why was it that on a Lowndes County Freedom Organization pamphlet that we had, why they had this charging black panther as the logo. Huey come up with some notion that if you drive a panther into a corner, if he can't go left and he can't go right, then he will tend to come out of that corner to wipe out or stop its aggressor. So I said, "That's just like black people. All the civil rights people are getting brutalized across this country for exercising the First Amendment of the Constitution, which is the law of the land. They can't go left. Other people have tried to control the police with law books and tape recorders and have been brutalized. They can't go right. Even the young whites who were protesting, I saw, who was in support of the black people, can't go left, can't go right. So we just like the black panthers." And in effect Huey Newton and I named the organization the Black Panther party. At first, it was the Black Panther Party for Self-Defense. Later, we dropped the "Self-Defense" because we didn't want to be classified as a paramilitary organization.

70. CITIZENS ORGANIZE AFTER WATTS

After the rebellion in Watts in the summer of 1965, the attention of the nation was riveted on this community in southwestern Los Angeles. Political and social pundits, journalists, and scholars dissected the uprising, trying to figure out what had gone wrong and why. Amid all the attention, the people of Watts picked up their lives and restored the routines of everyday living as best they could. Their efforts included activism in local civil rights circles. This document by community leader Clara James highlights some of the grassroots activism that emerged after Watts. According to James, in what ways had the recent Watts uprising changed daily life in the community? What are her greatest concerns about her community and her neighbors? Whom does she count as allies? What similarities can you find between this document and the other selections in this chapter?

Clara James

"The South Side Citizens Defense Committee"
1966[1]

The South Side Citizens Defense Committee was organized as a direct result of the Watts and South side rebellion. When 4,000 persons were rounded up and thrown in jail, including 750 juveniles; 700 hospitalized; and 34 killed; we were determined to band together for mutual protection and defense against any further onslaughts against our community or our people.

The statistics quoted represent not merely numbers but real . . . live . . . people . . . human beings, mind you, not monkeys as the distinguished Chief of Police William Parker has called them. They are human beings with flesh and bone and blood and soul who have wants, needs, hopes, desires, ambitions and aspirations just like all other human beings.

All men are created equal and are endowed by their Creator with certain inalienable rights that among these are life, liberty and the pursuit of happiness. So states a portion of the "Declaration of Independence" of the United States of America. But this has not applied to the Negro people and for this reason—WE HAVE HAD A WATTS.

Watts is a predominantly Negro community. There are Mexican, Asian and a few Caucasians living there. There are nice homes as well as shacks. There live the educated as well as the uneducated. Good people and bad people. Intelligent and the unintelligent. There are the employed and many unemployed.

Doctors, domestics, lawyers, merchants, students and drop-outs all are to be found there.

---

1. Los Angeles Committee for the Protection of the Foreign Born, *Defense: Sixteenth Annual Conference Journal* (Los Angeles: n.p., 1966), 32–34.

But Watts and South Los Angeles has been bypassed by the city administration in terms of servicing this community as it does others. It has needed street lights and parks, schools, banks, nurseries and all the things that other communities have. The unemployment rate is high and the underemployment is almost as serious. The man who is employed can hardly support his family on the low wages he receives and the man who is unemployed gradually succumbs to hopelessness and despair.

These key factors require that both mother and father work which leaves too many of the children unsupervised. Since most of the women are compelled to work as domestics way over on the other side of the city in the Valley or Westside where she tends some other person's children the problems of distance, travel, and long hours, leave her own children unattended.

Do you not think that the Negro mother would like to feed and dress her young child and to see her older child off to school? As it is, the children are left to fare for themselves. Wouldn't she like to be on hand when the family returns in the evening? Certainly . . . how can she? In far too many instances she is the sole breadwinner of the family. And because her child has to eat, she has to leave to earn food.

The husband and father of this same family would also like to be able to provide well for his family . . . but if he is employed, his wages are low and he can't make ends meet. He was the last hired and as the lowest paid he was the first fired.

When he looks for a job, he is told that the job has been filled, and yet, in line behind him is another man whose skin is different who may be less qualified who is picked for the already "filled" job. When this type of thing happens day after day or week after week how does one expect a man not to become discouraged and disillusioned?

Meanwhile, the wife becomes tired and irritable, overworked and underpaid, feels unappreciated and the children become unruly and unbearable. The children can sense the deprivations they bear while other children have things and cannot be blamed.

The result is a breakdown in family relations, the beginning of juvenile delinquency, infidelity, sickness, broken homes and finally welfare.

Of course not all families end up this way. Sometimes mother, father, and children work. Many times, grandmother, uncle and aunt pile into one house in order to help sustain the family. Added to these family handicaps are the higher prices charged for inferior foods they buy at the markets and higher rents they pay for inferior housing.

Young people in the community face even greater oppression. Like all young men, they face the possibility of the draft—but unlike other young men, they have no desire to fight for a freedom neither they nor their people enjoy. Their desire for an education is negated as they begin to realize how limited their opportunity is to exercise it, once obtained.

They have seen their fathers and mothers before them with college education forced to take menial jobs far below their preparedness and ability. They are a frustrated group of angry young men who see no way out of the dilemma in which they find themselves, and it is not their fault. We must dispel the idea which states, "Pull yourself up by your bootstraps." For where there are no boots, there are no straps by which to pull.

It becomes the duty of all thinking people—not Negroes alone—to erase the sordid conditions that abide in Watts. Some weeks ago, I asked a friend who lives there to give me his picture of Watts. His reply went something like the following:

"You want a picture of Watts . . . well here it is. Every morning, early, the milkman comes around, then the bread man, followed by the guys with rotten food from the stores. Next, the liquor stores open and there is one on almost every corner. About 8 A.M. in come the teachers from other communities and then the children start for school. About 10 A.M., the doctors, lawyers and storekeepers begin to arrive. None of them live in the area. Later come the door to door salesmen and the insurance agents. By this time the cops have begun to cruise the area and Watts is then in full bloom. About 3 P.M. the children get out of school. A little later the teachers all leave, and then about five, the storekeepers, doctors, lawyers get out of the area and the liquor stores are the only thing to remain open. But the boss-man is gone and so is his money. He takes that out to Beverly Hills, you know.

"And then the guys, the kids—with no place to go and nothing to do—start walking the streets, or gathering on corners, and the cops start beating heads."

This goes on day in and day out thruout the year. Add to this lack of decent housing, inferior education, low grade merchandise, police brutality and poverty . . . and you get the Rebellion.

For those who are not yet convinced that there is continuing police brutality, I suggest that you contact our office. We can show you or refer you to those who have documented proof.

The picture tho not a very pretty one is a true one altho I am happy to say that a change seems to be taking place. Many persons outside the Watts community have reacted in a most understanding manner and have been offering to assist the victims and their families. Also, the people within the community have allied and are responding to suggestions of ways by which to improve conditions.

It became evident to many persons that those arrested during the disorders included large numbers of persons whose only crime was that of their color and the fact that they were present. Understanding this, Mr. Hursel Alexander immediately decided that an organization of defense would be necessary. He appealed to the Los Angeles Committee for Defense of the Bill of Rights and Protection of the Foreign Born who opened their arms and their purse for such a purpose. Had it not been for the Committee's assistance the picture today would be much worse, indeed.

Thus we began the organization of the South Side Citizens Defense Committee.... And while our immediate efforts were absorbed in assisting those arrested and needing immediate defense, we have been evolving a concrete program, based on the needs of the community that will channel the frustrations and hatred into a collectively constructive fashion rather than individual and oftimes deadend explosive outbursts.

There are a great number of Negroes who are demanding a more militant type of organization than those which are presently in operation thru the churches, labor groups and in the community. They want an organization that is Negro-run that reflects the basic needs and aspirations of the Negro community. No one group can alone fullfill this desire.

Althou we shall concentrate in the area of defense, we call on and urge all organizations fighting for jobs, civil rights, housing and education to unite and work together toward the end that a total program of renewal and rebuilding can be accomplished.

Among the things our Committee hopes to develop in the community is a Co-op program in the form of a Thrift Shop and Employment agency. We appreciate that this, alone, is not the answer, we feel it is a start toward relieving some of the stifling conditions that now beset Watts and the surrounding area.

We sincerely hope that our white friends will support our efforts and appreciate the fact that the best kind of assistance from them to us will be to work in the white community and generate the kind of pressures on the city Administration to assist in our efforts of self-help.

This undertaking requires the help of all. White progressive persons can be more effective at this time among white groups and Negro progressive persons can be more effective among Negro groups. However, I venture to say if we work properly now, the day will come sooner than we think, when all can work hand in hand together.

71. THE LIBERATION OF ALCATRAZ ISLAND

Alcatraz, a small island in San Francisco Bay and site of a former maximum-security prison, may seem an odd target for civil rights activism. But the 1969 seizure and subsequent occupation of the island by a loose confederation of Native American activists was in many ways a masterstroke of propaganda. The island was under federal jurisdiction, thus ensuring widespread response to the action. It was also uninhabited, and such a prominent feature of the Bay Area skyline and tourist economy that it might as well have been in the middle of San Francisco itself. This document is a pronouncement released by the activists following their seizure of the island. Echoing the language of countless federal treaties and other documents, the manifesto mocks the supposed commitment of the federal government to the well-being of American Indians. How do the writers of this manifesto use history and past interactions between Native Americans and the US government to make their points? How do you think this manifesto was received by federal authorities? Do you imagine it won over members of the general public in San Francisco or in other parts of the West and the nation?

Indians of All Tribes
"Proclamation to the Great White Father and All His People"
1969[1]

We, the native Americans, re-claim the land known as Alcatraz Island in the name of all American Indians by right of discovery.

We wish to be fair and honorable in our dealings with the Caucasian inhabitants of this land, and hereby offer the following treaty:

We will purchase said Alcatraz Island for twenty-four dollars (24) in glass beads and red cloth, a precedent set by the white man's purchase of a similar island about 300 years ago. We know that $24 in trade goods for these 16 acres is more than was paid when Manhattan Island was sold, but we know that land values have risen over the years. Our offer of $1.24 per acre is greater than the 47 cents per acre the white men are now paying the California Indians for their land.

We will give to the inhabitants of this island a portion of the land for their own to be held in trust by the American Indian Affairs and by the bureau of Caucasian Affairs to hold in perpetuity—for as long as the sun shall rise and the rivers go down to the sea. We will further guide the inhabitants in the proper way of living. We will offer them our religion, our education, our lifeways, in order to help them achieve our level of civilization and thus raise them and all their white brothers up from their savage and unhappy state. We offer this treaty in good faith and wish to be fair and honorable in our dealings with all white men.

We feel that this so-called Alcatraz Island is more than suitable for an Indian reservation, as determined by the white man's own standards. By this we mean that this place resembles most Indian reservations in that:

1. It is isolated from modern facilities, and without adequate means of transportation.
2. It has no fresh running water.
3. It has inadequate sanitation facilities.
4. There are no oil or mineral rights.
5. There is no industry and so unemployment is very great.
6. There are no health care facilities.

---

1. Indians of All Tribes, *Alcatraz Is Not an Island*, ed. Peter Blue Cloud (Berkeley: Wingbow, 1969), 40–42.

7. The soil is rocky and non-productive; and the land does not support game.
8. There are no educational facilities.
9. The population has always exceeded the land base.
10. The population has always been held as prisoners and kept dependent upon others.

Further, it would be fitting and symbolic that ships from all over the world, entering the Golden Gate, would first see Indian land, and thus be reminded of the true history of this nation. This tiny island would be a symbol of the great lands once ruled by free and noble Indians.

What use will we make of this land?

Since the San Francisco Indian Center burned down, there is no place for Indians to assemble and carry on tribal life here in the white man's city. Therefore, we plan to develop on this island several Indian institutions:

1. A CENTER FOR NATIVE AMERICAN STUDIES will be developed which will educate them to the skills and knowledge relevant to improve the lives and spirits of all Indian peoples. Attached to this center will be traveling universities, managed by Indians, which will go to the Indian Reservations, learning those necessary and relevant materials now about.

2. AN AMERICAN INDIAN SPIRITUAL CENTER which will practice our ancient tribal religious and sacred healing ceremonies. Our cultural arts will be featured and our young people trained in music, dance, and healing rituals.

3. AN INDIAN CENTER OF ECOLOGY which will train and support our young people in scientific research and practice to restore our lands and waters to their pure and natural state. We will work to de-pollute the air and waters of the Bay Area. We will seek to restore fish and animal life to the area and to revitalize sea life which has been threatened by the white man's way. We will set up facilities to desalt sea water for human benefit.

4. A GREAT INDIAN TRAINING SCHOOL will be developed to teach our people how to make a living in the world, improve our standard of living, and to end hunger and unemployment among all our people. This training school will include a center for Indian arts and crafts, and an Indian restaurant serving native foods, which will restore Indian culinary arts. This center will display Indian arts and offer Indian foods to the public, so that all may know of the beauty and spirit of the traditional INDIAN ways.

Some of the present buildings will be taken over to develop an AMERICAN INDIAN MUSEUM which will depict our native food & other cultural contributions we have given to the world. Another part of the museum will present some of the things the white man has given to the Indians in return for the land and life he took: disease, alcohol, poverty and cultural decimation (as symbolized by old tin cans, barbed wire, rubber tires, plastic containers, etc.). Part of the museum will remain a dungeon to symbolize both those Indian captives

Alpine County, California, gay migration poster, 1970
Courtesy ONE Archives, University of Southern California.

who were incarcerated for challenging white authority, and those who were imprisoned on reservations. The museum will show the noble and the tragic events of Indian history, including the broken treaties, the documentary of the Trail of Tears, the Massacre of Wounded Knee, as well as the victory over Yellow Hair Custer and his army.

In the name of all Indians, therefore, we reclaim this island for our Indian nations, for all these reasons. We feel this claim is just and proper, and that this land should rightfully be granted to us for as long as the rivers shall run and the sun shall shine.

72. POWER TO THE PEOPLE? A SEPARATIST EFFORT IN THE FAR WEST

In 1969, gay activists in the Bay Area of Northern California, fighting discrimination, reprisals, and violence, hit upon an imaginative idea. Why not migrate en masse to another part of the West, a place where an influx of gay residents could swamp local votes and local people such that a gay community might exist free of the troubles found elsewhere in the West and the nation? Why not a gay separatist community? By 1970 the idea had become at least seemingly feasible, and the migration to Alpine County, California, a sparsely populated county nestled against Nevada in eastern California, began. Alpine had only a couple of hundred resident voters, and the theory was that the arrival of something like four or five hundred gay Americans could rewire the community's laws and customs to create, in the eyes of the project's promoters, a gay utopia. Fascinating though it was, the project came to little, as the gay rights movement began to accelerate demands and struggles for equality rather than try to pick up and leave in search of something probably mythical anyway. In the end, the San Francisco Bay Area became the center of the gay rights movement in the nation, if not the world.

FURTHER READING

Cobb, Daniel M., and Loretta Fowler, eds. *Beyond Red Power: American Indian Politics and Activism since 1900.* Santa Fe, NM: School for Advanced Research, 2007.

Cornell, Stephen. *The Return of the Native: American Indian Political Resurgence.* New York: Oxford University Press, 1988.

DeBenedetti, Charles, with Charles Chatfield. *American Ordeal: The Antiwar Movement of the Vietnam Era.* Syracuse, NY: Syracuse University Press, 1990.

Dochuk, Darren. *From Bible Belt to Sunbelt: Plain-Folk Religion, Grassroots Politics, and the Rise of Evangelical Conservatism.* W. W. Norton, 2012.

Echols, Alice. *Shaky Ground: The '60s and Its Aftershocks.* New York: Columbia University Press, 2002.

Farber, David R. *The Age of Great Dreams: America in the 1960s.* New York: Hill and Wang, 1994.

Franklin, H. Bruce. *The Vietnam War in American Stories, Songs, and Poems.* Boston: Bedford Books, 1996.

Gerstle, Gery. *American Crucible: Race and Nation in the Twentieth Century.* Princeton, NJ: Princeton University Press, 2001.

Gutierrez, David. *Walls and Mirrors: Mexican Americans, Mexican Immigrants, and the Politics of Ethnicity.* Berkeley: University of California Press, 1995.

Hillstrom, Kevin. *The Vietnam Experience: A Concise Encyclopedia of American Literature, Songs, and Films.* Westport, CT: Greenwood, 1998.

Horne, Gerald. *Fire This Time: The Watts Uprising and the 1960s.* Charlottesville: University Press of Virginia, 1995.

Karnow, Stanley. *Vietnam: A History.* New York: Viking, 1983.

Klatch, Rebecca. *A Generation Divided: The New Left, the New Right and the 1960s.* Berkeley: University of California Press, 1999.

Kushner, Sam. *Long Road to Delano: A Century of Farmworkers' Struggle.* New York: International, 1975.

Matthiessen, Peter. *In the Spirit of Crazy Horse.* New York: Viking, 1983.

Montejano, David. *Quixote's Soldiers: A Local History of the Chicano Movement, 1966–1981.* Austin: University of Texas Press, 2010.

Nickerson, Michelle. *Mothers of Conservatism: Women and the Postwar Right.* Princeton, NJ: Princeton University Press, 2012.

Nicolaides, Becky. *My Blue Heaven: Life and Politics in the Working-Class Suburbs of Los Angeles, 1920–1965.* Chicago: University of Chicago Press, 2002.

Nixon, Richard. *The Memoirs of Richard Nixon.* New York: Grosset and Dunlap, 1978.

Pawel, Miriam. *The Crusades of Cesar Chavez: A Biography.* New York: Bloomsbury, 2014.

———. *The Union of Their Dreams: Power, Hope, and Struggle in Cesar Chavez's Farm Worker Movement.* New York: Bloomsbury, 2009.

Rodriguez, Marc Simon. *Rethinking the Chicano Movement.* New York: Routledge, 2014.

Rorabaugh, W. J. *Berkeley at War: The 1960s.* New York: Oxford University Press, 1989.

Sides, Josh. *L.A. City Limits: African American Los Angeles from the Great Depression to the Present.* Berkeley: University of California Press, 2003.

———. *Post-Ghetto: Reimagining South Los Angeles.* Berkeley: University of California Press; San Marino, CA: Huntington Library, 2012.

Solnit, Rebecca, with cartographers Ben Pease and Shizue Siegel. *Infinite City: A San Francisco Atlas.* Berkeley: University of California Press, 2010.

Sonenshein, Raphael. *Politics in Black and White: Race and Power in Los Angeles.* Princeton, NJ: Princeton University Press, 1993.

Useem, Michael. *Conscription, Protest, and Social Conflict: The Life and Death of a Draft Resistance Movement.* New York: Wiley, 1973.

Antiwar protest in Los Angeles, 1972. The public furor over US involvement in the Vietnam War brought together diverse groups of protesters, many of them young and minorities. America's earlier wars had been fought mostly by men in their twenties, but a lower draft age meant that the Vietnam War was fought by much younger men, often still in their teens when they were sent to Southeast Asia. African Americans and Mexican Americans also protested the war because they believed they were disproportionately shouldering the burden of fighting. How does this antiwar march reveal the feelings that prompted people in the West, and the nation as a whole, to protest the Vietnam War?

Photograph by Joe Kennedy, the *Los Angeles Times*.

The West's Vietnam

T he Vietnam War shattered America: it divided families, generations, political parties, regions of the country, and communities, and it killed more than fifty thousand Americans. The nation has not gotten past it; the wounds and heartaches are yet fresh, and so too the divisions caused by what was until recently America's longest war.

The sheer velocity of deepening American involvement in Southeast Asia was startling. In the early 1960s, President John F. Kennedy committed US military advisors to South Vietnam, alongside a commitment to draw the United States more and more into Vietnam's domestic political activities. After Kennedy was assassinated in 1963, President Lyndon Johnson upped the ante, sending US fighters and bombers to strike North Vietnamese torpedo bases and oil storage facilities. This was done in supposed retaliation for the North's presumed attack on two US destroyers in the Gulf of Tonkin. The subsequent Gulf of Tonkin Resolution, which Congress passed in the summer of 1964 (the only dissenting votes were by two westerners) gave Johnson great leeway and power to act largely as he wished in pursuing what had already become a war. By the end of his presidency, Johnson had put more than half a million US troops in Vietnam; one in ten would die.

As with other regions in the county, Americans in the West fought in the war and they fought against it. That buildup in the Cold War era that had so changed the West now meant something different with an actual war, a hot war, going on. Military personnel at western bases now trained for actual combat and then went into it. Young cadets at the Air Force Academy in Colorado Springs trained to be fighter pilots and, upon graduating, became them, sent off on sorties high above North and South Vietnam. Young men in the US Army and Marine Corps went from basic training in the open spaces and under the spacious skies of the West into harm's way in the dense jungles of Southeast Asia.

Through the mid-1960s, American support for the war appeared strong. Americans believed that Communism had to be stopped, and they seemed willing to send young American men to help do the job. Then the mood began to shift. Johnson accelerated the war effort after promising he would not. American deaths increased: five thousand, ten thousand, twenty thousand, thirty thousand, and more. The antiwar movement, with powerful roots in the far West, began to gather steam, power, and numbers.

Look to Oakland, California, for an example. In 1967, more than ten thousand young people and other angry demonstrators blockaded a draft center for the US Army. A protest argument arose: the war in the Southeast was illegitimate and likely unwinnable as well. College campuses soon exploded in antiwar demonstrations both peaceful and not. California was at the epicenter of the movement opposed to the war.

Of course, the opponents of the war had opponents. The West was home to millions of Americans who believed that the war was just, right, and winnable. In their minds, the problem lay with the antiwar movement, which they viewed as wrong and harmful to the war effort. The polarization, which did not always occur along generational lines (it's not so easy to say that young people opposed the war and that their parents and grandparents supported it), created great bitterness on both sides, tension that is still discernible today, a half century later.

The differences spawned political arguments, and even entire presidential campaigns. John F. Kennedy's younger brother Robert, running for president in 1968 on an antiwar platform, won the Democratic primary in California, a very important step that might have taken him to the Oval Office. But his assassination in Los Angeles crushed the hopes of those who thought that the war could be de-escalated, if not ended. This was rendered all the more starkly upon the election that year of Californian Richard Nixon, a Republican who knew how to masterfully turn the nation's tensions into votes and who had neither interest in nor patience with the peace movement.

Nixon, along with his chief advisor Henry Kissinger, furthered the war effort and tried to force North Vietnam to the peace table through such maneuvers as a secret bombing campaign in neutral Cambodia. Once that plot was made public through a series of exposés, protests against the war, and the president, accelerated. Americans, including large numbers of disillusioned and often wounded veterans, took to the streets and demanded that the war be stopped. Students shut down their campuses and the draft centers that processed them as soldiers.

The antiwar movement had great internal cleavages—of ideology, of commitment to violence or nonviolence, of race, gender, and class. It was so big, it grew so fast, and it attracted such opposition that it could hardly be run with much commitment to consistency or efficiency. It was, after all, a movement, complete with all the exuberance and flaws of any other mass movement in history. It began to fall apart in the later 1960s, because it had so many opponents from without and so many problems from within. The United States eventually withdrew from the war in 1973, just as Nixon began his long, slow walk to disgrace after having been caught up in the scandals of Watergate.

Below are a number of perspectives on the war coming out of the West. We try to show that the war could be viewed, and was, from 360 degrees of vantage, ideology, and understanding.

AS YOU READ: Think of the reasons why this or that person, or this or that group or organization, held the opinions they did. How might they change? Can you see yourself holding similar views? What about the Vietnam War can you still see, hear, or feel in contemporary American settings? Fifty years ago is a long time, right? Or is it?

73. MEXICAN AMERICAN REACTIONS TO VIETNAM

As the war dragged on through the late 1960s and early 1970s, antiwar protests took on new dimensions. African Americans and Mexican Americans, increasingly angry that they appeared to be shouldering much of the burden of combat, linked the antiwar movement with civil rights activism. Such linkages energized the antiwar movement on the one hand, but also revealed tensions within the West's ethnic and racial communities.

Ruben Salazar, a journalist for the Los Angeles Times, *began to question the Vietnam War in his columns in the early 1970s. The first Mexican American to have a daily column in an English-language newspaper, Salazar had become a well-known and respected figure in the Mexican American community not only in California but across the Southwest. In August 1970, as many as twenty thousand young people, most of Mexican descent, staged a huge rally against the war in Los Angeles. Sheriff's deputies fired rounds of tear gas into the crowds. Salazar, who was there covering the rally for his newspaper, was killed when he was struck in the head by a tear gas canister fired into the bar where he had sought cover.*

Salazar wrote this column six months before his death. It describes how the war was fracturing the Mexican American community across different generations and points of view. What can you deduce from this article about the rising power of the antiwar movement among Mexican Americans? According to Salazar, what cultural issues divide antiwar Chicanos from more traditional Mexican Americans? From what you have read, how did the gap between differing points of view within the Mexican American community compare with that in other American communities? How does this portrayal of young Chicano activists compare with the perspectives of the antiwar students in Denver (see Document 74 on p. 268)?

Ruben Salazar
"Chicanos vs. Traditionalists"
1970[1]

Last Saturday's Chicano Moratorium and the activities of the Catolicos por La Raza[2] dramatize the gulf which exists between the traditional-minded Mexican-Americans and the young activists.

Unless this is understood, observers can fall easily into the simplistic conclusions that the traditionalists are Tio Tacos (Uncle Toms) or that the activists are irresponsible punks.

Either conclusion misses the essence of the present Mexican-American condition.

Traditional-minded Mexican-Americans blush at the mention of the word Chicano. They blanch at the thought of being called brown people. The reason for this, outside of personal views, is the psychological makeup of the Mexican in general.

Octavio Paz, the Mexican poet-essayist-diplomat, has tried to explain it this way: "The Mexican, whether young or old, white or brown, general or lawyer, seems to me to be a person who shuts himself away to protect himself. . . . He is jealous of his own privacy and that of others. . . . He passes through life like a man who has been flayed; everything can hurt him, including words and the very suspicion of words. . . ."

The Mexican, says Paz, "builds a wall of indifference and remoteness between reality and himself, a wall that is no less impenetrable for being invisible. The Mexican is always remote, from the world and from other people. And also from himself."

1. *Los Angeles Times*, March 6, 1970.
2. **Catolicos por La Raza:** Catholics for The People (or, literally, The Race), a group of liberal and left-leaning Mexican Americans who were questioning the social role of the Catholic Church during this period.

Is it any wonder, then, that the more conservative Mexican-Americans—and there are many of them—are embarrassed and angered at Chicanos (suspicious word) who say they don't want to fight the war in Vietnam and Catolicos who are questioning the church and the world about them?

The Mexican, says Paz, wears his face as a mask and believes "that opening oneself up is a weakness or a betrayal."

The Chicano activists are trying to rid themselves of their masks and to open themselves to themselves and to others. It is significant that in doing this they should pick as a means the Vietnam war and the Catholic Church.

That more than three thousand people braved torrential rains last Saturday to participate in the Chicano Moratorium is important not because so many people showed a distaste for the war—Anglos have done this in a bigger way—but because it was Mexican-Americans who did it.

Mexican-Americans, who include a disproportionate number of Medal of Honor winners and who, like the blacks, are suffering a disproportionate number of deaths in Vietnam, had up to now fought our wars without question.

It was part of the "machismo" tradition. When called to war, Mexican-Americans showed everyone how "macho" or manly they were and never questioned the justification for the war.

Mexicans, says Paz, judge manliness according to their "invulnerability to enemy arms or the impacts of the outside world. Stoicism is the most exalted of (Mexicans') military and political attributes."

The Chicano Moratorium strove to end this stoicism, which is hardly a democratic attribute.

"We weren't shedding our machismo," said a young marcher. "We were proving our machismo by asking the establishment the tough question: 'Why are we dying overseas when the real struggle is at home?'"

When the Catolicos por La Raza demonstrated during a midnight Christmas mass last year, they were also breaking with tradition and asking tough questions at the cost of going through the ordeal of being tried for disturbing the peace.

A San Antonio teacher, testifying before the U.S. Commission on Civil Rights last year, said he has noted that the difference between Anglo and Mexican-American students is that when "some situation befalls the Mexican-American," the Mexican-American tends to leave things up to God while the Anglo tries to solve it on his own.

Catolicos por La Raza, who greatly embarrassed the traditional-minded Mexican-Americans by their questioning of the Catholic Church's relevance to present society, were breaking with this concept.

Chicanos and traditional-minded Mexican-Americans are suffering from the ever-present communications gap. Traditionalists, more concerned with the, to them, chafing terms like Chicano, are not really listening to what the activists are saying. And the activists forget that tradition is hard to kill.

74. STUDENTS AGAINST THE WAR

This excerpt from a Denver, Colorado, newsletter, Stop the War Committee, *hints at the rising influence of the antiwar movement by 1966. The newsletter offers advice on rally chants and proper picketing strategies for antiwar demonstrators, and it keeps the membership up to date on key events and personnel. In the summer of 1966, as the newsletter notes, the war had already taken four thousand American lives. That number had risen more than tenfold by the war's end nearly a decade later. What are some of the tactics that the Stop the War Committee advocates to get its points across? Which tactics do you imagine were effective and which were not?*

Stop the War Committee Newsletter
1966[1]

. . . RECOMMENDATIONS OF PICKET CAPTAIN COMM.:

1. Don't argue with hecklers.
2. Respond to hecklers with chants. Suggested chants are, "Support our troops, bring them home now," and, "Freedom Now for Lt. Howe."
3. Stay two abreast throughout the march.
4. Notify picket captain immediately in case of violence or any other trouble.
5. Attempts to break up the line should be met by grasping the shoulder of the person in front.
6. Dress comfortably for walking. (High heels didn't work out too well the last time.)
7. On entering the capitol grounds, the march will go immediately to the State Capitol steps on the West side and link arms. (Watch for directions from picket captains on this one; they might change it to fit the circumstances.) . . .

SUGGESTED SLOGANS FOR AUGUST 6:

1. Johnson cries peace, makes war.
2. 1776 Self Determination USA.
   1966 Self Determination Vietnam.
3. Wipe out poverty, not people.
4. Yankees come home.
5. Support our GI's, bring them home.
6. Stop Johnson's crimes against humanity.

---

1. *Stop the War Committee Newsletter* (Denver), no. 13 (July 23, 1966).

7. 1945—Hiroshima—A-bomb.
    1966—Vietnam—napalm.
8. 4,000 US dead, 2,000 wounded.
    400,000 dead Vietnamese.
    End killing now!
9. Stop war profiteering. Bring our troops home.
10. There is no Ky[2] to peaceful settlement.
    (More slogans next time!)

---

2. **Ky:** a sly reference to South Vietnamese military leader *Nguyen Cao Ky* (1930–2011).

75. A CLASSIC ANTIWAR SONG

The singer Country Joe McDonald became an important voice of protest against US intervention in Vietnam. This song, the "I-Feel-Like-I'm-Fixin'-to-Die Rag," which he wrote in 1965 and recorded a few years later, was one of the antiwar movement's most popular anthems. Easy to remember and sing along with, it was played or shouted at countless rallies throughout the late 1960s and early 1970s. Its popularity—and its bitter lyrics—helped make Country Joe and his band, The Fish, one of the most important antiwar musical groups. The "Fixin'- to-Die Rag" also helped make Berkeley, California, where Country Joe lived and performed, into a national capital of war protest. How would you describe the song's point of view? How would groups supportive of the US war effort have reacted to it? How does this perspective compare with the point of view expressed by President Richard Nixon at the Air Force Academy in 1969 (see Document 78 on p. 272)?

Country Joe McDonald
"I-Feel-Like-I'm-Fixin'-to-Die Rag"
1965[1]

> Come on all of you big strong men,
> Uncle Sam needs your help again;
> He's got himself in a terrible jam,
> Way down yonder in Vietnam;
> So put down your books and pick up a gun,
> We're gonna have a whole lot of fun!
>
> Chorus:
> And it's one, two, three,

---

1. Words and music by Joe McDonald, © 1965, renewed 1993 by Alcatraz Corner Music Co.

What are we fighting for?
Don't ask me, I don't give a damn,
Next stop is Vietnam;
And it's five, six, seven,
Open up the pearly gates;
There ain't no time to wonder why,
Whoopie—we're all gonna die.

Come on, generals, let's move fast,
Your big chance has come at last;
Now you can go out and get those Reds,
The only good Commie is one that's dead;
You know that peace can only be won,
When we've blown 'em all to kingdom come!

(Chorus)

Come on, Wall Street, don't be slow.
Why, man, this is war Au-go-go;
There's plenty good money to be made,
Supplying the army with tools of the trade;
Just hope and pray if they drop the Bomb,
They drop it on the Viet Cong!

(Chorus)

Come on, mothers, throughout the land,
Pack your boys off to Vietnam;
Come on, fathers, don't hesitate.
Send your sons off before it's too late;
You can be the first one on your block
To have your boy come home in a box.

(Chorus)

76. "OUT NOW" *(SEE P. 271)*

Opposition to the escalation of US involvement in the Vietnam War grew and grew from the late 1960s into the early 1970s. Though often characterized as either solely a young people's movement or radical anger coming at the establishment from only the urban North and West, the truth is that opponents of the war could be found anywhere and could be anyone. As the war deepened, and as the administration of President Richard Nixon accelerated bombing campaigns against North Vietnam (both publicly and in secret), opponents of the war made bigger and bigger expressions of protest. This poster, like thousands of others of the era, called people to the streets to protest a war that would take the lives of more than fifty thousand Americans and end, at least as far as the United States was concerned, in (at best) a draw.

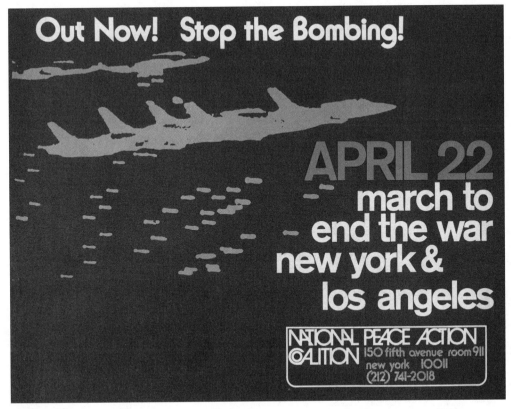

National Peace Action Coalition poster protesting the war in Vietnam, ca. 1972

Courtesy the Library of Congress, Prints and Photographs Division.

77. THE COUNTER-COUNTERCULTURE

"Okie from Muskogee" is the antithesis of Country Joe McDonald's "Fixin'-to-Die Rag," and Merle Haggard was, in many ways, the contemporary opposite of a protest singer like McDonald, although they both had western roots. Born in California's Central Valley, Haggard developed his musical talent while serving a prison sentence for armed robbery. By the late 1960s he had become an important country and western singer, his songs and ballads often tinged with a patriotic sensibility. In 1969 he wrote "Okie from Muskogee" as a response to the antiwar movement and youthful counterculture. It became a major hit and elevated Haggard to a perhaps unwanted role as spokesperson for American tensions over the war. How would you compare Haggard's point of view with McDonald's? Some have suggested that Haggard's song was meant more as irony than as straight political commentary. Do you find the song ironic?

Merle Haggard
"Okie from Muskogee"
1969[1]

We don't smoke marijuana in Muskogee.
We don't take our trips on LSD.
We don't burn our draft cards down on Main Street,
'cause we like living right and being free.

We don't make a party out of loving,
but we like holding hands and pitching woo.
We don't let our hair grow long and shaggy,
like the hippies out in San Francisco do.

And I'm proud to be an Okie from Muskogee,
a place where even squares can have a ball.
We still wave Ol' Glory down at the courthouse,
and white lightning's still the biggest thrill of all.

Leather boots are still in style for manly footwear.
Beads and roman sandals won't be seen,
'n' football's still the roughest thing on campus,
and the kids there still respect the college dean.

And I'm proud to be an Okie from Muskogee,
a place where even squares can have a ball.
We still wave Ol' Glory down at the courthouse,
and white lightning's still the biggest thrill of all.

And white lightning's still the biggest thrill of all.
In Muskogee, Oklahoma, USA.

———————————

1. Courtesy of Sony/ATV Music Publishing.

78. THE PRESIDENT'S SUPPORT FOR THE WAR

Unswayed by the rising antiwar movement, Richard Nixon moved boldly ahead with his plan to win the war in Vietnam. In this important speech before the graduates of the Air Force Academy in Colorado Springs, the president argues that the students and other Americans protesting the Vietnam War have no understanding of the nation's defense needs—that the United States must pursue an aggressive policy of military preparedness abroad while simultaneously attempting to reconcile domestic fissures at home. These sentiments, delivered at the gemstone of Cold War military installations in the West, undoubtedly resonated with the audience assembled to celebrate the new Air Force officers. How might antiwar activists respond to Nixon's arguments? What do you imagine the graduates of the Air Force Academy thought about the student protesters at western colleges and universities?

Richard Nixon

Speech at the Air Force Academy
1969[1]

For each of you, and for your parents and your countrymen, this is a moment of quiet pride.

After years of study and training, you have earned the right to be saluted.

But the members of the graduating class of the Air Force Academy are beginning their careers at a difficult moment in military life.

On a fighting front, you are asked to be ready to make unlimited sacrifice in a limited war.

On the home front, you are under attack from those who question the need for a strong national defense, and indeed see a danger in the power of the defenders.

You are entering the military service of your country when the nation's potential adversaries abroad were never stronger and your critics at home were never more numerous.

It is open season on the armed forces. Military programs are ridiculed as needless if not deliberate waste. The military profession is derided in some of the best circles. Patriotism is considered by some to be a backward, unfashionable fetish of the uneducated and unsophisticated. Nationalism is hailed and applauded as a panacea for the ills of every nation—except the United States.

This paradox of military power is a symptom of something far deeper that is stirring in our body politic. It goes beyond the dissent about the war in Vietnam. It goes behind the fear of the "military industrial complex."

The underlying questions are really these:

What is America's role in the world? What are the responsibilities of a great nation toward protecting freedom beyond its shores? Can we ever be *left* in peace if we do not actively assume the burden of *keeping* the peace?

When great questions are posed, fundamental differences of opinion come into focus. It serves no purpose to gloss over these differences, or to try to pretend they are mere matters of degree.

One school of thought holds that the road to understanding with the Soviet Union and Communist China lies through a downgrading of our own alliances and what amounts to a unilateral reduction of our arms—as a demonstration of our "good faith."

They believe that we can be conciliatory and accommodating only if we do not have the strength to be otherwise. They believe America will be able to deal with the possibility of peace only when we are unable to cope with the threat of war.

---

1. Congressional Quarterly Inc., *Nixon: The First Year of His Presidency* (Washington, DC: Congressional Quarterly Service, 1970), 66-A.

Those who think that way have grown weary of the weight of free world leadership that fell upon us in the wake of World War II, and they argue that we are as much responsible for the tensions in the world as any adversary we face.

They assert that the United States is blocking the road to peace by maintaining its military strength at home and its defense forces abroad. If we would only reduce our forces, they contend, tensions would disappear and the chances for peace brighten.

America's presence on the world scene, they believe, makes peace abroad improbable and peace in our society impossible.

We should never underestimate the appeal of the isolationist school of thought. Their slogans are simplistic and powerful: "Charity begins at home." "Let's first solve our own problems and then we can deal with the problems of the world."

This simple formula touches a responsive chord with many an overburdened taxpayer. It would be easy to buy some popularity by going along with the new isolationists. But it would be disastrous for our nation and the world.

I hold a totally different view of the world, and I come to a different conclusion about the direction America must take.

Imagine what would happen to this world if the American presence were swept from the scene. As every world leader knows, and as even the most outspoken of America's critics will admit, the rest of the world would be living in terror.

If America were to turn its back on the world, a deadening form of peace would settle over this planet—the kind of peace that suffocated freedom in Czechoslovakia.

The danger to us has changed, but it has not vanished. We must revitalize our alliances, not abandon them.

We must rule out unilateral disarmament. In the real world that simply will not work. If we pursue arms control as an end in itself, we will not achieve our end. The adversaries in the world today are not in conflict because they are armed. They are armed because they are in conflict, and have not yet learned peaceful ways to resolve their conflicting national interests.

The aggressors of this world are not going to give the United States a period of grace in which to put our domestic house in order—just as the crises within our society cannot be put on a back burner until we resolve the problem of Vietnam.

Programs solving our domestic problems will be meaningless if we are not around to enjoy them. Nor can we conduct a successful policy of peace abroad if our society is at war with itself at home.

There is no advancement for Americans at home in a retreat from the problems of the world. America has a vital national interest in world stability, and no other nation can uphold that interest for us.

We stand at a crossroad in our history. We shall reaffirm our aspiration to greatness or we shall choose instead to withdraw into ourselves. The choice will affect far more than our foreign policy; it will determine the quality of our lives. . . .

FURTHER READING

DeBenedetti, Charles, with Charles Chatfield. *An American Ordeal: The Antiwar Movement of the Vietnam Era.* Syracuse, NY: Syracuse University Press, 1990.

Eymann, Marcia A., and Charles Wollenberg, eds. *What's Going On?: California and the Vietnam Era.* Berkeley: University of California Press, 2004.

Farber, David. *The Age of Great Dreams: America in the 1960s.* New York: Hill and Wang, 1994.

Franklin, H. Bruce, ed. *The Vietnam War in American Stories, Songs, and Poems.* Boston: Bedford Books of St. Martin's Press, 1996.

Gilbert, Marc Jason. "Lock and Load High: The Vietnam War Comes to a Los Angeles Secondary School." In *The Vietnam War on Campus: Other Voices, More Distant Drums,* edited by Marc Jason Gilbert, 174–93. Westport, CT: Praeger, 2001.

Hillstrom, Kevin. *The Vietnam Experience: A Concise Encyclopedia of American Literature, Songs, and Films.* Westport, CT: Greenwood, 1998.

Karnow, Stanley. *Vietnam: A History.* New York: Viking, 1991.

McGirr, Lisa. *Suburban Warriors: The Origins of the New American Right.* Princeton, NJ: Princeton University Press, 2002.

Nickerson, Michelle, and Darren Dochuk. *Sunbelt Rising: The Politics of Place, Space, and Region.* Philadelphia: University of Pennsylvania Press, 2011.

Nixon, Richard. *The Memoirs of Richard Nixon.* New York: Grosset and Dunlap, 1978.

Perlstein, Rick. *Nixonland: The Rise of a President and the Fracturing of America.* New York: Scribner, 2008.

Richardson, Peter. *A Bomb in Every Issue: How the Short, Unruly Life of* Ramparts *Magazine Changed America.* New York: New Press, 2010.

Rorabaugh, W. J. *Berkeley at War: The 1960s.* New York: Oxford University Press, 1989.

Schulman, Bruce J., and Julian E. Zelizer, eds. *Rightward Bound: Making America Conservative in the 1970s.* Cambridge, MA: Harvard University Press, 2008.

Suri, Jeremy. *Power and Protest: Global Revolution and the Rise of Détente.* Cambridge, MA: Harvard University Press, 2005.

Unseem, Michael. *Conscription, Protest, and Social Conflict: The Life and Death of a Draft Resistance Movement.* New York: Wiley, 1973.

Matt Gainer, *LAPD Officers at Immigration Rally, Los Angeles,* 2006. In the early spring of 2006, more than half a million people filled the streets of downtown Los Angeles for a "Day without Immigrants" march and rally in favor of immigrant rights. Other cities, in the West and beyond, saw similar demonstrations, but the Los Angeles outpouring astounded observers, and was likely the largest mass gathering in the city's history.
Courtesy the photographer.

Immigration Roils the West

Immigration is an American tradition with deep roots in the history of the nation and the makeup of American identity. But debates over immigration, which spring from tensions over race, ethnicity, and the ability of national institutions to make Americans out of diverse peoples, are also part of American culture, history, and the American psyche. Such tensions continue to be a significant force in contemporary America, particularly in the West, which stands at the forefront of current controversies over immigration. This complex subject remains a hot-button issue in American politics and society, contested in the electoral arena as well as in the streets and neighborhoods of western American cities and towns.

Some background to the current debate is helpful. Harsh restrictions enacted between 1910 and 1930 halted Asian immigration to the United States and severely curtailed immigration from southern and eastern Europe. The Great Depression raised new anxieties, again with particular resonance in the West, as the nation embarked on a coercive repatriation program that sent tens of thousands of Mexicans, many of whom had migrated to the United States legally (and had become US citizens), back across the border. In the 1940s and 1950s the government reversed course, joining with giant agricultural corporations and Mexico to bring Mexican braceros, or "guest workers," here on temporary work permits. By the late 1950s, rising concern that Mexicans might be taking jobs away from Americans provoked a new round of immigration restrictions, even though the bracero program continued for years in one form or another. In the mid-1960s the United States changed gears again: the Immigration Act relaxed the former quotas on immigration for non-Europeans and help create what has come to be known as the "new immigration," especially of people moving to the United States from Asia. These sorts of push-me, pull-you contradictions and crosscutting policies have been endemic to American immigration.

In recent years, immigration to all parts of the nation continued to increase, changing the makeup of American society in dramatic, lasting ways. By the mid-1990s, nearly 10 percent of the US population had been born elsewhere. As they had in years and decades past, immigrants continue to congregate in cities. In the West, Los Angeles and San Francisco (and their immediate hinterlands) are magnets for immigrants. The greater Los Angeles region in particular is an immigration center for people arriving from sending sites such as Mexico, El Salvador, Guatemala, and all parts of Asia. One out of five immigrants to the United States in the 1990s settled in Southern California.

The West's larger cities, like Los Angeles, San Francisco, Seattle, and San Diego, often find that they are ill-equipped to handle the cultural and social challenges posed by hundreds of thousands of new immigrants. Big western urban school districts now record as many as eighty languages among enrolled pupils. Many immigrants arrive poor and in need of immediate help in the form of health care or other social services. On top of this, these newcomers discover that they are not always welcome in their new neighborhoods and communities, whether in cities, suburbs, or rural areas. The same tensions and fears that accompanied immigration in the past surround the issue today. Anti-immigrant sentiment plays out in a variety of complicated forms, but it often boils down to a few particular fears about immigrant populations. Some wonder whether new immigrants adopt American customs quickly enough; in the minds of many people, the traditional cultures and languages of immigrants pose a problem. The other major concern is broadly economic. Some question whether immigrants are taking jobs away from Americans and resent their access to social and educational services, especially those who arrive without legal documentation. On the other side of these debates are arguments that immigrants add to the West's economic and cultural well-being in significant ways, or that the agricultural and manufacturing industries in the West depend on the labor of immigrant workers to do jobs that native-born Americans continue to shun.

Recent legislation, especially in the far West, has recharged the immigration issue by making the debate more public and vocal. The following documents explore some of these responses. A reporter for a western newspaper looks at how the crackdown on undocumented immigration affects life in a famous

Rocky Mountain tourist resort. A former official of the Immigration and Naturalization Service offers his views on the immigration issue and characterizes
his support of California's Proposition 187 (see Document 80 on p. 285), a
measure designed to prevent undocumented immigrants from receiving a variety of social and educational services. Former California governor Pete Wilson,
a major supporter of Proposition 187, is lampooned in a newspaper cartoon
over his changing rhetoric. A newspaper columnist explores some of the complexities surrounding another California proposition designed to curtail bilingual education in public schools. We close with a speech given by President
Donald Trump, his first to Congress, in February 2017, in which he outlines his
administration's harsher and more punitive response not only to the US-Mexico international border itself but to those who have crossed it without legal
documentation, by choice or circumstance, in the recent past or long ago.

AS YOU READ: Think of the ways in which the American West has become a
focal point for the national debate on immigration. How do the issues raised in
these selections compare to what you know of earlier periods in the West?
From the documents reproduced here, how would you describe the major
themes of the immigration debate in the contemporary West? How and why is
the West different from other parts of the nation on the immigration issue?
What do you think of President Trump's promise to build a wall, "a beautiful
wall," as he calls it, across two thousand miles at the border between the United
States and Mexico? What is the likelihood that it will be built, and do you think
it's a good idea? Why or why not?

79. IMMIGRATION RESTRICTION IN THE ROCKIES

*In recent decades, the controversial issue of undocumented immigration has
become a national one, although it remains particularly germane to the American West. Politicians, political parties, and a variety of citizens' groups have
staked out territory, and many states have passed or proposed one anti-
immigrant measure or another. But the issue is far more complex than many
people believe, as this article from the Rocky Mountain newspaper* High Country News *tries to make clear. It discusses the impact of an Immigration and Naturalization Service raid on illegal immigrants in the ski and tourist town of
Jackson, Wyoming. As the author suggests, making hard policy choices about
immigration and citizenship status is inevitably linked to equally tough decisions about labor. In a world of tighter immigration controls and penalties, who
will do the work that immigrants (both documented and otherwise) now perform? What economic and demographic factors bring Latino workers to western
ski towns? According to this article, how does the current situation in a place
like northwestern Wyoming mirror the past?*

Lisa Jones

"El Nuevo West"
1996[1]

A week before Labor Day, the tourist town of Jackson, Wyoming, lost its labor force.

Teams of federal agents and local police entered hotels and restaurants, asking dark-skinned workers for their immigration papers. Those who couldn't produce them were taken away in police cars. One group was hauled off in a horse trailer.

Within three hours, with more than half of the sixty targeted establishments still unvisited, agents had already netted about four times the number of suspected illegal workers they'd expected. Overwhelmed, they stopped.

The chain-link enclosure outside the Teton County Sheriff's Department contained 151 Mexicans—about one-sixth of the town's Mexican population and a young pair from England. Numbers were inked on their forearms while their paperwork was processed.

The next day, 120 undocumented Mexicans were on their way back to Mexico by bus and airplane.

It was the biggest immigration bust in Wyoming's history. And, like most busts of undocumented Mexicans, it accomplished virtually nothing. A little over a week after leaving Jackson, all but four of the deportees were reportedly back on the job. One restaurant worker said that after a long bus ride in handcuffs, he spent two hours in the Ciudad Juarez jail. Then he and some friends got into a car, drove six hours west to the Arizona border, and headed back to the Rockies.

"That raid," he said, "it was really stupid."

When the man, whom I'll call Juan Sanchez, tells me this, I am sitting at the kitchen table in his trailer in the town of Driggs, Idaho. Hundreds of Jackson's workers live here, across the pass, where the Tetons' famously jagged skyline is obscured by the mild, forested western slope of the range. Only the tallest Teton, the Grand, pokes over the top.

In the trailer, there are enough chairs for me, another reporter, and Juan's wife. The room is crowded. A couple leans against the wall, alternately winding their limbs around each other, kissing and stopping to listen to us. A teenage boy sits with a couple of kids in front of the television. A young man comes to the door, looks in, and leaves.

Everyone is nervous. Juan is nervous because he doesn't know us; we're only there because a local activist he trusts told him she trusted us. Still, he answers our questions as if we're the police. We're nervous because we are talking in

---

1. *High Country News*, December 23, 1996, 1, 6, 8–11.

Spanish and our tape recorder keeps going dead. If this interview doesn't work, we don't know if we'll find any more undocumented workers who will talk to us. After the raid, even legal Mexicans stayed away from work for a week or more; many families were too frightened to even go to the grocery store. But when we ask Juan if he ever considered staying in Mexico, he looks at us like we're crazy. His wife is here, and his three children.

And there's work. In Jackson's classified ads, hotels and restaurants beg for applicants. There's construction work in Driggs, which is sprouting subdivisions the way its neighbors downvalley sprout potatoes. There's plenty of work, if you're willing to do it.

After finishing the interview and telling Juan that no, we didn't know when the next raid would be, we leave. Up the street we meet a man I'll call José Umaña. He has been in Idaho for about ten years, and has a green card and a full-time job pouring concrete for a construction company in Driggs. Evenings, he cleans the local slaughterhouse. Weekends, he milks cows twice a day. With his earnings, he paid $1,000 to have his wife, Milagro, smuggled from Tijuana into California behind a refrigerator on a moving van. Last summer, he bought the trailer we're sitting in.

"As soon as I have money, I spend it," says the thirty-year-old Umaña while his two children tumble, giggling, from sofa to floor in his warm trailer and Milagro makes piles of fragrant chicken and tortillas to serve the visitors. "But we never go hungry. We have to work hard because these kids are growing. We have to grow them up."

"We make $2 to $3 a day in Mexico. There, people work for beans and tortillas. Not meat, it's too expensive. In Mexico, you have to work for two weeks just for a pair of shoes."

People like Umaña and Sanchez are an employer's dream. The ski industry—no longer able to fill its $6-an-hour jobs with white college kids—is soaking up Latin labor.

The upside of this new relationship is that families like Juan's and José's can prosper in a way they never could in Mexico. The tourists and local merchants benefit, too: Beds are made quickly and well, eggs Florentine is delivered on time. The downside is that an estimated half of the Mexican workers in Jackson and some other resort towns are working illegally, making them and their employers vulnerable to Immigration and Naturalization Service raids, which, if not effective, are at least inconvenient and embarrassing. What's more, employers can be fined thousands of dollars for employing illegal workers.

The hunger of ski towns for cheap, energetic labor and the desire of the INS to uphold immigration law make for moral ambiguities, to put it politely.

After all, the ski industry has cultivated an image that is clean, athletic and non-seedy. We are used to illegal laborers working on farms. Nor do they seem out of place in gambling towns, where the opportunism and survival instincts of the visitors in many ways mirror those of the workers. But unlike a gambling vacation, which sells hope to people who want money, a $15,000 ski vacation sells perfection to those who already have it. Perfection is elusive; its gossamer threads can be strained by one foul look from a maître d'. Just think how the web would rupture if, upon returning from a lobster dinner, the family found the maid with the nice smile up against the wall being frisked by federal agents. The ski industry's use of illegal labor breaks its own logic.

Joseph Greene has thought about this. But he thinks about a lot of things. The holder of two philosophy degrees and the author of a position paper on the inviolability of churches as sanctuaries for refugees, Greene is a regional director for the Immigration and Naturalization Service. He oversees Colorado, Utah and Wyoming from an almost comically bland office complex in Denver....

As far as regional directorships in the INS go, Greene's looks fairly easy at first. Unlike his peers in California, Arizona and Texas, he doesn't have thousands of undocumented Mexicans and Central Americans playing cat-and-mouse with the Border Patrol every night. (Last May, for example, 67,282 Mexicans were arrested in the San Diego area alone.) Of the several million undocumented Latinos in the country, perhaps 38,000 are in this region. On demography maps, much of the area looks like a field of whitest snow.

But the area's number of Mexican workers, both legal and illegal, is expanding fast. The combined effects of stepped-up law enforcement along the border and the decision of California's voters in 1994[2] to make public health care and schooling off-limits to undocumented immigrants and their children have sent Mexicans pouring north and east.

Last winter the Colorado State Patrol found 1,209 undocumented Mexicans within a three-month period. "They'd pull over a U-Haul for weaving," says Greene, "and there would be thirty people in there." The number was twelve, or maybe fourteen, times what they'd found in the past.

Most were passing through to the slaughterhouses of Iowa and the fields of Missouri, but some were headed to join family and friends already holding down two or three jobs in ski country.

Workers in ski towns take the bus from the trailer courts of Glenwood Springs and El Jebel to the glittering streets of Aspen. They drive over Lizard Head Pass to work in the lavender-and-pink mining cabins-turned-restaurants of Telluride; and they make their way from rent-controlled apartment buildings to the brand new Victorian-style hotels of Park City, Utah.

Why are there so many jobs available in ski areas? Myles Rademan, who became town planner in Crested Butte, Colorado, in 1972 and now directs

---

2. **voters in 1994:** a reference to California's Proposition 187, passed in 1994, which barred illegal immigrants from receiving a variety of public services in the state. Proposition 187 was subsequently dismantled through a number of legal rulings that determined it to be unconstitutional.

public affairs in Park City, Utah, explains that the industry has experienced dizzying growth. During the same period, most of the ski bums—usually white baby boomers who worked in ski towns—grew up, got serious, and moved to the city.

As for their logical successors, Generation X, they were raised in a less prosperous, more competitive world. For the most part, they'd rather study law or computer programming than hang out in Jackson or Sun Valley for a semester. Even if they wanted to, the rising cost of living in those towns has made it harder to do. In five Colorado ski counties alone, 6,000 tourism jobs reportedly went unfilled in 1994.

"Not many people want to come and work three jobs so they can ski one afternoon a week," says Rademan. "A lot of the Mexicans aren't interested in skiing, they're just making a better wage than where they're coming from. At this point most resorts couldn't live without them."

There's a joke in Park City that goes, "Where can you get Mexican food here?" Answer: "In every restaurant." Indeed, about 700 Mexicans work there. In Jackson, about 1,000 of the town's 7,000 people are Mexican, about half of them working legally. The Roaring Fork Valley below Aspen is home to an estimated 10,000 to 12,000 Latinos, about three-quarters of whom are Mexican. Most of the rest are from Central America.

Although the INS has executed raids all over the region, Jackson's may have been the biggest bust a western ski town has ever seen. Its effects reached far beyond the Mexicans who were deported. . . .

One hotelier actually called Jackson Police Chief David Cameron—whose officers teamed up with the INS, the Teton Sheriff's Department and the Wyoming Division of Criminal Investigation to pull off the raid—and asked if the police were planning to help him make the beds.

The effects were felt immediately on Jackson's streets. It took twenty minutes to get a burrito at Taco Bell. The Westerner Family Restaurant lost its entire kitchen crew and had to close down. Manager Glenn McAfee told the *Jackson Hole News*, "I'm upset; I'm pissed off. I've hired a total of six (Anglo) people, and I've had two people actually show up for work. That's why we hire Mexicans."

He bristled at the *News'* suggestion that he hire less foreign labor to avoid paperwork pitfalls.

"Excuse the term," he said, "but most Americans are lazy."

Police Chief Cameron figures this is not his problem.

He says the raid's timing, right before one of the biggest tourist weekends of the year, was not a consideration: "We were not in a position, obviously, to say (to the INS), 'That weekend doesn't work for us.'"

But he admits the aftermath of the raid has been stressful.

Furious locals reported seeing a bicyclist being thrown to the ground and police hurling employees up against walls. Both Cameron and INS Regional Director Greene apologized for the fact that fifteen hotel workers were hauled off to the county jail in a horse trailer. Letters to the editor of both local newspapers alternately reviled and supported the raid. . . .

Cameron and other small-town police chiefs aren't just dealing with Latino immigration. They're also dealing with explosive growth which brings problems, regardless of the race of the newcomers.

An infusion of Anglo workers, who would demand better housing and pay than Latinos do, would disrupt mountain towns enormously. Downvalley from Aspen in Glenwood Springs, Police Chief Terry Wilson emphasizes that the first gang in his town was formed six years ago by Anglos who moved in from Reno, Nevada. But Latinos aren't immune from violence; there have been several altercations between Hispanics and Anglos up the road in Carbondale. Last month, a seventeen-year-old Latino, who had been involved in gangs while growing up in Los Angeles, pulled a gun at a party and pointed it at an Anglo teenager's head. He has since been arrested.

"Our juvenile delinquent problems are rising out of local American-born Hispanics and Anglos," says Carbondale Police Chief Fred Williams. "The teenager who was born in Chihuahua, he's not the problem."

Williams has been with his department for twenty years. "I think it's just like twenty-five years ago it was the cowboys and the hippies, and in time we all learned to get along. Right now that's what's happening here. . . . People from the city are finding valleys like this, and moving here."

You could argue that Carbondale's restive teenagers are just the latest product of a dynamic that started rolling with the Romantic poets: People like pristine mountain landscapes. As recent history in the West proves, what they like they will pay for. The rarer pristine mountain landscapes become, the more people will pay for access to them.

Over the last fifty years, richer and richer people have moved to the high mountain landscapes of the West. The people who worked in ski areas started to feel the squeeze of rising real estate prices. That squeeze turned into a pinch by the 1980s. But they good-naturedly commuted to work from outlying towns. When the outlying towns got gentrified, they drove for longer and longer distances, until their cheerfulness was expended and they quit.

Into this vacuum came the Latinos, to the horror of many of the people who had driven up the real estate prices. Finding the funky log cabins formerly rented by ski bums occupied by minor movie stars, the new workers moved into trailer courts. They shared their trailers with not only their own family but maybe one or two others. And they worked nonstop. . . .

The police—who know the deportees they're ushering south will probably rebound north as soon as humanly possible—don't share the politicians' unbridled enthusiasm for law enforcement as the solution to illegal immigration.

"From a global perspective," says Jackson Police Chief Cameron, "we don't have a border."

Says Joseph Greene, "We don't take the posture that the immigration service has the mission to arrest every single illegal alien that comes to this country. Practically, that's beyond our ability." Indeed, despite the *Sturm und Drang* surrounding the current immigration bill, the INS won't do more busts like Jackson's in the future, he says.

"We've got to try to be experimental; we've got to try temporary worker permits," he says. For nearly half a century, he explains, immigration law has assumed if a foreigner is in the country for a purpose other than being a student or a tourist, they want to stay here permanently.

"Our world is much more complex than that," he says. "This thing is absolutely huge." . . .

No one can predict how many more immigrants will reach the inland West, but one thing is clear: The world economy has sent a new wave of pioneers in this direction. And history shows that pioneers, with their fear of poverty and limitless energy, change everything.

80. RESTRICTING UNDOCUMENTED IMMIGRATION

Tensions over the presence of undocumented, or illegal, immigrants in California led to legislative action in the 1990s. This is an excerpt from the text of Proposition 187, a 1994 California ballot measure aimed at barring access to a variety of public services then available to illegal immigrants. The sweeping restrictions imposed by Proposition 187 included prohibiting illegal aliens in California from attending public elementary, secondary, or postsecondary schools. The legislation also prohibited access to public health services. A provision of the proposition insisted that public authorities notify the Immigration and Naturalization Service or other authorities of the presence of undocumented immigrants. Despite concerted opposition, Proposition 187 passed easily but was immediately challenged in federal court. Over the next several years, it was dismantled in a number of rulings that determined it to be unconstitutional, in part because individual states cannot make immigration law. What factors do you think motivated California's voters to pass this measure? How do the provisions and restrictions of Proposition 187 compare to earlier actions in the history of the American West? How do you think concerns about the economy affect concerns about immigration?

From California's Proposition 187
1994[1]

Section 1. Findings and Declaration

The People of California find and declare as follows:

That they have suffered and are suffering economic hardship caused by the presence of illegal aliens in this state.

That they have suffered and are suffering personal injury and damage caused by the criminal conduct of illegal aliens in this state.

That they have a right to the protection of their government from any person or persons entering this country unlawfully.

Therefore, the People of California declare their intention to provide for cooperation between their agencies of state and local government with the federal government, and to establish a system of required notification by and between such agencies to prevent illegal aliens in the United States from receiving benefits or public services in the State of California. . . .

Section 5. Exclusion of Illegal Aliens from Public Social Services . . .

Section 10001.5 is added to the Welfare and Institutions Code, to read:

10001.5. (a) In order to carry out the intention of the People of California that only citizens of the United States and aliens lawfully admitted to the United States may receive the benefits of public social services and to ensure that all persons employed in the providing of those services shall diligently protect public funds from misuse, the provisions of this section are adopted.

(b) A person shall not receive any public social services to which he or she may be otherwise entitled until the legal status of that person has been verified as one of the following:

(1) A citizen of the United States.
(2) An alien lawfully admitted as a permanent resident.
(3) An alien lawfully admitted for a temporary period of time.

(c) If any public entity in this state to whom a person has applied for public social services determines or reasonably suspects, based upon the information provided to it, that the person is an alien in the United States in violation of federal law, the following procedures shall be followed by the public entity:

(1) The entity shall not provide the person with benefits or services.

---

1. California Secretary of State's Office, Web site text of proposed law, https://ballotpedia.org/California_Proposition_187,_Illegal_Aliens_Ineligible_for_Public_Benefits_(1994).

(2) The entity shall, in writing, notify the person of his or her apparent illegal immigration status, and that the person must either obtain legal status or leave the United States.

(3) The entity shall also notify the State Director of Social Services, the Attorney General of California, and the United States Immigration and Naturalization Service of the apparent illegal status, and shall provide any additional information that may be requested by any other public entity.

Section 6. Exclusion of Illegal Aliens from Publicly Funded Health Care

Chapter 1.3 (commencing with Section 130) is added to Part 1 of Division 1 of the Health and Safety Code, to read:

CHAPTER 1.3. PUBLICLY FUNDED HEALTH CARE SERVICES: *130.* (a) In order to carry out the intention of the People of California that, excepting emergency medical care as required by federal law, only citizens of the United States and aliens lawfully admitted to the United States may receive the benefits of publicly funded health care, and to ensure that all persons employed in the providing of those services shall diligently protect public funds from misuse, the provisions of this section are adopted.

(b) A person shall not receive any health care services from a publicly funded health care facility, to which he or she is otherwise entitled until the legal status of that person has been verified as one of the following:

(1) A citizen of the United States.
(2) An alien lawfully admitted as a permanent resident.
(3) An alien lawfully admitted for a temporary period of time.

(c) If any publicly funded health care facility in this state from whom a person seeks health care services, other than emergency medical care as required by federal law, determines or reasonably suspects, based upon the information provided to it, that the person is an alien in the United States in violation of federal law, the following procedures shall be followed by the facility:

(1) The facility shall not provide the person with services.
(2) The facility shall, in writing, notify the person of his or her apparent illegal immigration status, and that the person must either obtain legal status or leave the United States.
(3) The facility shall also notify the State Director of Health Services, the Attorney General of California, and the United States Immigration and Naturalization Service of the apparent illegal status, and shall provide any additional information that may be requested by any other public entity.

(d) For purposes of this section "publicly funded health care facility" shall be defined as specified in Sections 1200 and 1250 of this code as of January 1, 1993.

Section 7. Exclusion of Illegal Aliens from Public Elementary and Secondary Schools

Section 48215 is added to the Education Code, to read:

48215. (a) No public elementary or secondary school shall admit, or permit the attendance of, any child who is not a citizen of the United States, an alien lawfully admitted as a permanent resident, or a person who is otherwise authorized under federal law to be present in the United States.

(b) Commencing January 1, 1995, each school district shall verify the legal status of each child enrolling in the school district for the first time in order to ensure the enrollment or attendance only of citizens, aliens lawfully admitted as permanent residents, or persons who are otherwise authorized to be present in the United States.

(c) By January 1, 1996, each school district shall have verified the legal status of each child already enrolled and in attendance in the school district in order to ensure the enrollment or attendance only of citizens, aliens lawfully admitted as permanent residents, or persons who are otherwise authorized under federal law to be present in the United States.

(d) By January 1, 1996, each school district shall also have verified the legal status of each parent or guardian of each child referred to in subdivisions (b) and (c), to determine whether such parent or guardian is one of the following:

(1) A citizen of the United States.
(2) An alien lawfully admitted as a permanent resident.
(3) An alien admitted lawfully for a temporary period of time.

(e) Each school district shall provide information to the State Superintendent of Public Instruction, the Attorney General of California, and the United States Immigration and Naturalization Service regarding any enrollee or pupil, or parent or guardian, attending a public elementary or secondary school in the school district determined or reasonably suspected to be in violation of federal immigration laws within forty-five days after becoming aware of an apparent violation. The notice shall also be provided to the parent or legal guardian of the enrollee or pupil, and shall state that an existing pupil may not continue to attend the school after ninety calendar days from the date of the notice, unless legal status is established.

(f) For each child who cannot establish legal status in the United States, each school district shall continue to provide education for a period of ninety days from the date of the notice. Such ninety day period shall be utilized to accomplish an orderly transition to a school in the child's country of origin. Each school district shall fully cooperate in this transition effort to ensure that the educational needs of the child are best served for that period of time. . . .

81. SUPPORT FOR PROPOSITION 187

Harold Ezell served for many years as the western commissioner of the Immigration and Naturalization Service. He also coauthored California's Proposition 187, the ballot measure that sought to deny public health care, education, and social service benefits to illegal immigrants. By the mid-1990s Ezell had become a well-known spokesperson for those who believed that stringent restrictions must be placed upon illegal immigrant access to public facilities and funds across the country. In this essay, Ezell outlines his position and that of other Proposition 187 supporters. How does Ezell seek to blunt the objections of opponents of Proposition 187? How does he use history to bolster his arguments? Compare Ezell's economic arguments to the points raised in Lisa Jones's essay in Document 79.

Harold Ezell
"Enough Is More Than Enough"
1994[1]

The issue of illegal immigration is color-blind; it is not a racial but a legal issue. It is an issue that taxpayers, who have seen our tax dollars squandered on programs that have nothing to do with American citizens or legal aliens, understand.

Each of us must ask ourselves: How many illegals can we educate, medicate, compensate and incarcerate before California goes bankrupt? Can we continue business as usual, wasting taxpayer dollars?

The opponents of 187 say it's flawed, poorly written, doesn't really answer the question of illegal immigration and costs too much. They agree that something must be done, but they have no solution. The Democratic Party elder statesman, former Senator Eugene McCarthy, says, "The 'save our state' initiative is a way to let the government know people aren't happy with things as they are."

Proposition 187 is not the total answer, but it is a piece of the puzzle. It will send a message that even the White House will understand. We must do something about our borders. Californians are not going to reward and underwrite those who come here illegally, whether by land, sea or air. Let the White House sue us for not paying for illegals.

---

1. *Los Angeles Times*, October 23, 1994, M5.

The widow of the late Howard Jarvis, founder of the taxpayers' revolt in the 1970s and the father of Proposition 13,[2] told me that she spent many hours gathering signatures for Proposition 187. "If Howard was alive," Estelle Jarvis said, "he would stand shoulder to shoulder with you and see that Proposition 187 becomes a reality."

Proposition 187 is the Proposition 13 of the 1990s. Just as Proposition 13 had its impact on all state and local candidates, so will Proposition 187. Governor Pete Wilson says *yes* on 187. What does your politician say?

We have heard the opponents say that $15 billion, which the federal government pays to California annually, will be taken away if Proposition 187 becomes law. That's baloney; the chances of that happening are as good as that of the Clinton Administration balancing the budget in 1996. Does anyone really believe that the Clinton Administration would take one dime from the most populous state in the nation?

Here's the truth behind the myth of the $15 billion. The federal government pays annually $3 billion for education costs in California. These funds would not be lost. Passage of 187 will require the attorney general to go to the U.S. Supreme Court to test the Plyler vs. Doe decision of 1982. This bad decision allows any five-year-old, here legally or not, to get a free, twelve-year education plus college. We can't afford this. Proposition 187 would force the Supreme Court to revisit the issue.

In addition, $9 billion is spent annually for medical reimbursement to the state of California. California taxpayers alone are paying $400 million per year to provide medical care to approximately 317,000 illegals. The California Medical Assn. wants our dollars without accountability. They say that we cannot ask a person if they are legally in the United States, that it's against federal law. This is not true. The First District Court of Appeals in California said in August that we can ask. The court upheld the 1992 state law requiring all medical applicants to disclose their Social Security numbers.

The additional $3 billion that our opponents say Uncle Sam will "take away" is for Aid to Families with Dependent Children, or welfare. Proposition 187 has nothing to do with children born here, who are citizens whether or not their parents are legal and thus entitled to the federal AFDC.

The Chicken Little opponents, who say the sky is falling if you vote *yes* on 187, are not telling the truth. California taxpayers are spending 10 percent of state general funds to underwrite illegal immigration—$3.4 billion per year. Proposition 187 would cost several million to implement, while saving billions. This is a good investment.

Our opponents ignore the Proposition 187 provisions that require law enforcement cooperation among state and local agencies and the Immigration

---

2. **Proposition 13:** a 1978 California referendum that cut local property taxes by more than 50 percent.

and Naturalization Service. This initiative requires local law enforcement agencies to cooperate when they come in contact with illegals. Maybe this is why L.A. County Sheriff Sherman Block is a "No on 187" spokesperson. It's hard for me to understand why Block, whose county has the largest population of illegals in the nation and who has sworn to uphold the laws of the land, will not allow his officers to cooperate with the INS.

Another important provision of Proposition 187 is a change in the state penal code that would make it a felony, with a five-year prison term and a $75,000 fine, to manufacture, sell or distribute phony documents. A $25,000 fine and five-year prison term would apply if an individual uses a phony document to get a benefit. This would be a major help in the enforcement of employer sanctions.

Proposition 187 is not enough, but it tells the federal government that California has had enough and we're not going to take it any more.

82. THE ENGLISH-ONLY BANDWAGON

On the heels of California's Proposition 187, Proposition 227, a ballot measure, called for a dramatic pullback in the state's commitment to bilingual education. To many supporters of the English for the Children measure, the continued use of their own languages by immigrants was an affront to American customs. Others believed that the state would be doing immigrants a favor by dismantling bilingual programs in the schools: forced by circumstance to learn English quickly, immigrant children would find their way into the economic mainstream more easily. Opponents believed the measure a front for anti-immigrant ideas and argued that attempting to legislate language use set a bad precedent. This selection from a newspaper column discusses some of the complexities of the ballot measure (which won easily), including support of the measure by Latinos who wished that their children would grow up proficient in English. How would you compare the arguments made in favor of Proposition 227 and those made in favor of Proposition 187? What arguments might be made by someone who was in favor of one but not the other? How do attitudes about education reflect beliefs about immigration and immigrants?

Joanne Jacobs
"Latino Vote Is Key to Depth of Prop. 227's Victory"
1998[1]

Vote *si* on Proposition 227, say the Mexican-American principal and the Mexican immigrant mother. Vote for *"Ingles para los Niños."* Most of the media

---

1. *San Jose Mercury News*, May 23, 1998.

dollars for Ron Unz's "English for the Children" initiative are paying for Spanish-language radio ads, which went on the air in Southern California this week. To end bilingual education, Unz is running "the most bilingual campaign" ever, he says, and perhaps the first in which the contents of the Spanish ads are the same as the English ads.

A software millionaire, Unz has spent $640,000 of his own money on the Proposition 227 campaign, more than half the total budget.

Get past the irony, and his logic becomes clear. Proposition 227 is favored by two out of three likely voters in recent polls. Almost certainly, it's going to win. But the way it wins will determine whether this is seen as a vote about educating immigrant children or about bashing immigrants. Unz needs to win with substantial Latino support.

In the Field Poll, conducted the last week in April, 73 percent of whites, 74 percent of Asians, 66 percent of blacks and 58 percent of Latinos said they planned to vote "yes." Only 1 percent of Latinos were undecided.

But a poll by the Public Policy Institute of California, done the first week in May, showed Latino voters split 48−48 on Proposition 227, down ten points from PPIC's April survey.

Proposition 227 calls for teaching students English by teaching them "overwhelmingly" in English. They'd start in a special class for students with limited English skills, moving to a mainstream class as soon as they picked up a "working knowledge" of English.

Bilingual education programs, which teach primarily in students' first language while they're learning English, would survive only if parents of twenty students in the same grade requested and qualified for a "special needs" waiver. It's likely the initiative will end most bilingual programs statewide.

Without Latino support, a victory for "English for the Children" could be a victory for divisiveness and distrust, nativism and nastiness. The context will be Proposition 187, which tried to bar illegal immigrants' children from public school, and Proposition 209, which ended race-based preferences, leading to a sharp drop in Latino and black admissions at Berkeley and UCLA.

To a remarkable extent, the debate so far has centered mostly on how to teach English, not on all the entangling issues of culture and ethnicity. It's been the education establishment, the ethnic establishment and the political establishment against Ron Unz and two-thirds of the multiethnic electorate.

The "no" campaign has been feeble. Latino politicians haven't been vocal, cowed by early poll numbers that showed overwhelming Latino support for 227. The teachers' unions have been distracted by fighting the anti-union Proposition 226. Only bilingual educators have defended their program with any energy.

On the "yes" side, the anti-immigration groups have stayed out. Anti-immigration activists hate Unz almost as much as they hate bilingual education because of his vocal opposition to Proposition 187. He ensured their opposition to Proposition 227 by including $50 million a year from the General Fund to teach English to adult immigrants who promise to tutor students who aren't fluent in English. (The tutoring pledge keeps the adult English classes within the single-subject rule for initiatives.)

It worked: The immigrant-bashers bashed 227.

It also created a line of attack for no-on-227 ads, which suggest teaching English to immigrants is a "new spending program" that will take money away from the schools and won't help kids learn English.

It's interesting to note that the "no" ads in Spanish don't hit adult English classes; the focus is on letting "parents and teachers decide what is best for us."

Raising the money issue could backfire. Voters think they'll save a bundle by not teaching children in Spanish—more than the cost of teaching English to their parents.

(The Legislative Analyst estimates total state education spending wouldn't change.)

Targeting English classes for adults also gives Unz another chance to stress that immigrants want to learn English, and want their children to learn English. They want to be able to help with homework and talk to the teacher. But those bilingual education zealots won't let them.

There's no doubt many "yes" votes for 227 will be motivated, at least in part, by fear that immigrants aren't assimilating, anger at multiculturalist claims and resentment because Grandpa never got Italian classes and Grandma never got taught in Slovak. Many Californians worry that our society is fracturing because we can't all talk to each other in the same language.

But I think most voters—whatever their family language or ethnicity—really do want the children of Mexican immigrant families to succeed in our schools and in our society. If nothing else, Californians want them to grow up to pay taxes and pay into the Social Security fund. They'll need to be proficient in English. The only question is how?

Foreign-born or native-born, Latino or non-Latino, we are not divided in our goals for our children. All our children. Let's hang on to that thought in the final weeks of the election season.

83. RALLYING FOR (AND AGAINST) IMMIGRANT RIGHTS

In March of 2006, as many as five hundred thousand people rallied and marched through downtown Los Angeles in support of immigrants and immigrant rights and against various aspects of immigration reform legislation or proposals viewed as anti-immigrant. This rally constituted one of the largest mass political gatherings in American history and further revealed the potent political power and potential—most on display in the American West—of Latino peoples. As we see here in photographs by Matt Gainer, opposition to the

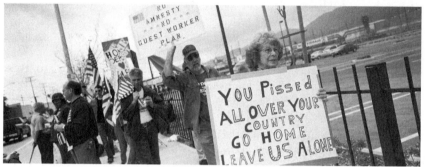

Immigrant rights rally, Los Angeles, 2006. In the spring of 2006, millions of people rallied across the United States in support of immigrant rights. The largest of these protests and rallies occurred in Los Angeles, where hundreds of thousands of people gathered to march and give voice to solidarity with immigrants, with and without legal sanction. Opponents gathered, too, insisting on the primacy of legal status over mere presence. The rallies—remarkable in their scale and impact—remind us how central the West is to one of the nation's most divisive, important, and complicated issues, cutting across matters of law, culture, race, and ethnicity.

Courtesy Matt Gainer.

marchers, and to immigrants more generally, was on display as well. Could it be that a pan-Latin or pan-Latino identity has been shaped, forged, and sustained in the cities of the West, as a result of political activism like that pictured here?

84. BUILDING A WALL

In his first speech to the United States Congress following his November 2016 election to the presidency, Donald J. Trump briefly addressed one of his major campaign issues: the building of a wall along the southern border of the United States adjacent to the Republic of Mexico. During the campaign, Trump had pledged to build the wall—embedded deeply in the earth and soaring thirty feet into the air—along the nearly two thousand miles of the international border between the nations. Much of that border is already fenced. Some of it is marked by the course of rivers or canyons; at other stretches, the border meanders through and across private land. The wall (and building it, as Trump campaigned, in such a way that Mexico would be forced to pay for it), proved to be a "red meat" issue for Trump supporters; opponents greeted the plan with fervent opposition of perhaps equal exuberance. That migration from Mexico into the United States (by Mexican nationals and others coming from Central and South America) had significantly slowed in recent years did nothing to temper Trump's claims about safety nor his pledge to build the wall. Here, the new president again champions the project that, in reference to a calendar or time frame perhaps only he understands, was apparently already "ahead of schedule." It remains to be seen if the Trump administration will build "the wall," or perhaps "a wall," or maybe just "part of a wall." What is not mysterious is the ways in which the idea and the rhetoric have riled up those in the region who would be most affected by the thing: the westerners and southwesterners and those who live just on the other side of the border.

President Donald Trump

Speech to Congress
February 28, 2017[1]

. . . I have further ordered the Departments of Homeland Security and Justice, along with the Department of State and the Director of National Intelligence, to coordinate an aggressive strategy to dismantle the criminal cartels that have spread across our Nation.

We will stop the drugs from pouring into our country and poisoning our youth—and we will expand treatment for those who have become so badly addicted.

At the same time, my Administration has answered the pleas of the American people for immigration enforcement and border security. By finally enforcing our immigration laws, we will raise wages, help the unemployed, save billions of dollars, and make our communities safer for everyone.

We want all Americans to succeed—but that can't happen in an environment of lawless chaos. We must restore integrity and the rule of law to our borders.

For that reason, we will soon begin the construction of a great wall along our southern border. It will be started ahead of schedule and, when finished, it will be a very effective weapon against drugs and crime.

---

1. https://www.cnn.com/2017/02/28/politics/donald-trump-congress-speech/index.html.

As we speak, we are removing gang members, drug dealers, and criminals that threaten our communities and prey on our citizens. Bad ones are going out as I speak tonight and as I have promised.

To any in Congress who do not believe we should enforce our laws, I would ask you this question: What would you say to the American family that loses their jobs, their income, or a loved one, because America refused to uphold its laws and defend its borders?

FURTHER READING

Cohen, Deborah. *Braceros: Migrant Citizens and Transnational Subjects in the Postwar United States and Mexico.* Chapel Hill: University of North Carolina Press, 2011.

Daniels, Roger. *Asian America: Chinese and Japanese in the United States since 1850.* Seattle: University of Washington Press, 1992.

———. *Coming to America: A History of Immigration and Ethnicity in American Life.* New York: Perennial, 2002.

Eig, Larry M. *California's Proposition 187: A Brief Overview.* Washington, DC: Congressional Research Service, 1995.

Gaouette, Teresa, and Nicole Watanabe. "Marchers Fill L.A.'s Streets." *Los Angeles Times*, May 2, 2006.

Glenn, Evelyn Nakano. *Unequal Freedom: How Race and Gender Shaped American Citizenship and Labor.* Cambridge, MA: Harvard University Press, 2004.

Gold, Scott. "Measuring Distance by Miles and Attitudes; Driving West on Ventura Boulevard Reveals Lives Untouched by the Debate over Immigration." *Los Angeles Times*, May 2, 2006.

Gutierrez, David. *Walls and Mirrors: Mexican Americans, Mexican Immigrants, and the Politics of Ethnicity.* Berkeley: University of California Press, 1995.

Ngai, Mae M. *Impossible Subjects: Illegal Aliens and the Making of Modern America.* Princeton, NJ: Princeton University Press, 2004.

Pawel, Miriam. *The Crusades of Cesar Chavez: A Biography.* New York: Bloomsbury, 2014.

———. *The Union of Their Dreams : Power, Hope, and Struggle in Cesar Chavez's Farm Worker Movement.* New York: Bloomsbury, 2010.

Peck, Gunther. *Reinventing Free Labor: Padrones and Immigrant Workers in the North American West, 1880–1930.* Cambridge and New York: Cambridge University Press, 2000.

Rodriguez, Richard. *Days of Obligation: An Argument with My Mexican Father.* New York: Viking, 1992.

Streitfeld, David. "Throngs Show Their Potent Role in Economy." *Los Angeles Times*, May 2, 2006.

Suro, Roberto. *Strangers among Us: Latino Lives in a Changing America.* New York: Vintage, 1999.

Takaki, Ronald. *Strangers at the Gates Again: Asian American Immigration after 1965.* New York: Chelsea House, 1995.

Yi, Daniel. "Koreatown Immigrants Blending In; Necessity Is Helping Strengthen Ties and Bridge the Cultural Divide between Latinos, the Largest Ethnic Group in the Area, and Asians." *Los Angeles Times*, May 3, 2006.

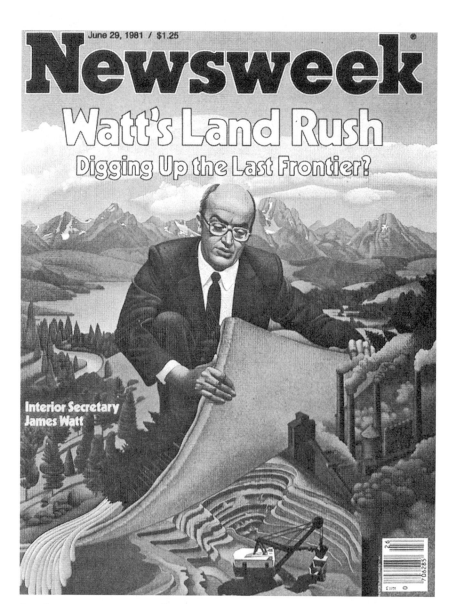

June 29, 1981 / $1.25

Newsweek

Watt's Land Rush
Digging Up the Last Frontier?

Interior Secretary
James Watt

Development versus preservation. Wyoming-born James Watt became secretary of the interior in 1980 under President Ronald Reagan. His tenure in office was controversial and short. Depicted on this 1981 cover of *Newsweek* magazine, Watt became known as pro-development, willing to open federal lands up to industrial and commercial uses that had previously been prohibited. Hugely unpopular with environmentalists of all stripes, from moderates to radicals, he nonetheless had many supporters in the West among those who resented federal authority over the western landscape. Watt resigned before the end of Reagan's first term in office. What does the reference to the "last frontier" mean?

Environmental Challenges and Environmental Imperatives

Over the last half century or so, the American West has become an increasingly critical region in regard to environmental consciousness, change, and controversy across the nation and around the world. In some respects, this importance is not surprising and fits within continuities of western environmental importance drifting back to much earlier periods of US history. For example, the creation of the national park system, beginning in 1872 with Yellowstone National Park, had everything to do with the awareness of nature inspired by the beauty and natural resources of the American West. By the early twentieth century, westerners were closely involved in the conservation movement. Even "westerners by adoption" played significant political and other roles. The naturalist John Muir, one of the earliest environmentalists and founder of the Sierra Club in 1892, was born in Scotland.

The relationship between environmental thinking and the landscapes of the American West has only become closer in the years since the first Earth Day in 1970. The West has been the birthplace of a variety of environmental groups with different viewpoints. Some have embraced fairly modest goals: the cleanup of local rivers, parks, or public beaches. Others, often with federal help, have attempted to clean up toxic sites or move environmentally dangerous industries out of beleaguered neighborhoods and communities. Still others fight against the suburban sprawl creeping outward from the West's cities and towns.

The West is also home to far more radical environmental groups whose political agendas call for action outside the traditional political arena. Inspired by figures like the writer, naturalist, and activist Edward Abbey, some of these western (and now national and even international) groups believed, and continue to believe, that acts of civil disobedience, including what has been called "ecoterrorism," are legitimate in response to the widespread degradation of Western lands. In the West, these groups have been represented since the late 1970s by opponents of western logging, some of them affiliated with the radical Earth First! movement. Some activists have chained themselves to trees or perched in treetop structures to keep logging companies at bay. In a few rare cases, they have hammered metal spikes into tree trunks to disable chainsaws.

Another important development in the environmental history of the West during the 1970s and 1980s was the so-called Sagebrush Rebellion. Less an actual rebellion than a modern version of an older struggle between states' rights and federal control, the Sagebrush movement claimed that federal control of the West's resources (particularly land) was an outdated and backward approach. Sagebrush rebels, western politicians most prominent among them, wanted federal agencies to loosen their grip on western lands, which, they claimed, ought to be in the hands of western states, not (for instance) the federal Bureau of Land Management or the Forest Service. But the catch, at least according to their opponents, was that the most vehement proponents of this loosened control wanted *access* to federal lands but did not advocate for local or state *protection* of these lands. On the contrary, the "rebellion" had a real strain of old-fashioned western growth advocacy running through it. If only the federal government would back off, Sagebrushers claimed, the West could grow at the pace and to the level that it "should." But the federal government was not interested in stepping aside, and the Sagebrush Rebellion fell apart (though vestiges of it still exist throughout the West in the form of antigovernment sentiment).

If the environmental activists of such groups as Earth First! represent one end of a western spectrum, and the Sagebrush Rebellion the other, what of the great majority in the middle? What do they think? In some ways, we just don't know: historians have only recently begun to examine contemporary attitudes on environmental issues. We do know that people in the West think about the environment and that they worry about it in the face of continued growth, sprawl, pollution, and degradation. But beyond that, it is not clear what impact the environmental awakening of the 1970s and 1980s will have in the years to come.

The documents chosen for this chapter offer a number of perspectives on environmentalism and the environmental movements arising out of, or centered in, the American West. The first-ever celebration of Earth Day in 1970, an event marked around the world, helped push environmental thinking and consciousness forward, perhaps nowhere more significantly than in the West. One indication of this is the environmental curriculum developed in one Northern California high school.

We can easily find environmentalism pushed in other directions and with other intentions in the West, beyond educational perspectives and points of view. Edward Abbey, a writer and important public figure and activist, promoted environmental "monkey wrenching" with his 1975 novel *The Monkey Wrench Gang*, which we excerpt here. Abbey became a touchstone figure for those who took ideals of environmentalism, and in some cases anarchy, into western spaces in order to disrupt the systems they saw as antithetical to the health of the West and the planet.

In more recent years, the threats to the environment have only grown more complicated and perhaps even insoluble. Western aridity, long a part of the environmental equation of vast reaches of the region, has deepened by way of drought that threatens to stretch into a "mega-drought" timescale. Climate change, pushed along so obviously and inexorably by fossil fuel use and consequences, interacts with drought in an intricate relationship not yet fully understood beyond what *is* abundantly clear: that environmental perspectives on the West must reconcile expectations of beauty with frightening presumptions of catastrophe and collapse. Environmental consciousness rose in the West as a preservation-of-nature impulse; it must now address, alongside that, imperatives about the preservation of all life: plant, animal, and human.

85. PLANS FOR EARTH DAY

Earth Day, an international celebration of environmental awareness first held on April 22, 1970, helped awaken an environmental sensibility across the nation. Environmental thinking had been stirring for a number of years, thanks in part to the alarm sounded by Rachel Carson in her pivotal book Silent Spring *(1962), and the increasing political influence of conservation groups like the Sierra Club. But the 1970s saw an expansion of the environmental movement. Young people especially became more environmentally active, seeking redress for such endemic problems as air and water pollution and the destruction of the nation's timber reserves. Students also tried to encourage environmental awareness among their parents and peers, as this selection attests. The rising consciousness among young people is illustrated by the following plans of two Palo Alto, California, high school students for an ecological awareness program on the first Earth Day in 1970. Although their ideas hardly seem revolutionary, it is important to remember that such a perspective was uncommon at the time. A movement was building, but its progress was gradual. What environmental issues are mentioned in this piece? What do the initiators of this curriculum expect to accomplish? Do you imagine that they were able to reach their goals?*

Claire Boissevain and Jim Harding
"Curriculum for Cubberley High School"
1970[1]

Why is it so important to develop environmental awareness in high school students? Because high school reaches all but the most disadvantaged youth, including those who do not go on to college; because the first years in college should not be wasted with introductory concepts that can easily be taught in high schools; because eighteen-year-olds will soon have the vote; and because we high school students *want* to know how we can contribute—*now*—to the quality of the world that we shall live in for the rest of our lives.

In response to these motives, we are preparing an "ecology awareness program" to be a workshop aimed at the April 22 Environmental Teach-In—the first national day of environmental concern. We hope that this can be a model for other high schools to consider, because we are calling for the second annual national day of environmental concern in 1971 to be oriented primarily toward the high schools. By including ourselves this year in what is mainly a college effort, perhaps we can show the value of high school participation next year.

Palo Alto High School, another in our city, recently held an antipollution forum, in which speakers representing both sides of several pollution issues presented their cases for student consideration. The organizers of the forum worked extremely hard to present a balanced program. They wanted to introduce their classmates to some of the primary forces that cause pollution, to help them see areas in which solutions can be found, and to motivate them to seek these solutions.

But the Palo Alto High School program was voluntary, and barely 200 out of [a] senior-high student body of 1,500 felt it worth their while to attend. Only those who were already concerned were reached, leaving 1,300 students who were untouched by this excellent program. Further, there was no follow-up to the forum—no continuity to the efforts resulting from the forum.

We chose to make our ecology awareness program mandatory. With a senior high enrollment of 1,200, this challenged us to offer considerable variety. And we wanted to frame our program so that it would be a beginning, leading to efforts that would extend through the rest of our school year, hopefully producing some useful results.

Here is why [a] national environmental day of concern, or an environmental teach-in day, is of such value. Our environmental program, slated for January,

---

1. Garrett De Bell, ed., *The Environmental Handbook* (New York: Ballantine, 1970), 297–300.

becomes a workshop, focused on developing ideas and activities that will grow and carry on, culminating in April on the teach-in day. Instead of just listening to speakers for the educational values of what they have to say, we shall be evaluating what they say, and participating in debates and seminars, in order to define what we can do and what programs and changes we should call for. And the cooperation of our teachers in all of this, certainly to the extent that large portions of the class work after the ecology awareness program are devoted to pursuing ideas introduced during the program, will assure the continuity of our efforts.

Although any program should be developed by the students from their own ideas, let us describe ours as an example. The program will be three days long, from January 26 to 28. Each day there will be a principal speaker to help focus attention on some of the issues. David Brower, president of Friends of the Earth, will open the conference Monday morning. Stephanie Mills will highlight the population discussions in her talk on Tuesday. And Dr. Donald Aitken, Stanford University physicist and a director of Friends of the Earth, will summarize the three-day program in a talk on Wednesday afternoon on "Where do we go from here?" Dr. Aitken's talk will be based on his appraisal of our performance over the three-day program.

These talks will be to assemblies for the entire student body. For the rest of the time there will be forty seminars, field trips, and movies, all repeated on an almost continuous basis for the entire three days. Although attendance during the three days is compulsory, the students will select which seminars they wish to attend, and work out their own time schedules in advance of the program. Each student must think of what he wants to do, or what he might want to learn, ahead of time. For example, does he want to learn all aspects of a single issue, such as the San Francisco Bay, or does he want to learn something of several issues, to see how different ecological problems are related? This is his choice.

Here are some specific examples from our agenda. A population debate will be offered, featuring a woman with thirteen children who opposes population control. A pesticide debate will be offered, featuring a defendant of DDT. Oil companies and electric utility companies will be on hand to defend their policies.

The field trips will include a Bay-walk ecology tour; a trip to Half Moon Bay to pick up trash from the shore and to analyze the types of containers and other articles that contribute to the greatest amount of litter; and a trip to the DuPont factory in Antioch, to inspect their recent installations of antipollution devices, as well as to ask questions about their general program.

The seminars will cover fields represented by the discussion leaders. Among these will be our own teachers, outside conservationists, and county officials. Subjects covered will include ecology programs for high schools; high-school student participation in local political decision-making and in community conservation activities; technical aspects of certain types of pollution control;

legal aspects of environmental defense; and other subjects along these general lines.

The program will be closed by a pantomime presented by the Ecology Action Theater group from the University of California at Berkeley. In pantomime, this group traces the entire cycle of ecological destruction from plants to fish to animals to man. At the end, a human machine is formed which is about to destroy the last life on earth. The students themselves must run from the audience to stop the machine, symbolic of the urgent need for our own participation in the global environmental battle.

Our goal in this program is fivefold: (1) we want to set a precedent for future workshops of this type, especially for the high-school teach-in for 1971; (2) we want to impart an awareness of the dependence of man on his environment to every student in the school; (3) we want to motivate our classmates to involve themselves in the preservation of the environment; (4) we want to make legislative recommendations to our legislators for action; and (5) we want to offer curriculum additions to our own school, to provide a long-term benefit resulting from our first efforts this year.

Material resulting from our studies initiated by the program will be assembled, along with photographs from the program and from the field trips, into a book for action. This book will be released on April 22, when we will send it to all who might be affected by our suggestions.

The only missing ingredient is the assurance that *you*, the high-school student reading this, will join with us this year, on April 22, in calling for the second annual day of environmental concern in 1971 to be directed at an environmental teach-in for high schools, and to join with us next year in developing programs that focus the national attention on what we can do in the high schools to help keep the earth a nice place to live on.

86. ECO-SABOTAGE AS CIVIL DISOBEDIENCE

One of the West's most ardent environmental defenders in the second half of the twentieth century was Edward Abbey. A prolific and opinionated writer on a variety of environmental issues centered mostly in his beloved West and Southwest, Abbey became a literary and spiritual leader of many radical environmentalists by the late 1970s. This selection from his well-known 1975 novel The Monkey Wrench Gang *highlights tactics that would soon become known as "monkey wrenching." Monkey wrenching, which included the destruction of tools and machines, rapidly became a controversial strategy. Proponents, many of whom pushed Abbey's examples to further extremes, saw their deeds (such as chaining themselves to trees or spiking tree trunks to prevent logging) as part of an American tradition of civil disobedience stretching at least as far back as the civil rights protests of the 1960s. Opponents of monkey wrenching saw such acts as lawless, violent, and unnecessarily obstructionist. The only clear thing in all of this is that opposing sides continue to disagree. How does the novelist use images of death and resurrection to reveal his, or his characters', feelings about environmental degradation? Does Abbey present Smith and Hayduke as heroes or villains?*

Edward Abbey

From *The Monkey Wrench Gang*
1975[1]

Hayduke and Smith restocked the beer chest and drove on, sunward, downward, riverward, upwind, into the red-rock rimrock country of the Colorado River, heart of the heart of the American West. Where the wind always blows and nothing grows but stunted juniper on the edge of a canyon, scattered blackbrush, scrubby cactus. After the winter rains, if any, and again after the summer rains, if any, there will be a brief flourish of flowers, ephemeral things. The average annual rainfall comes to five inches. It is the kind of land to cause horror and repugnance in the heart of the dirt farmer, stock raiser, land developer. There is no water; there is no soil; there is no grass; there are no trees except a few brave cottonwoods deep in the canyons. Nothing but skeleton rock, the skin of sand and dust, the silence, the space, the mountains beyond.

Hayduke and Smith, jouncing down into the red desert, passed without stopping (for Smith could not bear the memories) the turnoff to the old road which formerly had led to the hamlet of Hite (not to be confused with Hite Marina). Hite, once home for Seldom Seen and still official headquarters of his business, now lies underwater.

They drove on, coming presently to the new bridge that spanned the gorge of White Canyon, the first of the three new bridges in the area. Three bridges to cross one river?

Consult the map. When Glen Canyon Dam plugged the Colorado, the waters backed up over Hite, over the ferry and into thirty miles of canyon upstream from the ferry. The best place to bridge the river (now Lake Powell) was upstream at Narrow Canyon. In order to reach the Narrow Canyon bridge site it was necessary to bridge White Canyon on the east and Dirty Devil Canyon on the west. Thus, three bridges.

Hayduke and Smith stopped to inspect the White Canyon bridge. This, like the other two, was of arch construction and massive proportion, meant to last. The very bolt heads in the cross members were the size of a man's fist.

George Hayduke crawled about for a few minutes underneath the abutments, where nomads already, despite the newness of the bridge, had left their

---

1. Edward Abbey, *The Monkey Wrench Gang* (Philadelphia: J. B. Lippincott, 1975), 108–16.

signatures with spray paint on the pale concrete and their dung, dried and shriveled, in the dust. He came up shaking his head.

"Don't know," he says, "don't know. It's one big motherfucker."

"The middle one's bigger," says Smith.

They stared down over the railing at the meandering trickle, two hundred feet below, of White Canyon's intermittent, strictly seasonal stream. Their beer cans sailed light as Dixie cups into the gloom of the gorge. The first flood of the summer would flush them, along with all other such detritus, down to the storage reservoir, Lake Powell, where all upstream garbage found a fitting resting-place.

On to the middle bridge.

They were descending, going down, yet so vast is the scale of things here, so complex the terrain, that neither river nor central canyon become visible until the traveler is almost on the rim of the canyon.

They saw the bridge first, a high lovely twin arch rising in silvery steel well above the level of its roadway. Then they could see the stratified walls of Narrow Canyon. Smith parked his truck; they got out and walked onto the bridge.

The first thing they noticed was that the river was no longer there. Somebody had removed the Colorado River. This was old news to Smith, but to Hayduke, who knew of it only by hearsay, the discovery that the river was indeed gone came as a jolt. Instead of a river he looked down on a motionless body of murky green effluent, dead, stagnant, dull, a scum of oil floating on the surface. On the canyon walls a coating of dried silt and mineral salts, like a bathtub ring, recorded high-water mark. Lake Powell: storage pond, silt trap, evaporation tank and garbage dispose-all, a 180-mile-long incipient sewage lagoon.

They stared down. A few dead fish floated belly up on the oily surface among the orange peels and picnic plates. One waterlogged tree, a hazard to navigation, hung suspended in the static medium. The smell of decay, faint but unmistakable, rose four hundred and fifty feet to their nostrils. Somewhere below that still surface, down where the cloudy silt was settling out, the drowned cottonwoods must yet be standing, their dead branches thick with algae, their ancient knees laden with mud. Somewhere under the heavy burden of water going nowhere, under the silence, the old rocks of the river channel waited for the promised resurrection. Promised by whom? Promised by Capt. Joseph "Seldom Seen" Smith; by Sgt. George Washington Hayduke; by Dr. Sarvis and Ms. Bonnie Abbzug, that's whom.

But how?

Hayduke climbed down the rocks and inspected the foundations of the bridge: very concrete. Abutments sunk deep into the sandstone wall of the canyon, huge I beams bolted together with bolts the size of a man's arm, nuts big as dinner plates. If a man had a wrench with a 14-inch head, thinks Hayduke, and a handle like a 20-foot crowbar, he might get some leverage on those nuts.

They drove on to the third bridge, over the now-submerged mouth of the Dirty Devil River. On the way they passed an unmarked dirt road, the jeep trail leading north toward the Maze, Land of Standing Rocks, the Fins, Lizard Rock and Land's End. No-man's land. Smith knew it well.

The third bridge, like the others, was of arch construction, all steel and concrete, built to bear the weight of forty-ton haulers loaded with carnotite, pitchblende, bentonite, bituminous coal, diatomaceous earth, sulfuric acid, Schlumberger's drill mud, copper ore, oil shale, sand tar, whatever might yet be extracted from the wilderness.

"We're going to need a carload of H.E.," says George Hayduke. "Not like them old wooden truss and trestle bridges over in 'Nam."

"Well, hell, who says we have to blow all three?" Smith says. "If we take out any one it will cut the road."

"Symmetry," says Hayduke. "A nice neat job on all three would be more appreciated. I don't know. Let's think about it. Do you see what I see?"

Leaning on the rail of the Dirty Devil bridge, they looked south to Hite Marina, where a few cabin cruisers floated at their moorings, and at something more interesting closer by, the Hite airstrip, which appeared to be undergoing expansion. They saw a quarter mile of cleared land, a pickup truck, a wheeled loader, a dump truck and, coming to a halt, a Caterpillar D-7 bulldozer. The airstrip was laid out north and south on a flat bench of land below the road, above the reservoir; one edge of the airstrip was no more than fifty feet from the rim of the bench, with a vertical drop-off of 300 feet to the dark green waters of Lake Powell.

"I see it," Smith said at last, reluctantly.

Even as they watched, the dozer operator was getting off the machine, getting into the pickup and driving down to the marina. Lunchtime again.

"Seldom," says Hayduke, "that guy shut off the engine but he sure as hell didn't remove anything."

"No?"

"Absolutely not."

"Well . . . "

"Seldom, I want you to give me a lesson in equipment operation."

"Not here."

"Right here."

"Not in broad daylight."

"Why not?"

Smith seeks an excuse. "Not with them motorboaters hangin' around the marina."

"They couldn't care less. We'll have our hard hats and your pickup truck, and people will think we're construction workers."

"You ain't supposed to make a big wake near the boat docks."

"It'll make one fine helluva splash, won't it?"

"We can't do it."

"It's a matter of honor."

Smith thinking, reflecting, meditating. Finally the deep creases shifted position, his leathery face relaxed into a smile.

"One thing first," he says.

"What's that?"

"We take the license plates off my truck."

Done.

"Let's go," says Smith.

The road wound about the heads of side canyons, rose, descended, rose again to the mesa above the marina. They turned off and drove out on the airstrip. Nobody around. Down at the marina, half a mile away, a few tourists, anglers and boaters lounged in the shade. The Cat operator's pickup stood parked in front of the café. Heat waves shimmered above the walls of red rock. Except for the purr of a motorboat far down the lake, the world was silent, drugged with heat.

Smith drove straight to the side of the bulldozer, a middle-aged dust-covered iron beast. He shut off his engine and stared at Hayduke.

"I'm ready," says Hayduke.

They put on their hard hats and got out.

"First we start the starting engine, right?" Hayduke says. "To warm up the diesel engine, right?"

"Wrong. It's warmed up for us already. First we check the controls to make sure the tractor is in correct starting position."

Smith climbed into the operator's seat, facing an array of levers and pedals. "This," he said, "is the flywheel clutch lever. Disengage." He pushed it forward. "This here is the speed selector lever. Put in neutral."

Hayduke watched closely, memorizing each detail. "That's the throttle," he said.

"That's right. This is the forward and reverse lever. It should be in neutral too. This is the governor control lever. Push forward all the way. Now we apply the right steering brake"—Smith stepped on the right pedal—"and we lock it in position." He flipped forward a small lever on the floorboards. "Now—"

"So everything's in neutral and the brake is locked and it can't go anywhere?"

"That's right. Now"—Smith got out of the seat and moved to the port side of the engine—"now we start the starting engine. The new tractors are a lot simpler, they don't need a starting engine, but you'll find plenty of these old ones still around. These big tractors will last for fifty years if they're taken good care of. Now this here little lever is called the transmission control lever. It goes in HIGH speed position for starting. This is the compression release lever; we put it in START position. Now we disengage the starting-engine clutch with this handle here." He pushed the lever in toward the diesel block.

"Oh, Jesus," mutters Hayduke.

"Yep, it's a little complicated. Now . . . where was I? Now we open the fuel valve by unscrewing this little valve, right . . . here. Now we pull out the choke. Now we set the idling latch in position. Now we turn on the switch."

"That's the ignition switch for the starting engine?"

"Yep." Smith turned on the switch. Sound of a positive click. Nothing else.

"Nothing happened," Hayduke says.

"Oh, I reckon something happened," Smith said. "We closed a circuit. Now if this was a fairly old-model tractor the next thing you'd have to do is get the crank and crank up the engine. But this model has an electric starter. Let's see if she works." Smith put his hand on a lever under the clutch handle and pushed it back. The engine growled, turned over, caught fire. Smith released the starter lever, adjusted the choke; the engine ran smoothly.

"That's only the gasoline engine," Hayduke said. "We still have to get the diesel started, right?"

"That's right, George. Anybody coming?"

Hayduke climbed to the driver's seat. "Nobody in sight."

"All right." The starting engine was warm; Smith closed the choke. The engine throbbed at a comfortable idling speed. "Okay, now we grab these two levers here." Hayduke watching again, all attention. "This upper one is the pinion control and the lower one is the clutch control. Now we push the clutch lever all the way in"—toward the diesel engine block—"and pull the pinion lever all the way out. Now we move the idle latch to let the starting engine run at full speed. Now we engage the starting-engine clutch." He pulled the clutch lever out. The engine slowed, almost stalled, then picked up speed. He moved the compression release lever to RUN position. "Now the starting engine is cranking the diesel engine against compression," Smith said, shouting above the roar of the meshing motors. "It'll start right off."

Hayduke nodded but was no longer sure he followed it all. The tractor was making a great noise; black smoke jetted up, making the hinged lid dance on top of the exhaust stack.

"Now the diesel is running," Smith shouted, looking at the exhaust smoke with approval. He came back to the operator's seat, beside Hayduke. "So now we give it more speed. Pull the governor back to half speed. Now we're about ready to go," he shouted. "So we shut off the starting engine."

He moved forward again and disengaged the starting engine clutch, closed the fuel valve, shut off the ignition switch and returned to Hayduke. They sat side by side on the wide leather-covered operator's seat.

"Now we're ready to drive this thing," he shouted, grinning at Hayduke. "You still interested or would you rather go drink a beer?"

"Let's go," Hayduke shouts back. He scanned the road and marina again for any sign of hostile activity. All seemed to be in order.

"Okay," shouted Smith. He pulled a lever, lifting the hydraulic dozer blade a foot off the ground, "Now we select our operating speed. We have five speeds forward, four in reverse. Since you're kind of a beginner and that cliff is only a hundred yards away we'll stick to the slowest speed for right now." The tractor faced toward the big drop-off. He shifted the speed selector from neutral into first, pulled the forward-and-reverse lever *back* to the *forward* position. Nothing happened.

"Nothing's happening," says Hayduke, nervous again.

"That's right and ain't supposed to neither," says Smith. "Keep your shirt on. Now we rev up the engine a bit." He pulled the throttle back to full speed. "Now we engage the flywheel clutch." He pulled the clutch lever back; the great tractor started to tremble as the transmission gears slid into meshing position. He pulled the clutch lever all the way back and snapped it over center. At once the tractor began to move—thirty-five tons of iron bearing east toward St. Louis, Mo., via Lake Powell and Narrow Canyon.

"I reckon I'll get off now," Smith said, standing up.

"Wait a minute," Hayduke shouts. "How do you steer it?"

"Steering too, huh? Okay, you use these two levers in the middle. These are steering clutch levers, one for each track. Pull back on the right lever and you disengage the clutch on the right side." He did as he said; the tractor began a ponderous turn to the right. "Pull back on the other for a left turn." He released the right lever, pulled back on the left; the tractor began a ponderous turn to the left. "To make a sharper turn you apply the steering clutch brakes." He stepped on first one then the other of the two steel pedals that rose from the floor panels. "You catch on?"

"I get it," shouted Hayduke happily. "Let me do it."

Smith got up, letting Hayduke take over. "You sure you understand the whole thing?" he said.

"Don't bother me, I'm busy," Hayduke shouted, big grin shining through his shaggy beard.

"All right." Smith stepped from the fender to the drawbar of the slow-moving machine and jumped lightly to the ground. "You be careful now," he shouted.

Hayduke didn't hear him. Playing with clutch levers and clutch brakes he wove a crazy course toward the loading machine at the side of the airstrip. At the rate of two miles per hour the bulldozer smashed into the loader, a great mass of metal colliding with a lesser mass. The loader yielded, sliding sideways over the ground. Hayduke steered toward the edge of the runway and the plunge beyond, pushing the loader ahead. He grinned ferociously. Dust clouds billowed above the grind, the crunch, the squeal and groan of steel under stress.

Smith got into his pickup and started the motor, ready to take off at the first hint of danger. Despite the uproar there seemed to be no sign of alarm in any quarter. The yellow pickup remained at the café. Down at the marina a boater refueled his runabout. Two boys fished for channel cat from the end of the dock. Tourists picked over trinkets in the curio shop. A pair of hawks soared high above the radiant cliffs. Peace. . . .

Standing at the controls Hayduke saw, beyond the clouds of dust, the edge of the mesa coming toward him. Beyond that edge, far below, lay the waters of Lake Powell, the surface wrinkled by the wake of a passing boat.

He thought of one final point.

"Hey!" he shouted back at Smith. "How do you stop this thing?"

Smith, leaning against the door of his truck, cupped his ears and shouted back, "What's that?"

"How do you stop this thing?" Hayduke bellowed.

"What?" bellowed Smith.

"HOW DO YOU STOP THIS THING?"

"CAN'T HEAR YOU. . . ."

The loader, pushed by the dozer blade, arrived at the verge, wheeled over, vanished. The bulldozer followed steadily, chuffing black smoke from the burnt metal of the exhaust stack. The steel treads kept firm grip on the sandstone ledge, propelling the machine forward into space. Hayduke jumped off. As the tipover point approached the tractor attempted (so it seemed) to save itself: one tread being more advanced into the air than the other, the tractor made a lurching half-turn to the right, trying to cling to the rim of the mesa and somehow regain solid footing. Useless: there was no remedy; the bulldozer went over, making one somersault, and fell, at minimal trajectory, toward the flat hard metallic-lustered face of the reservoir. As it fell the tracks kept turning, and the engine howled.

Hayduke crawled to the edge in time to see, first, the blurred form of the loading machine sinking into the depths and, second, a few details of the tractor as it crashed into the lake. The thunder of the impact resounded from the canyon walls with shuddering effect, like a sonic boom. The bulldozer sank into the darkness of the cold subsurface waters, its dim shape of Caterpillar yellow obliterated, after a second, by the flare of an underwater explosion. A galaxy of bubbles rose to the surface and popped. Sand and stone trickled for another minute from the cliff. That ceased; there was no further activity but the cautious advance of one motorboat across the dying ripples of the lake: some curious boatman drawn to the scene of calamity.

"Let's get out of here!" Smith called, as he noticed finally, down at the marina, the pickup truck pulling away from the café.

Hayduke stood up dripping dust and jogged toward Smith, a great grim grin on his face.

"Come on!" yelled Smith. Hayduke ran.

They pulled away as the yellow truck ascended the switchbacks leading from marina to road. Smith headed back the way they'd come, across the bridge over the Dirty Devil and on toward the Colorado, but braked hard and turned abruptly before they reached the center bridge, taking the jeep road north

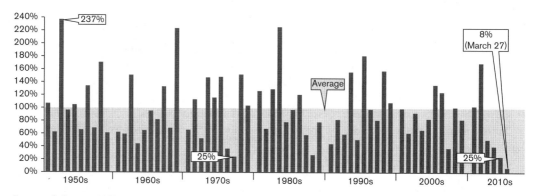

Snowpack data, ca. 1950–present

California Department of Water Resources.

around a bend which concealed them from direct view of anyone passing on the highway.

Or did it? Not entirely, for a cloud of dust, like a giant rooster tail hovering in the air, revealed their passage up the dirt road.

Aware of the rising dust, Smith stopped his truck as soon as they were behind the rocks. He left the engine idling in case it became necessary to move on quickly.

They waited.

They heard the whine of the pursuing truck, the vicious hiss of rubber on asphalt as it rushed past on toward the east. They listened to the diminishing noise of its wheels, the gradual return of peace and stillness, harmony and joy.

87. CLIMATE CHANGE, DROUGHT, AND THE FATE OF THE WEST *(SEE GRAPHIC ABOVE)*

Western snowfall, especially that which falls in the Rockies and Sierra Nevada mountains, plays a critical role in the availability of downstream fresh water as winter gives way to spring—and runoff—each year. But the snow is coming in lesser amounts, and high country places that hold snow year-round are becoming fewer and fewer. This does not bode well for the West. In fact, the situation looks dire. Snowfall has always been variable, with alternating heavy, mid-range, and light years. But look closely at this diagram—the falloff is obvious. Heavy years are less heavy, middle-amount years are similarly off, and light snowfall years are modest to the point of almost nonexistence. No snow, no water.

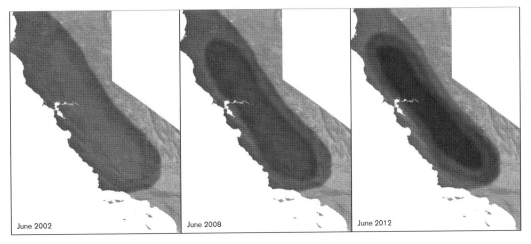

Far Western drought from space

GRACE (NASA) https://svs.gsfc.nasa.gov/4363.

88. THE VELOCITY OF ARIDITY *(SEE GRAPHIC ABOVE)*

Utilizing soil moisture data and a range of modeling techniques, NASA scientists have been able to depict the deepening of western drought in recent years. Forecasting suggests that by the end of the twenty-first century, much of the American Southwest and Great Plains will experience so-called mega-droughts: periods of extreme aridity decades, not years, in duration.

89. FIGHTING THE TYRANNY OF TURF

Given the deepening western drought of recent years, as seen so sharply in the from-space photographs in Document 88 above, as well as the consensus around the certainties of human-caused climate change, westerners are reconsidering the ways they use, and often waste, water. Water in the West is wrapped in complex cultural, legal, environmental, and political realities, and how water is used, by whom, and at what cost is increasingly controversial, fraught with differences of both opinion and influence. Certain facets of change and dynamism are more readily noticeable than others. In recent years, the giant Metropolitan Water District (MWD), like other water suppliers across the West, has created monetary incentives for residential customers to alter the plantings around their homes. Pulling up grass and laying in more drought-tolerant plantings (or none at all) has become a sign of rising consciousness about the preciousness of water in places getting hotter and drier. There will be no new sources of water in the West. What is here—on the surface, below the earth, and falling as rain and snow—will simply have to be more carefully conserved and more thoughtfully used and utilized. There is no other way.

Metropolitan Water District Pays Customers to Kill Grass
2015[1]

While Southern California's population and economy continue to grow, its water supply doesn't. In the next 15 years, our region is expected to gain as many as 2.6 million new residents. That's almost like having everyone in the state of Kansas move west. Meeting this future demand is what we are hard at work on every day.

Funding for the SoCal Water$mart program is through a partnership between the Metropolitan Water District of Southern California (Metropolitan) and its 26 member agencies throughout Southern California. Their commitment to developing an affordable balance between supply and demand has made "finding" water a mission. . . .

WHY SHOULD I CONSIDER REMOVING TURF FROM MY LANDSCAPE?   Turf grass is a commonly used landscape. But it is an expensive option, which often consumes a large percentage of a property's water use and requires regular maintenance. Conversion to a [turfless] landscape may dramatically reduce both water and maintenance expenses. An example of potential savings is an experiment conducted using two properties in Santa Monica. One was a traditional turf landscape and the other was [a] converted landscape. Over the years, the [converted] landscape has used 83% less water and required 68% less maintenance than the traditional turf landscape. . . .

Often times, turf is located in places where it is underutilized or not needed, such as side yards, parkways, street medians, around parking lots, and in business landscapes without pedestrians. Many customers find that they can remove turf in their landscape while improving the usefulness and curb appeal of their property. In fact, [reimagined] landscapes not only save water and money, but they can be a beautiful, unique, and interesting replacement for traditional turf.

---

1. Metropolitan Water District.

90. NATIONAL MONUMENTS COME UNDER RENEWED SCRUTINY

As the presidency of Barack Obama came to a close in the late winter of 2016 and early weeks of 2017, presidential acts created public land protections, in the form of national monument status and other preservation tools, of large parcels of wilderness lands in the West and elsewhere. The Obama administration also placed mining and other natural resource extraction prohibitions on public lands deemed at peril. In sum, the Obama actions, both at the last moments and throughout his two-term presidency, were responses to several impulses. These included a desire to protect lands of natural beauty and fragility; a willingness to honor indigenous religious and cultural attachment to landforms and landscapes; a commitment to lower reliance on fossil fuel extraction and dependency; and a willingness to move public lands away from the corporate gaze of big mining, big oil, or big uranium interests. As one presidency transitioned to another, these viewpoints and commitments were not carried through. On the contrary, as we see in this executive order signed early in President Trump's administration, much is now open for new scrutiny. What land gets protected, what constitutes protection, and how might Obama and others from previous administrations and periods see their efforts undone? Much remains unknown. But, given the vastly different public pronouncements from the back-to-back presidents of the early twenty-first century, it seems likely that the American West, its people and its spaces, will remain focal points of decision-making of lasting consequences. How might you construct a meaningful debate on the merits and otherwise of this executive order? What would the two (or more) sides argue in favor or opposition? What do you think this presidential order will lead to or leave in its wake?

Presidential Executive Order on the Review of Designations under the Antiquities Act

2017[1]

The White House
Office of the Press Secretary
For Immediate Release
April 26, 2017

Executive Order

Review of Designations under the Antiquities Act

By the authority vested in me as President by the Constitution and the laws of the United States of America, and in recognition of the importance of the Nation's wealth of natural resources to American workers and the American economy, it is hereby ordered as follows:

---

1. https://www.federalregister.gov/documents/2017/05/01/2017–08908/review-of-designations-under-the-antiquities-act.

Section 1. Policy. Designations of national monuments under the Antiquities Act of 1906, recently recodified at sections 320301 to 320303 of title 54, United States Code (the "Antiquities Act" or "Act"), have a substantial impact on the management of Federal lands and the use and enjoyment of neighboring lands. Such designations are a means of stewarding America's natural resources, protecting America's natural beauty, and preserving America's historic places. Monument designations that result from a lack of public outreach and proper coordination with State, tribal, and local officials and other relevant stakeholders may also create barriers to achieving energy independence, restrict public access to and use of Federal lands, burden State, tribal, and local governments, and otherwise curtail economic growth. Designations should be made in accordance with the requirements and original objectives of the Act and appropriately balance the protection of landmarks, structures, and objects against the appropriate use of Federal lands and the effects on surrounding lands and communities.

Sec. 2. Review of National Monument Designations. (a) The Secretary of the Interior (Secretary) shall conduct a review of all Presidential designations or expansions of designations under the Antiquities Act made since January 1, 1996, where the designation covers more than 100,000 acres, where the designation after expansion covers more than 100,000 acres, or where the Secretary determines that the designation or expansion was made without adequate public outreach and coordination with relevant stakeholders, to determine whether each designation or expansion conforms to the policy set forth in section 1 of this order. In making those determinations, the Secretary shall consider:

(i) the requirements and original objectives of the Act, including the Act's requirement that reservations of land not exceed "the smallest area compatible with the proper care and management of the objects to be protected";

(ii) whether designated lands are appropriately classified under the Act as "historic landmarks, historic and prehistoric structures, [or] other objects of historic or scientific interest";

(iii) the effects of a designation on the available uses of designated Federal lands, including consideration of the multiple-use policy of section 102(a)(7) of the Federal Land Policy and Management Act (43 U.S.C. 1701(a)(7)), as well as the effects on the available uses of Federal lands beyond the monument boundaries;

(iv) the effects of a designation on the use and enjoyment of non-Federal lands within or beyond monument boundaries;

(v) concerns of State, tribal, and local governments affected by a designation, including the economic development and fiscal condition of affected States, tribes, and localities;

(vi)   the availability of Federal resources to properly manage designated areas; and

(vii)   such other factors as the Secretary deems appropriate.

(b) In conducting the review described in subsection (a) of this section, the Secretary shall consult and coordinate with, as appropriate, the Secretary of Defense, the Secretary of Agriculture, the Secretary of Commerce, the Secretary of Energy, the Secretary of Homeland Security, and the heads of any other executive departments or agencies concerned with areas designated under the Act.

(c) In conducting the review described in subsection (a) of this section, the Secretary shall, as appropriate, consult and coordinate with the Governors of States affected by monument designations or other relevant officials of affected State, tribal, and local governments.

(d) Within 45 days of the date of this order, the Secretary shall provide an interim report to the President, through the Director of the Office of Management and Budget, the Assistant to the President for Economic Policy, the Assistant to the President for Domestic Policy, and the Chairman of the Council on Environmental Quality, summarizing the findings of the review described in subsection (a) of this section with respect to Proclamation 9558 of December 28, 2016 (Establishment of the Bears Ears National Monument), and such other designations as the Secretary determines to be appropriate for inclusion in the interim report. For those designations, the interim report shall include recommendations for such Presidential actions, legislative proposals, or other actions consistent with law as the Secretary may consider appropriate to carry out the policy set forth in section 1 of this order.

(e) Within 120 days of the date of this order, the Secretary shall provide a final report to the President, through the Director of the Office of Management and Budget, the Assistant to the President for Economic Policy, the Assistant to the President for Domestic Policy, and the Chairman of the Council on Environmental Quality, summarizing the findings of the review described in subsection (a) of this section. The final report shall include recommendations for such Presidential actions, legislative proposals, or other actions consistent with law as the Secretary may consider appropriate to carry out the policy set forth in section 1 of this order.

Sec. 3. General Provisions. (a) Nothing in this order shall be construed to impair or otherwise affect:

(i)   the authority granted by law to an executive department or agency, or the head thereof; or

(ii)   the functions of the Director of the Office of Management and Budget relating to budgetary, administrative, or legislative proposals.

(b) This order shall be implemented consistent with applicable law and subject to the availability of appropriations.

(c) This order is not intended to, and does not, create any right or benefit, substantive or procedural, enforceable at law or in equity by any party against the United States, its departments, agencies, or entities, its officers, employees, or agents, or any other person.

Donald J. Trump
The White House

FURTHER READING

Abbey, Edward. *The Journey Home: Some Words in Defense of the American West.* New York: Dutton, 1977.

Brower, David R. *For Earth's Sake: The Life and Times of David Brower.* Salt Lake City: Peregrine Smith, 1990.

Cawley, R. McGreggor. *Federal Land, Western Anger: The Sagebrush Rebellion and Environmental Politics.* Lawrence: University Press of Kansas, 1993.

Dant, Sara. *Losing Eden: An Environmental History of the American West.* Chichester, England, and Malden, MA: John Wiley and Sons, 2017.

Davis, Mike. *Ecology of Fear: Los Angeles and the Imagination of Disaster.* New York: Metropolitan, 1998.

Deverell William, and Greg Hise, eds. *The Land of Sunshine: An Environmental History of Metropolitan Los Angeles.* Pittsburgh: University of Pittsburgh Press, 2005.

Deverell, William, and Tom Sitton. *Water and Los Angeles: A Tale of Three Rivers, 1900–1941.* Oakland: University of California Press, 2017.

Dowie, Mark. *Losing Ground: American Environmentalism at the Close of the Twentieth Century.* Cambridge, MA: MIT Press, 1995.

Foreman, Dave. *Confessions of an Eco-Warrior.* New York: Harmony, 1991.

Ingram, B. Lynn, and Frances Malamud-Roam. *The West without Water: What Past Floods, Droughts, and Other Climatic Clues Tell Us about Tomorrow.* Berkeley: University of California Press, 2013.

Kirk, Andrew G. *Counterculture Green: The Whole Earth Catalog and American Environmentalism.* Lawrence: University Press of Kansas, 2007.

Nash, Linda. *Inescapable Ecologies: A History of Environment, Disease, and Knowledge.* Berkeley: University of California Press, 2006.

Nash, Roderick Frazier, ed. *American Environmentalism: Readings in Conservation History.* New York: McGraw-Hill, 1990.

Righter, Robert W. *The Battle over Hetch Hetchy: America's Most Controversial Dam and the Birth of Modern Environmentalism.* New York: Oxford University Press, 2005.

Rome, Adam. *The Genius of Earth Day: How a 1970 Teach-in Unexpectedly Made the First Green Generation.* New York: Hill and Wang, 2013.

Shabecoff, Philip. *A Fierce Green Fire: The American Environmental Movement.* New York: Hill and Wang, 1993.

Turner, James Morton. *The Promise of Wilderness: American Environmental Politics since 1964.* Seattle: University of Washington, 2012.

Woodhouse, Keith Mako. *The Ecocentrists.* New York: Columbia University Press, 2018.

Worster, Donald. *Rivers of Empire: Water, Aridity, and the Growth of the American West.* New York: Pantheon, 1985.

Index

Note: *Italic* page numbers indicate illustrations.